Statelessness, governance, and the problem of citizenship

MANCHESTER
1824

Manchester University Press

Statelessness, governance, and the problem of citizenship

Edited by

Tendayi Bloom and Lindsey N. Kingston

MANCHESTER UNIVERSITY PRESS

Published by Manchester University Press
Oxford Road, Manchester M13 9PL
www.manchesteruniversitypress.co.uk

British Library Cataloguing-in-Publication Data is available

ISBN 978 1 5261 5641 9 hardback
ISBN 978 1 5261 7175 7 paperback

First published by Manchester University Press in hardback 2021

This edition first published 2023

Typeset by Newgen Publishing UK

Contents

Contributors

Edwin O. Abuya is Associate Professor at the University of Nairobi School of Law. He has published several articles and presented papers at international conferences on the rights of vulnerable populations, including refugees, internally displaced persons, persons living with disabilities, and those at risk of statelessness. Abuya is also part of a Kenyan network that works on issues relating to persons at risk of statelessness.

Heather Alexander is an expert on nationality, statelessness, and refugee law. She previously worked for the United Nations High Commissioner for Refugees (UNHCR) in Chad, Sri Lanka, Kosovo, and Côte d'Ivoire. In 2020, she completed a PhD in law at Tilburg University in the Netherlands. Her dissertation is on the nationality and statelessness of nomadic and mobile peoples. She has also published on climate change, statelessness, and refugee law. She is based in Montreal, Canada.

Areej Alshammiry is a doctoral student in Social Justice and International Studies at the University of Alberta under the supervision of Dia Da Costa. She researches nationalism, statelessness, and belonging in Kuwait. Her work also explores the post-stateless experiences of the Bidoon who migrated from Kuwait and settled in Canada. She is a former stateless person from Kuwait who is now a Canadian citizen residing in Canada.

Thiago Assunção is Assistant Professor of International Relations at Positivo University in Brazil. He holds a PhD in International Law from the University of São Paulo (USP) and he received the UNHCR Brazil Office 2018 award for best doctoral research. Assunção has worked for RFK Human Rights in Italy, at the UNESCO headquarters in Paris, and as adviser for the regional government of Paraná (Brazil). Currently, he works as an independent consultant on ESG, sustainable development and human rights.

Haqqi Bahram is a PhD candidate at the Institute for Research on Migration, Ethnicity and Society (REMESO) at Linköping University, Sweden. His research focuses on the legacy of statelessness in relation to forced migration and identity formation through the experiences of Syrian Kurds in Europe. Bahram has previously worked as a Senior Officer on humanitarian and development programmes implemented in Syria. Alongside his research, he is actively involved in international refugee-led advocacy.

Ahmad Benswait is from the Indigenous populations of Arabia. He was born and grew up in Kuwait, and he became an asylum seeker in the United Kingdom in 2019. He studies applied linguistics at UCL Institute of Education and has configured his research into diasporic political activism. His current research focuses on the nexus between language and identity in unbalanced power relations. He is writing his dissertation on the Bidoon community's activism against social categorisations and control during the current global crisis. He is also preparing a PhD thesis on the same topic.

Tendayi Bloom is a political and legal theorist who focuses particularly on noncitizenship and engages from this perspective in UN and civil society processes relating to migration governance. She is author of *Noncitizen Power: Agency and the Politics of Migration* (Bloomsbury, forthcoming) and *Noncitizenism: Recognising Noncitizen Capabilities in a World of Citizens* (Routledge, 2018). She is co-editor of *Understanding Statelessness* (Routledge, 2017). She lectures in politics and international studies at the University of Birmingham, UK.

Deirdre Brennan is a PhD candidate at the Peter McMullin Centre on Statelessness, University of Melbourne, Australia. Brennan has published research on the nexus between statelessness and human trafficking, gender discriminatory nationality laws, and femicide in the United Kingdom. She also co-authored the children's book *The Girl Who Lost Her Country* in collaboration with the Institute on Statelessness and Inclusion.

Natalie Brinham (also known as Alice Cowley) is an Economic and Social Research Council-funded PhD student at Queen Mary University of London. Her thesis focuses on Rohingya experiences and understandings of the slow and ongoing production of their statelessness in Myanmar. Brinham has also worked for many years in NGOs in the United Kingdom and Southeast Asia on forced migration, trafficking, and statelessness in both frontline service provision roles and research and advocacy roles.

Jan Lukas Buterman is a Canadian transgender activist and PhD student at the University of Alberta. His Master's research investigated the technological effects of the birth certificate, revealing it to be a fetish object used to prove both identity and citizenship. He currently researches the intersections of identity and technology.

Janepicha Cheva-Isarakul is a Lecturer at the School of Social and Cultural Studies, Victoria University of Wellington, in New Zealand. Her research focuses on everyday experiences and the long-term impact of statelessness on children and adolescents. She has conducted long-term ethnographic research in northern Thailand on how stateless Shan youth make sense of the 'statelessness' label, make decisions about their future, challenge the idea of national identity, and negotiate their place within a society that simultaneously includes and excludes them.

Manal Deeb is a Palestinian-American visual artist who works between the Washington D.C. area, USA and Ramallah, Palestine. Since personality extends itself beyond present existence to what is the past, Deeb's self-consciousness to preserve her Palestinian identity made her concerned and accountable for her past, just upon the same ground and for the same reason as she does for the present. A desire for happiness, which is the unavoidable attendance of consciousness of pleasure and pain, Deeb's work is an attempt to reach a conscious happiness away from home (in exile). Deeb studied art and psychology disciplines in U.S. universities.

Ekaterina E is an artist and human rights activist originally from Soviet Central Asia. She has been living on the West Coast of the United States as a stateless person for more than twenty years. In 2017, Ekaterina co-founded United Stateless – an organisation dedicated to human rights advocacy for stateless people in the U.S. She currently serves on the board of United Stateless, as well as the advisory council for the Institute on Statelessness and Inclusion.

Thana Faroq is a Yemeni documentary photographer and educator based in The Netherlands. Her work aims to achieve a personal reportage that negotiates themes of memory, boundaries, and violence. Previously, Faroq worked with various international non-governmental organisations in Yemen to tell stories of displaced women and children there.

Anoshay Fazal is a lawyer and Senior Research Associate at the Shaikh Ahmad Hassan School of Law, Lahore University of Management Sciences

(LUMS). Fazal holds an LLM from the University of London with a specialisation in Law and Development and has ten years of experience in academic and policy research focusing on constitutionalism and legal history, human rights and humanitarian law, environmental justice, and other areas within the South Asian region. She has also worked on implementing and coordinating projects with the UN Refugee Agency in Pakistan and the American Bar Association – Rule of Law Initiative, focusing on Refugee Law, Business and Human Rights, and more recently the Rights of the Child in Pakistan, respectively. Fazal also serves as an advisory member with the Lahore Education and Research Network (LEARN).

Katharine Fortin is Associate Professor in Public International Law and Human Rights at Utrecht University's Netherlands Institute of Human Rights. The focus of her research is the legal framework that applies to non-international armed conflicts, with a particular focus on intersections between international humanitarian law and international human rights law.

Karina Gareginovna Ambartsoumian-Clough, born of Armenian descent in the former U.S.S.R., has been stateless since the age of eight. Ambartsoumian-Clough lives in sanctuary in Philadelphia, Pennsylvania, with her husband Kevin. In 2017, Karina helped found United Stateless and now leads the organisation, aiming to build and inspire community among those affected by statelessness, and advocating for their human rights.

Dilli Gautam is President of the Bhutanese Community of Michigan (BCM), which started and continues to be operated by resettled Bhutanese refugees. Gautam is Associate Director of Community Engagement of Bethany Refugee Services in Grand Rapids, Michigan, USA. Gautam has an extensive background working with refugee and immigrant students in Michigan. He holds a Master's in Public Health from Eastern Washington University. His graduate research focused on mental health among immigrant youth.

Odessa Gonzalez Benson is Assistant Professor at the University of Michigan School of Social Work and Detroit School of Urban Studies in the United States. Her research areas include refugee resettlement, participatory approaches to urban governance with refugees, state–civil society relations, and critical policy studies. She also conducts research on migrant advocacy in Tunisia and climate displacement in the Philippines.

Nataliia Kasianenko is an Assistant Professor in the Department of Political Science at California State University, Fresno. She received her PhD in political science from the University of Nevada, Reno. Her research focuses on comparative politics and international relations, with an emphasis on nationalism, identity, and politics in the countries of the former Soviet Union. Her work explores how political elites may intentionally intensify nationalism to gain legitimacy or advance to power.

Pefi Kingi is a daughter of Niue and a Pacific civil society leader. Her background is in education, mental health, and public health management. An Indigenous language activist, her passion and specialisation focuses on Pacific community development and effectiveness. She contributes to several global committees, with a high commitment to advancing the Blue Pacific agenda for Pacific prosperity as a regional legacy.

Lindsey N. Kingston is Associate Professor of International Human Rights at Webster University in Saint Louis, Missouri, United States, where she directs the Institute for Human Rights and Humanitarian Studies. Kingston is a Fulbright Scholar (*Università degli Studi di Milano*) and previously edited *Human Rights in Higher Education: Institutional, Classroom, and Community Approaches to Teaching Social Justice* (Palgrave Macmillan, 2018). Her monograph *Fully Human: Personhood, Citizenship, and Rights* (Oxford University Press, 2019) was awarded the 2020 International Studies Association 'Human Rights Best Book Award'.

Bart Klem is Associate Professor in Peace and Development at Gothenburg University, Sweden. His main research interest lies in rebel governance, de facto sovereignty, public authority, the positioning of civil servants, and international intervention in the complicated political landscapes of armed conflict. He edited a special issue in *Modern Asian Studies* (52/3) titled 'The Politics of Order and Disturbance: Public Authority, Sovereignty and Violent Contestation in South Asia' and he is completing a book manuscript on sovereign enactment and contestation within the Tamil nationalist insurgency in Sri Lanka.

Arison Kul is a self-taught artist from Tirokave village in the Eastern Highlands of Papua New Guinea. He started painting in 2003 and it has not been an easy journey. He is fascinated by colours and explores various styles and techniques. He is now based in Lae, Papua New Guinea.

Fred Kuwornu is an Italian-born film producer, director, and activist now based in the United States. He is perhaps best known for his films *Inside Buffalo* (2010), *18 Ius Soli* (2011), and *Blaxpolitalian* (2016).

Yoana Kuzmova is a lawyer practising in the areas of immigration, citizenship, and refugee law. Her work focuses on protracted displacement, statelessness, and the future of citizenship. She has worked as a Clinical Instructor at the Boston University School of Law International Human Rights Clinic and held a fellowship at the Forced Migration and Human Trafficking Initiative at Boston University. Previously, Kuzmova represented asylum seekers and worked on federal appeals challenging deportation from the United States. She holds a JD and an MA in International Relations from Boston University, and is a member of the Massachusetts and New York bars.

Jamie Chai Yun Liew is Associate Professor at the Faculty of Law, University of Ottawa, and a lawyer, called to the Bar of Ontario (Canada). She appeared before the Supreme Court of Canada representing Amnesty International and the Canadian Council for Refugees on two cases involving stateless persons (relating to immigration detention and the interpretation of the Citizenship Act). Her research focuses on how the law marginalises immigrants, refugees, and stateless persons. She is also the daughter of a previously stateless person.

Danielle Legros Georges is a Haitian-born American writer, translator, academic, and author of several books of poetry. She directs Lesley University's MFA programme in creative writing and has received numerous fellowships and awards in literature and the arts. Between 2015 and 2019, she served as the second Poet Laureate of the City of Boston.

Pragna Paramita Mondal is a PhD scholar at the Women's Studies Research Centre, University of Calcutta, and Assistant Professor at Narajole Raj College, India. She completed her M.Phil as UGC Junior Research Fellow at the Institute of Development Studies Kolkata. She is conducting ongoing multi-sited research on surrogacy in India. She has published in the *Economic & Political Weekly* (2018) and has contributed to *Population Dynamics in Eastern India and Bangladesh: Demographic, Health and Developmental Issues* (Springer, 2020), which is listed under STICERD LSE India Observatory Publications.

Nina Murray is Head of Policy and Research at the European Network on Statelessness (ENS), a civil society alliance committed to addressing statelessness in Europe. She leads work on ENS's Statelessness Index and coordinates ENS's research, training, and law and policy development in priority thematic areas – including forced migration, child rights, immigration detention and access to justice, and minority rights. Her professional experience has focused on migration, asylum, and gender equality in a range of roles, including with the Scottish Refugee Council and the Board of Scotland's leading feminist organisation, Engender.

Shabu Mwangi was born in Nairobi, Kenya, in 1985. He lives and works as an artist in Mukuru slum, where he established the Wajukuu Art Project with the deep conviction that his work could highlight the lives of disadvantaged minorities in his community. His work has been exhibited in Kenya, the United Kingdom, and Germany.

Yoosun Park is Associate Professor at the University of Pennsylvania School for Social Policy and Practice in the United States. Park's scholarship, framed within the broad substantive area of immigration, is informed by poststructuralist theories of discourse and methods of inquiry, and pursues two overlapping lines of inquiry: social work's history with immigrants and immigration, and the study of contemporary issues pertinent to immigrants and the issue of immigration.

Allison J. Petrozziello is a migration researcher and human rights advocate who is currently pursuing a PhD in Global Governance at the Balsillie School of International Affairs, Wilfrid Laurier University, Canada. Her doctoral research takes a feminist approach to the study of exclusionary birth registration practices that generate a risk of statelessness, building upon prior research in the Dominican Republic. She has consulted for UN Women and ILO, among others, and is affiliated with the International Migration Research Centre and the Caribbean Migrants Observatory (OBMICA).

Mawa Rannahr is a self-taught, undocumented stateless painter living in the United States since 1994.

Melissa Schnyder is Professor of International Relations and Global Security at American Public University and Co-Director of the Multidisciplinary Research Council. Her research examines civil society advocacy to address human security policy issues, with a focus on the European Union context. In addition to books published by Rowman & Littlefield International (*Activism, NGOs and the State: Multilevel Responses to Immigration Politics in Europe*, 2015) and Lexington Books (*Advocating for Refugees in the European Union: Norm-Based Strategies by Civil Society Organizations*, 2020), she has published numerous articles in peer-reviewed journals including the *Journal of Contemporary European Research*, *Journal* *of European Integration, Comparative European Politics,* and *Social Movement Studies.*

Marika Sosnowski is an Australian-qualified lawyer and a Research Fellow with the German Institute for Global and Area Studies. Her primary research interests are in the fields of critical security studies, complex political order, local/rebel governance, and legal systems. Her geographical area of specialisation is the Middle East, particularly Syria.

Christoph Sperfeldt is Senior Research Fellow at the Peter McMullin Centre on Statelessness at Melbourne Law School, Australia. Prior to this, Sperfeldt was Deputy Director at the Asian International Justice Initiative, a joint programme of the East-West Center and the Center for Human Rights and International Justice, Stanford University, where he has supported human rights and rule of law capacity-building efforts in Southeast Asia. From 2007 to 2011, he was Senior Advisor with the Gesellschaft für Internationale Zusammenarbeit (GIZ) in Cambodia. He holds a PhD from the School of Regulation and Global Governance (RegNet), Australian National University.

Francis Tom Temprosa is a Doctor of the Science of Law candidate and Michigan Grotius Fellow at the University of Michigan Law School (USA), where he also obtained his Master of Laws degree with a certificate of merit under a DeWitt Fellowship. He is an Adjunct Professor of Law at the Ateneo de Manila University Law School and a Professorial Lecturer at the De La Salle University Manila College of Law in the Philippines, teaching human rights law and international criminal law, among other courses. He is the Director of the Human Rights Education and Promotion Office of the Commission on Human Rights (Philippines) and worked for the UN High Commissioner for Refugees from 2009 to 2012. He writes on human rights, international law, refugee law, and the law on statelessness.

Jason Tucker is Researcher in Global Political Studies, Malmö University, Sweden. His main area of focus is the relationship between statelessness and forced migration. He has researched and published on asylum and refugee law, citizenship, integration, and migration theory. Prior to his current position, Tucker worked on statelessness for UNHCR Central Asia and UNHCR Northern Europe. He completed his PhD on statelessness in Lebanon in 2014 at the Centre for Development Studies at the University of Bath, United Kingdom.

Maarja Vollmer is a Senior Analyst with Civitta Estonia. She holds a Master's degree in International Migration and Ethnic Relations from Malmö University in Sweden. Vollmer specialises in research on migration and fundamental rights issues and has previously carried out both qualitative and quantitative research projects. These have included: research on the stateless youth in Estonia and their citizenship choices (2015), the comparison of rights of children in irregular status in Sweden and the United Kingdom (2015), the reality of free movement for young European citizens (2016), and human rights and human rights education in Estonian schools and education policy (2017).

Kate Wilkinson Cross is a Senior Lecturer in Public International Law, Gender and the Environment at De Montfort University's School of Law. Her main research areas lie in ecofeminist legal theory and representations of the environment in international law. Her research focuses on discourses of technology, modernisation and knowledge in international environmental law, with a focus on the role of technology in the context of food security and biodiversity conservation. Drawing on ecofeminist theory, her work explores how discourses of ecological modernisation and technology shape negotiations in the Convention on Biological Diversity. Other areas of interest include environmental security, statelessness, and desertification.

Bridget Wooding is a researcher, advocate, writer, trainer, and expert witness on statelessness and related issues. She has coordinated the Caribbean Migration and Development Observatory (OBMICA), based in Santo Domingo (www.obmica.org), since its inception in 2009. She is the author of numerous publications and in 2013, she delivered an expert witness testimony in the case of *Expelled Dominicans and Haitians v. Dominican Republic*, which led to significant jurisprudence on the right to nationality for Dominicans of foreign ancestry (IACtHR, 2014). Under her leadership, OBMICA is a founding member of the Americas Network on Nationality and Statelessness, established in late 2014.

Acknowledgements

We are grateful to those who supported the production of this volume in various important ways. Many thanks to our colleagues Katherine Tonkiss, Kelly Staples, and Phillip Cole, who have been supportive of this project from the beginning and have encouraged and counselled from the sidelines. Thank you to those who participated in the 'Understanding Statelessness' session at the World Conference on Statelessness (27 June 2019) in The Hague, The Netherlands. Discussions at that event helped us think through the framing of this project and the organisation of this book. Lindsey is indebted to Michelle Foster and colleagues at the Peter McMullin Centre on Statelessness at Melbourne Law School, where she held a visiting fellowship during a key phase of this project. Tendayi thanks the Leverhulme Trust for the research fellowship which enabled her to begin work on this project, all those who welcomed her to the Graduate Institute in Geneva's Global Migration Center at that time, and her new colleagues at the University of Birmingham who were supportive during the final stages of this project. We are both grateful to Eve Hopkins, who provided logistical help and advice at the start of the project, and to Sean Waite, who helped with copy editing towards its completion. It has been wonderful to work with Lucy Burns, Robert Byron, Jonathan de Peyer, Jen Mellor, and their colleagues at Manchester University Press. They have shared our vision for the book from the outset. We thank them, the anonymous reviewer, and the production team, including Katie Finnegan, Nancy Gerth, Judi Gibbs, and Sophie Robinson, for making the book a reality.

The sustained commitment and camaraderie of the authors and artists involved in this project has been incredible. Contributors have overcome often substantial challenges alongside their work for this book, and we appreciate their unwavering dedication in seeing this project through – including finishing it in the midst of the COVID-19 pandemic. It is the product of engagement among more than forty people based around the world. Everyone involved in this endeavour hopes it may contribute to the larger aim of bringing about societies in which people are empowered to seek social justice and pursue happiness – no matter their citizenship status.

Tendayi Bloom and Lindsey N. Kingston

A Stateless Poem

Danielle Legros Georges

If you are born, and you are stateless,
if you are born, and you are homeless,

if your state and your home are not
yours – and yet everything you know –

what are you? Who are you? And who
am I without the dark fields I walk upon,

the streets I know, the blue corners
I call mine, the ones you call yours...

Who am I to call myself citizen, and
human and free? And who are you

to call yourself landed and grounded,
and free. And who is judge enough?

Who native? Who other?

And who are we who move so freely
without accents of identification,

without skin of identification, with
all manner of identification. With

gold seals of approval. With stamps
of good fortune. With the accident

of blameless birth. Who are we to be
so lucky?

Introduction: Opening a conversation about statelessness, governance, and the problem of citizenship

Tendayi Bloom and Lindsey N. Kingston[1]

> A stateless person is 'a person who is not considered as a national by any State under the operation of its law'.
> Article 1.1, 1954 Convention relating to the Status of Stateless Persons

For too long, the study of 'statelessness' has focused on technical legal issues. While these are vital in understanding and addressing people's urgent needs, they represent only one aspect of a complex and messy reality. This project examines the often-confusing ways in which the structures that govern society move people into or out of recognition – from the role of local administrators, through national policy makers, regional courts, and global organisations. Using governance as a lens for understanding the realities of statelessness helps to uncover a commonality among perspectives and contexts. It becomes clear that the underlying problem is not statelessness itself, but rather it is citizenship – including both the ways in which citizenship is governed and how it is used as a governance tool.

In this book, we meet young people experiencing statelessness in Thailand and Estonia who express similar feelings of displacement and frustration, but adopt different strategies to realise their aims (Cheva-Isarakul, this volume; Vollmer, this volume). We discover how formerly stateless persons in the United Arab Emirates who have been allocated Comoros citizenship still face challenges, albeit now as members of an artificial 'Comorian' minority (Kuzmova, this volume). Individual legal statelessness alone cannot explain the challenges of Syrian Kurds, some of whom have Syrian citizenship while others do not (Bahram, this volume). In the Pacific region, the experiences of statelessness can be driven by cultural displacement rather than the question of documents (Wilkinson Cross and Kingi, this volume). The terminology of statelessness is also contested; while activists experiencing statelessness in some contexts find this terminology empowering, others reject it as undermining their struggle for recognition (E, this volume; Brinham, this volume).

In order to interrogate the complex nature of the relationship between statelessness and governance, this edited volume combines a diversity of approaches. The project team of more than forty contributors is diverse, interdisciplinary, and global. It includes academics, activists, affected persons, and artists. Central to this endeavour is the unique expertise contributed by those with direct experience with statelessness, who draw on this insight both explicitly and implicitly in their analyses. The inclusion of more traditional-style essays alongside poetry and visual artwork is intended to provide a deepened understanding. Ultimately, we set out both to enrich the research literature and to provide a resource for those seeking to address real-world challenges: practitioners, policy makers, activists, and those who engage with them.

The aim of this introduction is to open a conversation about statelessness, governance, and the problem of citizenship. We first redefine the 'problem' that needs to be addressed from one of statelessness to one of citizenship, showing how this conversation has been affected by practices and policies tied to the logics of colonialism, decolonisation, security, and migration control. Second, we introduce the many-layered relationship between statelessness and governance. We look at how statelessness forces a re-examination of both the role of governance systems and the function of citizenship itself. Third, we outline the organisation of the book, which encompasses one poem, twenty-six substantive chapters, and seven images, and provides an initial step in a larger agenda of examining the relationship between statelessness and governance – and indeed, in addressing the problem of citizenship that is so often ignored by scholars and practitioners alike.

Redefining the 'problem'

This book started life as a project with the working title *Statelessness and Governance*. The contributors shared a recognition that the relationship between statelessness and governance needed to be interrogated, and that new ways of thinking needed to be developed. However, another commonality emerged as the project progressed; repeated across the work was the assertion, in various manifestations, that the problems associated with statelessness boiled down to problems in the governance structures relating to citizenship, and to the use of citizenship as an 'international sorting system'.[2] Interrogating the relationship between statelessness and governance laid bare the problem of citizenship and showed that it was tied to larger logics of colonialism and decolonisation on the one hand, and security and migration control on the other. This book therefore departs from standard theoretical and practical approaches to statelessness and suggests different responses.

It is generally accepted that statelessness is a global phenomenon (e.g. UNHCR, 2014; ISI, 2019). It can leave people without the tools to demonstrate their existence and to claim even the most basic rights. Yet on the global level, the problems associated with statelessness have only recently garnered significant attention within the United Nations system and among a small network of advocates and scholars (Kingston, 2013 and 2019). Until now, the focus of work on statelessness as a global consideration has been on ending legal statelessness. This includes the United Nations High Commissioner for Refugees' (UNHCR) #IBelong Campaign to End Statelessness by 2024 (UNHCR, 2014; Staples, 2017; Swider, 2017; Schnyder, this volume). There has so far been little work to investigate the wider relationship between statelessness and governance, or the problems created by the governance of citizenship.

The framings of citizenship and identity that have emerged from colonialism and decolonisation have been particularly powerful in producing today's logics of citizenship and in defining the communities now experiencing entrenched statelessness. Those framings can be seen in more recent moves towards denationalisation and 'migration control'. Indeed, many affected populations can trace their statelessness, in one way or another, to colonialism and/or decolonisation. For some, ruling elites supported by retreating colonial powers created citizenship policies that excluded unwanted minorities or unwanted ways of life. Migration during colonial periods has also given rise to communities seen as symbolic of the colonial power, who became unwanted minorities in newly independent states (consider Russian speakers in Estonia, as shown in Vollmer, this volume). Processes of decolonisation have themselves given rise to stranded populations who do not fit into any of the remaining citizenship regimes (for instance, stateless Palestinians, as represented in Deeb, this volume). More recently, there is also an increasing trend towards denationalisation within the logic of security and 'migration control' (Kingston, this volume). That is, people are told that their citizenship is no longer recognised, often leading to attempts to remove them from their home country. In this way, citizenship is no longer seen as a right but as a privilege, and one which can be leveraged as a tool of coercion.

Three key tensions run through these various dimensions of statelessness and are found in different forms throughout this book. First, while on the one hand citizenship is presented as an emancipatory, presumed good, there are those who reject citizenships or pursue alternative forms of identity (Kochenov, 2019; Bloom, 2017). Second, identity documents serve multiple purposes: they recognise and empower individuals; they order and categorise them; and they provide mechanisms and technologies of control (e.g. essays in Caplan and Torpey, 2001). Finally, emotional elements of identity and membership intertwine with legal, political, and social elements, so that it can be difficult to separate one from another.

It becomes clear, through these many different lenses and contrary to common discourses, that statelessness is not the key 'problem' to be solved. Instead, both the theoretical inconsistencies and the real-world harms associated with statelessness are driven by a more fundamental problem – the 'problem of citizenship' (Bloom, this volume; Bloom, 2019). If we are to understand the realities of statelessness, this study must not focus on some problem of statelessness itself, but on the problems produced by the governance of citizenship and by the uses – both implicit and explicit – of citizenship in all levels of governance.

New directions for studying statelessness and governance

'Governance' refers broadly to the activity of institutions, policies, and norms that maintain order, stability, and well-functioning societies. The concept is intentionally fuzzy to allow the study of a broad range of entities, mechanisms, and power structures – and the relations between them (Finkelstein, 1995). 'Governance' can encompass government institutions as well as 'informal, non-governmental institutions operating in the public realm' (Bøås, 1998), and indeed it has long been understood to go further, to include 'systems of rule at all levels of human activity – from the family to the international organization' (Rosenau, 1995: 13). Applied to citizenship and statelessness, the versatility of the language of governance enables examination of a variety of structures, from the personal to the global, and the interplay between them. However, the study of statelessness also presents challenges for traditional approaches to governance. This is because it brings to light dimensions of governance that are often unseen by that majority of theorists who do not themselves have experience with statelessness (e.g. Cole's 'Insider Theory', 2017).

Statelessness functions at all these levels in interrelated ways. Consider, for instance, how the mundane day-to-day decisions of petty administrators in Malaysia can effectively bar some people from citizenship (Liew, this volume), while global governance structures which defer to state citizenship in defining their scope may translate such local exclusions into exclusion from consideration in the international system (Bloom, this volume). Different levels of governance structures may also interact more explicitly, such as how the national government in the Dominican Republic has interacted with both the national Constitutional Court and the Inter-American

Court in citizenship decision-making (Wooding, this volume). In this way, the study of statelessness and governance provides a crucial next step in the emerging discipline of governance.

Meanwhile, the language of governance provides the interdisciplinarity and flexibility needed in order to begin to develop a deeper understanding of how statelessness functions. In breaking down boundaries between discourses, theories of governance allow a 'fundamental transformation in how we understand existing orders' (Zumbansen, 2014: 84). As a political theory, the concept of governance provides a way to examine concerns that are of both theoretical and real-world importance (Peters, 2014: 20). Statelessness as a topic benefits from this approach, since it simultaneously presents puzzles to theory and urgent challenges to people in the real world.

Though the notion of governance is older, the contemporary tradition in governance scholarship as we understand it here emerged in the 1980s and 1990s in three main dimensions: 'global governance', 'good governance', and what we might refer to as 'legitimate governance' (though these three traditions also merge). The study of statelessness helps to interrogate the relationships between these dimensions. The literature on 'global governance' is interested in all areas of governance insofar as they have 'transnational repercussions' (Rosenau, 1995: 13). This includes both those systems and actors that maintain the status quo and those that that seek to reform it (Weiss and Wilkinson, 2019). It also includes, whether implicitly or explicitly, a concern with the governance of the process of globalisation itself (Buzdugan and Payne, 2016). The literature on 'good governance' largely focuses on the relationships between actors within states and that between 'society' and 'the state'. This began life by focusing on states that receive aid or development assistance, many of which have a history of colonialism and decolonisation, with a particular focus on those in Africa (Nanda, 2006; Gisselquist, 2012). This includes a consideration of the potential role of the global system in promoting internal structures of 'good governance' within states (Weiss, 2000), as well as the risk that this is part of a neo-colonial agenda (Mkandawire, 2007). Relatedly, a discourse of legitimacy in governance takes into account 'dynamics of identity, power, wealth, and inequality' that reinforce existing formal political structures and frame individuals as 'necessarily the repositories of governmental power' (Gathii, 2000: 2018, in response to Roth, 1999). This also allows consideration of a wider range of social and political arrangements (Anghie, 1999).

The relationship between statelessness and governance is complex, with a rich mix of formal and informal contributing factors. On the one hand, there is the 'non-decisionism' of states, officials, and functionaries, which can leave people effectively stateless when action fails to be taken – as happens to elderly Bhutanese refugees in the United States (Benson et al., this volume). On the other hand, there are explicit and intentional efforts within state policies to 'weaponise' citizenship, as can be seen in a growing range of countries that use the removal of citizenship, or threat of that removal, as punishment (Kingston, this volume). Both of these extremes, and the many and mixed contexts in between, must be part of our understanding of the relationship between statelessness and governance, and the governance of citizenship in particular.

Moreover, the reality of statelessness forces a reappraisal of structures of membership in the international community. This becomes particularly clear by considering the implications of citizenships (and lack of citizenships) in contexts where governance structures themselves are being contested. For example, consider situations in which competing state and non-state governments claim control over the same territorial space – and over the people that live within it (Kasianenko, this volume). Competing governance frameworks may also have competing understandings of membership. At the extreme, where principal governance is not provided by states but rather by so-called 'rebel groups', the meaning of 'citizenship' is complicated further and so is the relationship between statelessness and governance (Fortin et al., this volume). These analyses of statelessness and governance force a reassessment of the role of systems that govern and a reappraisal of the function of citizenship.

Organisation of the book

Statelessness is often understood as an indication of rupture in law and policy, and is presented as anomalous. This leads to a focus on 'fixing' or 'solving' statelessness, rather than addressing the context which makes statelessness so problematic for those affected. The poem that opens this book, 'A Stateless Poem' by Danielle Legros Georges, illustrates the seemingly arbitrary way in which citizenship comes with good fortune for some while being unavailable to others – and the challenges this creates for citizenship's legitimacy.

Statelessness, Governance, and the Problem of Citizenship is organised into three sections. In Part I, 'Producing and maintaining statelessness', chapters explore how the problem of citizenship serves as a root cause of statelessness and raises key questions about governance at all levels. The chapters in Part II, 'Living with the problem of citizenship', highlight how statelessness is experienced throughout a person's life course – from conception and birth through old age. In Part III, 'Rethinking governance', contributors consider existing efforts to 'solve' statelessness and propose ways to refocus energy in order to address the overlooked problem of citizenship.

Part I: Producing and maintaining statelessness

In Part I, we present how statelessness is facilitated by governance structures. It opens with Shabu Mwangi's painting of an indistinct figure whose face is clear and expression complex (Figure 1: 'New Democracy II'). For Mwangi, the figure signifies people who are unrepresented. This figure provides a focus for the chapters that follow. In the first chapter, Tendayi Bloom argues that statelessness raises fundamental questions for global governance (Chapter 1: 'The problem of citizenship in global governance'). She shows that when projects and programmes of the United Nations defer to national citizenships, they risk either passing over or targeting people who do not have citizenship of any state.

Global governance is realised in diverse contexts, affected by complex relationships between citizenship policies and national, regional, and international politics. Kate Wilkinson Cross and Pefi Kingi then show how the real-world experiences of statelessness in the Pacific region affect understandings of governance, even in the context of the ultimate existential crisis: the potential disappearance of a state under the sea (Chapter 2: '*Fonua* cultural statelessness in the Pacific and the effects of climate change').

Regional politics can also impact national situations. Anoshay Fazal presents how national policies, as well as the perceived geopolitical implications of those policies, affect the status of people with Afghan roots living in Pakistan (Chapter 3: 'A regional politics of foreignness and Pakistan's Afghan refugees'). Individuals of Afghan descent are caught up in diplomatic and other challenges that don't, at first glance, seem to have much to do with citizenship. Seen neither as Pakistanis nor as stateless refugees, members of this community are sometimes simply labelled as 'foreign'.

Jason Tucker highlights how the statelessness of stateless refugees is often overlooked, but may be of primary importance for ensuring that rights are recognised and protected (Chapter 4: 'The statelessness of refugees'). Prioritising the label of 'refugee' in governance relating to stateless refugees and overlooking statelessness risks missing key elements of their experience – one which cannot be tied officially to a home country. Relatedly, Mawa Rannahr's painting figuratively evokes this experience of having nowhere to stand (Figure 2: 'Dissolution of the moonbeam union'). The figures are bare; they gather on what looks like a crescent moon, sinking beneath the waves of what Rannahr describes as a metaphorical sea. Some cling to each other, while one falls into the swell. There is no state in the painting, no infrastructure. They are caught in some no-place in between.

Administrative categories are important in the construction of this liminality. Jamie Chai Yun Liew shows how legal structures along with the administrative practices of state and local officials impact everyday statelessness in Malaysia (Chapter 5: 'Statelessness and the administrative state: The legal prowess of the first-line bureaucrat in Malaysia'). She demonstrates that statelessness can be produced on the ground in administrative offices and in the places where paperwork is processed, with profound effects on people's access to rights and recognition. The labelling of people as 'stateless' can also be organised from the top down, as illustrated through Ahmad Benswait's analyses and personal reflections as a linguist who is also member of Kuwait's Bidoon community (Chapter 6: 'Language and statelessness: The impact of political discourses on the Bidoon community in Kuwait'). Benswait's chapter presents how official and centralised state policies use both language and objects to create symbolic exclusions that cement people's perceived 'foreignness' and so also appear to legitimise their legal statelessness.

Citizenship policies can therefore be used as part of a strategy of social control – whether in withholding citizenship, removing citizenship, or even enforcing it. Lindsey N. Kingston shows how citizenship can be wielded by powerful states to reward or punish – including for the purposes of repression and erasure (Chapter 7: 'The weaponisation of citizenship: Punishment, erasure, and social control'). She challenges the belief that legal nationality is always a social good and contends that it can also be weaponised in deeply harmful ways. In the case of the Donetsk People's Republic (DPR), Nataliia Kasianenko illustrates how individuals navigate a complex context where Russian citizenship is sometimes imposed, Ukrainian citizenship is sometimes retained or rejected, and many claim the citizenship of the DPR even though it is not recognised externally as a state (Chapter 8: 'Statelessness and governance in the absence of recognition: The case of the "Donetsk People's Republic"'). This lack of international recognition challenges the meaning of citizenship. Katharine Fortin, Bart Klem, and Marika Sosnowski interrogate in more detail the implications of registration within territories controlled by so-called 'rebel governments' (Chapter 9: 'Legal identity and rebel governance: A comparative perspective on lived consequence of contested sovereignty'). For instance, people given citizenship of the Islamic State, or whose births and marriages were registered by its administration, must now seek recognition in states that have never recognised the validity of either the Islamic State or its bureaucracy. For such individuals, civil registration and its recognition are also weaponised.

Part II: Living with the problem of citizenship

Part II focuses on the real-world experiences of statelessness and governance throughout a person's life course. Manal Deeb stares out from the image which opens this section (Figure 3: 'Obsession'). As a Palestinian

American, she describes herself in this image as looking out through layers of identity. This includes fronds that look like writing. The viewer may try to make them into something meaningful, but on closer inspection they are meaningless. Instead, Deeb explains, the statehood is inside her. This is her obsession.

The need for a person to have documents that prove the reality of their existence emerges as a theme throughout the book. Crucial among these documents is the birth certificate. In the first chapter in this section, Pragna Paramita Mondal's analysis of transnational surrogacy in India provides a vehicle for exploring how the governance of citizenship begins at conception (Chapter 10: 'Transnational surrogacy, biocitizenship, and statelessness: India's response to the "ghosts of the republic"'). Before a child is born, the conditions for their access to citizenship are already being set. Jan Lukas Buterman adds that identity documents like the birth certificate can become 'fetishised', used to shape and reinforce gender and sexuality norms, and in turn create situations of statelessness (Chapter 11: 'The birth certificate as fetish object in the governance of citizenship and its presumed sex and gender norms'). This includes the almost universal practice of requiring every person to be identified as either male or female.

Transitioning from infancy to youth, we find that statelessness can have different consequences for young people depending on context. It is helpful to consider Janepicha Cheva-Isarakul's presentation of children made stateless by labour migration policies in Thailand (Chapter 12: 'Seeking "a right to belong": A stateless Shan youth's journey to citizenship in northern Thailand') alongside Maarja Vollmer's analysis of citizenship choices among youth in Estonia (Chapter 13: 'Being excluded or excluding yourself? Citizenship choices among the stateless youth in Estonia'). Cheva-Isarakul follows one young woman from Thailand's Shan community as she seeks novel ways to access a citizenship and fulfil her ambitions, while Vollmer examines why some Estonian young people adopt similar strategies while others opt to remain stateless.

Following these chapters is a letter written by Karina Gareginovna Ambartsoumian-Clough, one of the founders of the organisation United Stateless (Figure 4: 'Letter'). In the letter, the author reflects on how, as a young woman, she came to realise the extent of the implications for her own situation of statelessness at the moment she discovered that she was diabetic, and her life suddenly seemed impossible. Handwritten and personal, without salutation, it is unclear whether the author is addressing a general reader, or perhaps writing the letter to herself. It demonstrates that macro realities of statelessness must be understood through real, hidden, and often devastating personal consequences. It also illustrates the strength that it takes to live despite these difficulties.

Different ways of life can create different experiences of citizenship and of statelessness. For example, Christoph Sperfeldt analyses research into the experiences of so-called 'nomadic' populations in Thailand, Côte d'Ivoire, and Lebanon (Chapter 14: 'Statelessness and governance at the periphery: "Nomadic" populations and the modern state in Thailand, Côte d'Ivoire, and Lebanon'). Populations associated with traditional practices involving regular movement – whether they in fact continue to move – face discrimination in accessing citizenship. In this way, the governance of citizenship constructs and determines what is to be a 'nation' and a 'state' and who is to be included in it.

The governance of citizenship continues to affect people in older age. Whereas earlier chapters showed how citizenship policies can be directly used by states, Odessa Gonzalez Benson, Yoosun Park, Francis Tom Temprosa, and Dilli Gautam show how inaction of states can also be deleterious (Chapter 15: 'Ageing and stateless: Non-decisionism and state violence across temporal and geopolitical space from Bhutan to the United States'). The United States has not rejected Bhutanese refugees from citizenship, but it will not make them citizens until they pass a language test. Inability to pass that test leaves people, even into their advanced years, without any citizenship. In this chapter, those who are no longer of working age express different struggles to those expressed by younger people in earlier chapters affected by statelessness. Poignantly, some mention a desire to 'belong' somewhere before they die; to be remembered as someone who was a citizen.

The many-layered and complex implications of statelessness – and how they intertwine with other dimensions of peoples' lived realities – are presented throughout this book. Deirdre Brennan, Nina Murray, and Allison J. Petrozziello use cases from the European context to show the necessity of intentionally adopting an intersectional approach to understanding lived experiences of statelessness, and suggest ways in which this could be achieved (Chapter 16: 'Asking the "other questions": Applying intersectionality to understand statelessness in Europe'). They conclude this section by setting out why it is essential that stateless persons themselves are part of the project of understanding statelessness, governance, and the problem of citizenship.

Part III: Rethinking governance

The third and final section of this book interrogates efforts to 'solve' statelessness. Contributors propose new directions in efforts to address the problem of citizenship. This final section opens with Thana Faroq's photograph of a woman behind clouded, rain-spattered glass alongside her handwritten note

(Figure 5: 'I don't recognize me in the shadows'). Through the note, the photographed woman communicates directly with the viewer while her identity remains obscured. Together, the image and the note demonstrate the complexity of the difficulties associated with statelessness. While the problem of her citizenship is left unaddressed, she has been forced to navigate the borders around her in strategic and uncomfortable ways. She explains that as a stateless person in Syria, she was unable to travel to visit family in neighbouring countries. She has only been able to do so thanks to residence in The Netherlands while she remains without a citizenship. She flags this arrangement as peculiar.

Efforts to 'solve statelessness' commonly start with projects to quantify the number of stateless persons on the one hand and systems of mass civil registration on the other. Heather Alexander raises fundamental difficulties with efforts to quantify the complex reality of statelessness (Chapter 17: 'The ethics of quantifying statelessness'). She argues that trying to map and to count stateless persons carries methodological challenges, while identifying and mapping stateless persons risks putting people at risk of state coercion or violence. On the other hand, Edwin O. Abuya shows problems with a mass documentation project in Kenya (Chapter 18: 'Registering persons at risk of statelessness in Kenya: Solutions or further problems?'). While some stateless persons hoped that registration with Kenya's new biometric 'Huduma Namba' system would help to alleviate difficulties associated with their lack of status, the system's failure to engage with the registration barriers facing stateless persons has left them disappointed.

It is often supposed that the best way to 'solve statelessness' would be to allocate citizenship. However, this does not address those problems underlying the governance of citizenship which make statelessness so burdensome. For example, Haaqi Bahram demonstrates how allocating citizenship can create divisions (Chapter 19: 'Too little too late? Naturalisation of stateless Kurds and transitional justice in Syria'). The decision to give Syrian citizenship to some Kurds and not others has effectively created two new quasi-ethnic groups. Even if everyone is allocated a citizenship, this may not address the difficulties associated with being stateless. Yoana Kuzmova interrogates the United Arab Emirates' policy to purchase citizenship of a third country, Comoros, for those who were stateless in the country (Chapter 20: 'Statelessness elimination through legal fiction: The United Arab Emirates' Comorian minority'). Rather than addressing the problems associated with statelessness, this has merely produced a new Comorian minority community of illegal immigrants, whose names and details have now been documented by the state.

Addressing the governance of citizenship requires an interdisciplinary and multi-actor approach. Bridget Wooding presents how the Dominican

Republic's Constitutional Court and the Inter-American Court have challenged the Dominican policy to deprive citizens of their citizenship (Chapter 21: 'Supra-national jurisprudence: Necessary but insufficient to contest statelessness in the Dominican Republic'). While the courts play a key role, she argues that they rely on civil society actors to bring cases to trial. Civil society is diverse, as is demonstrated by Arison Kul in the second image of this section (Figure 6: 'All faces'). For Kul, it reaches beyond the human realm. The mix of human and bird eyes gaze steadily out from his image at the observer. Inspired by his home in Papua New Guinea, he illustrates a strength that derives from interconnection between people and nature, which comes before the laws of states and citizenships.

Civil society includes the movements that engage with UNHCR in Geneva or in country offices, as well as the grassroots efforts of both stateless persons and their advocates. Melissa Schnyder presents how civil society actors have worked with the UNHCR Action Plan to promote the rights of stateless persons and those at risk of statelessness (Chapter 22: 'Civil society advocacy to address statelessness: Using norms to promote progress on the Global Action Plan to End Statelessness'). Building on this, Thiago Assunção explores how specific campaigns in Brazil have effected policy change and influenced regional policy development (Chapter 23: 'The construction of a Brazilian "hospitality policy" and the adoption of a new legal framework for stateless persons'). In particular, he highlights the successful activism of formally stateless sisters in Brazil who engaged multiple actors in their own struggle for Brazilian citizenship and set a new precedent in the process.

Addressing the challenges associated with statelessness requires radical rethinking. The first step will be to revisit the contemporary meaning and relevance of 'nation' and the assumptions that produce it. This is what Areej Alshammiry does in her analysis of the construction of Bidoon 'foreignness' in Kuwait (Chapter 24: 'Ideological governance of citizen and noncitizen others in Kuwait'). She argues that the nation cannot be taken as given, but rather is produced by underlying assumptions which can appear to legitimise locating some people outside it. To address the problem of citizenship, it will be necessary to interrogate the theoretical structures that produce it.

Throughout this book, contributors demonstrate the need to centre the perspectives of stateless persons within any efforts to address statelessness, governance, and the problem of citizenship. This includes acknowledging that there is diversity among the experiences and perspectives of stateless persons. Natalie Brinham presents arguments made by Rohingya activists for abandoning the 'stateless' label (Chapter 25: ' "We are *not* stateless! You can call us what you like, but we are citizens of Myanmar!": Rohingya resistance and the stateless label'). Such activists argue that labelling people as stateless risks reconfirming and entrenching the state's denial of their citizenship. Ekaterina E wraps up the section and concludes the book with an activist's reflections on the work of United Stateless, an advocacy organisation founded by and for stateless persons living in the United States (Chapter 26: 'United Stateless in the United States: Reflections from an activist'). She presents how her own experiences of statelessness, and those of her colleagues in the organisation, frame a unique approach to advocacy and to activism. She argues that centring persons with experience of statelessness has the potential to improve governance structures for everyone, including those who are not affected by statelessness directly.

In the final image of the book, a young man looks to the future (Figure 7: 'We are not immigrants'). He wears a baseball cap, which is blue in the original image, with the words '18 ius soli' written on it. 'Ius soli' (or 'jus soli' in English) refers to the Latin phrase meaning 'rule of the soil' and the idea that a person should receive the citizenship of the country in which they are born. This hat marks him as part of a movement of young Italians, born in the country to immigrant parents, who have now reached the age of 18 and are still unable to access their Italian citizenship. This still image is drawn from Fred Kuwornu's film *18 Ius Soli*, which highlights this situation and young people's efforts to remedy it. Kuwornu selected this image to represent the film; flanked by the iconography of the Italian state, the young man asserts that he is Italian, even if the state will not recognise it.

While statelessness is associated with significant challenges for those affected, we suggest that the underlying problem is not statelessness itself, but rather it is citizenship and how citizenship is both governed and used as a governance tool. We demonstrate how the problem of citizenship emerges, time and again, when we consider the relationship between statelessness and governance. This book is not intended to represent a finished project, but rather to serve as an invitation to join a conversation about statelessness, governance, and the problem of citizenship.

Notes

1 The authors thank Nicola Smith, Katherine Tonkiss, and the anonymous reviewer for their helpful comments on earlier drafts of this chapter.
2 With thanks to the anonymous reviewer for suggesting this turn of phrase.

References

Anghie, A. (1999) 'Universality and the concept of governance in international law', in E. K. Quashigah and O. C. Okafor (eds) *Legitimate Governance in*

Africa: International and Domestic Legal Perspectives (Leiden: Martinus Nijhoff): pp. 21–40.

Bloom, T. (2017) 'Members of colonised groups, statelessness and the right to have rights', in T. Bloom, K. Tonkiss, and P. Cole (eds) *Understanding Statelessness* (Abingdon: Routledge): pp. 153–172.

Bloom, T. (2018) *Noncitizenism: Recognising Noncitizen Capabilities in a World of Citizens* (Abingdon: Routledge).

Bloom, T. (2019) 'When migration policy isn't about migration: Considerations for implementation of the Global Compact for Migration', *Ethics and International Affairs*, 33:4, 481–497.

Bøås, M. (1998) 'Governance as multilateral bank policy', *European Journal of Development Research*, 10:2, 117–134.

Buzdugan, S., and Payne, A. (2016) *The Long Battle for Global Governance* (Abingdon: Routledge).

Caplan, J., and Torpey, J. (2001) *Documenting Individual Identity* (Princeton, NJ: Princeton University Press).

Cole, P. (2017) 'Insider theory and the construction of statelessness', in T. Bloom, K. Tonkiss, and P. Cole (eds) *Understanding Statelessness* (Abingdon: Routledge): pp. 255–267.

Finkelstein, L. (1995) 'What is global governance?', *Global Governance*, 1:3, 367–372.

Gathii, J. T. (2000) 'Neoliberalism, colonialism and international governance: Decentering the international law of governmental legitimacy', *Michigan Law Review*, 98, 1996–2055.

Gisselquist, R. M. (2012) 'Good governance as a concept, and why this matters for development policy', *WIDER Working Paper* No. 2012/30. Helsinki: The United Nations University World Institute for Development Economics Research.

Institute for Statelessness and Inclusion (2019) 'Statelessness in numbers: 2019' [Online]. Available at https://files.institutesi.org/ISI_statistics_analysis_2019.pdf (Accessed 29 July 2020).

Kingston, L. N. (2013) '"A forgotten human rights crisis": Statelessness and issue non(emergence)', *Human Rights Review*, 14, 73–87.

Kingston, L. N. (2019) 'Conceptualizing statelessness as a human rights challenge: Framing, visual representation, and (partial) issue emergence', *Journal of Human Rights Practice*, 11:1, 52–72.

Kochenov, D. (2019) *Citizenship* (Boston, MA: Institute of Technology Press).

Mkandawire, T. (2007) '"Good governance": The itinerary of an idea', *Development in Practice*, 17:4, 679–681.

Nanda, V. P. (2006) 'The "Good Governance" concept revisited', *The Annals of the American Academy*, 603, 270–283.

Peters, B. G. (2014) 'Governance as a political theory', in D. Levi-Faur (ed.) *Oxford Handbook of Governance* (Oxford: Oxford University Press): pp. 19–32.

Rosenau, J. (1995) 'Governance in the twenty-first century', *Global Governance*, 1:1, 13–43.

Roth, B. R. (1999) *Governmental Illegitimacy in International Law* (New York: Oxford University Press).

Staples, K. (2017) 'Recognition, nationality, and statelessness', in T. Bloom, K. Tonkiss, and P. Cole (eds) *Understanding Statelessness* (Abingdon: Routledge): pp. 173–188.

Swider, K. (2017) 'Why end statelessness?', in T. Bloom, K. Tonkiss, and P. Cole (eds) *Understanding Statelessness* (Abingdon: Routledge): pp. 191–209.

United Nations (1954) 'Convention relating to the Status of Stateless Persons', *United Nations Treaty Series* 360 117 [Online]. Available at www.un.org/en/ genocideprevention/documents/atrocity-crimes/Doc.24_convention%20stateless. pdf (Accessed 27 July 2020).

United Nations High Commissioner for Refugees (UNHCR) (2014) 'Ending statelessness within 10 years', UNHCR Special Report. Geneva: UNHRC [Online]. Available at www.unhcr.org/en-us/protection/statelessness/546217229/ special-report-ending-statelessness-10-years.html (Accessed 13 August 2020).

Weiss, T. (2000) 'Governance, good governance and global governance: Conceptual and actual challenges', *Third World Quarterly*, 21:5, 795–814.

Weiss, T. G. and Wilkinson, R. (2019) *Rethinking Global Governance* (Cambridge: Polity).

Zumbansen, P. (2014) 'Governance: An interdisciplinary perspective', in D. Levi-Faur (ed.) *Oxford Handbook of Governance* (Oxford: Oxford University Press): pp. 83–96.

Part I

Producing and maintaining statelessness

Figure 1

New Democracy II

Shabu Mwangi

Shabu Mwangi's work focuses on structural violence in society, notions of rootlessness and alienation (particularly the trauma of forced migration), and the reality of finding oneself excluded from a society's vision of itself. His work examines identity and the constant struggle of negotiating one's perception of self against socially established and enforced collective identities. Mwangi's work studies various forms of violence arising from social, economic, and political divisions. He looks at our interaction with one another (and our situations) and the motivation behind action taken during volatile political periods.

1

The problem of citizenship in global governance

Tendayi Bloom[1]

Today's global governance structures suffer from an underlying 'citizenism'. That is, in order to be seen as a full participant in the global system, usually a person must first be recognised as a citizen of a state.[2] This produces contradictions in global governance projects, which I show in this chapter through two examples. First, while a stated aim of the United Nations Sustainable Development Goals (SDGs) is to 'leave no one behind', stateless persons are often unaccounted for in the implementation and monitoring of global development efforts. As a result, they can be left out entirely. Second, presuming citizenship means that policies ostensibly contributing to the global governance of migration target people without any citizenship, including those who have never crossed a border, as 'illegal immigrants'. In both cases, the implications for stateless persons seem to follow at least in part from an underlying presumption of, and deference to, citizenship. The mandate for addressing statelessness officially sits with the United Nations High Commissioner for Refugees (UNHCR) (e.g., discussed in Seet, 2016). However, the obligation to address the problem of citizenship falls much wider.

The problem of citizenship here is particularly insidious. This is because it affects not only the content of global governance, but also who is able to participate in constructing, maintaining, and reforming it. This exclusion from participation both in the world and in the conference rooms makes it less likely for the problem of citizenship to be challenged, and makes the project of developing more inclusive systems more difficult. I conclude this chapter by arguing that rather than merely seeing statelessness as a problem in the international system, it is crucial to problematise the citizenism that makes statelessness so burdensome – including unpicking the common conflation of 'citizen' with person in global governance discourses. Given citizenism may often be invisible to citizens, any project to address it will need to seek out and defer to the expertise of those with direct experience of the problems it creates, and to that of stateless persons in particular.

Ideological and administrative understandings of citizenship

Citizenship is a powerful concept in global governance, both ideologically and administratively. The relationship between the ideological and administrative faces of citizenship's power can create tensions. Ideologically, modern citizenship includes the idea that a citizen of a state is more than a subject of a ruler. The conditions and implications of citizenship are, then, tied up with state sovereignty and self-determination, and so with a presumption that a state has the right to choose its citizens.

This means that citizenship can be made dependent on a person's place of birth, the immigration or marital status of their parents, and even the ethnicity or religion of their family. Naturalisation, or obtaining citizenship after birth, can be made dependent on even more factors, including a person's bank balance, adherence to a set of values, or passing a series of knowledge or language tests. Throughout this book, authors present the challenges posed by making participation in one's home society dependent upon such factors. However, when seen on the global level, additional challenges emerge from a state's unilateral ability to govern citizenship.

Administratively, citizenship is the dominant way in which people are organised globally. It is how we know which state has which responsibilities towards a particular person. In practice, it should not be surprising that the ideological governance of access to citizenship may leave some people out. Difficulties for global governance emerge because administrative citizenship and ideological citizenship are assumed to be coextensive. Consequently, the ideological governance of citizenship has significant implications for global administrative structures. In the work towards the Sustainable Development Goals, people without any citizenship can be left out of consideration entirely, while in migration governance those without citizenship risk being targeted specifically. In both of these cases, problems arise because mechanisms based on the governance of nationhood are made fundamental to the administration of global governance.[3]

Citizenship and development

Citizenship of a state is often implicitly necessary for a person's inclusion in global development efforts. Adopted in 2015, the UN Sustainable Development Agenda set out seventeen goals (the Sustainable Development Goals, or 'SDGs') for the following fifteen years (United Nations, 2015b). These goals address issues such as poverty, hunger, and sanitation; they address access to education, to justice, and to finance; and sustainability in industry, in agriculture, and in aquaculture. There is a series of targets within each goal, and for each target there are indicators for measuring progress. For example, Goal One (to end poverty) includes targets such as eradicating extreme poverty (Target 1.1) and implementing 'nationally appropriate social protection systems' (Target 1.3).

While these targets may seem universal, in practice they risk bypassing people without citizenship. First, populations without citizenship may go uncounted in demographic poverty measures. Uncounted, they are more easily overlooked by Target 1.1 (see Chattopadhyay, 2016). Second, without any recognised status, such persons may be defined as ineligible for the social protection of Target 1.3 by the state in which they live (van Waas and de Chickera, 2017). For example, in this volume Ahmad Benswait describes how, as members of the Bidoon community in Kuwait, he and his family have struggled to access education and healthcare. The problem of citizenship produces invisibility and exclusion of stateless persons in various ways across the Sustainable Development Agenda.

Criticisms of the Millennium Development Goals (MDGs), on whose heels the Sustainable Development Goals followed, included the concern that it reinforced a status quo in which some states, and so also their citizens, are dependent upon others. That is, it focused on aid and on transferring resources (with particular focus on development in Africa) rather than engaging with the structures that produce this dependence and domination (Aleyomi and IseOlorunkanmi, 2012; Durokifa and Ijeoma, 2018; see also United Nations, 2000). I suggest that another side of this status quo is the presumption that individual people participate at the grace of recognised states, and that existing states not only select who to include in their own citizenries but also decide which other entities to recognise as citizenship-granting states.

The MDGs, then, were accused of incentivising states to aim for 'low-hanging fruit': to focus on those whose situations could be improved most easily within existing arrangements, rather than confronting problematic structures that help to keep people poor and excluded (Creppeau, 2014; see also United Nations, 2015b). For example, while Goal One of the MDGs was to eradicate extreme poverty and hunger, its targets ended up focusing merely on reducing the proportion of people in poverty in various dimensions. Some critics observed that the natural increase in the global population alone significantly weakened this commitment (e.g. Pogge, 2004: 319). It also made it possible to overlook people whose inclusion in development would be most politically sensitive (ODI, 2010: 9, 13). This included populations living in states that refuse to recognise their rights or even their existence (Kingston, 2017; van Waas and de Chickera, 2017). In leaving out stateless persons, the MDGs 'could be failing to meet the needs of some of the world's poorest' (Tucker, 2013: 2).

As the period of the MDGs was ending and the SDGs were being developed, it was observed that some groups are often excluded from development decision-making (see United Nations, 2012: 58[j] and 58[k]). This led to the key principle that in order to avoid some of the failings of the MDGs, in the SDGs, 'no one should be left behind' (see United Nations, 2015b: preamble; United Nations 2015a). Within the SDGs, 'status' is given as one of the categories according to which a person should not experience discrimination (United Nations, 2015b: para 19). Since people without any citizenship may well suffer discrimination based on their lack of 'status', this could be seen as referring to stateless persons. However, this is not how it plays out. While the SDGs do include the eradication of absolute poverty in Target 1.1, states are relied upon to decide who to include in this measure. This reliance risks importing national-level exclusions into global-level governance. That is, groups excluded from development efforts within particular states are also excluded from consideration in global development governance.

The benefits of the SDGs can sometimes be framed as 'universal', but 'differentiated' (e.g. Long, 2015). For example, Target 1.3's commitment to implementing 'social protection systems and measures for all' includes the caveat that this be understood as 'nationally appropriate' (United Nations, 2015b).[4] While this might refer to domestic material capacity, it also allows that the scope of who is included in that universal system can be limited on the basis of domestic politics and exclusionary practices (Sengupta, 2016).

The implications of this become clearer if we consider Target 16.9, which commits to the following: '[b]y 2030, provide legal identity for all, including birth registration' (United Nations, 2015b). On first glance, this looks like it might support the inclusion of those affected by statelessness, but it is ambiguous. There is no internationally agreed way to recognise legal identity (Dahan and Gelb, 2015; ISI, 2017). The indicator instituted to track progress on this target (Indicator 16.9.1) measures the '[p]roportion of children under 5 years of age whose births have been registered with a civil authority, by age' (United Nations, 2020: 22). However, civil registration is insufficient to allocate either recognition of legal status or access to rights, and it certainly does not equate to citizenship. Registering and identifying a population may help a state to plan school places and health facilities for those that it intends to serve, without benefitting those who are intentionally excluded (Gerber et al., 2011; Dunning et al., 2014: 2; Alexander, this volume).

Indeed, 'legal identity' also carries risks for some people. For example, legal identification as a 'stateless Palestinian' in Lebanon excludes a person from Lebanese citizenship (Akram, 2002). In Estonia, members of the Russian-speaking minority are given a specific legal identity of non-citizen of

Estonia in lieu of citizenship (Vollmer, this volume). Even citizenship status *per se* may carry risks. The United Arab Emirates (U.A.E.), for example, has created a Comorian minority community by buying Comoros citizenship for those residents excluded from U.A.E. citizenship, producing additional challenges for those affected (Kuzmova, this volume). There is a risk that if the role of citizenship in global development efforts is not addressed explicitly, work to realise Target 16.9 may contribute to, rather than ameliorate, the exclusion of some people entirely.

States are, then, able to restrict who falls within the scope of the SDGs' targets. In 2013, the Dominican Republic effected a large-scale programme of denationalisation, which left many Dominicans without citizenship (Blake, 2017; Wooding, this volume). Apart from anything else, this removed people from consideration in its twenty-year 2030 Action Plan for Sustainable Development. In the lead-up to the adoption of the SDGs, the Dominican Republic planned programmes to ensure all its citizens would have access to identity documents (República Dominicana, 2012), while at the same time removing tens of thousands of people from Dominican citizenship. Rather than merely incentivising 'low-hanging fruit' as mentioned above, deference to citizenship in this Agenda risks incentivising removing people from consideration entirely.

There were efforts by those drafting the SDGs to broaden participation in its creation (Gellers, 2016). This included mapping exercises, the use of social media, and an online survey[5] which could be completed by anyone with an internet connection. While this has been lauded as enacting a democratic shift in the production of a key UN governance framework (Fox and Stoett, 2016), it has also been criticised as window-dressing which obscures business as usual (Geller, 2016). The MyWorld survey continues to gather responses to a constrained set of questions, but the principal follow-up tool is a High Level Political Forum (HLPF), which convenes annually. This is state led, but international organisations and non-governmental organisation (NGO) members of the UN's Economic and Social Council (ECOSOC) can provide expert interventions.

In preparation for the 2019 HLPF, a coalition of organisations and academics presented a submission that explicitly addressed the question of statelessness (Bloom et al., 2019). However, such a submission requires at least one member of the coalition to be a member of ECOSOC. This makes it difficult for informal and grassroots organisations, including stateless persons themselves, both to become aware of the opportunities for contributing to such discussions and then to contribute to them. Discourses around sustainable development have long emphasised the need to include stakeholders and 'citizens' when creating and enacting development policy (see Meadowcroft, 2004). This is undermined if stateless persons are omitted.

The underlying citizenism of the SDGs is apparent in its opening declaration: 'On behalf of the peoples we serve, we have adopted a historic decision on a comprehensive, far-reaching and people-centred set of universal and transformative goals and targets' (United Nations, 2015b). That is, it is framed in terms of 'peoples' rather than 'people', and we have seen that in practice this means that state citizenship policies can remove a person from consideration within this global agenda. If this citizenism remains unchecked, stateless persons will continue not merely to be left behind in the realisation of the SDGs, but they risk being left out entirely.

Migrants without moving

Someone without citizenship of a state can become targeted as a 'migrant' even if they have never left their hometown. The person that may be invisible to development governance may, at the same time, be hyper-visible to migration governance. In practice, those who are not citizens of any state may be defined as 'migrants' in relation to every state, and even as 'illegal immigrants' in the state where they were born (Bloom, 2019).

For example, in Myanmar, members of the Rohingya minority have long been referred to as 'illegal immigrants' to justify their exclusion from citizenship, while their consequent lack of status has been used to justify their designation as 'illegal immigrants' (ERT, 2010; Fullerton, 2014). This has provided a basis for escalation of violence in recent years, which is now being monitored by the International Court of Justice within the purview of the Genocide Convention (ICJ, 2020; see also Brinham, this volume). If discourses around global migration governance do not explicitly address the problem of citizenship, they risk legitimising such practices.

The Sustainable Development Agenda's Target 10.7 commits states to '[f]acilitate orderly, safe, regular and responsible migration and mobility of people, including through the implementation of planned and well-managed migration policies' (United Nations, 2015b: 21). Building on this, in 2016 UN Member states declared that they would develop a Global Compact for Safe, Orderly and Regular Migration, alongside a Compact on Refugees (United Nations, 2016: appendix 2, appendix 1). The New York Declaration, which introduced the processes towards these compacts, observed that 'statelessness can be a root cause of forced displacement and that forced displacement, in turn, can lead to statelessness' (United Nations, 2016: para 72). It was initially assumed that if statelessness should be considered at all in the context of the governance of human mobility, it would be as a refugee issue. This was subsequently recognised to be inadequate, as is evidenced in the eventual inclusion of Action 4 in the Global Compact for

Migration, under the heading: '[e]nsure that all migrants have proof of legal identity and adequate documentation', which goes on to address statelessness explicitly (United Nations, 2018).

While statelessness is not a migration status, stateless people can often be treated as if it is. Abraham Zere, a stateless man living in the United States, recalls that a bank manager, referring to Zere's statelessness, once told him: '…you can't open an account with us as your immigration status does not fit into our categories' (Zere, 2015). In a world built for citizens, many official forms and social categorisations do not include the possibility that a person might not have any citizenship at all (see Liew, this volume). This often leaves stateless persons treated as 'illegal immigrants', facing barriers to regular labour markets, legal redress, healthcare systems, education, and social security, for example. Such individuals are often even subject to immigration detention and, without any other state to which to be deported, this detention may be indefinite and arbitrary (ERT, 2012; ENS, 2017). People without citizenship of any state often also lack travel documents and so, alongside perhaps being treated as migrants everywhere, they are blocked from systems of international mobility.[6] If such individuals want or need to migrate, they must circumvent legal channels, possibly risking exploitation (UNODC, 2008: 433–435).

Migration and migration controls can also put people at risk of statelessness. Migration, particularly when it is urgent, may sever links between a person and their country of citizenship. In addition, some people may be afraid to register births and marriages because they fear either immigration authorities or home country authorities, while some are barred from such civil registration because of their status. Without birth or marriage certificates, people can struggle to prove their eligibility for citizenship (Ferris, 2016). Policies aimed at stopping people from settling in a new country can even create situations of statelessness that prevent them from leaving it. Consider the experience of a Cuban couple, both engineers on temporary contracts in South Africa, who only intended to stay a couple of years. During that period, in 2008, they had a child. The child was rendered stateless because they were unable to register their baby as a citizen of Cuba because they had been outside the country for too long, while South African authorities said that as the child should be Cuban it could not receive South African citizenship (Muller, 2016). Without legal means to travel internationally with their stateless child and unwilling to leave the child behind, the family ended up stranded in South Africa for over a decade (LHR, 2019).

The relationship between statelessness and migration governance may be overwhelming for those affected by it, while those who are not affected are oblivious to it. This presents a problem, since it can be difficult for those confronted by the problem of citizenship to be heard in global decision-making fora. The Global Compact for Migration process engaged in new ways with new communities of civil society actors. However, it did not explicitly include those who are affected by migration governance because they are stateless as a key constituency. A major reason for this may be that the implications for stateless persons are easy to overlook for those who are not stateless. Work is needed specifically to interrogate the role of citizenship and lack of citizenship in people's experiences of migration governance.

Dislocating citizenship from global governance

Both of the examples of global governance discussed in this chapter suffer from contradictions produced by the problem of citizenship, though the problem manifests in each in different ways. In each case, the invisibility (in the case of the SDGs) or hyper-visibility (in the case of migration governance) of those without any citizenship makes it difficult for such individuals to intervene and for them to be heard in discussions of global governance. This means that addressing the problem of citizenship in global governance requires that those who experience the international system primarily as citizens actively make space for stateless persons to intervene and support mechanisms to ensure that their interventions are central to the creation, maintenance, and reform of global governance processes. While UNHCR may hold the official mandate to coordinate responses to statelessness, the responsibility to address the problems produced by the governance of citizenship sits with a much broader range of actors.

Interrogating the problem of citizenship is made more difficult by the fact that three main uses of 'citizenship' can be found in the discourse relating to these agendas. First, there are two ideological uses of citizenship: the 'citizen' who carries out morally good and socially responsible civic activities; and the 'citizen' who has a legal status bestowed by a state. Second, the latter also contributes to an administrative use of 'citizenship'. Finally, 'citizen' is used as if it were synonymous with 'person'. This last factor is even seen among those who highlight existing exclusions and advocate methods to address them.[7] There is a risk, when citizenship is used in these three ways within the same discourse, that they become conflated. When this happens, access to goods to which all people may be entitled becomes dependent upon being a 'good citizen' or on meeting the arbitrary requirements for legal citizenship set by some state.

As discussed above, states often make access to citizenship conditional on a range of attributes. This may include: birth in a particular place, or to particular parents; it may relate to the immigration or marital status of parents, or to membership of a particular ethnic group. In order to naturalise, individuals may need to declare fealty to certain values, prove knowledge of certain presentations of history, or demonstrate certain skills, income, or other resources. This is justified on the grounds that access to membership of a polity needs to reflect its particular needs, history, and experiences. Irrespective of the implications domestically (which are addressed throughout this book), the concatenation of multiple local conditions of membership also drives a global problem. That is, an individual's access to recognition in the international system becomes dependent upon these local arbitrary characteristics.

This occurs in two main ways. First, it occurs explicitly, since stateless persons are largely unrepresented in national politics and by extension have no state to represent their interests at the UN General Assembly. Policy makers may have little motivation to seek them out, to fulfil their needs, or to advocate on their behalf. When people are unregistered and undocumented, their existence even denied, they are most likely also absent from population data. This makes it difficult to address their needs, even if there were a desire to do so.

Second, this lack of representation means that the conflation between 'citizen' and 'person' can more easily be left unchecked. This produces two often conflated international communities (Conklin, 2014): first, there is the international community made up of all people insofar as they are citizens of states; second, there is the international community made up of all people. Global governance institutions may gain their moral legitimacy from the latter, while in practice they gain their political legitimacy from the former. As a result, those who are not citizens of states are both overlooked (as in the case of sustainable development), and targeted (as in the case of migration governance). This risks a 'global governance' that is not really global or sustainable.

The problem of citizenship can seem intractable, but it isn't. Addressing it will rely not on 'surfacing' statelessness,[8] but rather on highlighting and rectifying problems caused by international regimes of citizenship and the deference of global systems to them. This effort will rely heavily on the expertise of those who have the clearest insights into citizenship: those currently labelled as 'stateless'. Framing this as a 'problem of statelessness' is distracting. It risks identifying stateless persons as anomalous, problematic, or abject. This belies a reality in which: neither citizenship nor statelessness is natural; and individuals affected by statelessness are agents. That is, stateless persons, though forced to act despite the governance structures that both ignore and target them, still live out their lives with agency.

Karina Gareginovna Ambartsoumian-Clough, a founding member of United Stateless – an organisation set up by and for stateless persons in the United States (see also E, this volume) – observes[9]: 'A lot of the framing of statelessness is as a victim. We don't want to be seen as a victim (sic.). We are strong. We don't want people to feel sorry for us. We want to be empowered.' Far from being abject, activists like Ambartsoumian-Clough have valuable expertise regarding the problem of citizenship. Their long-running experiences of addressing it in their own lives and those of their families, as well as wider advocacy efforts, make them well placed to lead work to address the global problem of citizenship. However, as set out in this chapter, those who bear the greatest burden of the problem of citizenship also face the most barriers to addressing it, while those who are currently in a position to effect administrative change may never have confronted it (Cole, 2017; Kingston, 2019). I suggest that it will be crucial to ensure that those with direct experience of the problem of citizenship are included as participants in the construction, maintenance, and reform of global governance, if they are willing to do so. However, while the role of such individuals is vital, the responsibility to address the problems sketched here sit with everyone who has a stake in the governance of citizenship.

Conclusion

Living one's life as a citizen, it is easy to overlook the problems that citizenship creates for others in the international system. That is, it is easy not to notice those left out of development efforts, and to presume that where people are targeted by migration governance, this is appropriate. This means that the move to address the problem of citizenship in global governance must be driven by the insights of those with direct experience of it, and by the insights of stateless persons in particular. This will only be possible if the people with the power to do so facilitate those confronted with the international system's citizenism to participate across the development and the critique of global governance. The problem of citizenship affects the ability of global governance to be sustainable, global, or legitimate. Wherever the governance of citizenship makes it difficult for individuals to access core rights or participate in development, responsibility to address the situation sits with all those involved. However, the expertise of stateless persons will be crucial in diagnosing the problem of citizenship and in framing a more sustainable and more equitable approach to global governance.

Notes

1 I am grateful to Phillip Cole, May Darwich, Charlotte Galpin, Andrew Kaye, Lindsey Kingston, Yoana Kuzmova, Richard Shorten, Kelly Staples, Katherine

Tonkiss, and Susan Williams, as well as the anonymous reviewer, for their comments on earlier drafts. Any remaining errors are mine.

2 The language of 'citizenism' is developed in Bloom (2018).

3 For an analysis of the conflation of 'nationality' and 'citizenship', see Tonkiss (2017).

4 This wording of national appropriateness also appears in Target 5.4's commitment to recognise unpaid care and domestic work in social protection policies and to promote shared household responsibility, suggesting that national appropriateness might also allow gendered discrimination, for example.

5 This can be found and completed at http://myworld2030.org (accessed 31 July 2020).

6 Though note that the 1954 Convention Relating to the Status of Stateless Persons, Article 28, commits states to provide travel documents to stateless persons in their territory.

7 For example, even the important report by Thinyane (2008) adopts this convention.

8 With thanks to Yoana Kuzmova for suggesting this turn of phrase.

9 Personal communication, 27 December 2019. Quoted with permission.

References

Akram, S. (2002) 'Palestinian refugees and their legal status', *Journal of Palestine Studies*, 31:3, 36–51.

Aleyomi, M. B. and IseOlorunkanmi, J. O. (2012) 'Africa and the Millennium Development Goals: Constraints and possibilities', *International Journal of Politics and Good Governance*, 5:1, 53–73.

Blake, J. (2017) 'Race-based statelessness in the Dominican Republic', in T. Bloom, K. Tonkiss, and P. Cole (eds) *Understanding Statelessness* (New York: Routledge): pp. 102–116.

Bloom, T. (2018) *Noncitizenism* (Abingdon: Routledge).

Bloom, T. (2019) 'When migration policy isn't about migration', *Ethics and International Affairs*, 33:4, 481–497.

Bloom, T., Manby, B., and Badri, K. (2019) 'Why citizenship is relevant to sustainable development', European Network on Statelessness policy brief [Online]. Available at www.statelessness.eu/sites/www.statelessness.eu/files/attachments/resources/ENS-Citizenship-SDGs-High_Level_Political_Forum_2019-briefing.pdf (Accessed 13 August 2020).

Chattopadhyay, S. (2016) 'What gets measured, gets managed: Challenges ahead for the UN's data-driven development agenda', Overseas Development Institute Briefing, December 2016 (London: Overseas Development Institute).

Cole, P. (2017) 'Insider theory and the construction of statelessness', in T. Bloom, K. Tonkiss, and P. Cole (eds) *Understanding Statelessness* (New York: Routledge): 255–267.

Conklin, W. (2014) *Statelessness* (London: Bloomsbury).

Creppeau, F. (2014) 'Report of the special rapporteur on the human rights of migrants', Human rights of migrants: Note by the Secretary General to the sixty-ninth session of the General Assembly (A/69/302): paragraph III.A.12.

Dahan, M., and Gelb, A. (2015) 'The role of identification in the post-2015 development agenda', Centre for Global Development [Online]. Available at www.cgdev.org/publication/role-identification-post-2015-development-agenda (Accessed 29 August 2020).

Dunning, C., Gelb, A., and Raghavan, S. (2014) 'Birth registration, legal identity, and the post-2015 agenda', Center for Global Development Policy Paper 046 [Online]. Available at www.cgdev.org/publication/birth-registration-legal-identity-and-post-2015-agenda (Accessed 29 August 2020).

Durokifa, A. A., and Ijeoma, E. C. (2018) 'Neo-colonialism and Millennium Development Goals (MDGs) in Africa', *African Journal of Science, Technology, Innovation and Development*, 10:3, 355–366.

Equal Rights Trust (ERT) (2012) *Guidelines on the Detention of Stateless Persons* (London: Equal Rights Trust) [Online]. Available at www.equalrightstrust.org/ertdocumentbank/guidelines%20complete.pdf (Accessed 29 August 2020).

Equal Rights Trust (ERT) (2010) *Unravelling Anomaly: Detention, Discrimination, and the Protection Needs of Stateless Persons* (London: Equal Rights Trust).

European Network on Statelessness (ENS) (2017) *Protecting Stateless Persons from Arbitrary Detention* (London: European Network on Statelessness).

Ferris, E. (2016) 'Displacement and statelessness', *International Affairs Forum*, 1:1, 79–81.

Fox, O., and Stoett, P. (2016) 'Citizen participation in the UN Sustainable Development Goals consultation process', *Global Governance*, 22, 555–574.

Fullerton, M. (2014) 'The intersection of statelessness and refugee protection in asylum policy', *Journal on Migration and Human Security*, 2:3, 144–164.

Gellers, J. (2016) 'Crowdsourcing global governance', *International Environmental Agreements*, 16, 415–432.

Gerber, P., Gargett, A., and Castan, M. (2011) 'Does the right to birth registration include a right to a birth certificate?', *Netherlands Quarterly of Human Rights*, 29:4, 434–459.

Institute on Statelessness and Inclusion (ISI) (2017) 'Statelessness, human rights and the Sustainable Development Agenda', Working paper [Online]. Available at https://files.institutesi.org/SDG_working-paper2017.pdf (Accessed 13 August 2020).

International Court of Justice (ICJ) (2020) 'Application of the Convention of the Prevention and Punishment of the Crime of Genocide (The Gambia v Myanmar)' [Online]. Available at www.icj-cij.org/en/case/178 (Accessed 16 November 2020).

Kingston, L. N. (2017) 'Worthy of rights: Statelessness as a cause and symptom of marginalisation', in T. Bloom, K. Tonkiss, and P. Cole (eds) *Understanding Statelessness* (New York: Routledge): pp. 17–34.

Kingston, L. N. (2019) 'Conceptualizing statelessness as a human rights challenge: Framing, visual representation, and (partial) issue emergence', *Journal of Human Rights Practice*, 11:1, 52–72.

Lawyers for Human Rights (LHR) South Africa (2019) 'Press release: High court dismisses attempt to revoke stateless child's citizenship', 30 May, Citizenship Rights in Africa Initiative [Online]. Available at https://citizenshiprightsafrica.org/press-release-high-court-dismisses-attempt-to-revoke-stateless-childs-citizenship/ (Accessed 13 August 2020).

Long, G. (2015) 'The idea of universality in the Sustainable Development Goals', *Ethics and International Affairs*, 29:2, 203–222.

Meadowcroft, J. (2004) 'Participation and sustainable development', in W. M. Lafferty (ed.) *Governance for Sustainable Development: The Challenge of Adapting Form to Function* (Cheltenham: Edward Elgar): pp. 162–190.

Muller, L. (2016) 'South African courts confirm the right to nationality of a stateless child', European Network on Statelessness blog, 13 September [Online]. Available at www.statelessness.eu/blog/south-african-courts-confirm-right-nationality-stateless-child-20-year-old-legal-principle (Accessed 16 August 2020).

Overseas Development Institute (ODI) (2010) *Millennium Development Goals Report Card* (London: Overseas Development Institute).

Pogge, T. (2004) 'The first UN Millennium Development Goal', in A. Follesdal and T. Pogge (eds) *Real World Justice: Grounds, Principles, Human Rights, and Social Institutions* (New York: Springer): pp. 317–338.

República Dominicana (2012) *Ley de Estrategia Nacional de Desarollo 2030*. Ministerio de Economía, Planificación y Desarrollo de la República Dominicana.

Seet, M. (2016) 'The origins of UNHCR's global mandate on statelessness', *International Journal of Refugee Law*, 28:1, 7–24.

Sengupta, M. (2016) 'The Sustainable Development Goals', E-International Relations, 18 January [Online]. Available at www.e-ir.info/2016/01/18/the-sustainable-development-goals-an-assessment-of-ambition/ (Accessed 16 August 2020).

Staples, K. (2014) *Retheorising Statelessness* (Edinburgh: Edinburgh University Press).

Thinyane, M. (2018) 'Engaging citizens for sustainable development', United Nations University Institute on Computing and Society [Online]. Available at https://collections.unu.edu/eserv/UNU:6646/UNU-CS-Data_SD-Report-Engaging_Citizens-20181004-compressed.pdf (Accessed 13 August 2020).

Tonkiss, K. (2017) 'Statelessness and the performance of citizenship-as-nationality', in T. Bloom, K. Tonkiss, and P. Cole (eds) *Understanding Statelessness* (New York: Routledge): pp. 241–254.

Tucker, J. (2013) 'The humanitarian side of statelessness: Statelessness within the framework of the Millennium Development Goals', SSRN [Online]. Available at https://papers.ssrn.com/sol3/papers.cfm?abstract_id=2220802 (Accessed 13 August 2020).

United Nations (2000) *United Nations Millennium Declaration*, Resolution adopted by the General Assembly 18 September 2000 [A/55/L.2].

United Nations (2012) *The Future We Want*: Outcome document of the United Nations Conference on Sustainable Development.

United Nations (2015a) *The Millennium Goals Report* (New York: United Nations).

United Nations (2015b) *Transforming Our World* [A/RES/70/1] (New York: United Nations).

United Nations (2016) *New York Declaration for Refugees and Migrants*, Resolution adopted by the General Assembly on 19 September 2016 [A/71/L.1].

United Nations (2018) *Global Compact for Safe, Orderly, and Regular Migration*. Intergovernmentally negotiated and agreed outcome, 13 July 2018.

United Nations (2020) 'Global indicator framework for the Sustainable Development Goals and targets of the 2030 Agenda for Sustainable Development', Resolution adopted by the General Assembly on 6 July 2017, including annual amendments [A/RES/71/313; E/CN.3/2020/2].

United Nations High Commissioner for Refugees (UNHCR) (n.d.) 'The Sustainable Development Goals and addressing statelessness', Briefing note [Online]. Available at www.refworld.org/docid/58b6e3364.html (Accessed 26 August 2020).

United Nations Office on Drugs and Crime (UNODC) (2008) *Toolkit to Combat Trafficking in Persons* (New York: United Nations).

Van Waas, L., and de Chickera, A. (2017) 'Unpacking statelessness', in T. Bloom, K. Tonkiss, and P. Cole (eds) *Understanding Statelessness* (New York: Routledge): pp. 53–69.

Zere, A. (2015) 'Being stateless in America', *Al Jazeera* Opinion, 7 September [Online]. Available at www.aljazeera.com/indepth/opinion/2017/09/stateless-america-170903125426485.html (Accessed 13 August 2020).

2

'Fonua' cultural statelessness in the Pacific and the effects of climate change

Kate Wilkinson Cross and Pefi Kingi[1]

The Pacific Ocean is at the heart of our Blue Pacific narrative and critical for our future. As Leaders of the Pacific Islands Forum, custodians of the world's largest ocean and carbon sink, and representatives of our Pacific peoples, we call for immediate action and not just discussion of ambition. Action must be taken in our region, and internationally, to support clean, healthy, and productive oceans, the sustainable management, use and conservation of marine resources, growth in the blue economy and address the impacts of climate change on ocean health.

Kainaki II Declaration for Urgent Climate Action Now
(Pacific Islands Forum Secretariat, 2019a)

For many Pacific nation groups, the ritual of burying a newborn child's *fonua*, or placenta,[2] ensures that the child will be connected to their lands and seas. It is grounded in the belief that the buried *fonua* will forge their identities, link them with their families, protect their lives, and connect them spiritually and emotionally to their environment. In the broadest sense, *fonua* 'carries the meaning of placenta, land, people of the land, and grave' (Ka'ili, 2017: 40). As a concept and practice, *fonua* reflects how Pacific peoples view the world as a 'sea of islands' in which society and nature form a complementary relationship (Mahina, 1999). It also means that when people move from where their *fonua* is buried, they may no longer perceive a connection to their community, nor are they able to easily access membership to the community in their new location. Therefore, forced or voluntary migration can produce something tantamount to statelessness for Pacific Island peoples, based on rooted Indigenous notions of identity and belonging as expressed in the burial of *fonua*. Notably, this may also produce legal statelessness.

Anecdotal *talanoa* in almost all Pacific community *fono* (meetings) on climate change reveals how such a disruption cuts to the core, affecting peoples of the Pacific collectively, nationally, regionally, spiritually, emotionally, and psychologically. *Talanoa* is a Pacific traditional approach which engages communities in 'inclusive, participatory and transparent dialogue' (United Nations Framework Convention on Climate Change, 2017). Its purpose is to 'share stories, build empathy and trust', thus enabling participants to 'advance their knowledge through common understanding [and creating] a platform of dialogue [resulting] in better decision making for the collective good' (United Nations Framework Convention on Climate Change, 2017: 7). Recent *talanoa* highlight the existential threat posed by climate change for Pacific Island Countries (PICs), and how climate change causes statelessness by destroying the sites in which the *fonua* are buried, or by forcing communities to migrate for increased opportunities (Tunufa'i, 2016).

Due to the extent of climate change, sea-level rise is accelerating the regularity of extreme sea-level events (Intergovernmental Panel on Climate Change, 2014a; Oppenheimer et al., 2019). Further, warmer sea temperatures, hazards such as cyclones, tropical storms, and hurricanes have more force (Holland, 2014; Wu et al., 2016). This, in combination with rising sea levels, presents severe risks for PICs (Intergovernmental Panel on Climate Change, 2014a). Recent projections indicate that extreme sea-level events will become increasingly common and affected low-lying coastal areas will experience such events annually by 2050 (Oppenheimer et al., 2019). Even now, these types of extreme events disproportionately affect PICs, and any increases in such events will have a disastrous impact on local communities, including the loss of food security, livelihood, cultural practices, and connection with homelands.

As a result, climate change will force many Pacific peoples to leave their homelands. Even internal migration between islands within a state may result in something like statelessness for Pacific individuals and groups forced to leave their *fonua* and community. This cultural citizenship, expressed through *fonua*, is not acknowledged in regional and international law and policy. This means that responses to migration and displacement are incomplete, and do not recognise the consequences of climate change faced by Pacific communities.

Furthermore, some Pacific peoples unable to establish legal citizenship may face a dual form of cultural and legal statelessness. This *talanoa* of statelessness highlights the current and potential loss of land, nationality, and rights in the Pacific region. In recognition of the implications of cultural statelessness, we call for pro-active policy solutions to create pathways for migration – new routes and roots and a collective project of rerouting/rooting – while also coming together in *talanoa* to unpack and develop a collective narrative around this important issue.

This chapter relates some key experiences of statelessness in the Pacific region. Focusing on PICs, we contend that the historical context of colonialism has shaped contemporary reactions to migration and state-lessness by Pacific Indigenous communities. These reactions towards statelessness are ignored or discounted in regional responses to, and solutions for, climate change induced migration and displacement. We explore the implications of this in the context of climate change and evaluate the regional responses and proposed solutions for statelessness. We argue that such solutions are limited because they fail to account for cultural statelessness and how *fonua* is central to the identities and experience of Pacific peoples.

Historical experiences of cultural and legal statelessness in the region

The *talanoa* of statelessness is not new in the Pacific region. Many Pacific nation groups were the targets of 'blackbirding', where they were kidnapped or coerced through deception to work as slave or indentured labourers for colonial enterprises (Summy, 2009; Connell, 2010). Up to 63,000 Pacific Islanders were taken to Australia as indentured and slave labourers on sugarcane and cotton farms (Flanagan et al., 2003). Known as Kanakas or South Sea Islanders, they were stateless because many of the stolen people were never granted official documentation by the colonising countries who purchased them as indentured and slave labourers (Maude, 1981). This term has long been considered derogatory by South Sea Islanders due to the historical connotations. In Australia, South Sea Islanders were subsequently deported in order to 'racially purify' Australia and to 'protect' white Australians from the threat of cheap labour (Flanagan et al., 2003; Banivanua Mar, 2006).

These historical experiences of forced migration continue to affect Pacific communities and their perceptions of migration and displacement. Stolen South Sea Islanders lost their ancestral *fonua*, died stateless, and few were able to establish *fonua* links through marriage with local Indigenous peoples. Some have managed to trace their ancestral lines back to their original homeland, but this is uncommon because legal documentation recording their removal was lost or did not exist in the first place.

More recently, regional discourses around migration and security have reinforced the negative perception of migration and displacement at a time when climate change is forcing increased numbers of Pacific groups to migrate or prepare to vacate their homelands. Therefore, migration is a profoundly emotive political agenda. This may affect how effectively the region successfully provides safe and orderly solutions for migration by Pacific communities.

The impact of climate change in the Pacific region

Direct and indirect effects of climate change have already affected Pacific communities and will continue to affect the wider region. PIC leaders have reiterated this point in the Pacific Islands Forum (PIF), a regional intergovernmental organisation. In 2018, the PIF affirmed that climate change is the 'single greatest threat to the livelihoods, security and wellbeing of the peoples of the Pacific' (Pacific Islands Forum Secretariat, 2018a). This recognised that climate change exacerbates existing sources of insecurity and has a profound impact on the people's relationship with their land and their community, particularly those who live on low-lying atolls such as Kiribati and Tuvalu.

However, while there is consensus that climate change is extremely dangerous for PICs and Pacific peoples specifically, regional climate change mitigation and adaptation strategies have been piecemeal and ad hoc. This changed to an extent with the creation of the Pacific Resilience Facility in 2018, which seeks to consolidate all climate change matters and reaffirms the importance of member-driven, inclusive, and coordinated regional actions on climate and disaster resilience (Pacific Islands Forum Secretariat, 2018b). Nevertheless, strategies for integrating migration and statelessness, as understood by Pacific peoples, remain absent from regional strategies for climate change (Pacific Islands Forum Secretariat, 2019b). This highlights that *talanoa* of cultural and legal statelessness by Pacific peoples are underdeveloped in regional and international climate change mitigation and adaptation strategies.

This response to climate change reflects the complex views held by PICs and Pacific communities concerning the likelihood of being directly affected by climate change. The Pacific Islands region is historically prone to natural disasters and has experienced natural hazards, such as storm surges, flooding, earthquakes, tsunamis, and tropical cyclones.[3] Many communities pass down stories of earlier storms and have experienced devastating impacts in low-lying atolls, inter-tidal zones, and inland areas (King et al., 2018). These phenomena are their 'normal' and, as a result, many country people do not discern significant differences between climate-induced phenomena and hydrometeorological hazards. Instead, communities place faith in the belief that these hazards will 'blow over' and they will clean up as per normal, as they do with a cyclone, and life will continue.

Further, many communities believe that *their* community will not be as badly affected by climate-induced natural hazards as neighbouring islands (Rubow and Bird, 2016; Brown et al., 2018). This belief means that many communities do not envision the possibility that they will become stateless due to extreme hazards caused by climate change. For them, this 'new normal' happens to other island communities, not theirs. For a few island nations, this has translated to a range of responses, from 'high alert' to 'business as usual' to 'tired apathy'.

For a few island nations on high alert, such as Kiribati, statelessness is a feared possibility. That is, the territory of Kiribati is predicted to disappear beneath the sea by 2100 (Intergovernmental Panel on Climate Change, 2014b; Hoegh-Gudlberg et al., 2018). For these communities, sovereignty is tied to *fonua*. Therefore, sovereignty would be lost should they voluntarily or involuntarily relocate to a newly found *fonua* – especially where that land is in another sovereign nation.[4] This means that there are many economic, social, and cultural costs associated with climate change migration, which have profound consequences including the loss of tradition, language, identity, livelihoods, and community cohesion. Therefore, PICs focus on adaptation so they can remain on their home islands and mitigate the impact of climate change rather than vacating them for a safer environment elsewhere.

These strategies reflect the shared *talanoa* of allegiances to protect the homelands with dying breaths. For many proud Pacific peoples, leaving their community, lands, and *fonua* is incomprehensible. However, the decision whether to leave or remain will be forced. Pacific leaders and international experts affirm that it is only a matter of time before *fonua* – atoll islands and habitable lands as they are currently known – will cease to exist.

This discussion highlights the complex understanding and/or lack of appreciation of statelessness and migration among Pacific communities. For many, migration is akin to cultural statelessness, and is therefore incomprehensible or feared. Many communities do not wish to leave their home because the consequence is losing their culture and identity. Even where they recognise the likelihood of becoming stateless, the existing legal framework does not recognise their situation. Subsequently, many Pacific communities have normalised the impacts of climate change in their lives.

Regional responses to cultural statelessness

Regional responses to climate change and migration fail to recognise that Pacific communities experience such migration as cultural and legal statelessness. Metropolitan countries such as Australia reinforce the view of stateless peoples and migrants as 'other' and as coming from outside the region because of war, political unrest, economic stagnation, or persecution.

Australia's border protection operations such as the 'Pacific Solution' and 'Operation Sovereign Borders' subject asylum seekers arriving in Australia by boat to offshore processing in the Republic of Nauru or on Manus

Island. Under this highly controversial and criticised policy, around 1,660 individuals were detained on Nauru, Manus Island, and in Australia under regional processing arrangements in March 2020 (Australian Human Rights Commission, 2016; Office of the High Commissioner for Human Rights, 2019; Armbruster, 2020). These actions reinforce the view of migrants as a source of danger and instability to the Australian way of life. While many Pacific peoples are not subject to offshore processing, the maintenance of such centres sustains a sense of distrust and anti-migrant discourse in Australia.

A consequence of this approach is that most of the focus and budget of the Pacific Islands Forum is directed at securing borders against 'illegal' migrants and addressing the criminal activities of other migrants (Oceania Customs Organisation Secretariat, n.d.; Pacific Islands Forum Secretariat, n.d.). Given that PICs in the Forum are dependent on their geopolitical and aid/donor relationships with New Zealand and Australia, they are limited in how far they can challenge the conventional understanding and definition of 'statelessness' within the region. In reality, cultural and legal statelessness is tied to migration and the effects of climate change, and this is a wider and more inclusive understanding of migration, statelessness, and asylum than currently conceived in the region.

A consequence of the influence of these external forces on PICs is that the definitions of statelessness and migration are derived from the experiences of these issues in other global regions. These definitions are unable to account for the extent to which climate change, sea-level rise, and other extreme weather events shape Pacific peoples' choices to migrate. Therefore, they fail to recognise the specific experiences of cultural statelessness felt by Pacific peoples who are tied to their *fonua*, and instead adopt a more traditional understanding of these issues, such as policing the inter-regional movement of peoples. This undermines regional solutions for statelessness and planning for the potential extinction of PICs due to climate change.

Regional solutions to cultural statelessness

In 2018, the United Nations General Assembly adopted the Global Compact for Safe, Orderly and Regular Migration (GCM). The GCM recognises that climate change interacts with the drivers for migration, and the resulting need to develop solutions for migrants leaving their homes because of natural disasters, climate change, and environmental degradation (United Nations General Assembly, 2018). Under Objective 4, the GCM seeks to strengthen measures to reduce statelessness by registering migrants' births, facilitating participation in community life, and issuing means of identification so that migrants may access relevant services and authorities. These measures acknowledge that some people may become stateless because of their migration experience (see also Bloom, this volume).

However, the overarching objectives of the GCM reflect a 'traditional' understanding of the drivers of migration and do not consider the way in which migration can be understood as statelessness in the Pacific context. For example, the objectives of the GCM refer to the need to minimise 'adverse drivers and structural factors that compel people to leave their country of origin' and to 'facilitate fair and ethical recruitment and safeguard conditions that ensure decent work' (United Nations General Assembly, 2018). These objectives adopt a technical response to migration that does not reflect diverse worldviews, such as cultural statelessness experienced by Pacific peoples. This is because the GCM does not incorporate the principles of *fonua* or acknowledge that climate change will ultimately force Pacific peoples to migrate from their countries of birth and origin. Therefore, the unique experience of statelessness by PICs has not been incorporated into international strategies for migration. While some countries acknowledge the impact of climate change on migration and statelessness, their immediate concerns relate to the management and governance of migration flows – as is reflected in the technical objectives of the GCM. This concern does not address the cultural and legal statelessness that such migration produces.

That this focus on technical solutions to migration are limiting in the Pacific context has been recognised by some regional actors. For example, in 2017 New Zealand introduced a humanitarian visa for 100 people from the Pacific affected by climate change (Anderson, 2017). This was a world first and the 'pilot visa' would enable Pacific Islanders who faced rising sea levels, salt-water intrusion, and other adverse effects of climate change to relocate to New Zealand. The introduction of this pilot visa was a 'breakthrough as no other government has pledged so concretely to assist those displaced directly by climate change' and indicated that New Zealand would take the lead in in assisting Pacific communities worst affected by climate change (Hall, 2019). More recently, researchers from the Kaldor Centre for International Refugee Law have recommended that Australia introduce a new 'Pacific visa' for 3,000 migrants impacted by climate change (McAdam and Pryke, 2020).

However, given the extent of the environmental crises, Pacific Island leaders and the PIF have not been able to take pro-active steps to facilitate migration. Some, such as the former president of Kiribati, actively lobbied for 'migration with dignity' (Oakes et al., 2016). Kiribati is a low-lying atoll state which is extremely vulnerable to climate change and sea-level rise, and this may explain the leadership taken by Kiribati on this issue. However, other PICs, such as Fiji, can internally relocate communities, thus delaying the need to consider international migration strategies (Farbotko, 2018).

To date, very few PICs have solid plans for external migration in the case of emergency. Little time and attention has been directed to safeguarding the legal status of migrants displaced from Pacific states by climate change, especially in circumstances that threaten the continued existence of their *fonua* and sovereignty. Where groups have relocated to nearby metropolitan countries, such as New Zealand or Australia, such migration has not been attributed to climate change-induced phenomena. There have been few groups who have applied for special visa entry because such a notion was not conceivable, even a few years ago.

Instead, PIC leaders prioritise alternative solutions to the threat of statelessness or 'homelessness'. First, they argue that all members of the global community should reduce their greenhouse gas emissions and limit the global average temperatures to 1.5 degrees Celsius. Second, they argue that all interested parties should adopt a 'Pacific-tailored' approach to climate change, which prioritises the desire of Pacific peoples to remain in their home countries and to preserve their societies and cultures in the first instance (Pacific Islands Forum Secretariat, 2008).

Therefore, there has been extensive movement in adaptation strategies. For example, Papua New Guinea, Vanuatu, and Timor Leste are strengthening early warning systems for low-lying coastal areas and improving resilience to natural disasters (Internal Displacement Monitoring Centre, 2020a). Other countries have been working with partners to identify risk hotspots and map evacuation centres to inform adaptation plans that will enable communities to remain in their heritage countries (Internal Displacement Monitoring Centre, 2020b).

This indicates that PIF leaders view migration as a last resort. This approach undermines efforts to develop a holistic solution for climate change migration or displacement, and that is a lost opportunity to negotiate best terms of relocation for nation groups that will benefit from better economic, educational, health, and welfare opportunities. Such a strategy is detrimental to the relative success of climate-induced migration or displacement strategies in the future. Because of inadequate and ad hoc planning for the future loss of land to rising sea-levels and sudden-onset disasters, there is an increased risk of PICs' citizens becoming 'climate refugees' instead of 'climate migrants' who have followed a coherent and dignified migration policy to relocate.

For many Pacific peoples, the label 'refugee' does not reflect their understanding of their situation (McNamara and Gibson, 2009; Farbotko and Lazrus, 2012; Connell, 2016). Refugee status indicates a permanent separation between community and the land. Without land, one is without a place to stand and is lost. This is because the land and one's sovereignty over it is what you hold in your heart. It is your collective identity; it clothes you and your cultural memories and feeds your soul. Pacific *fonua* are heavily contested spaces because of their understood capacity to determine collective, familial and individual rights, customary legacies, powers, and privileges. Adopting strategies that encourage a strong sense of 'involvement and ownership in climate-change planning by communities, many of which follow tradition in making decisions at the village level' would enable Pacific peoples the autonomy to move with dignity and consider ways in which one's *fonua* or sovereignty could be moved, as well (Farbotko, 2018).

Against this background, people from different Pacific communities are leaving their Indigenous foundations to seek work and opportunities in New Zealand, Australia, and elsewhere. In 2017, a total of 450,787 PIC citizens migrated away from their homelands, with half the migrants moving to Australia or New Zealand (ILO Office for Pacific Island Countries, 2019). However, the extent to which they are leaving their homes as a result of sea-level rise and climate change is less understood. Due to reporting limitations, it is difficult to untangle which migrants are leaving for environmental, economic, or a combination of reasons. Some migrants may not make the connection between their drive to migrate and the impact of climate change on their home community, and because the data is not disaggregated, it has been difficult to link such exodus to climate-focused drivers. The work by the Internal Displacement Monitoring Centre is intended to address this paucity in data and enable more informed policy development, risk modelling, and training (Internal Displacement Monitoring Centre, 2020a).

Pacific leaders must explore possible solutions for migration that do not culminate in legal or cultural statelessness. One such solution would be the introduction of free movement agreements (FMAs). Approximately 120 countries across the globe participate in regional arrangements that incorporate free movement provisions (Chetail, 2014). FMAs have been introduced in the Caribbean against the backdrop of increased natural disasters and extreme weather events caused by climate change (Francis, 2019). FMAs have been incorporated in the European Union's regional economic scheme to liberalise migration restrictions between participating member states by providing protection benefits in the absence of a governing legal framework and guaranteed legal rights (Publications Office of the European Union, 2009; Coleman, 2016).

PIF leaders could prioritise flexible understandings of citizenship and membership and how these could complement national cultural-specific needs. For example, an Italian citizen living in Spain can function as a European citizen in Spain, and this is very similar to functioning as a

Spanish citizen. Importantly, this citizen retains their ties to Italy. Perhaps the Pacific should consider integrating a similar arrangement for the advantage of their migrating populations. Adopting a similar FMA in the Pacific region could enable some degree of autonomy for those forced to move, and confer greater freedom of movement for Pacific population groups. Should a Niue person have rights as a citizen of Niue, Pacific, and Aotearoa New Zealand, it will formally recognise the historical context of forced migration within the region, as well as the traditional and historical ancestral interconnections between the Niue citizen and their other lands. This evolving concept may take a while to be considered, but this dialogue best not be too far away.

Any discussion of future solutions to statelessness, displacement, and migration are limited by adopting the 'traditional' understanding of statelessness imported from other regions. This understanding does not recognise how cultural statelessness is shaped through the disconnection of a person from their *fonua*. Furthermore, the possibility of pro-active solutions to facilitate migration in advance of land loss or state extinction are limited by the legacy of forced migration and by the significant connection between peoples and land. If considered, FMAs would allow Pacific peoples to migrate with dignity and maintain ties with their homelands and their *fonua*.

Conclusion

Pacific understandings of statelessness are different to the definition of the concept in international policy documents and by other countries. Pacific peoples have a complex relationship with their land, which is manifested through *fonua*. To leave one's land means leaving one's *fonua* and becoming stateless, though this may not always lead to legal statelessness. This means that any form of internal or external migration results in cultural statelessness in the Pacific context – a worldview that is not recognised in the current legal or policy framework. This is compounded by the historical experiences of blackbirding and the forced migration of Pacific peoples during the colonial period, which still shapes the understanding of migration for Pacific communities. Consequently, many Pacific communities are hesitant to discuss the likelihood of statelessness and its implications for their community, identity, and sovereignty.

In light of the existential threat of climate change to developing Pacific states, it is essential to develop solutions for how to either regenerate *fonua* elsewhere, or to develop alternative understandings of 'home', so that PIC citizens may retain, constitute, or reconstitute their citizenship. This chapter has shown how responses to statelessness in the Pacific adopt an understanding of statelessness which does not reflect the experiences or specific cultural understanding of *fonua* as peoples' connection to the land and sea, their identity, ethnicity, and culture. Therefore, existing regional frameworks focus on responding to inter-regional migration of peoples fleeing from 'traditional' drivers of war, political unrest, economic stagnation, or persecution. This is to the detriment of Pacific peoples, who are facing a different form of statelessness through the complete eradication of their land and *fonua* due to climate change.

Given that climatic changes threatening Pacific states are unlikely to be averted, existing law and policy needs to incorporate a more nuanced and multifaceted understanding of statelessness caused by climate change migration and displacement. Regional consultations and national dialogue must develop specific legislation and policies on statelessness and what it means to Pacific peoples. This dialogue should address as part of broader discussion, pre-evaluation from country of origin, evacuation in transit (negotiating safe passage with countries concerned), and post-evacuation at country of destination. There needs to be focused dialogue on a number of issues, including intellectual property, cultural assets, heritage sites, Indigenous language[s], arts and crafts, and how to conserve or maintain the burial sites for those left behind.

Such a dialogue would facilitate local, national, and regional actions to adopt more effective strategic plans acknowledging the cultural and social impacts of statelessness on Pacific communities. In doing so, relevant actors can engage respectfully with Pacific peoples who resist any discussion around migration and statelessness, and collaboratively develop mechanisms or solutions to regenerate *fonua* in a new setting. At present, these cultural and spiritual ties to the land are ignored and devalued in global and regional solutions to statelessness and migration, to the detriment of those who disproportionately experience the effects of such statelessness. Unless the fundamental ties between a community and their land are recognised, any policy addressing migration and statelessness will negatively impact the future spiritual, physical, cultural, and social wellbeing of Pacific peoples, wherever they are located. It is essential that any process encompassing their relocation facilitates the recreation of their sense of *fonua* in their new *fonua*.

Notes

1 Oue Tulutulou, we acknowledge the contributions made by the Pacific Advisory Group on early drafts of this chapter. Maalo Nui: Tutagaloa Tutose Tuhipa

MNZM (Niue); Dr. Jenny Rankine (Australian-New Zealand); Suzanna Tiapula JD (American Samoa); Emeline Siale 'Ilolahia (Tongan); High Chief Tanealaepa Pepe Tanuvasa (Samoan); Deborah Misiuepa (Māori-Niue, Aoteaora New Zealand), and TAMM Kingi-Falakoa (Niue).

2 In many Pacific nation groups, a *fonua* is a newborn's placenta and all parts resulting from childbirth. *Fonua* also refers to 'land' in many Polynesian and the Tongic-Samoic languages.

3 For more information, see: www.nhc.noaa.gov/prepare/hazards.php (accessed 14 November 2020).

4 As is the case of Kiribati purchasing land in Vanua Levu, Fiji (see Republic of Kiribati, 2014).

References

Anderson, C. (2017) 'New Zealand considers creating climate change refugee visas', *The Guardian*, 31 October [Online]. Available at www.theguardian.com/world/2017/oct/31/new-zealand-considers-creating-climate-change-refugee-visas (Accessed 10 December 2019).

Armbruster, S. (2020) 'Dozens of refugees flown from Australia and PNG to US despite coronavirus travel bans', Special Broadcasting Service News [Online]. Available at www.sbs.com.au/news/dozens-of-refugees-flown-from-australia-and-png-to-us-despite-coronavirus-travel-bans (Accessed 21 May 2020).

Australian Human Rights Commission (2016) 'Immigration detention and human rights' [Online]. Available at www.humanrights.gov.au/our-work/asylum-seekers-and-refugees/projects/immigration-detention-and-human-rights (Accessed 16 October 2019).

Banivanua Mar, T. (2006) *Violence and Colonial Dialogue: The Australian-Pacific Indentured Labor Trade* (Honolulu: University of Hawaii Press).

Brown, P., Daigneault, A. J., Tjernström, E., and Zou, W. (2018) 'Natural disasters, social protection, and risk perceptions', *World Development*, 104, 310–325.

Chetail, V. (2014) 'The transnational movement of persons under general international law – Mapping the customary law foundations of international migration law', in V. Chetail and C. Bauloz (eds) *Research Handbook on International Law and Migration* (Cheltenham: Edward Elgar): pp. 1–72.

Coleman, C. (2016) 'Schengen Agreement: A short history', House of Lords Library, Briefing Note LLN 2016/013 [Online]. Available at https://lordslibrary.parliament.uk/research-briefings/lln-2016-0013/ (Accessed 1 July 2020).

Connell, J. (2010) 'From blackbirds to guestworkers in the South Pacific: "Plus ça change?"', *Economic and Labour Relations Review*, 20:2, 111–122.

Connell, J. (2016) 'Last days in the Carteret Islands? Climate change, livelihoods and migration on coral atolls', *Asia Pacific Viewpoint*, 57:1, 3–15.

Farbotko, C. (2018) 'No retreat: Climate change and voluntary immobility in the Pacific Islands', Migration Policy Institute [Online]. Available at www.migrationpolicy.org/article/no-retreat-climate-change-and-voluntary-immobility-pacific-islands (Accessed 9 March 2020).

Farbotko, C., and Lazrus, H. (2012) 'The first climate refugees? Contesting global narratives of climate change in Tuvalu', *Global Environmental Change*, 22:2, 382–390.

Flanagan, T., Wilkie, M., and Iuliano, S. (2003) 'Australian South Sea Islanders: A century of race discrimination under Australian law', Australian Human Rights Commission [Online]. Available at www.humanrights.gov.au/our-work/race-discrimination/publications/australian-south-sea-islanders-century-race#1 (Accessed 23 March 2020).

Francis, A. (2019) 'Free movement agreements & climate-induced migration: A Caribbean case study', Sabin Center for Climate Change Law [Online]. Available at https://ssrn.com/abstract=3464594 (Accessed 11 December 2019).

Hall, N. (2019) 'New Zealand: A global leader on climate and displacement?', Asia and the Pacific Policy Society [Online]. Available at www.policyforum.net/new-zealand-a-global-leader-on-climate-and-displacement/ (Accessed 1 October 2019).

Hoegh-Gudlberg, O., Jacob, D., Taylor, M., Bindi, M., Brown, S., Camilloni, I., Diedhiou, A., Djalante, R., Ebi, K. L., Engelbrecht, F., Guiot, J., Hijioka, Y., Mehrotra, S., Payne, A., Seneviratne, S. I., Thomas, A., Warren, R., and Zhou, G. (2018) 'Impacts of 1.5°c global warming on natural and human systems', The Intergovernmental Panel on Climate Change (IPCC) [Online]. Available at www.ipcc.ch/sr15/chapter/chapter-3/ (Accessed 24 June 2020).

Holland, P. (2014) 'Hydrometeorological disasters in the Pacific', SPC Applied Geoscience and Technology Division (SOPAC) Report No. 187 [Online]. Available at https://library.wmo.int/doc_num.php?explnum_id=6381 (Accessed 30 November 2019).

ILO Office for Pacific Island Countries (2019) 'Labour mobility in Pacific Island countries' [Online]. Available at www.ilo.org/suva/publications/WCMS_712549/lang--en/index.htm (Accessed 30 November 2019).

Intergovernmental Panel on Climate Change (2014a) *Climate Change 2014: Impacts, Adaptation, and Vulnerability Part A: Global and Sectoral Aspects Working Group Ii Contribution to the Fifth Assessment Report of the Intergovernmental Panel on Climate Change* (Cambridge: Cambridge University Press) [Online]. Available at www.ipcc.ch/report/ar5/wg2/ (Accessed 31 March 2020).

Intergovernmental Panel on Climate Change (2014b) 'Climate Change 2014: Synthesis report. Contribution of Working Groups I, II and III to the Fifth Assessment Report of the Intergovernmental Panel on Climate Change' [Online]. Available at https://archive.ipcc.ch/pdf/assessment-report/ar5/syr/SYR_AR5_FINAL_full_wcover.pdf (Accessed 1 July 2020).

Internal Displacement Monitoring Centre (2020a) *Pacific Response to Disaster Displacement Project* [Online]. Available at www.internal-displacement.org/pacific-disasters (Accessed 16 November 2020).

Internal Displacement Monitoring Centre (2020b) *Fiji: Disaster Displacement Risk Profile* [Online]. Available at www.internal-displacement.org/publications/fiji-disaster-displacement-risk-profile (Accessed 16 November 2020).

Ka'ili, T. O. (2017) *Marking Indigeneity: The Tongan Art of Sociospatial Relations* (Tucson, AZ: University of Arizona Press).

King, D. N., Shaw, W. S., Meihana, P. N., and Goff, J. R. (2018) 'Māori oral histories and the impact of tsunamis in Aotearoa-New Zealand', *Natural Hazards Earth System Sciences*, 18:3, 907–919.

Mahina, O. (1999) 'Food me'akai and body sino in traditional Tongan society: Their theoretical and practical implications for health policy', *Pacific Health Dialogue*, 6:2, 276–287.

Maude, H. E. (1981) *Slavers in Paradise: The Peruvian Slave Trade in Polynesia* (Canberra: Australian National University Press).

McAdam, J., and Pryke, J. (2020) *Policy Brief 10, Climate Change, Disasters and Mobility: A Roadmap for Australian Action* [Online]. Kaldor Centre for International Refugee Law. Available at www.kaldorcentre.unsw.edu.au/ publication/policy-brief-10-climate-change-disasters-and-mobility-roadmap-australian-action (Accessed 16 November 2020).

McNamara, K. E., and Gibson, C. (2009) '"We do not want to leave our land": Pacific ambassadors at the United Nations resist the category of "climate refugees"', *Geoforum*, 40:3, 475–483.

Oakes, R., Milan, A., and Campbell, J. (2016) 'Kiribati: Climate change and migration', United Nations University Institute for Environment and Human Security (UNU-EHS), Report no. 20 [Online]. Available at https://collections.unu. edu/eserv/UNU:5903/Online_No_20_Kiribati_Report_161207.pdf (Accessed 9 March 2020).

Oceania Customs Organisation Secretariat (n.d.) 'Law enforcement and border security' [Online]. Available at www.ocosec.org/law-enforcement-border-security/ (Accessed 29 June 2020).

Office of the High Commissioner for Human Rights (2019) 'Mandates of the Special Rapporteur on the Right of Everyone to the Enjoyment of the Highest Attainable Standard of Physical and Mental Health; the Working Group on the Use of Mercenaries as a Means of Violating Human Rights and Impeding the Exercise of the Right of Peoples to Self-determination; the Special Rapporteur on the Human Rights of Migrants; and the Special Rapporteur on Torture and Other Cruel, Inhuman or Degrading Treatment or Punishment', AL AUS 4/2019 [Online]. Available at https://spcommreports.ohchr.org/TMResultsBase/DownLo adPublicCommunicationFile?gId=24482 (Accessed 16 October 2019).

Oppenheimer, M., Glavovic, B., Hinkel, J., Van De Wal, R., Magnan, A. K., Abd-Elgawad, A., Cai, R., Cifuentes-Jara, M., Deconto, R. M., Ghosh, T., Hay, J., Isla, F., Marzeion, B., Meyssignac, B. and Sebesvari, Z. (2019). 'Sea Level Rise and Implications for Low-Lying Islands, Coasts and Communities', Pörtner, H.-O., Roberts, D. C., Masson-Delmotte, V., Zhai, P., Tignor, M., Poloczanska, E., Mintenbeck, K., Alegría, A., Nicolai, M., Okem, A., Petzold, J., Rama, B. and Weyer, N. M. (eds.) IPCC Special Report on the Ocean and Cryosphere in a Changing Climate [Online]. Available at https://www.ipcc.ch/srocc/chapter/ chapter-4-sea-level-rise-and-implications-for-low-lying-islands-coasts-and-communities/ (Accessed 15 November 2019).

Pacific Islands Forum Secretariat (2008) *The Niue Declaration on Climate Change* [Online]. Available at www.forumsec.org/the-niue-declaration-on-climate-change/ (Accessed 5 December 2019).

Pacific Islands Forum Secretariat (2018a) *Boe Declaration on Regional Security* [Online]. Available at www.forumsec.org/boe-declaration-on-regional-security/ (Accessed 17 October 2019).

Pacific Islands Forum Secretariat (2018b) 'The Pacific resilience facility' [Online]. Available at www.forumsec.org/2018-femm-the-pacific-resilience-facility/ (Accessed 5 March 2019).

Pacific Islands Forum Secretariat (2019a) *Kainaki II Declaration for Urgent Climate Action Now* [Online]. Available at www.forumsec.org/2020/11/11/kainaki/ (Accessed 24 June 2020).

Pacific Islands Forum Secretariat (2019b) 'Pacific Islands Forum Foreign Ministers Meeting: Outcomes', Australian Department of Foreign Affairs and Trade [Online]. Available at https://dfat.gov.au/international-relations/regional-architecture/pacific-islands/Pages/pacific-islands-forum-foreign-ministers-meeting.aspx (Accessed 10 December 2019).

Pacific Islands Forum Secretariat (n.d.) 'Security' [Online]. Available at www.forumsec.org/security/ (Accessed 16 October 2019).

Publications Office of the European Union (2009) 'The Schengen Area and cooperation', EUR-Lex [Online]. Available at https://eur-lex.europa.eu/legal-content/EN/TXT/?uri=LEGISSUM:l33020 (Accessed 1 July 2020).

Republic of Kiribati (2014) 'Kiribati buys a piece of Fiji' [Online]. Available at www.climate.gov.ki/2014/05/30/kiribati-buys-a-piece-of-fiji/ (Accessed 24 June 2020).

Rubow, C., and Bird, C. (2016) 'Eco-theological responses to climate change in Oceania', *Worldviews: Global Religions, Culture & Ecology*, 20:2, 150–168.

Summy, H. (2009) 'Fiji's forgotten people: The legatees of "blackbirding"', *Social Alternatives*, 28:4, 39–44.

Tunufa'i, L. (2016) 'Pacific research: Rethinking the Talanoa "methodology"', *New Zealand Sociology*, 31:7, 227–239.

United Nations Framework Convention on Climate Change (2017) 'Decision 1/CP.23 Talanoa Dialogue', FCCC/CP/2017/11/Add.1 Annex II [Online]. Available at https://unfccc.int/documents/65126 (Accessed 29 June 2020).

United Nations General Assembly (2018) *Global Compact for Safe, Orderly and Regular Migration* [Online]. Available at https://undocs.org/en/A/RES/73/195 (Accessed 31 March 2020).

Wu, H., Huang, M., Tang, Q., Kirschbaum, D. B., and Ward, P. (2016) 'Hydrometeorological hazards: Monitoring, forecasting, risk assessment, and socioeconomic responses', *Advances in Meteorology*, vol. 2016, Article ID 2367939, 1–3. https://doi.org/10.1155/2016/2367939.

3

A regional politics of foreignness and Pakistan's Afghan refugees

Anoshay Fazal[1]

> The conception of human rights, based upon the assumed existence of a human being as such, broke down at the very moment when those who professed to believe in it were for the first time confronted with people who had indeed lost all other qualities and specific relationships – except that they were still human. The world found nothing sacred in the abstract nakedness of being human.
>
> Hannah Arendt (1973: 299–300)

The Partition of British India in 1947 gave way to the two independent states of India and Pakistan, resulting in the largest human migration in history. In this chapter, I explore the linkages between statelessness, citizenship laws, and migration in the Indian sub-continent. The citizenship regime that emerged in 1947 in Pakistan is studied in order to contextualise and further analyse the status conferred upon a sizeable population of persons of Afghan origin residing in Pakistan over the last forty years.

Geopolitics and the consequent politics of national exclusion play a formative role in putting populations at risk of statelessness. Such measures not only go against the basic fabric of the international regime focused on the reduction and prevention of statelessness, but also go against the 'universality' of human rights, particularly 'non-discrimination'. Geopolitics dictate a number of policies that impact migrant populations in the sub-continent. On the one hand, there is bitterness between India and Pakistan; any loyalty to India from Afghanistan has been met with significant hostility towards the Afghan population in Pakistan. Conversely, Kashmiri migrants have been accorded a number of favourable conditions, including the right to vote in Pakistan.

David Weissbrodt and Clay Collins (2006) state that 'the right not to be stateless, or the right to a nationality, is widely recognised as a fundamental human right' (246). Nonetheless, historically (and currently) the assertion of state sovereignty is often at the expense of basic human rights (Blitz and Lynch, 2009; Staples, 2012: 3). Therefore, the tension between the state as an independent and sovereign nation-state and the granting of human rights is deeply rooted in the environment that creates stateless beings. We can see this particularly through the example of Afghan refugees in Pakistan and how Pakistan's national policies and legal system interact with international law on statelessness.

'Statelessness'

'Statelessness', or being denied or being born without the nationality of a particular state, has a strong connection to the state's nationality laws, socio-political history, and the protection of fundamental rights of individuals within that state's jurisdiction (Bianchini, 2018). Acquiring citizenship bears even more prominence in the context of migration coupled with protracted refugee crises, such as the case of Afghan refugees in Pakistan. The ensuing limbo due to this precarious legal status guarantees a denial of the basic necessities of human life, fundamentals only available to 'nationals' or 'citizens'.

The Convention relating to the Status of Stateless Persons was adopted in 1954 and the Convention on the Reduction of Statelessness was adopted in 1961. Unfortunately, the international community has rarely focused on these Conventions; they have been eclipsed by the refugee crisis (Goodwin-Gill, 1994). A welcome step has been the New York Declaration for Refugees and Migrants, which states: 'We recognize that statelessness can be a root cause of forced displacement and that forced displacement, in turn, can lead to statelessness' (United Nations General Assembly, 2016).

Strictly speaking, refugees of Afghan descent in Pakistan may be able to seek cover of Afghan citizenship (although this is debatable as it will depend on the provision of adequate documentation required by Afghan authorities) (Khan, 2019). However, it may well be termed largely 'ineffective' due to the deteriorating security situation in the country over the past several decades (Athayi, 2017). Furthermore, since the recent Afghan Peace Deal, many Afghans feel that an enhanced and uninhibited Taliban rule equates very much to them being 'thrown under the bus' (George, 2020). The 'Agreement for Bringing Peace to Afghanistan' comes at a time when the current Afghan government stands contested. This, coupled with a rise in attacks that are being attributed to the Taliban, creates serious concerns regarding the potential of the Taliban to gain control of the political arena in Afghanistan (Farr, 2020).

Hannah Arendt's (1949 and 1973) views on the rights of humankind and statelessness help us to understand the resettlement and citizenship regime that transpired with the 1947 'Partition'. First, she correctly identifies that even if all persons are theoretically eligible for human rights, 'citizenship' effectively functions as a prerequisite to the exercise of those so-called 'universal' human rights. Not only can 'humans exist in a place called nowhere', but once they have lost their position in the political community, they can never be certain of regaining it (Gessen, 2018). Therefore, the enjoyment of fundamental rights will very much depend on political membership within society.

The second observation made by Arendt focuses on the making of the 'nation-state' and the politics of exclusion. Citizenship was identifiable with nationality and therefore led to the assertion of rights that were in line with the 'national interest'. In practice, this results in the exclusion of certain minority groups from nationality entirely. In Patrick Hayden's (2008) words: 'In the new statist era only membership within a particular nation-state could guarantee rights their legal status… those persons excluded from having a recognized place within a polity were compelled to live "under conditions of absolute lawlessness"' (252). These 'conditions of lawlessness' present themselves in human form as the stateless being. Afghan refugees in Pakistan, having fallen between national citizenships and borderlands, often find themselves in a condition of lawlessness. In this thread, Ayten Gündogdu (2015) correctly reiterates Arendt's 'insistence that human rights cannot be deduced to the rights attached to citizenship status' (13–14).

The 1947 Partition and Pakistani citizenship

This section illustrates the unfolding and establishment of the citizenship regime in Pakistan following the 1947 Partition. It then progresses to the application of this regime (or lack of) in the context of the Afghan refugees residing and born in Pakistan.

The 1947 Partition uprooted around 18 million individuals who crossed boundaries into the newly created nation-states of India and Pakistan, thus becoming one of the largest human migrations in history. In the context of partition, the '*Muhajir*' (or 'refugee') was a central figure. While some populations, specifically those from the Punjab, suffered painful and violent episodes in their migration fitting the 'refugee' definition, various populations migrated willingly and therefore were not forcibly displaced (Talbot, 2011).

Looking at state policy vis-à-vis citizenship at this juncture means being attentive to what Ravinder Kaur (2009) writes about this particular migration and how it was accommodated: 'The core principle of the official resettlement policy was self-rehabilitation, that is, the ability to become a productive citizen of the new nation state without state intervention' (434).

The adaptation of such policies on both sides gives us an early indication of the politics of exclusion that emerged and strengthened over the decades. Certain populations were never accorded citizenship to begin with and have therefore lived on the margins, at risk of becoming stateless (Ansari and Gould, 2019).

Recalling Arendt, nationality forms the premise of nation-states; this nationality is sometimes perceived and dependent on an allegiance to the state. Created as a state for Muslims, the Islamic Republic of Pakistan (through its turbulent Constitutional history) has converged state policy and legislation in a particular direction (Aziz, 2018). The implementation of a 'selective' Citizenship Amendment Bill in India paints a similar picture.

The 1951 Citizenship Act (the '1951 Act') was promulgated to accommodate the 6.5 million Muslim migrants settling in Pakistan. The 1951 Act covers both the acquisition of citizenship and instances that may result in a loss of citizenship. Section 3 of the Act introduces four categories of persons that may acquire citizenship.[2] It is apparent from the language of this section that it was intended as a post-partition facilitating legislation. Incoming immigrants were allotted immovable property under the Displaced Persons (Compensation and Rehabilitation) Act of 1958. The regime to deal with 'Muslim' partition migrants was wide-ranging, and various other laws were also enacted to accommodate this populace between 1955 and 1971. Having served their purpose, this set of laws was repealed in 1975 under the Evacuee Property and Displaced Persons Laws (Repeal) Act of 1975.

Section 4 of the 1951 Act covers grounds for *jus soli* citizenship, or birthright citizenship. A person born in Pakistan at the commencement of the 1951 Act or later can claim citizenship (although a person cannot claim citizenship if his father enjoys diplomatic immunity in the country or if his father was classified as an alien or an enemy of the state). The citizenship regime does not provide for refugees residing in Pakistan. It does, however, accord special status to migrants settling in Pakistan from Jammu and Kashmir, a disputed territory/region in the border area between China, India, and Pakistan, and currently administered by India. Such individuals are covered in Section 14B of the 1951 Act: 'Those persons who have migrated to Pakistan with the intention of residing therein until such time as the relationship between Pakistan and that State is finally determined, shall, without prejudice to his status as such subject, be a citizen of Pakistan.'

For Afghans, under Section 5 of the 1951 Citizenship Act, citizenship may be passed on through blood. Therefore, children of Afghan refugees who have a Pakistani spouse should be bestowed citizenship. Under section 10 of the Act, women of non-Pakistani origin who have married Pakistani citizens can acquire nationality by virtue of their marriage to a Pakistani citizen. Notably, section 3 of the Naturalization Act 1926 allows those who have resided in Pakistan for eight years, have a good character, and knowledge of at least one Pakistani language to apply for citizenship by naturalisation.

Pakistan's Afghan refugees

The United Nations High Commissioner for Refugees (UNHCR) identifies 1.4 million registered Afghan refugees in Pakistan (UNHCR Operations Portal Refugee Situations, n.d.), but others contend that the number of refugees is closer to 3 million considering those who remain unregistered. Historically, the Afghan population has followed nomadic migratory patterns, often travelling into present-day Pakistan (the lowlands) to find work. These tribes have been referred to as 'Kuchis', 'Powindah', and 'Bangriwalas' (Kakar, 2011). Excerpts from government files also feature 'Powindahs', perhaps even prior to 1972.

The drawing of the international border between Afghanistan and Pakistan, the 'Durand line', effectively converted this regional migration into 'international' migration. The border has long held a contested status between Afghanistan and Pakistan. In the 1880s, with the Russians advancing closer to Afghanistan, the British Empire was compelled to formalise the borders of British India. In an interesting turn of events, when the border was almost agreed to between the then-Amir of Afghanistan and Sir Mortimer Durand, Durand 'possibly as a concession to allow the Amir to gain a little face, suddenly allowed the Amir to keep the Birmal tract of Waziristan. This was not the best of ideas, since it involved splitting Waziristan and the tribal people in two' (Omrani, 2009: 185). The line then created an imaginary split, cutting tribes and ethnic factions into two (Dupree, 1980). I use the word 'imaginary' because it did not adversely impact the fluidity of identity in these regions and populations continued to travel to and fro across the Durand line (Kronenfeld, 2008). Due to their shared Pashtun origin and familial links on the Pakistani side of the border, a number of Afghans (including refugees) tried to acquire citizenship through naturalisation. This was denied through both administrative and judicial mechanisms (Nazir, 2016: 5).

Following the 1979 Soviet invasion, the Afghan populace was devastated and forced to flee the country. Afghan migration to Pakistan began as early as 1973 with rising political instability in the country. The influx of Afghans into Pakistan's Khyber-Pakhtunkhwa and Balochistan provinces and their protracted stay considerably impacted the economy, demographics, and social structure in the provinces. With the local administrations of these two provinces as host communities, the president of Pakistan assigned the issue of the Afghan refugees to the Ministry of States and Frontier Regions (SAFRON) in 1980 (Ahmad, 2017).

Despite hosting Afghan refugees for forty years, Pakistan does not have a national framework for determining the legal status of refugees in the country. The UNHCR (2011) states: 'The core protection challenge in Pakistan is the absence of a specific legal regime for the protection of refugees' (183). Recently, attempts were made to draft a national refugee law but sadly these efforts bore no fruit. The UNHCR has been the primary support agency in managing Afghan refugees in the country. The government of Pakistan and the UNHCR have periodically agreed to a number of mechanisms and programmes for the settlement, voluntary repatriation, and registration of Afghan refugees in the country (Zieck, 2008). In the absence of a legal framework, the Afghan refugee population has been awarded *prima facie* refugee status, as defined by the UNHCR in its 2006 guidelines:

> This means that each individual member of a particular group is presumed to qualify for refugee status. This presumption is based on objective information on the circumstances causing their flight. Prima facie recognition is appropriate where there are grounds for considering that the large majority of those in the group would meet the eligibility criteria set out in the applicable refugee definition.
>
> (United Nations High Commissioner for Refugees, 2006: 9)

With the end of the Cold War drawing near, foreign aid previously pouring in from Western countries began to dwindle. Thus, the government of Pakistan allowed for a 'freedom of movement to work' approach for refugees who were previously confined to camps (Ahmad, 2017: 616). This urbanisation created significant gaps in data on the refugee population in Pakistan (Kronenfeld, 2008). Arguably, this population and specifically those born in Pakistan are no longer 'refugees' – they are part of the workforce, as well as the social and economic structure in Pakistan. The UNHCR and the government of Pakistan have also launched initiatives such as the 'Solutions Strategy for Afghan Refugees', which facilitates the provision of Proof of Registration (POR) cards allowing Afghans to register and remain in Pakistan while the cards are valid (Bhoyroo, 2019).

The 'urbanisation' of this refugee population is at the basis of the conundrum surrounding protracted refugee status, citizenship regimes, and statelessness. The protracted existence of Afghan refugees in Pakistan (in camps and subsequently into urban cities such as Karachi, Peshawar, and Lahore) and the birth of second and third-generation Afghans in Pakistan gives rise to debates about the denial of citizenship in Pakistan. With 74% of the Afghan refugee population born in Pakistan, both the 1951 Act and section 3 of the 1926 Naturalization Act theoretically bestow the right to

acquire *jus soli* citizenship for those born in Pakistan, as well as naturalisation rights to those who married a Pakistani – yet they are frequently
unable to access such status. Despite having acquired POR cards, Afghan
refugees are subjected to illegal arrests, harassment, and blatant discrimination (Alimia, 2013).

The courts and Afghan refugees as 'aliens'

The structural application of a state's citizenship regimes can significantly
impact populations at risk. Administrative frameworks, specifically in relation to documentation and birth registration, can also render many people
stateless (see Liew, this volume). This section illustrates how the judicial
system is used to deny the right to nationality by excluding refugee populations from the citizenship regime.

The quandary for the Afghan refugee population continues while they
are governed as aliens under the Foreigners Act of 1946 (which stands in
contrast to Kashmiri refugees who have equal status as citizens in Pakistan).
The Foreigners Act allows for wide-ranging powers in the treatment meted
out to refugees and migrants. Under Section 3(2) (g) of the Foreigners Act,
a foreigner may be arrested and detained 'in the interest of the security of
Pakistan' for up to two months and subsequently deported. The legislation
is vague because it does not define what may or may not amount to 'security
of Pakistan'. Therefore, authorities are able to detain, deport, and arrest
Afghan refugees under the guise of 'national security'.

Domestic courts in Pakistan have rarely taken favourable views regarding the legal status of refugees, yet some safeguards are available to individuals under the fundamental rights category in the Constitution of Pakistan.
Regarding detention, for instance, in the case of *Muhammad Akbar Cheema*,
the Lahore High Court held that Section 3(2) (g) of the Foreigners Act must
be read in subordination and in line with Article 10(4) of the Constitution of
Pakistan. Thus, the Court held that the safeguards in Article 10 are extended
and cover not only citizens of Pakistan, but every person – immigrants and
refugees included.

However, the judiciary's approach has not been so favourable regarding issues of citizenship and nationality. In *Ghulam Sanai v. The Assistant
Director, National Registration Office* (PLD 1999 Peshawar 18), the facts of
the case centred on the legal status (nationality) of the petitioner, a son of an
Afghan refugee who was born in Pakistan. This decision is a prime example
of how legislation and policies can be used to deny rights otherwise applicable to individuals. The Peshawar High Court held that, as per Section 4 of
the Pakistan Citizenship Act of 1951, every person born in Pakistan after

the promulgation of the Act is allowed to be a citizen of Pakistan by birth (the only impediments being the child of a diplomat or enemy of the state). Furthermore, Section 3 allows the person born in Pakistan to be a 'citizen by descent' if his father was a citizen at the time of his birth. However, these provisions did not apply to the petitioner because he was an Afghan refugee and was thus governed by the Foreigners Act of 1946.

Two further cases illustrate the judicial system's attitudes towards the movement of Afghan refugees and, interestingly, the attitude of local ethnic factions towards Afghan refugees. In the case of *Abdul Majeed and another v. The S.H.O. Police Station Naulakha, Lahore* (PLD 1989 Lahore 223), the Lahore High Court held that Afghan refugees have been given temporary political asylum in Pakistan until foreign forces withdraw from Afghan territory. It was reiterated once again that refugees are governed by the Foreigners Act of 1946. Highlighting the national security narrative, the Court also states that 'in the garb of refugees foreign agents have entered into the holy land of Pakistan and they are busy in the implementation of their nefarious designs'. A rise in internal terrorism has often been followed by a backlash against Afghan refugees, especially in the Khyber-Pakhtunkhwa province. Host communities have also feared a change in the proportion of the population made up of Afghan refugees (Achakzai, 2018). Similar concerns have also been voiced in the Balochistan province (Baloch, 2017). In *Senator Abdul Malik v. Government of Pakistan*, a petition was filed to prevent a census from being carried out in the province, citing the rise in Afghan populace as the basis of an inaccurate reflection of the Balochi interest.

The application of the Foreigners Act has been significant following the rise of militancy and anti-terrorism initiatives following the terrorist attacks of September 11, 2001 in the United States. The scapegoating of Afghan refugees by the authorities and law enforcement agencies has escalated in the last two decades. Detentions and forced returns have been commonplace in this context (Human Rights Watch, 2002: 28). Human Rights Watch (HRW) (2002) noted that the government of Pakistan issued public orders in 2001 to strictly monitor the border for illegal immigrants, while authorising the police to detain and deport newly arriving refugees. The argument was that 'Afghan refugees were economically displaced persons. They are not refugees. They are illegal immigrants and we insist they go back' (Human Rights Watch, 2002).

During my 2007 and 2011 visits to Peshawar, Khyber-Pakhtunkhwa in the North-West of Pakistan near the Afghan border, I observed the antagonism and hostility towards what the locals called 'Kabulis' – that is, Afghan refugees. In December 2014, following the Peshawar Attack on an army public school that killed more than 130 children, the government of

Pakistan launched its National Action Plan, amidst other counter-terrorism measures. The twenty-point agenda underscored the need to repatriate all Afghans by the end of 2015. However, with the deteriorating situation in Afghanistan, officials from both the UNHCR and the Human Rights Commission of Pakistan agree that Afghan refugees do not want to 'voluntarily' repatriate back to Afghanistan. Furthermore, the ability to incorporate and integrate these returnees is not strong in the current security climate (Asia Foundation, 2019).

Conclusion

The preceding discussion leads us back to Arendt's views. Her experience with the inherent dependency of freedom and rights on nationality and the making of 'nation-states' is increasingly relevant given rising trends in denationalisation and deprivation of the right to a nationality in autocratic regimes. For instance, a case in point would be the exercise to update the 'National Register of Citizens' (NRC) in Assam, India. Minority subjects (or citizens) have been stripped of their citizenship status for not being able to produce adequate documentation, thus leaving them stateless. The extension of the NRC across India will adversely impact Muslims in the country.

The fate of Afghan refugees is still precarious given the Taliban's impending mainstreaming into power politics. For Pakistan, which has hosted one of the largest refugee populations for more than forty years, it is crucial to have a comprehensive refugee policy in line with the international laws that recognise populations that are stateless, or at risk of becoming stateless. Important steps for preventing and reducing statelessness include reassessing the status of refugee populations as an asset (rather than a burden), their inclusion within society, and providing interim measures protecting the right to education (such as offering technical and vocational training) and other fundamental rights. It is important for the region and the world to curtail the alarming trends in South Asia vis-à-vis citizenship and nationality and to protect the fundamental rights of those most vulnerable (refugees, migrants, and the stateless). Inclusive societies offer the prelude to regional peace, which is the prelude to strengthened democracies.

Notes

1 Dedicated to my mother, Abida Fazal, for her immeasurable love and support directed toward everything I do and to (my late father) Mr. Kanwer Fazal-ur-Rehman. I am greatly indebted to Dr. Sadaf Aziz and Sikander A. Shah for their continued support, encouragement, and supervision throughout the years. They

have had an immense impact on my academic evolution and for that, I offer my heartfelt gratitude. I am also immensely grateful to Mr. Khalid Aziz for directing my interest to this pertinent subject area. Last but certainly not the least, deep and sincere gratitude to my unfaltering support system: Angela Williams, Amelia, Olivia, Saba Rehman, Kanwer Khan, Meher, Mahnoor and Jehangir Aziz Hayat.

2 1) A person whose parents or grandparents were born within the territory of Pakistan around Partition and are now permanently resident in the country. 2) Persons who were born in territories that now form part of India but are currently residing in Pakistan. 3) This category addresses persons that were naturalised as British subjects in Pakistan and have in fact renounced their British (or foreign) citizenship before the commencement of the 1951 Act. 4) Those '[w]ho before the commencement of this Act migrated to the territories now Included in Pakistan from any territory in the Indo-Pakistan sub-continent outside those territories with the intention of residing permanently in those territories'.

References

Abdul Majeed and another v. The S.H.O. Police Station Naulakha, Lahore (1989), PLD Lahore 223.

Achakzai, M. (2018) 'Who can be Pakistani?', *The Diplomat*, 11 October [Online]. Available at https://thediplomat.com/2018/10/who-can-be-pakistani/ (Accessed 22 February 2020).

Ahmad, W. (2017) 'The fate of durable solutions in protracted refugee situations: The odyssey of Afghan refugees in Pakistan', *Seattle Journal for Social Justice*, 15:3, 591–661.

Alimia, S. (2013) 'The quest for humanity in a dehumanised state: Afghan refugees and devalued citizens in urban Pakistan, 1979-2012' (PhD thesis, SOAS, University of London).

Ansari, S., and Gould, W. (2019) *Boundaries of Belonging: Localities, Citizenship and Rights in India and Pakistan* (Cambridge: Cambridge University Press).

Arendt, H. (1949) '"The rights of man": What are they?' *Modern Review*, 3:1, 24–36.

Arendt, H. (1973) *The Origins of Totalitarianism* (Boston, MA: Houghton Mifflin Harcourt).

Asia Foundation (2019) 'A survey of the Afghan Refugees' [Online]. Available at https://asiafoundation.org/publication/a-survey-of-the-afghan-returnees-2018/ (Accessed 16 June 2020).

Athayi, A. (2017) 'Report on citizenship law: Afghanistan', European University Institute [Online]. Available at https://cadmus.eui.eu/bitstream/handle/1814/45933/GLOBALCIT_CR_2017_09.pdf (Accessed 24 June 2020).

Aziz, S. (2018) *The Constitution of Pakistan: A Contextual Analysis.* (London: Bloomsbury Publishing).

Baloch, S. (2017) 'Problems with census in Balochistan', *Express Tribune*, 30 March [Online] Available at https://tribune.com.pk/story/1370062/problems-census-balochistan/ (Accessed 25 June 2020).

Bhoyroo, F. (2019) 'New SSAR support platform refocuses international attention on displaced Afghans', UNHCR Iran [Online]. Available at www.unhcr.org/ir/2019/12/19/new-ssar-support-platform-refocuses-international-attention-on-displaced-afghans/ (Accessed 24 June 2020).

Bianchini, K. (2018) *Protecting Stateless Persons: The Implementation of the Convention Relating to the Status of Stateless Persons Across EU States* (Leiden: Brill).

Blitz, B. K., and Lynch, M. (2009) *Statelessness and the Benefits of Citizenship: A Comparative Study* (Geneva: Geneva Academy of International Humanitarian Law and Human Rights and International Observatory on Statelessness).

The Displaced Persons (Compensation and Rehabilitation) Act 1958 (XXVIII of 1958).

The Displaced Persons (Land Settlement) Act 1958 (XLVII of 1958).

Dupree, L. (1980) *Afghanistan* (Princeton, NJ, Princeton University Press).

Farr, G. (2020) 'The Afghan peace agreement and its problems', E-International Relations, 6 April [Online]. Available at www.e-ir.info/2020/04/06/the-afghan-peace-agreement-and-its-problems/ (Accessed 1 June 2020).

The Foreigners Act 1946 (XXXI OF 1946) [Online]. Available at www.ilo.org/dyn/natlex/docs/ELECTRONIC/37905/128188/F1951227926/PAK37905%202016.pdf (Accessed 25 June 2020).

George, S. (2020) '"Thrown under the bus": Some Afghans view U.S.-Taliban peace deal with mix of disbelief and anger', *The Washington Post*, 7 March [Online]. Available at www.washingtonpost.com/world/asia_pacific/afghanistan-us-taliban-peace-deal-anger/2020/03/07/25be7fde-5e46–11ea-ac50–18701e14e06d_story.html (Accessed 15 March 2020).

Gessen, M. (2018) '"The right to have rights" and the plight of the stateless', *The New Yorker*, 3 May [Online]. Available at https://www.newyorker.com/news/our-columnists/the-right-to-have-rights-and-the-plight-of-the-stateless (Accessed 3 September 2019).

Ghulam Sanai v. The Assistant Director, National Registration Office (1999), PLD Peshawar 18.

Goodwin-Gill, G. (1994) 'The rights of refugees and stateless persons', in K. P. Saxena (ed.) *Human Rights Perspectives & Challenges (in 1900's and Beyond)* (New Delhi: Lancers Books): pp. 394–395.

Gündogdu, A. (2015) *Rightlessness in an Age of Rights: Hannah Arendt and the Contemporary Struggles of Migrants* (Oxford: Oxford University Press).

Hayden, P. (2008) 'From exclusion to containment: Arendt, sovereign power, and statelessness', *Societies Without Borders*, 3:2, 248–269.

Human Rights Watch (2002) 'Closed door policy: Afghan refugees in Pakistan and Iran', 27 February [Online]. Available at www.refworld.org/docid/3c7ce78a4.html (Accessed on: 20 March 2020).

Kakar, H. K. (2011) *Government and Society in Afghanistan: The Reign of Amir 'Abd al-Rahman Khan* (Vol. 5) (Austin, TX: University of Texas Press).

Kaur, R. (2009) 'Distinctive citizenship: Refugees, subjects and post-colonial state in India's partition', *Cultural and Social History*, 6:4, 429–446.

Khan, T. (2019) 'Stateless millions', *DAWN NEWS*, 26 November [Online]. Available at www.dawn.com/news/1518883 (Accessed 20 February 2020).

Kronenfeld, D. A. (2008) 'Afghan refugees in Pakistan: Not all refugees, not always in Pakistan, not necessarily Afghan?', *Journal of Refugee Studies*, 21:1, 43–63.

Muhammad Akbar Cheema, Advocate v. Superintendent Jail, Kot Lakhpat (1994) PCRLJ 2362, Lahore High Court.

Nazir, F. (2016) 'Report on citizenship law: Pakistan', European University Institute [Online]. Available at https://cadmus.eui.eu/bitstream/handle/1814/44544/EudoCit_2016_13Pakistan.pdf?sequence=1 (Accessed 24 June 2020).

Omrani, B. (2009) 'The Durand line: History and problems of the Afghan-Pakistan border', *Asian Affairs*, 40:2, 177–195.

The Pakistan (Administration of Evacuee Property) Act 1957 (XII of 1957).

The Pakistan Citizenship Act 1951. [Online]. Available at www.refworld.org/pdfid/3ae6b4ffa.pdf (Accessed 24 June 2020).

The Pakistan Rehabilitation Act 1955 (XLII of 1955).

The Price of Evacuee Property and Public Dues (Recovery) Regulation 1971.

The Registration of Claims (Displaced Persons) Act 1956 (III of 1956).

Senator Abdul Malik v. Government of Pakistan (2012) PLD Quetta 11.

The Scrutiny of Claims (Evacuee Property) Regulation 1961.

Staples, K. (2012) *Retheorising Statelessness: A Background Theory of Membership in World Politics: A Background Theory of Membership in World Politics* (Edinburgh: Edinburgh University Press).

Talbot, I. (2011) 'Punjabi refugees' rehabilitation and the Indian state: Discourses, denials and dissonances', *Modern Asian Studies*, 45:1, 109–130.

UNHCR Operations Portal Refugee Situations (n.d.) 'Islamic Republic of Pakistan' [Online]. Available at https://data2.unhcr.org/en/country/pak (Accessed 2 July 2020).

United Nations (1954) *Convention relating to the Status of Stateless Persons* [Online]. Available at www.unhcr.org/ibelong/wp-content/uploads/1954-Convention-relating-to-the-Status-of-Stateless-Persons_ENG.pdf (Accessed 16 June 2020).

United Nations General Assembly (2016) *New York Declaration for Refugees and Migrants*, 3 October, A/RES/71/1.

United Nations High Commissioner for Refugees (UNHCR) (2006) 'UNHCR Guidelines on the Application in Mass Influx Situations of the Exclusion Clauses of Article 1F of the 1951 Convention relating to the Status of Refugees', 7 February [Online]. Available at www.refworld.org/docid/43f48c0b4.html (Accessed 3 March 2020).

United Nations High Commissioner for Refugees (UNHCR) (2011) 'Pakistan', *Global Appeal 2012–2013* [Online]. Available at www.unhcr.org/4ec231040.pdf (Accessed 16 June 2020).

Weissbrodt, D., and Collins, C. (2006) 'The human rights of stateless persons', *Human Rights Quarterly*, 28:1, 245–276.

Zieck, M. (2008) 'The legal status of Afghan refugees in Pakistan, a story of eight agreements and two suppressed premises', *International Journal of Refugee Law*, 20:2, 253–272.

4

The statelessness of refugees

Jason Tucker

According to the Office of the United Nations High Commissioner for Refugees (UNHCR), there were 22.5 million refugees globally in 2014 (UNHCR, 2017). Research shows that of these 22.5 million, at least 6.6 million were stateless (Institute on Statelessness and Inclusion, 2014). This year was by no means exceptional. The number of stateless refugees makes up a substantial proportion of the total refugee population, year upon year. While a few large groups constitute a significant proportion of these displaced stateless persons, statelessness impacts nearly every refugee movement. Yet since the 1950s, policy related to refugees has rarely mentioned statelessness.

This chapter critically engages with a central policy norm developed over the last three decades by key international actors working on statelessness: for stateless refugees, their 'refugeeness' effectively trumps their statelessness. I term this norm, which separates and ranks statelessness and refugeeness, the 'protection hierarchy'. This norm is increasingly being called into question as a result of growing research on stateless refugees, which shows that statelessness is both very impactful and highly intertwined with refugeeness.

The 'protection hierarchy'

Stateless refugees are simultaneously under the scope of the 1951 Convention Relating to the Status of Refugees (hereafter the 1951 Convention; United Nations General Assembly, 1951) and the 1954 Convention Relating to the Status of Stateless Persons (hereafter the 1954 Convention; United Nations General Assembly, 1954). There is no ranking, comparison, or friction between international protection stemming from either their statelessness or their refugeeness.[1] However, in reality policy relating to stateless refugees has traditionally ranked these two, with refugeeness frequently eclipsing statelessness.

I use the term 'protection hierarchy' here to refer to this norm in the state-less and refugee policy fields. It is a norm that frames the causes, impacts, and consequences of – as well as solutions to – the statelessness of stateless refugees as secondary, or even inconsequential, compared to those stemming from their refugeeness. This has been the policy position shaped and perpetuated by UNHCR, the organisation with mandates for both the 1951 and 1954 Conventions, as well as other key international actors working on statelessness. This position has been moulded through policy and practice of UNHCR during the last fifty or sixty years, and made explicit as their policy position over the last five to ten years. A recent UNHCR statement expresses this framing: 'Although an individual can be both stateless as per the 1954 Convention and a refugee as per the 1951 Convention, at a minimum, a stateless refugee must benefit from the protection of the 1951 Convention and international refugee law' (UNHCR, 2014b: 7).

UNHCR's justification for this position is that protection for stateless refugees can be most effectively achieved under refugee law, with the 1951 Convention adding rights (such as non-refoulment and the right not to be penalised for illegal entry) that are not present in the 1954 Convention (United Nations General Assembly, 1951: 31, 33). This justification is based on the premise that the statelessness of refugees does not impact their ability to claim or be recognised as refugees. Further, it is assumed that in all states, stateless refugees can receive better protection if they are recognised as refugees rather than as stateless persons.

However, this policy position is not based on purely normative legal considerations. While UNHCR is a main agenda setter on statelessness, they are far from the only one. Giulia Scalettaris' (2007) claim that a 'distinctive characteristic of Refugee Studies is its intimate connection with international policy, more precisely the international refugee regime' (36) can also be said about Statelessness Studies. The protection hierarchy was developed by a collective of international actors and academics working on statelessness. Ten years ago, there were only a handful of people working on the issue. This small group (who were overwhelmingly from a legal background) were trying to carve out and maintain the fragile field of statelessness. This fragility, along with the politically sensitive nature of statelessness (both for states but also internally for some organisations), meant that pragmatic decisions about the scope of this new field had to be made.

Key international actors demarking stateless persons as one 'problem' and refugees (including stateless refugees) as another, was an example of this. With the vast majority of states not providing stateless people with any form of protection or status at all, refugee status was seen as the only viable way to protect stateless people who were also refugees. It was also hoped that by separating the two, there would be a greater opportunity to frame as many stateless people as possible as being *in situ*, in 'their' country. The perceived danger of negatively impacting refugee protection meant that stateless refugees were sidelined for the greater good.[2] By doing so, states could avoid the uncomfortable truth that potentially large numbers of the refugees they were hosting would need to be granted a permanent protection status or citizenship in line with international standards on statelessness. Developing this norm also meant that UNHCR could better cope with internal and external tensions of being a refugee organisation that was beginning to work regularly on statelessness. By framing stateless refugees' statelessness as insignificant compared to their refugeeness, statelessness and refugeeness could be separate organisational areas of operation. It also meant that complex questions related to the identification, protection, and provision of solutions for stateless refugees – along with how this would impact nearly all areas of UNHCR's work – did not need to be raised.

These justifications are based on normative or pragmatic concerns that do not draw on an evidence-based evaluation of the actual relationship between statelessness and refugeeness. This is understandable; it was only very recently that a significant body of research on stateless refugees has become available. The policy of isolating statelessness from refugeeness, thus allowing for its incubation, has arguably paid off. Yet a consequence of this success is that the protection hierarchy is now coming under increasing scrutiny, based on empirical foundations.

There is now a substantial and growing body of research that calls into question the idea that we can distinguish, rank, or detach the negative causes and consequences of statelessness from those of refugeeness. It is to this literature, and three multidisciplinary themes related to the protection hierarchy, that I now turn.

Statelessness and recognition as a refugee

The first theme (and arguably one that questions the policy that stateless refugees should, at a minimum, be protected as refugees from the outset) is that statelessness can be a barrier to being recognised as a refugee in a range of contexts. In 2005, when statelessness was being 'rediscovered', Maryellen Fullerton (2005) began to raise concerns about the causes and consequences of seeing statelessness as a homogenous vulnerability with regard to how to ensure protection. Drawing on court cases involving stateless individuals seeking protection as refugees in Canada, the United Kingdom, and the United States, Fullerton (2005, 2014) argued that there was a clear overlap between refugee and statelessness law, highlighting the difficulty – or impossibility – of trying to detach a claimant's statelessness from their refugeeness during refugee status determination (RSD).

Kate Darling (2009) analyses court cases by incorporating international human rights law, international relations, and domestic decision-making. Darling reflects on why international refugee law has been weakened with regard to its ability to protect stateless persons (refugees or otherwise). However, it is only in the last few years that we can see a surge in research on the challenges that stateless refugees face in being recognised as refugees. For example, there is now an ongoing debate about very central aspects of the 1951 Convention, such as how stateless refugees' claims should be assessed (Lambert, 2014; Fripp, 2016a and 2016b). This debate focuses mostly on technical aspects of nationality assessments, country of origin/ former habitual residence, and how to assess statelessness as an aspect of persecution. More recently, Michelle Foster and Hélène Lambert (2019), in their comprehensive review of international refugee law and stateless-ness, argue that there has been inadequate development or understanding of how the 1951 Convention should be used to protect stateless persons. They problematise the separation of the two, claiming that the 1951 Convention 'is clearly relevant to the protection of *de jure* stateless persons on the move' (Foster and Lambert, 2019: 216).

Others have highlighted more practical concerns with regard to this rec-ognition. Bronwen Manby (2016) discusses how the lack of identification documents can lead to particular obstacles for stateless persons seeking refuge. Research also shows that stateless communities fleeing Syria and Myanmar have been forced to undertake extremely risky migration path-ways and are highly vulnerable to smugglers and traffickers due to their statelessness (Kaveri, 2017; Tucker, 2018b; Institute on Statelessness and Inclusion et al., 2019). In other instances, stateless refugees have been rejected *due* to their statelessness, such as Palestinian refugees in Egypt (BADIL, 2015) or where states have misapplied Article 1D of the 'exclusion clause' of the 1951 Convention and rejected Palestinian refugees (Fiddian-Qasmiyeh, 2015).[3]

Zezen Zaenal Mutaqin (2018) argues that whether framed as refugees or stateless people, neither of these labels provide many tangible benefits for Rohingya refugees in South East Asia given the lack of refugee or asylum systems in most states in the region (see also Brinham, this volume). Maissaa Almustafa (2018), using the case of the Palestinian refugees with their mul-tiple instances of forced migration, argues that the current international refugee regime was created, and is perpetuated, by Eurocentric concerns. This has led to significant structural flaws in how the international refugee regime is designed, so that many Palestinian refugees are excluded from receiving the same protection as other refugees (Almustafa, 2018).

Vulnerability, protection and refugees' statelessness

While the above discussion has been primarily dominated by legal scholars, research on the impact of statelessness on refugees' lives is far broader in terms of discipline and methodology. One subtheme that has arisen is the impact of statelessness on the health of refugees. Andrew Riley et al. (2017) undertook a cross-sectional study focusing on trauma history, daily environmental stressors, and mental health outcomes for 148 Rohingya refugees in Bangladesh. They found a high prevalence of mental health concerns and claim that the participants' past and present experiences, as well as future aspirations, can only be understood by acknowledging that their refugeeness *and* statelessness are both critical factors (Riley et al., 2017). Similar findings can be seen in research on conflict-related trauma and ongoing stressors for 230 West Papuan refugees in Papua New Guinea (Tay et al., 2015). In that study, 88.3% of respondents reported that the lack of legal rights and access to citizenship was a daily stressor (Tay et al., 2015).

The impact of statelessness on the health of Rohingya refugees can also be seen on a much larger scale. A. K. Tay et al. (2019) analysed the literature on the mental health and psychosocial wellbeing of Rohingya refugees, including an examination of associated cultural factors. They found that the persecution the population faced in Myanmar, as well as the uncertainty and vulnerability stemming from their prolonged statelessness, increased their vulnerability to psychological distress and mental disorders. Tay et al. (2019) also note that one spillover of this vulnerability was high rates of sexual and gender-based violence faced by the community. Annekathryn Goodman and Iftkher Mahmood (2019) further show that Rohingya women and children in Bangladesh are especially vulnerable to human trafficking and sexual exploitation, as well as sexual violence before, during, and after their journey as a result of their statelessness. The relationship between gender, statelessness and forced migration is one that arises again and again. For example, consider Mariangela Veikou's (2017) exploration of statelessness, forced migration, and lack of belonging among women and children in Greece and Mohamed Farahat's (2017) research on refugees in Egypt and the statelessness of their children born of rape.

The agency of stateless refugees to resist or reject either the refugee or stateless label(s) has also been the subject of research. For example, Michael Vicente Pérez's (2011) work explores Gaza Palestinians' claim for Jordanian nationality and how they negotiate their statelessness and rightlessness. Later, Pérez (2018) investigated how this population undertook repetitive ordinary daily activities as a form of agential effort – a form of survival in their highly unstable lives. Research also considers: the resistance of Palestinian refugees in Europe to their labelling as stateless

(Fiddian-Qasmiyeh, 2015); the resilience of stateless migrants in South East Asia (McAuliffe, 2017); the impact of statelessness on asylum destination decision-making (Tucker, 2018b); the use of the language as a form of resistance to statelessness (Alsahafi, 2019); and work exploring the various reasons why stateless refugees flee (Kader and Choudhury, 2019).

Statelessness and 'durable solutions' for refugees

Local integration

There is a growing body of research on the integration challenges facing stateless refugees. The difficulties the Rohingya face integrating in India and Malaysia has been linked to their lack of basic education (due to their exclusion from education in Myanmar), making language learning problematic (Azis, 2014; Velath and Chopra, 2015). Furthermore, their economic marginalisation in Myanmar has been shown to increase the barriers they face in securing adequate employment (Azis, 2014; Velath and Chopra, 2015).

Research also shows that when refugee status ends, statelessness continues and can prove to be an insurmountable obstacle to naturalisation (Kingston, 2017; Tucker, 2018a; Benson et al., this volume). Thus, for some refugees, local integration will always remain less accessible due to their statelessness. Research such as that by Katalin Berényi (2016) and David Howard (2017) highlights the dangers of refugees' children being born stateless, drawing attention to the multigenerational integration challenges that stateless refugees and their families may face. Isolating stateless refugees in camps, where local integration is not possible, is also shown as highly problematic in the case of the Sahrawi refugees in Algeria (Martín, 2017).

Some work also explores how, at a national and even regional level, the statelessness of some refugees has a significant impact on the local integration prospects for other populations, including *in situ* stateless and non-stateless migrant populations. For example, Marie McAuliffe (2017) argues that the intertwined phenomena of irregularity, statelessness, and protection in South East Asia has led to a situation whereby the discourse surrounding migrants' rights more generally has become muted. Susan Akram (2018) makes a similar argument, though with a focus on the Palestinians in the context of the Middle East and North Africa.

Repatriation

Research on the repatriation of stateless refugees is most prevalent with regard to the Rohingya. The multiple, and often disastrous, attempts to repatriate the population have failed because they did not address the statelessness of the population (Kiragu et al., 2011). Furthermore, and worryingly, there were instances of involuntary repatriation (Faulkner and Schiffer, 2019). Here, Esther Kiragu et al. (2011) and Christopher Faulkner and Samuel Schiffer (2019) argue that detaching statelessness and refugee-ness is not only questionable in terms of durability of solutions, but also exacerbates the vulnerability already faced by the Rohingya. Faulkner and Schiffer (2019) compare the failed repatriation attempts of the Rohingya to the successful repatriation of refugees to Angola, where the absence of statelessness improved the prospects of successful repatriation. Similarly, Bill Berkley (2009) discusses how the repatriation of Black Mauritanians faced significant challenges because their statelessness was not resolved. Where citizenship is offered as part of the solution, this can also be ham-pered by procedures that stateless refugees may be unable to meet, as was the case for some Faili Kurds and their repatriation from Iran to Iraq (Tucker, 2014).

Resettlement

Lindsey Kingston and Kathryn Stam (2017) interviewed two stateless refugee groups who recently had been resettled to the U.S. The participants noted that statelessness was a contributing factor to the human right abuses they suffered in the past *as well as* present. They noted how, post resettle-ment, their statelessness continued to impact their access to education, language learning, and access to employment (Kingston and Stam, 2017). Another study in the U.S. by Odessa Gonzalez Benson and Yoosun Park (2018) focuses on elderly monoglot Bhutanese refugees and highlights barri-ers they faced in acquiring U.S. citizenship due, in part, to their statelessness (also see Benson et al., this volume). More generally, while some stateless refugees have benefited from resettlement (the vast majority being from the Bhutanese-Nepali refugee community), stateless refugees have been shown to face exclusion from, or extra barriers to be included in, resettlement pro-grammes as compared to non-stateless refugees (Institute on Statelessness and Inclusion and Norwegian Refugee Council, 2016; McGee, 2016).

Moving beyond the protection hierarchy

The large body of empirical research on how people experience stateless-ness and refugeeness, as well as innovative legal and policy perspectives on managing this relationship, all point in one direction: the justifications for the protection hierarchy norm are now untenable. Research shows that refugeeness does not always trump statelessness in terms of protection concerns, that protection and solutions for stateless refugees under refugee law is not sufficient (or sometimes even possible), and that some vulnerabilities stem from refugees' statelessness. While this policy norm served a purpose, it has now been empirically and normatively found wanting.

Does this new understanding mean that the time has arrived for more evidence-based policy on stateless refugees? Here we can turn to the policy and operational themes of the key international and regional organisations working on statelessness, who are the main agenda setters on the issue.[4] Since 2014, we can see that some are moving beyond the protection hierarchy norm and centralising refugees who are stateless within their discourse on statelessness more generally (see Norwegian Refugee Council and Tilburg University, 2015; European Network on Statelessness, 2018a and 2018b; Citizenship Rights in Africa Initiative, 2019).

While many academics and key actors who previously perpetuated the protection hierarchy have now turned away from it (myself included), the same cannot be said for UNHCR. In their #IBelong Campaign and the associated 'Global Action Plan to End Statelessness' (2014–2024), the organisation continues to propagate this policy norm (UNHCR, 2014a). Despite a few brief references to the link between statelessness and refugees (in the case of children, solutions, protracted refugee situations, and deprivation of nationality), the language of the 'Global Action Plan to End Statelessness' consistently tries to detach refugeeness and statelessness. For example, the populations of concern are continually referred to as 'non-refugee stateless people/situations/communities' (UNHCR, 2014a).

However, since the launch of the #IBelong Campaign in 2014, UNHCR has (on rare occasions) explicitly noted that due to stateless-specific concerns, there is a need to identify and be sensitive to the statelessness of refugees. For example, UNHCR's Department for International Protection stated that they are looking into ways to include 'trigger questions' in RSD procedures so that statelessness can be identified (Li-Rosi, 2017). Furthermore, UNHCR (2017) produced guidance on the identification of stateless persons in arbitrary detention, noting that in addition to complicating durable solutions, the statelessness of refugees may have other consequences for refugees and/or their children. The Chief of UNHCR's Statelessness Section also said that not identifying the statelessness of asylum seekers 'may affect negatively their recognition as refugees' (Khanna and Garlick, 2017).

Despite recognising the significant flaws in how they frame the statelessness of refugees, this is far from an evolution in UNHCR's position on the subject. Where stateless refugees are mentioned by the organisation, the protection hierarchy is still used to justify the norm of detaching and ranking statelessness as less impactful than refugeeness.

In moving beyond the protection hierarchy norm, we open a complex set of questions relating to how governance frameworks engage with stateless refugees. For example, how should statelessness among refugees be identified in practice? How would the additional label of 'stateless' impact those upon whom it is imposed? How do we shape refugee regimes to be sensitive to statelessness? How, given the often highly politicised nature of citizenship, should this be framed to minimise the risk of stateless refugees having (further) negative impacts on broader migration asylum discourses? These challenges may seem daunting, but for the first time we have the possibility to draw on a wealth of research to use an evidence-based approach to meet these challenges.

Notes

1 This is not to say that this did not exist during the drafting of the Conventions; see Van Waas (2014).
2 In some cases, both refugee and non-refugee stateless populations were sidelined (Moas, 2010).
3 For details on the 'exclusion clause', see Akram (2002).
4 These include UNHCR, European Network on Statelessness, Institute on Statelessness Inclusion, Norwegian Refugee Council, American Network on Statelessness and Nationality (ANSN), Citizenship Rights in Africa Initiative and the Statelessness Network Asia Pacific (SNAP).

References

Akram, S. (2002) 'Palestinian refugees and their legal status: Rights, politics, and implications for a just solution', *Journal of Palestine Studies*, 31:3, 36–51.

Akram, S. (2018) 'The search for protection for stateless refugees in the Middle East: Palestinians and Kurds in Lebanon and Jordan', *International Journal of Refugee Law*, 30:3, 407–443.

Almustafa, M. (2018) 'Relived vulnerabilities of Palestinian refugees: Governing through exclusion', *Social & Legal Studies*, 27:2, 164–179.

Alsahafi, M. (2019) 'Language proficiency and usage among second- and third-generation Rohingya refugees in Mecca', *Journal of Multilingual and Multicultural Development*, 42:1, 32–51.

Azis, A. (2014) 'Urban refugees in a graduated sovereignty: The experiences of the stateless Rohingya in the Klang Valley', *Citizenship Studies*, 18:8, 839–854.

BADIL (2015) 'Palestinian refugees from Syria in Egypt: An overview' [Online]. Available at www.badil.org/en/publication/periodicals/al-majdal/item/2075-article-4.html (Accessed 2 August 2019).

Benson, O. G., and Park, Y. (2018) 'Resettled yet stateless: Elderly monoglot refugees in the United States as a limit case to citizenship', *Journal of Human Rights Practice*, 10, 423–438.

Berényi, K. (2016) 'Statelessness and the refugee crisis in Europe', *Forced Migration Review*, 53, 63–64.

Berkley, B. (2009) 'Stateless people, violent states', *World Policy Journal*, 26:1, 3–15.

Citizenship Rights in Africa Initiative. (2019) 'Nationality and refugees' [Online]. Available at http://citizenshiprightsafrica.org/theme/nationality-and-refugees/ (Accessed 10 September 2019).

Darling, K. (2009) 'Protection of stateless people in international asylum and refugee law', *International Journal of Refugee Law*, 21:4, 742–767.

European Network on Statelessness. (2018a) 'Addressing statelessness in Europe and the nexus with forced migration' [Online]. Available at www.rsc.ox.ac.uk/news/addressing-statelessness-in-europe-and-the-nexus-with-forced-migration-chris-nash (Accessed 5 December 2019).

European Network on Statelessness. (2018b) 'Solving statelessness in Europe, our strategic plan 2019–2023' [Online]. Available at www.statelessness.eu/sites/www.statelessness.eu/files/attachments/resources/ENS-Strategic-Plan-2019-23.pdf (Accessed 11 September 2019).

Farahat, M. (2017) 'Children of rape of refugee women, and statelessness, in Egypt', *Forced Migration Review*, 55, 79.

Faulkner, C., and Schiffer, S. (2019) 'Unwelcomed? The effects of statelessness on involuntary refugee repatriation in Bangladesh and Myanmar', *The Round Table*, 108:2, 145–158.

Fiddian-Qasmiyeh, E. (2015) 'On the threshold of statelessness: Palestinian narratives of loss and erasure', *Ethnic and Racial Studies*, 39:2, 301–321.

Foster, M., and Lambert, H. (2019) *International Refugee Law and the Protection of Stateless Persons* (Oxford: Oxford University Press).

Fripp, E. (2016a) 'Deprivation of nationality, "The Country of his Nationality" in Article 1A(2) of the Refugee Convention, and non-recognition under international law', *International Journal of Refugee Law*, 28:3, 453–479.

Fripp, E. (2016b) *Nationality and Statelessness in the International Law of Refugee Status* (Oxford: Hart Publishing).

Fullerton, M. (2005) 'Comparative perspectives on statelessness and persecution', *Kansas Law Review*, 63, 863–902.

Fullerton, M. (2014) 'The intersection of statelessness and refugee protection in U.S. asylum policy', *Journal of Migration and Human Security*, 2:3, 144–164.

Goodman, A., and Mahmood, I. (2019) 'The Rohingya refugee crisis of Bangladesh: Gender-based violence and the humanitarian response', *Open Journal of Political Science*, 9, 490–501.

Howard, D. M. (2017) 'Analyzing the causes of statelessness in Syrian refugee children', *Texas International Law Journal*, 52:2, 281–312.

Institute on Statelessness and Inclusion (2014) *The World's Stateless* (Oisterwijk: Wolf Legal Publishers).

Institute on Statelessness and Inclusion and Norwegian Refugee Council (2016) *Understanding Statelessness in the Syria Refugee Context* [Online]. Available at http://reliefweb.int/report/syrian-arab-republic/understanding-statelessness-syria-refugee-context (Accessed 15 May 2019).

Institute on Statelessness, ASKV, and European Network on Statelessness. (2019) 'From Syria to Europe: Experiences of stateless Kurds and Palestinian refugees from Syria seeking protection in Europe' [Online]. Available at www.statelessness.eu/sites/www.statelessness.eu/files/attachments/resources/ENS-ISI-From_Syria_to_Europe_Jan-2019.pdf (Accessed 11 June 2020).

Kader, M. F., and Choudhury, A. H. (2019) 'Historical background of the Rohingya refugee crisis and the implication of their statelessness', *International Journal of Social Sciences and Economic Review*, 1:1, 8–15.

Kaveri. (2017) 'Being stateless and the plight of the Rohingyas', *Peace Review*, 29:1, 31–39.

Khanna, M., and Garlick, M. (2017) 'Avoiding detention of stateless persons: UNHCR's new tool for identification and enhanced protection of stateless persons in detention' [Online]. Available at www.statelessness.eu/blog/avoiding-detention-stateless-persons-unhcrs-new-tool-identification-and-enhanced-protection (Accessed 10 December 2017).

Kingston, L. N. (2017) '"Bringing Rwandan refugees 'home' ": The cessation clause, statelessness, and forced repatriation', *International Journal of Refugee Law*, 29:3, 417–437.

Kingston, L. N., and Stam, K. (2017) 'Recovering from statelessness: Resettled Bhutanese-Nepali and Karen refugees reflect on the lack of legal nationality', *Journal of Human Rights*, 16:4, 389–406.

Kiragu, E., Li-Rosi, A., and Morris, T. (2011) 'States of denial, a review of UNHCR's response to the protracted situation of stateless Rohingya refugees in Bangladesh' [Online]. Available at www.refworld.org/docid/4a40d29f7f.html (Accessed 15 May 2019).

Lambert, H. (2014) *Refugee Status, Arbitrary Deprivation of Nationality, and Statelessness within the Context of Article 1A(2) of the 1951 Convention and its 1967 Protocol Relating to the Status of Refugees* [Online]. Available at www.unhcr.org/protection/globalconsult/5433f0f09/33-refugee-status-arbitrary-deprivation-nationality-statelessness-context.html (Accessed 3 January 2018).

Li-Rosi, A. (2017) 'Protecting stateless people from arbitrary detention', ENS Annual Conference (4 May, Budapest).

Manby, B. (2016) 'Identification in the context of forced displacement', International Bank for Reconstruction and Development/The World Bank [Online]. Available at http://documents.worldbank.org/curated/en/375811469772770030/pdf/Identification-in-the-Context-of-Forced-Displacement-Identification-for-Development-ID4D.pdf (Accessed 10 September 2019).

Martín, C. G. (2017) 'Rethinking the concept of "durable solutions": Sahrawi refugee camps four decades on', *Ethics & International Affairs* [Online]. Available at www.ethicsandinternationalaffairs.org/2017/rethinking-concept-durable-solution-sahrawi-refugee-camps/ (Accessed 10 September 2019).

McAuliffe, M. (2017) 'Protection elsewhere, resilience here: Introduction to the special issue on statelessness, irregularity, and protection in Southeast Asia', *Journal of Immigrant & Refugee Studies*, 15:3, 221–231.

McGee, T. (2016) 'Statelessness displaced: Update on Syria's stateless Kurds' [Online]. Available at www.institutesi.org/WP2016_02.pdf (Accessed 22 July 2018).

Moas, T. (2010) '62 years of human rights, yet no rights since '62' [Online]. Available at http://tagheemoas.blogspot.com/2010/12/62-years-of-human-rights-yet-no-rights.html (Accessed 18 February 2020).

Mutaqin, Z. Z. (2018) 'The Rohingya refugee crisis and human rights: What should ASEAN do?', *Asia-Pacific Journal on Human Rights and the Law*, 19, 1–26.

Norwegian Refugee Council and Tilburg University. (2015) 'Statelessness and displacement: Scoping paper' [Online]. Available at www.nrc.no/globalassets/pdf/reports/statelessness-and-displacement.pdf (Accessed 8 June 2019).

Pérez, M. V. (2011) 'Human rights and the rightless: The case of Gaza refugees in Jordan', *The International Journal of Human Rights*, 15:7, 1031–1054.

Pérez, M. V. (2018) 'The everyday as survival among ex-Gaza refugees in Jordan', *Middle East Critique*, 27:3, 275–288.

Riley, A., Varner, A., Ventevogel, P., Taimur Hasan, M. M., and Welton-Mitchell, C. (2017) 'Daily stressors, trauma exposure, and mental health among stateless Rohingya refugees in Bangladesh', *Transcultural Psychiatry*, 54:3, 304–331.

Scalettaris, G. (2007) 'Refugee studies and the international refugee regime: A reflection on a desirable separation', *Refugee Survey Quarterly*, 26:3, 36–50.

Tay, A. K., Rees, S., Chen, J., Kareth, M., Lahe, S., Kitau, R., David, K., Sonoling, J., and Silove, D. (2015) 'Associations of conflict-related trauma and ongoing stressors with the mental health and functioning of West Papuan refugees in Port Moresby, Papua New Guinea (PNG)', *PLOS One* [Online]. Available at https://journals.plos.org/plosone/article?id=10.1371/journal.pone.0125178 (Accessed 11 June 2020).

Tay, A. K., Riley, A., Islam, R., Welton-Mitchell, C., Duchesne, B., Waters, V., Varner, A., Moussa, B., Mahmudul Alam, A. N. M., Elshazly, M. A., Silove, D., and Ventevogel, P. (2019) 'The culture, mental health and psychosocial wellbeing of Rohingya refugees: A systematic review', *Epidemiology and Psychiatric Sciences*, 28, 489–494.

Tucker, J. (2014) 'Exploring statelessness and nationality in Iran: Gaps in the nationality law, populations of concern and areas for future research' [Online]. Available at https://papers.ssrn.com/sol3/papers.cfm?abstract_id=2441850 (Accessed 16 July 2020).

Tucker, J. (2018a) 'Sweden's temporary asylum law and the indefinite statelessness of refugees', *Oxford Monitor of Forced Migration*, 7:2, 21–36 [Online]. Available at http://mhi.hi.is/sites/mhi.hi.is/files/nalsfiles/5/nals_paper_tucker.pdf (Accessed 12 March 2019).

Tucker, J. (2018b) 'Why here? Factors affecting stateless Palestinian refugees from Syria in choosing Germany or Sweden as asylum destination countries', *Comparative Migration Studies*, 6:29 [Online]. Available at https://comparativemigrationstudies.springeropen.com/articles/10.1186/s40878-018-0094-2 (Accessed 9 July 2019).

United Nations General Assembly (1951) *Convention Relating to the Status of Refugees* [Online]. Available at www.refworld.org/docid/3be01b964.html (Accessed 20 October 2018).

United Nations General Assembly (1954) *Convention Relating to the Status of Stateless Persons* [Online]. Available at www.refworld.org/docid/3ae6b3840. html (Accessed 10 May 2018).

United Nations High Commissioner for Refugees (UNHCR) (2014a) 'Global Action Plan to End Statelessness' [Online]. Available at www.refworld.org/docid/ 545b47d64.html (Accessed 10 September 2019).

United Nations High Commissioner for Refugees (UNHCR) (2014b) *Handbook on Protection of Stateless Persons* [Online]. Available at www.unhcr.org/53b698ab9. html (Accessed 16 June 2016).

United Nations High Commissioner for Refugees (UNHCR) (2017) 'Stateless persons in detention: Guidance for their identification and enhanced protection' [Online]. Available at www.refworld.org/pdfid/598adacd4.pdf (Accessed 23 December 2017).

Van Waas, L. (2014) 'The UN statelessness conventions', in A. Edwards and L. Van Waas (eds) *Nationality and Statelessness under International Law* (Cambridge: Cambridge University Press): pp. 64–87.

Veikou, M. (2017) 'Back to basics: Stateless women and children in Greece', *Journal of Balkan and Near Eastern Studies*, 19:5, 557–570.

Velath, P. M., and Chopra, K. (2015) 'The stateless people – Rohingya in Hyderabad, India', *Policies and Practices: Mahanirban Calcutta Research Group*, 71, 25–39.

Figure 2

Dissolution of the moonbeam union

Mawa Rannahr

This work is a record of human activity expressed as layers of paint applied onto canvas with the intent to serve as proof that I – the artist – do exist and that I am, in fact, human. Shouldn't my humanity alone be enough?

5

Statelessness and the administrative state: The legal prowess of the first-line bureaucrat in Malaysia

Jamie Chai Yun Liew[1]

Do you remember your last visit to a government counter to apply for or renew your driver's licence? What did the government official say to you? What did the forms look like? Do you remember the questions that were asked of you?

Some of us can treat the acquisition of a driver's licence as, at best, an exciting moment of privilege to join others on the road, and at worst an administrative hassle or one of many errands on a particular day. This kind of encounter is seemingly innocuous, even forgettable. For stateless persons applying for citizenship however, the encounter at a government counter can be a perilous experience filled with denials, refusals, obstructions, misunderstandings, judgements, and deceptions leading to life-altering outcomes.

There is rich analysis in scholarly writing about 'administrative justice' and how law is practised and experienced at the 'street-level', including how government officials interpret and understand the law (Adler, 2010: 204; Hertogh, 2010; Pottie and Sossin, 2005; Lipsky, 1980; Raso, 2019). This chapter aims to further our understanding of administrative justice, but also provide clarity of when and how statelessness occurs in the administrative state from the point of view of the stateless person. Rather than presume that the administrative state functions as it should or as one may expect, this chapter suggests that the government counter is a frontier that should receive greater attention when legal accountability is sought. The following discussion uses the case study of stateless persons in Malaysia, but the insights gained from this case study pertain to any jurisdiction that relies on a regulatory state in implementing government regimes and policies.

The administrative state and administrative justice

The rise of the regulatory state in democratic, common law states has affected the way people interact with government. Malaysia is a post-colonial, multi-juridical, democratic state that deploys an administrative system to implement government policies. Thus, the case study of Malaysia provides an apt site to investigate how statelessness intersects with the administrative state.

Policies and programmes are now implemented and delivered by agencies, tribunals, and registrars. These offices employ government officers, bureaucrats, and officials who have been delegated decision-making power by a democratically elected government. Their power includes deciding the procedures by which to process these policies and programmes, but also the substantive power to make actual decisions about whether to confer benefits or make decisions.

Despite the role of law in creating the administrative state, legal discussion has 'focused largely on the construction of a set of boundaries designed to distinguish the legal from the administrative aspects of decision-making' (Potte and Sossin, 2005: 147). Deference is given to administrative bodies to allow them to deliver the policies and programmes mandated to them by an elected government. There are, however, new calls for a 're-examination of whether these boundaries are tenable or desirable' given how decisions in the administrative state 'often affect vulnerable people with few alternative recourses' (Pottie and Sossin, 2005: 147).

Simon Halliday (2004) describes administrative law, the law practised by the administrative state, as encompassing two concepts: 'the principles which police the lawfulness of government behaviour' and 'the law of the administration – the substantive powers and duties of public agencies' (8). Administrative law encompasses both procedural fairness and substantive justice. As Michael Adler (2010) suggests, procedural fairness is concerned with process where substantive justice is concerned with outcomes. In other words, 'procedural fairness focuses on how individuals are treated while substantive justice focuses on what they end up with' (Adler, 2010: 131, quoting Richardson, 1984). Naturally then, the term 'administrative justice' is used to convey the goal of fair treatment of those encountering government officials and outcomes that are seen as just (Adler, 2010: 129). In this sense, 'the just state of affairs is one in which each individual has exactly those benefits and burdens which are due to him [or her] by virtue of his [or her] personal characteristics and circumstances' (Adler, 2010: 130, quoting Miller, 1979: 19–20). Fair process can be seen as linked or even essential to a substantively just decision.

This chapter is preoccupied with administrative action at the counter – that is, frontline government officials who meet with stateless persons and what power they yield in exercising their power to interpret law and policies to make what are ultimately profound and lasting decisions about the citizenship of the people before them. The chapter is a call to pay closer attention to the administrative state when it comes to the creation and maintenance of statelessness.

The stateless at Malaysian registration offices

Between 1 January and 26 April 2018, I conducted unstructured interviews with forty-five people in various locations in Malaysia[2] (eight lawyers, two paralegals, thirteen NGO representatives, three academics, and nineteen stateless persons). It is important to point out that interviews were not conducted with any person working in the administrative state and the encounters described below are from the point of view of the stateless person or their advocate only. Thus, this research does not purport to explain *why* the stateless person experiences certain things at the government counter, but rather illuminates the effect or impact of such encounters on the stateless person. Similarly, this chapter does not provide a full legal account or description of how one obtains citizenship, but rather provides some background information when needed to understand how a stateless person may have experienced a particular face-to-face meeting with a government official. This chapter represents a small slice of a larger research project that interrogates who are stateless and what are the legal barriers to obtaining citizenship from the point of view of the stateless person (Liew, 2019).

The number of stateless persons in the world and in Malaysia is difficult to quantify because stateless persons do not have a legal identity and may avoid contact with the state for fear of repercussions, such as detention and removal from the country. At the time the research was conducted in 2018, the Malaysian government figures showed the population of Malaysia as 32.4 million, with 3,323 non-citizens (Department of Statistics Malaysia, 2018). Demographic information does not indicate whether stateless persons were included in the statistical figures or whether they comprise any of the 'non-citizens' counted or estimated. DHRRA Malaysia, with the United Nations High Commissioner for Refugees (UNHCR, n.d.), conducted a mapping project and found there were approximately 12,400 stateless persons of Tamil descent in Malaysia. In November 2016, the former home minister Datuk Seri Dr. Ahmad Zahid Hamidi said there were more than 290,000 stateless children in Malaysia (Buang, 2019). This chapter does not attempt to resolve the debate about the number of stateless persons, but rather acknowledges that there is a significant population of persons without any citizenship in Malaysia.

The qualitative interviews conducted for this study revealed specific encounters stateless persons had with Malaysia's administrative state. The first experience relates to people who had citizenship, but became stateless at the counter. The second experience is that of a series of barriers to applying for citizenship, including: (a) government officials not willing to help; (b) denial of access to forms, the giving of the wrong form, and/or the refusal to accept documentation; (c) misleading or wrong advice/information; and (d) racism of government officials.

Becoming stateless at the counter

At least five persons interviewed for this project explained that persons became stateless after applying for an Identification Card (IC) when eligible (at 12 years of age). What was supposed to be a routine application for identification turned into an interrogation and investigation into the validity of birth certificates, which led to some losing their birth certificate and therefore their citizenship (Liew, 2019). For example, one stateless person interviewed relayed how she went with her mother to apply for an IC when she became eligible at the age of 12. At the government counter, the official openly commented that the girl did not look like her mother and started examining her birth certificate. Indeed, the girl was adopted by her mother. Nevertheless, even though the girl's mother had believed she had legally adopted her, the birth certificate issued at the time of the adoption (when the girl was a baby) was deemed fraudulent. Her birth certificate was confiscated and a new one was issued, indicating she was not a citizen. All of this occurred at the counter (the birth certificate is examined in more detail in Buterman, this volume).

Government officials not willing to help

One of the most common barriers at the counter faced by stateless persons is the lack of assistance given by government officials. Eleven of nineteen stateless persons reported that they did not receive any helpful assistance from government officials when they approached them about applying for or inquiring about the status of their citizenship application.

Stateless persons approaching a government official to inquire about the process, or for information about how to apply, were met with responses that told them what needed to be done in piecemeal fashion. One person stated: 'We were never told what the whole process was. They just kept telling me one step at a time and didn't tell me what I needed to do after that step. There was no information and no list given. They were being deliberately uncooperative'. Another stateless person had a similar experience where government officials would ask for a different thing every time they attended the registrar. 'We went back and forth to the JPN [registration office] and each time the JPN was asking for different things.' Another stateless person was told to go to a different registration office, even though there was no information given and no apparent reason as to why the office they were at could not help them.

An NGO representative stated that when a person goes to a government office, 'it does not mean they will get the service or treatment they expect. We get complaints. People get stopped, denied. There is no clear direction from the government'. Another NGO representative said that sometimes it is a waste of time to go to a registrar's office.

When stateless persons asked about the status of their citizenship application, officers would not take any information from the persons or look into the system, but simply replied that applicants (or persons assisting them) had to just wait. Occasionally, stateless persons were told the government official would inquire and follow up or call them once they found the answer, but no follow-up ever materialised.

Denial of access to forms/refusal to accept documents

Another barrier is the complete denial of the accepting or giving of documents and forms necessary to apply for citizenship. Six of the nineteen stateless persons interviewed said they were either given the wrong application form, were denied a specific form or had to fight vigorously to acquire one, and/or experienced government officials refusing to take their documents.

In Malaysia, there are different kinds of citizenship applications depending on where your legal entitlement lies: (a) by operation of law; (b) by registration; or (c) by naturalisation. Applications for citizenship by naturalisation are governed by Article 19 of the Malaysian Constitution. There is also a different application form associated with this process (*The Federal Constitution of Malaysia* 1957, art. 19). Applications for citizenship by operation of law are known as Article 14 applications, since they arise from Article 14 of the Malaysian Constitution (*The Federal Constitution of Malaysia* 1957, art. 14). There is current legal debate about the scope of 'by operation of law', and whether simply being born within the territory of Malaysia is sufficient for automatic conferral of citizenship (for example: *Yun Sheng Meng*, 2016; *Than Siew Beng*, 2015; *Than Siew Beng*, 2017). Nevertheless, persons who have a Malaysian citizen parent are entitled to citizenship 'by operation of law' depending on who the parent is (mother or father) and when and if the parents are married (i.e. children with unmarried parents whose mothers do not have Malaysian citizenship cannot acquire citizenship by descent from their father).

Applications for citizenship by registration are called Article 15A applications – again, because they are derived from Article 15A of the Malaysian constitution (*The Federal Constitution of Malaysia* 1957, art.

15A). Unlike 'by operation of the law', citizenship applications under registration or Article 15A require the meeting of some requirements, as well as positive discretion on the part of the Minister of Home Affairs or a delegate (government official) of the Minister. While this legal avenue may seem like a viable method for acquiring citizenship, a conferral of citizenship under Article 15A is neither legally nor normatively as powerful as Article 14. This is because it relies on the whim/discretion of the Minister or his/her delegate, as well as certain criteria, and going through this application means that the applicant is not entitled to citizenship automatically.

Interviews highlighted the challenges associated with accessing proper forms. One stateless interviewee did not understand the difference between the various application forms and took for granted that the government official would give them the appropriate one. Stateless persons interviewed discussed the difficulty of getting Article 14 applications. They also mentioned how government officials preferred giving Article 15A applications instead of Article 14 applications (if any applications were given at all), implying that they, as particular applicants, did not have automatic legal entitlement to citizenship. One stateless person explained that it was only when a paralegal intervened that they received the proper form and that the paralegal had to 'fight with the government official' to give out the correct application form. Lawyers and other advocates are aware of this barrier and instruct their clients to ask for a particular form, warn persons of the resistance they may face, and sometimes intervene on their clients' behalf.

Misleading/wrong information

Government officials sometimes gave misleading or wrong advice about the citizenship application process. Seven of nineteen stateless persons said they received misleading or wrong advice from government officials. One father of a stateless person relayed an experience where he visited the registration office. He told a government official that his wife (who is not a Malaysian citizen) was advised to have bed rest for the remainder of her pregnancy, and asked if their marriage could be registered after the child was born. The government official not only said yes, but encouraged the applicant to wait until the child was born before registering the child. The father learned, after the birth of his child, that there were serious ramifications for this. In effect, because the marriage was not registered and therefore not legal at the time the child was born, the child was deemed 'illegitimate' in Malaysian law and could not acquire citizenship by descent from the father, who was a Malaysian citizen. A few persons interviewed for this project were also told, erroneously, to adopt their biological children in order to facilitate a citizenship application.

Racism

Malaysia considers itself a multicultural state and its Department of Statistics collects census information about ethnicity. In 2018, government statistics divided its population into the following categories: Bumiputera (Malay & Indigenous peoples) (62%), Chinese (20.6%), Indian (6.2%), other (0.9%), and non-citizens (10.3%) (Department of Statistics Malaysia, 2019). The United Nations Statistics Division has stated that '[e]thnic data is useful for the elaboration of policies to improve access to employment, education and training, social security and health, transportation and communications, etc.' (UN Stats, 2003: 2). The collection of this data, therefore, assists governments and other organisations in discerning not only who there is within a state, but whether some people are treated differently because of their race or ethnicity.

In the Malaysian context, interviewed stateless persons (and their advocates) claimed that they were treated differently at the government counter when applying for citizenship, and that this treatment was based on their race or ethnicity. Four of the nineteen stateless persons spoke of how government officials made comments to them about their race or the legitimacy of their application due to their race. One stateless person stated that a government official noticed 'she did not look like her mother' when she was applying for her Identification Card (IC) for the first time. At the counter, the government official decided to investigate her birth certificate, deemed it fraudulent and wrong, and took it away, effectively making the applicant stateless on the spot.

Lawyers, paralegals, and NGO representatives also expressed that since many government officials are Muslim and Malay, Muslims and Malays are given better treatment by government officials. They contend that race is not an indication of whether a person has actual legal entitlement to citizenship, and that persons who are not Muslim or Malay are often prompted, by government officials, to apply for citizenship in other countries.

Intersection of barriers

Finally, some of the above barriers meet at an intersection. In one case, the combination of misinformation and the denial of the taking of documents contributed to a stateless person's inability to apply for citizenship. For example, one person I interviewed recalled how a government official said that a copy of a marriage certificate was sufficient and that no certification or notarisation was necessary. However, when the stateless person came back with the original and a copy of the marriage certificate, another official denied the acceptance of the copy and said it needed to have an official notary stamp. When asked where the requirement for this came from, the government official simply reiterated that a certified, notarised copy was needed.

The social construction of stateless persons at the counter

The everyday understanding of a person's interaction with the administrative state is that a person visits an agency, office, or registrar and is asked to be served. Michael Lipsky (1980) writes:

> People come to street-level bureaucracies as unique individuals with different life experiences, personalities, and current circumstances. In their encounters with bureaucracies they are transformed into clients, identifiably located in a very small number of categories... The processing of *people* into *clients*, assigning them to categories for treatment by bureaucrats, and treating them in terms of those categories, is a social process (59).

In the case of the stateless person, however, the experience at the counter with 'street-level bureaucrats' is one of erasure, invisibility, and denial. Unlike Lipsky's (1980) observations, stateless persons are sometimes not processed at all, preventing them from even entering the legal realm as a client. Stateless persons expressed various thoughts in interviews on the impact of their encounters with government officials at the registrar. One stateless person commented: 'I want to have a life. I don't have one'. A parent of a stateless child asked: 'How can the government blame us for not sending our children to school when they do not even help our children?' Another parent felt like his child was banished as 'foreign' even though he was born in Malaysia to a Malaysian parent.

The procedural decision made by government officials to deny access to forms and deny the taking of documents, as well as the lack of assistance and the giving of erroneous advice, amounts to substantive decisions that refuse stateless persons the status of client. They cannot get one foot in the door in the administrative process of acquiring citizenship in some cases. These decisions do not consider the specific circumstances or unique characteristics of the individual, but are made during the course of one conversation at a counter. The effect of these procedural decisions is that persons are deemed as a foreigner and rendered stateless. Further, these encounters not only make citizenship discretionary and political but construct the stateless figure.

What this means is that stateless persons must be persistent in their efforts to ask for that to which they are entitled – which sometimes requires assistance from advocates, paralegals, and lawyers if necessary. There is immense administrative and emotional labour in preparing for an encounter with a government official at a registrar. Conceptually, however, lawyers and legal scholars should reconsider the way we view the administrative state and how much deference we give to those operating in that legal realm. Decisions in the administrative state are not akin to political choices in terms of what policies an elected government will embrace or ignore, or decisions that should be given deference by the judiciary. The experience of stateless persons shows us that greater accountability must be had in the way people are treated when serviced at government offices, even if officials are delegated by an elected government.

Lawyers and legal scholars may point to the system of judicial review, where courts can review the decisions of government officials – to see if they were made in a procedurally fair manner, to see whether they had the authority to make that decision, and whether they interpreted the law correctly. There is much discussion in scholarly work and in the courts about the extent to which courts should intervene in administrative decision-making. Despite this, courts hear a very limited number of cases of judicial review and therefore courts provide little procedural protection for administrative decisions (Adler, 2010: 145). Further, how can one conceive of bringing a judicial review to a court arguing the denial of a form? How does one show that such a decision has been made? There are multiple barriers to accessing the judicial review process for stateless persons. Beyond judicial remedies, we can further ask whether persons can access an administrative tribunal, ombudsperson, manager at a registrar office, or appeal directly to a member of parliament (Birkinshaw, 2010; Mullen, 2010; Lipsky, 1980).

The aim of this chapter is not to propose reforms for boosting accountability at the front lines of the administrative state, however, since that is beyond the scope of this work. Instead, this piece invites people to include the administrative state in their gaze and not limit the conversation to only legislatures, international conventions, and the courts. It is at the government counter that we can see what barriers are experienced by stateless persons, and so begin a conversation about how to keep the administrative state more accountable to all that ask for service.

The Malaysian experience may not be unique. In any state where there is an administrative state, we must turn our gaze towards the government counter to ask how stateless persons are treated. As interview data highlights, much power is exercised by government bureaucrats; while many may view their everyday decisions as procedural, the effect is substantive. A stateless person's very existence sometimes depends on an encounter with a government official.

Notes

1 This research was supported by a Research Development Grant from the Office of the Vice Dean of Research, University of Ottawa, and with in-kind support from Lawyers for Liberty and Eric Paulsen, most notably interpretation and research assistance. A special thank you to Nursyahirah Mohd Daud (Syaz) for her invaluable legal research assistance and interpretation on the ground in Malaysia and to Amanda Cheong for her collaborative research assistance in identifying participants, co-conducting interviews, and providing information on the Malaysian context. Thank you also to Paul Daly for his helpful suggestions related to administrative justice. Thank you to the editors, Tendayi and Lindsey, for their work on this important project. Most of all, thank you to all the stateless persons who bravely shared their stories, and the lawyers, civil society representatives, and researchers for sharing their valuable time. I hope I have conveyed your stories with respect.

2 Interviews took place in Kuala Lumpur, Kuala Selangor, Klang, Penang, Miri, and Kota Kinabalu, covering both West (peninsular) and East (Borneo Island) Malaysia. While many interviews were in English, I was able to communicate with persons using Hokkien Chinese, and some were conducted with the interpretive assistance of my research assistant Syaz, who spoke both Mandarin Chinese and Malay.

References

Adler, M. (2010) 'Understanding and analysing administrative justice', in M. Adler (ed.) *Administrative Justice in Context* (London: Hart Publishing): pp. 129–160.

Buang, S. (2019) 'Stateless kids' plight', *New Straight Times*, 13 February [Online]. Available at www.nst.com.my/opinion/columnists/2019/02/459991/stateless-kids-plight (Accessed 8 April 2020).

Department of Statistics Malaysia (2019) 'Press release: Current population estimates, Malaysia 2017–2018' [Online]. Available at www.dosm.gov.my/v1/index.php?r=column/cthemeByCat&cat=155&bul_id=aWJZRkJ4UEdKcUZpT2tVT090Snpydz09&menu_id=L0pheU43NWJwRWVSZklWdzQ4TlhUUT09 (Accessed 22 June 2020).

The Federal Constitution of Malaysia (1957) The Commissioner of Law Revision, Malaysia [Online]. Available at www.agc.gov.my (Accessed 22 June 2020).

Halliday, S. (2004) *Judicial Review and Compliance with Administrative Law* (Portland, OR: Hart Publishing).

Hertogh, M. (2010) 'Through the eyes of bureaucrats: How front-line officials understand administrative justice', in M. Adler (ed.) *Administrative Justice in Context* (London: Hart Publishing): pp. 203–226.

Liew, J. (2019) 'Homegrown statelessness in Malaysia and the promise of the principles of genuine and effective links', *Statelessness and Citizenship Review*, 1:1, 95–135.

Lipsky, M. (1980) *Street-Level Bureaucracy: Dilemmas of the Individual in Public Services* (New York: Russell Sage Foundation).

Mullen, T. (2010) 'A holistic approach to administrative justice?', in M. Adler (ed.) *Administrative Justice in Context* (London: Hart Publishing): pp. 383–420.

Pottie, L., and Sossin, L. (2005) 'Demystifying the boundaries of public law: Policy, discretion and social welfare', *University of British Columbia Law Review*, 38:1, 147–187.

Raso, J. (2019) 'Unity in the eye of the beholder? Reasons for decision in theory and practice in the Ontario Works Program', *University of Toronto Law Journal*, 71:1, 1–39.

Than Siew Beng & Anor v Ketua Pengarah Jabatan Pendaftaran Negara & Ors (2015) MLJU 2059.

Than Siew Beng & Anor v Ketua Pengarah Jabatan Pendaftaran Negara & Ors (2017) 5 MLJ 662.

United Nations High Commissioner for Refugees (UNHCR). (n.d.) 'Ending statelessness in Malaysia' [Online]. Available at www.unhcr.org/ending-statelessness-in-malaysia.html (Accessed 22 June 2020).

United Nations Statistics Division (UN Stats). (2003) 'Ethnicity: A review of data collection and dissemination' [Online]. Available at https://unstats.un.org/unsd/demographic/sconcerns/popchar/Ethnicitypaper.pdf (Accessed 22 June 2020).

Yu Sheng Meng v Ketua Pengarah Pendaftaran Negara & Ors (2016) 7 MLJ 628.

6

Language and statelessness: The impact of political discourses on the Bidoon community in Kuwait

Ahmad Benswait

I began writing this chapter when I was under the siege of statelessness as a member of the Bidoon community in Kuwait, and now I have completed it while I am in London pursuing my doctoral studies at UCL Institute of Education. Having started my journey in studying the role of language in society, I wish to comment on the situation of the Bidoon, and that of stateless people more generally, from the perspective of language. 'Bidoon' means without and refers to those people left without citizenship when modern Kuwait was formed, as well as their descendants. The Bidoon population is diverse, but includes many members of Bedouin tribes who lived in the land that is now modern Kuwait (Alshammiry, this volume).

In this chapter I will particularly draw on Critical Discourse Analysis (CDA), which studies language as a social practice that shapes and is shaped by social reality (Fairclough, 1995). CDA is concerned with the exercise of power and social inequalities through language; it addresses social and power relations in their semiotic forms (Fairclough et al., 2011). Power in this sense refers to the social differential through which one's ideas and interests are promoted at the expense of those of others (Brown and Levinson, 1987). Semiotics refers to any verbal or non-verbal move that occurs in a social interaction and communicates meaning. This includes spoken and written words, gestures, pose, signs, ways of dressing, and even silence – which at times is more expressive than anything else.

I will start with the premise that language is a form of social action through which social relations, ideologies, and identities are constructed. There is ample literature on the role of language in society, and I direct the reader to relevant scholarly accounts (e.g. Mehan, 1996; Blommaert, 2005; Milani, 2010; O'Regan and Betzel, 2016; Rheindorf and Wodak, 2018). In this chapter, I will present language as a social action through three examples from Kuwait. These examples illustrate how dominant discourses (re)produce social inequality and maintain hegemonic control of marginalised people.

In the first example, I use an excerpt from a speech of a state official in Kuwait rationalising oppressive practices against the Bidoon community. In the second example, I show how a card issued by the Central Apparatus for Remedying the Status of Illegal Residents in Kuwait (henceforth the Central Apparatus) is used as a semiotic resource of control and coercion. Finally, I broaden the discussion away from state-produced communication to shed light on the role of the international institutional discourse in naturalising social categorisations and the political and economic interests vested in it. This will be through an analysis of a 2019 statement by Amnesty International on the case of the Bidoon.

I have chosen these examples for what they show about the impact of political and ideological discourses on human rights and minority communities. Using this relatively small data sample makes it possible to provide a more detailed analysis of the sources that are selected. Although I do not aim to achieve generalisability, the samples are illustrative of the practices inflicted on the Bidoon community as a whole. The argument that makes up this chapter is that the life of stateless people is greatly shaped by what people say – or do not say – about the root causes of statelessness. As an entry point to the situation of the Bidoon community in Kuwait, I am using my personal story, and then I will delve into the history of the problem before addressing it from the point of view of language.

'Born a crime' and growing up illegal

The phrase 'born a crime' is used by the political commentator Trevor Noah, whose birth as a biracial child in apartheid South Africa was illegal due to laws prohibiting interracial relationships. Noah's story, which is narrated in his 2016 book *Born a Crime*, is reminiscent of my life trajectory and the ordeals I have experienced. The difference between Noah's story and mine is that apartheid has become part of the past, whereas statelessness for the Bidoon in Kuwait continues to persist. My story began in 1984 when I was born to a stateless family in Kuwait. My mother and father did not read or write, as their tribal and semi-nomadic lifestyle embraced education of a different type. In spite of this and the difficulties my family suffered after my father's forced disappearance in the early 1990s, my mother did everything she could to send me to school. Perhaps she wanted to spare me the harsh life she had been through.

As Bidoons are typically denied access to public schools, my mother wove garments to afford sending me to for-profit schools that charged expensive fees. I tried to help. I collected aluminium cans from the trash and sold them, but that did not pay much. During my childhood, I had to see my mother cry while entreating school secretaries to let me join until we could arrange the fees. I still feel guilty that I used to blame my mother for sending me late to school. I did not know, or perhaps did not understand, that it was a larger apparatus that did not want me to go to school.

As I grew up, I learned more about our reality. I realised that statelessness is the label for a life full of ordeals. This label made it legal for the state to prevent me from attending school. It allowed the police to arrest me even when I was a child because I tried to support my family. It was legal for sports clubs to turn me down. Privileged Kuwaiti children made fun of me because I lived in a slum neighbourhood. Because I did not have citizenship, Kuwaiti policemen bullied me for celebrating 'their' National Day. The state considered my fruit vending in the street to be illegal, while abuse against Bidoon children like myself was not illegal. When I got married, my wife and I could not have a stable life because we were considered 'illegal residents'. The list is long, but the common thread is how language is deeply rooted in all of this.

My mother's sacrifices, hopefully, were not without fruits. She has helped me become the first of my siblings, and one of a few in my community, to make it into higher education. In 2009, I joined a private university in Kuwait, where I completed an undergraduate programme in English language and literature. My studies enabled me to learn about the history of different nations and their struggles for liberty. It was an eye-opening experience that awakened me to my own cause. And it is what enables me now to comment on what it means to be Bidoon, stateless or 'illegal'. I explore how language is used in these framings in the next sections.

How we became 'Bidoon' (stateless) then 'illegals'

It is necessary to understand how the ideological and political categorisations in language that produce statelessness are rooted in the history of colonialism. Part of the colonial legacy in the Middle East has been the imposition of artificial borders and authoritarian regimes on peoples that have or had no choice. The conflict among European powers over prospective zones of influence in lands controlled by the Ottoman Empire in the Middle East culminated in the Sykes-Picot Agreement between Britain and France in 1916 (Fromkin, 2001) that 'ignored local identities and political preferences' (Wright, 2016: para. 4). The Sykes-Picot Agreement, as well as the Uqair Protocol of 1922, (re)shaped the life and destiny of the Indigenous populations of the Arabian Peninsula. In the context of Kuwait, the impact began to materialise in the 1930s during the oil drilling operations (Burne, 2003). The oil industry in Kuwait resulted in stripping the Bedouins of their right to free movement in their traditional lands. Moreover, when the hard borders were effectuated, the Bedouins found themselves stranded and members of the same tribes were split between different countries in the Arabian Peninsula. As of 1959, 'a tenth or more of Kuwait's indigenous national population' have been deprived of the right to citizenship, and thus became 'Bidoon' (Amnesty International, 2019: 3).

The discourse of indigeneity may invoke endless controversies. However, I refer to it in the context of Kuwait to indicate that the 'Bidoon' belong to Bedouin tribes, such as *Aniza, Shammar, Dhafir*, and *Muntafiq*, whose ethnic identities had been established in, and remain intrinsically connected to, the territories of northern Arabia (including Kuwait), centuries before modern state formations (see e.g. Jabal Shammar and Tuwal Al-Dhafir on the 'Northern Arabia' map in Ingham, 2016). This framing, I believe, would allow for better contextualisation of statelessness in Kuwait and challenge the reductive and violent 'Bidoon' term.

The term 'Bidoon' means 'without'. It comes from the Arabic phrase 'bidoon jinsiya', or 'without nationality'. While those constructed as 'Bidoon' are diverse, the process of alienation exerted through the new Bidoon identity, I suggest, has especially enabled the northern Bedouins to be dispossessed from their lands and natural resources. The case of the Bidoon in Kuwait is worth investigation because it may be a good link to exploring the displacement and alienation processes ensuing from the colonial treaties, including political borders and modern-state formation – processes which relied heavily on language, including both discursive and semiotic resources.

The phenomenon of statelessness in Kuwait should be ascribed to the formation of Kuwait's 1948 and 1959 nationality laws that treated nationality as a bespoke rather than universal human right. The effectively used 1959 version of the law came to define more precisely who to be included as 'Kuwaiti citizen', and among its stipulations was a proof of 'regular residence' in the country prior to 1920 and up to 1959 (Bjorklund, 2020; Amnesty International, 2019). This stipulation suggests an intention to alienate the northern Bedouin for multiple reasons. First, the proof that the law demanded was at odds with the 'migratory lifestyle' of northern Bedouin (Amnesty International, 2019). Second, during the naturalisation process around 50% of Kuwait's adult population were illiterate and did not possess the paperwork demanded of them (Hammoud, 2006; Cohen and Keinan-Cohen, 2019: 110). Third, the naturalisation process was made too brief to accommodate all the inhabitants of the country. The process lasted from 1959 to 1965, and it is often referred to in Kuwait as 'the early bird catches the worm'. What has happened later suggests that exclusion from citizenship was part of an alienation process. This begun with labelling the northern Bedouin as 'Bidoon' (stateless), then constructing them as 'illegals' (Kennedy, 2017). The role of language in these constructions is important to interrogate.

In 1987, the state passed legislation (Law No. 41/1987) defining the Bidoons as 'illegal residents'. Former speaker of the Kuwaiti parliament Ahmed Al-Sadoun revealed that the state has used different labels to forge the Bidoons' 'citizenship status for economic and (geo)political ends' (Al-Naqeeb, 2018). Another process that perpetuates statelessness in Kuwait is 'the government's frequent amendment of the Citizenship Law in order to restrict eligibility [of the Bidoon]' (Abu-Hamad, 1995). For example, consider the clause that deemed that a child who might be eligible for Kuwaiti nationality, but whose father was stateless, would be removed from Article 3 of Kuwait nationality law (Abu-Hamad,1995). In this way, nationality law is used as a semiotic tool for exclusion. Furthermore, the arbitrary labelling of 'Bidoon' and 'illegal residents', for instance, goes beyond citizen–noncitizen categorisations. It legitimises the discrimination against (and marginalisation of) the Bidoon people and subjugates them to punitive measures (Amnesty International, 2019). I suggest that the use of language in the case of the Bidoon is rooted in a calculated enterprise to convert them from Indigenous people who are stateless and have rights as per international law to 'illegal residents' who are liable to punitive measures (Amnesty International, 2019).

Language and power

This section demonstrates how the analysis of language is an analysis of power. It shows that the extent to which people are able to speak and to be heard is a reflection of how much power they have (Blommaert, 2005: 2). Language use by people in authority does reflect their power to change reality. 'You are fired' spoken by a decision-maker in a workplace provides an illustrative example of this (Mann, 2009). The same goes for state officials who use language to identify and categorise people.

Language as a tool for 'social and psychological' pressure

In 2015, Major General Sheikh Mazen Al-Jarrah, a member of the Kuwaiti ruling family and Kuwait's Assistant Undersecretary for Citizenship, Passport and Residency Affairs, appeared in a televised interview to talk about the country's position in addressing the Bidoon case. It was rare that an official from the executive authority (the government) in Kuwait would talk in public about the state's policy towards the Bidoon. This interview is important because it sums up the governance of statelessness in Kuwait in two words: denial and pressure. Throughout the interview, Al-Jarrah insisted that there were no stateless people in Kuwait and that the Bidoon were 'illegal residents'. The host responded by quoting the prominent political science professor at Kuwait University, Ghanem Alnajjar, who had described the term 'illegal residents' as a form of psychological pressure. Not only did Al-Jarrah acknowledge the implications of the term, but he also emphasised that he was using it as a means to pressure the Bidoon 'socially and psychologically' (Al Mehwar Channel, 2015). Alnajjar (2001) has established himself as a human rights theorist in Kuwait (see also Kennedy, 2017), yet he did not comment on Al-Jarrah's statement when it went viral. Neither did anyone else. As someone who was born and lived in Kuwait for thirty-five years, I understand the impunity Al-Jarrah enjoys so that he is able to intimidate the Bidoon community on mainstream media, while media censorship in Kuwait restricts freedom of expression (Human Rights Watch, 2015). I also appreciate how difficult it is for any academic or activist to challenge the regime in Kuwait.

Through the words of Al-Jarrah and the silence of the rest of the society, one may be able to make sense of what 'the analysis of language is an analysis of power' means. Al-Jarrah's use of language to exert violence on the Bidoon community is not an individual act. This is further compounded by the fact that he spoke while wearing the uniform of the Ministry of Interior. This provided a symbolic statement of the state's authority invested in him. It helped to add official authority to his statement. In this case then, the wearing of uniform plays a key role as a semiotic tool for making truth-claims about who the Bidoon are and conveying an 'authoritative' description of them as 'illegal residents'.

Semiotic control and coercion: The 'security card'

Semiotics is the study of verbal and non-verbal signs and symbols and the meanings they communicate. To explore the systematicity of the prejudices inflicted on the Bidoon through language, I will now examine another form of the semiotic practices. This time the example involves a state-established bureau exercising coercion and control over the life of the Bidoon people through a 'security card'. The 'security card' that is issued by the Central Apparatus exerts control and coercion on the Bidoon community in different ways. It identifies the Bidoon as 'illegal residents', and thus subjugates them to social stigma and mental pressure. In addition, it restricts the Bidoons' access to social and public spaces that require legal status, such as political institutions, sport clubs, schools, and job centres. In a personal experience, I was denied access to public schools from primary to graduate levels because of this card. Controlling the Bidoons' entry into social and public spaces is one effect of the card. The other is coercion.

The card has been used to convert the Bidoon into foreigners through the use of foreign 'nationality indicators', a processes that Amnesty International (2019) explains as follows:

> The Central System has arbitrarily assigned many Biduns [sic] who applied for renewed IDs in recent years a false, non-Kuwaiti nationality (typically Iraqi or Syrian), which then appears in both the database records system and on their new official documents. By doing so, the Central System has effectively been pressuring Biduns in need of ID cards into waiving their national rights in exchange for the documentation they need in order to manage their daily lives (2).

The arbitrary forging of the Bidoons' legal status is part of the alienation practices that have been inflicted on the community since 1959. This tactic has been used to aggravate pressure on the Bidoon. It forces the Bidoon person to live in constant fear of the legal implications of his or her de facto 'illegal status'. You could be stopped, probed, or even detained at any time just because you are Bidoon. This fear is mixed with humiliation that the Bidoon have to hold cards that demonise them.

Being identified as an 'illegal resident' with a foreign nationality puts the holders of these cards at constant fear and risk of arbitrary policing. Some Bidoon have taken their lives in protest against the precarity of their 'illegal status' (Amnesty International, 2019: 1–3). I have witnessed family members attempting suicide. Among people I know, paranoia is also common. I have personally been through this. It is so persistent that even though I am now in London, I still feel uneasy whenever I see police. I cannot help recalling memories of state abuse since I was a child. The terror that is cast on the Bidoon is beyond the limit of words. Visual symbols also accompany the text on the 'security card', contributing to its semiotic effects. For example, the card features an image of Nayef Palace, a site where capital punishment is executed in the form of hangings (Amnesty International, 2002). Importantly, Nayef Palace has been used as the headquarters of the Central Apparatus that deals with the Bidoon, although it is still a historical symbol of capital punishment in Kuwaiti culture. Ultimately, the card puts the Bidoon in a catch-22. In order to obtain the card, a Bidoon person must relinquish his or her claim for citizenship and be ready for the unknown. It feels like signing one's death warrant. On the other hand, if a Bidoon decides to boycott the card, he or she cannot have access to public and private services, even the essential ones.

These hostile practices are semiotic instances of the social and psychological pressure policy that was publicly advocated by Al-Jarrah, as discussed above. The policy of pressuring the Bidoon spills over into the discourse of even well-meaning international organisations, which reproduce official histories and political categorisations of people in Kuwait.

International human rights discourse: Amnesty International statement

Amnesty International issued a statement on November 21, 2019. Analysing this statement helps show how the discourse of international human rights organisations can reproduce state categorisations. The statement purportedly responds to draft legislation that had been proposed by Marzouq Al-Ghanim, the speaker of Kuwait's National Assembly, and the Kuwaiti Lawyers'Association, to address 'the Bidun problem' [sic] (Amnesty International, 2019). The statement reflects on the protracted plight of the Bidoon in Kuwait and the ordeals that the community endure as a result of being denied citizenship rights. It particularly criticises the legislation that Al-Ghanim 'put forth' because it mobilises a 'xenophobic rhetoric' against the Bidoon and describes them as a 'burden on national security' (Amnesty International, 2019: 2).

The Amnesty International statement addresses the Bidoon case from legal, historical, and humanitarian perspectives. It examines the historical context of Kuwaiti nationality law and how different factors have contributed to creating statelessness in the country. It also highlights how the ruling family in Kuwait stipulated that only those who could prove residence in Kuwait before 1920 would qualify for citizenship. Other factors that perpetuated statelessness in Kuwait, the statement suggests, are:

i.   the Bidoons' 'migratory' lifestyle;
ii. the brevity and inadequacy of the nationality registration and outreach; and
iii. the state's lack of 'prior experience of a national bureaucracy'.

                                        (Amnesty International, 2019: 3)

The statement concludes with recommendations to release detained Bidoon activists and to find a comprehensive solution 'that guarantees... access to employment and state services, particularly health care and education' (Amnesty International, 2019: 4). Amnesty International's statement puts the Bidoon cause in the spotlight. This reflects its institutional role of advocacy and consultancy as it calls on Kuwait to, 'in consultation with national and international civil society, determine and publish clear, objectively verifiable assessment criteria for naturalization' (Amnesty International, 2019: 3). The Bidoon community is in dire need of such advocacy, but the institutional discourse remains problematic as it seems to be governed by political priorities.

Institutional discourses, including those produced by international non-governmental organisations (INGOs), can be 'platform[s] to regulate international relations for the benefit of the strongest power'(Duchêne, 2008: 44). The logic of institutional language entails discussing problems outside their original contexts, thus leaving crucial facts unsaid. In our context, the institutional discourse reproduces the state's ideological construction of the Bidoon community. For example, Amnesty International's statement does not adequately engage with the impact of colonialism and competing local interests in the region. As a result, it erases crucial context. This jeopardises the Bidoons' legitimate claims for Indigenous rights and reparation for the decades of persecution they have suffered. Moreover, decontexualising the case reframes the reality of the Bidoon community's existence in Kuwait.

When crucial facts are omitted, new realities are created (Mehan, 1996: 253–257). For example, when the history of Kuwait nationality law is discussed in this particular statement, responsibility is partially placed on the Bidoons' migratory lifestyle. This problematisation of the northern tribes' lifestyle has two implications. One is that it consolidates Kuwait's exclusive nationality that confers the right to citizenship only on those who maintained 'regular residence' in Kuwait prior to 1920 and up to 1959. Problematising the northern tribes' lifestyle – as opposed to the stipulated 'regular residence' – seems to rationalise the exclusion of the Bidoon community. In addition, such use of language imposes a framing on the Bidoon as immigrants who (may) have transgressed the official borders. This, in turn, can support the official narrative that the Bidoons are 'illegal residents'. This is regardless of the fact that the statement itself acknowledges that the Bidoon 'amount to a tenth or more of Kuwait's [I]ndigenous national population' (Amnesty International, 2019: 3). In steering clear from interrogating the new colonial borders and regimes, the statement risks reinforcing an official history that is used to justify the exclusion of certain peoples.

Examining Amnesty International's statement also raises the question of definitions. It is necessary to look at the words used to refer to the persecution of the Bidoon people and the terminology of 'statelessness' and 'indigeneity'. Amnesty International's statement acknowledges that suicide incidents among the Bidoon are consequences of the conditions inflicted on the community. It frames the situation as a problem, without acknowledging it as a systematic process of exclusion, marginalisation, demonisation, and persecution. I argue that this, in fact, fits more accurately within the definition of the United Nations' Convention on the Prevention and Punishment of the Crime of Genocide. Article II identifies genocide as possibly including: Causing serious bodily or mental harm to members of the group, and deliberately inflicting on the group conditions of life calculated to bring about its physical destruction in whole or in part (United Nations, 1948). Failing to consider this hugely downplays the atrocities inflicted on the Bidoon community. This in turn denies the community access to the international legal framework that may address their case more effectively.

Another issue with definitions is the conflict between Indigenous and stateless peoples. While the Amnesty International statement emphasises that the Bidoon belong to the Indigenous population of Kuwait, it calls on the State of Kuwait and the United Nations to recognise the community as a stateless people. This call is problematic because it mystifies the Bidoons' history and hides the political and ideological links to their case. Statelessness in Kuwait is a consequence of a complex political process that involved excluding the northern Bedouins. The role of language in this is important. A better way to address the Bidoons' case is to recognise that they are an Indigenous people who became stateless when their lands and right to citizenship were confiscated.

Conclusion

This chapter has demonstrated how political and ideological use of language can create and perpetuate a social reality. Statelessness in Kuwait is rooted in complex political and ideological underpinnings entrenched in the history of colonialism and modern state formation. This history involved a process of alienation that drew heavily on strategic uses of language.

I have used language as an entry point to the case of the Bidoon. The three examples used in this chapter have illustrated how language may be a tool for legitimising, exercising, and normalising control and coercion. To reiterate, by language I mean the verbal and non-verbal discursive and semiotic practices including the use of terminology and silence. In the first example, a state official acknowledges that language, in the form of the 'illegal residents' label, allows the state to pressure the Bidoon community socially and psychologically. This is presented as an acceptable state strategy and is an illustration of the (ab)use of language to legitimise persecution. The second example illustrates how the Central Apparatus builds on the legitimised 'illegal status' of the Bidoon to exercise control and coercion against the community. That is done through the use of the 'security card' that depicts the Bidoon as 'outlaws'. Finally, the third example highlights how international human rights discourses that draw on official history may normalise the status quo while ostensibly challenging it. This is especially the case when discourses such as those relating to 'statelessness' result in crucial historical and political facts being decontexualised or omitted. While the first two examples illustrate the role of language in perpetuating the blatant pressure of policies against the Bidoon community, the third example indicates a gap in representing the case by reinforcing the official history and by marginalising the voice of Bidoon peoples.

As long as the discourse of statelessness continues in the absence of the voices of stateless people, hope for change will remain futile. The 'hope' is in ourselves. This is the space that should be worked on. We need our existence to be recognised. We need our existence to respected. We need our existence as humans to be understood. When the world realises this, then and only then, we can talk of a better reality.

References

Abu-Hamad, A. (1995) 'The Bedoons of Kuwait: "Citizens without citizenship"', Human Rights Watch [Online]. Available at www.hrw.org/reports/1995/Kuwait.htm (Accessed 1 June 2020).

Al Mehwar Channel (2015) 'Point of order: Major General Sheikh Mazen Al-Jarrah' [Online]. Available at www.youtube.com/watch?v=Ds1As5si29s&t=744 (Accessed 27 February 2020).

Alnajjar, G. (2001). 'Human rights in a crisis situation: The case of Kuwait after occupation', *Human Rights Quarterly*, 23:1, 188–209.

Al-Naqeeb, A. (2018). 'Former Parliament Speaker stresses importance of solving Bedoun issue', *Arab Times*, 13 December [Online]. Available at www.arabtimesonline.com/news/former-parliament-speaker-stresses-importance-of-solving-bedoun-issue/ (Accessed 1 June 2020).

Amnesty International (2002) 'Kuwait: Imminent execution' [Online]. Available at www.amnesty.org/en/documents/MDE17/003/2002/en/ (Accessed 13 May 2020).

Amnesty International (2019) 'Kuwait: Rising signs of despair among Bidun highlight cruelty of draft law' [Online]. Available at www.amnesty.org/download/Documents/MDE1713622019ENGLISH.pdf (Accessed 25 January 2020).

Bjorklund, A. (2020). 'The Bidoon in Kuwait, history at a glance', Salam for Democracy and Human Rights [Online]. Available at https://salam-dhr.org/?p=4170 (Accessed 21 November 2020).

Blommaert, J. (2005) *Discourse: A Critical Introduction* (Cambridge: Cambridge University Press).

Brown, P., and Levinson, S. (1987) *Politeness* (Cambridge: Cambridge University Press).

Burne, L. H. (2003) *Chronological History of US Foreign Relations: 1932–1988* (New York: Routledge).

Cohen, R. A., and Keinan-Cohen, Y. (2019) 'The issue of citizenship for the Bidun minority in Kuwait after the Arab Spring', *Digest of Middle East Studies*, 28:1, 107–123.

Duchêne, A. (2008) *Ideologies across Nations: The Construction of Linguistic Minorities at the United Nations* (Berlin and Boston, MA: De Gruyter Mouton).

Fairclough, N. (1995). *Critical Discourse Analysis: The Critical Study of Language* (New York: Longman).

Fairclough, N., Mulderrig, J., and Wodak, R. (2011) 'Critical discourse analysis', in T. van Dijk (ed.) *Discourse Studies: A Multidisciplinary Introduction*, 2nd edition (London, Sage): pp. 357–378.

Fromkin, D. (2001) *A Peace to End All Peace: The Fall of the Ottoman Empire and the Creation of the Modern Middle East* (New York: Henry Holt and Company).

Hammoud, H. R. (2006) 'Illiteracy in the Arab world', *Adult Education and Development*, 66, 83–106.

Human Rights Watch (2015) 'Kuwait: Cybercrime law a blow to free speech' [Online]. Available at www.refworld.org/docid/55b20beb4.html (Accessed 11 June 2020).

Ingham, B. (2016) *Bedouin of Northern Arabia: Traditions of the Āl-Ḏhafīr* (Abingdon: Routledge).

Kennedy, S. (2017) 'The stateless Bedoun in Kuwait society: A study of Bedouin identity, culture and the growth of an intellectual ideal' (PhD thesis, University of Adelaide) [Online]. Available at https://digital.library.adelaide.edu.au/dspace/bitstream/2440/119698/2/02whole.pdf (Accessed 16 July 2020).

Mann, S. T. (2009) '"You're fired": An application of speech act theory to 2 Samuel 15.23–16.14', *Journal for the Study of the Old Testament*, 33:3, 315–334.

Mehan, H. (1996) 'The construction of an LD student: A case study in the politics of representation', in M. Silverstein and G. Urban (eds) *Natural Histories of Discourse* (Chicago, IL: Chicago University Press): pp. 230–253.

Milani, T. (2010) 'What's in a name? Language ideology and social differentiation in a Swedish print-mediated debate', *Journal of Sociolinguistics*, 14:1, 116–142.

Noah, T. (2016) *Born a Crime* (Toronto: Doubleday Canada).

O'Regan, J., and Betzel, A. (2016) 'Critical discourse analysis: A sample study of extremism', in Z. Hua (ed.) *Research Methods in Intercultural Communication* (London: Blackwell): pp. 281–296.

Rheindorf, M., and Wodak, R. (2018) 'Borders, fences, and limits – Protecting Austria from refugees: Metadiscursive negotiation of meaning in the current refugee crisis', *Journal of Immigrant & Refugee Studies*, 16:1–2, 15–38.

United Nations (1948) *Convention on the Prevention and Punishment of the Crime of Genocide* [Online]. Available at www.un.org/en/genocideprevention/documents/atrocity-crimes/Doc.1_Convention%20on%20the%20Prevention%20and%20Punishment%20of%20the%20Crime%20of%20Genocide.pdf (Accessed 1 June 2020).

Wright, R. (2016) 'How the curse of Sykes-Picot still haunts the Middle East', *The New Yorker* [Online]. Available at: www.newyorker.com/news/news-desk/how-the-curse-of-sykes-picot-still-haunts-the-middle-east (Accessed 31 May 2020).

7

The weaponisation of citizenship: Punishment, erasure, and social control

Lindsey N. Kingston

Governments in the nineteenth and early twentieth centuries regularly leveraged statelessness as a punishment against those who threatened the social order, and Hannah Arendt (1966) called denationalisation a 'tool of totalitarian politics' in the wake of the World Wars. From those injustices and atrocities arose the 'right to a nationality' under international human rights law – as well as the widespread assumption that legal nationality was a social good that guaranteed political membership and rights protection. Yet today we see troubling shifts in how states view citizenship and nationality rights. At the individual level, denationalisation (the involuntary loss of citizenship)[1] is increasingly used globally as a method to punish enemies and reward others, thus de-valuing the concept of citizenship as a fundamental right and instead positing it as a privilege. At the group level, denationalisation sometimes targets entire identity groups in the quest to create and isolate 'strangers', particularly in times of rising nationalism. There is growing reliance on deportation, the deprivation of nationality, and extradition – which, together, Nisha Kapoor (2018) categorises as 'twenty-first century state extremism'. States are increasingly chipping away at nationality rights and bypassing obligations to citizens. This weakening of the relationship between state and citizen signals serious consequences for the protection of human rights, particularly since the international community continues to rely on governments as the legal duty-bearers of these fundamental needs.

My previous work focuses on the connection between legal recognition and human rights protection (Kingston, 2019), and in this chapter I further problematise common assumptions about citizenship. I challenge the belief that legal nationality is always a social good and contend that legal nationality – the assumed marker of political membership in our world system – can be weaponised as a tool of repression and erasure, as well as used as a bargaining chip for social control. First, modern citizenship and its resulting documentation exist in many communities with deeply harmful consequences. I've previously argued that the postwar international community built fatal errors into modern human rights frameworks by assuming that everyone has citizenship and can count on their governments to be responsible duty-bearers (Kingston, 2019). Yet we can dig deeper by considering the ways that citizenship (as well as accompanying things like ID cards and passports) was constructed to manage and order populations, and by evaluating how that legacy continues to do harm. This perspective challenges the dominant narrative that citizenship is always a tool of empowerment and a form of protection.

Second, citizenship (or its stripping away) is approached by some political leaders as both a reward for exceptionally good deeds, as well as a punishment for bad behaviour deemed threatening to the state. There are increased calls to denationalise citizens as part of anti-terrorism measures, to quell activists' voices, and even to punish people for domestic crimes. Indeed, recent debates and legislation have prompted Audrey Macklin (2018) to declare that, after decades in exile, 'banishment is back' – thus 'making legal citizenship contingent on performance.' At the same time, the granting of citizenship garners international headlines when it is issued as a reward for exceptional behaviour. Consider how some members of the Wild Boars soccer team were granted Thai citizenship after being rescued from a cave in 2018, or how France's 'Spider Man' (Mamoudou Gassama, a migrant from Mali) was granted French citizenship after saving a boy dangling from a balcony. We again see a move away from viewing legal nationality as a human right, thus privileging states' rights to deny, revoke, or grant citizenship as punishment or reward.

Third, the statelessness that results from the revocation or denial of citizenship serves as a method for the erasure of particular identity groups. I have already argued that statelessness is both a cause and consequence of marginalisation (Kingston, 2017b) – it leads to further human rights violations, but it begins as a result of discrimination and repression. I further contend that statelessness serves as a strategy for erasure that enables the theft of land, as well as mass atrocity crimes. Unwanted minority populations, including the Rohingya in Myanmar, are forced out of national territories (and national histories and identities) through the strategic use of statelessness, combined with surveillance, ethnic cleansing, and even genocide.[2]

Challenging assumed citizenship-as-empowerment

The international community largely views citizenship as an instrument of empowerment, not merely a set of passive rights, and the modern human rights system relies on legal nationality to serve as an essential link between an individual and a state government. Indeed, human rights ideals that arose after World War II made assumptions about political membership that inherently limited the scope of 'universal' rights, forcing people to rely on government duty-bearers for basic protection (Kingston, 2019). Yet if we set aside this notion that citizenship is an instrument of empowerment (or is intended to be), this relationship between legal nationality and rights takes on a new dimension: In some cases, the conferral of citizenship and the use of its accompanying documentation actually contribute to extensive social control and rights violations. John Torpey's (2000) scholarship on the modern passport regime, for instance, highlights how such documentation gave state governments control over 'legitimate' means of movement and bolstered surveillance capabilities. The creation of what James C. Scott (1998) calls 'legible people', or people who are open to the scrutiny of officialdom, illustrates an increasing dependency on states for the possession of individual identity that is required of rights claimants. European efforts to classify citizen populations and issue ID cards led to violent ethnic division in countries such as Thailand (Scott, 1998) and Rwanda (van Brakel and Van Kerckhoven, 2014), showing the negative impacts associated with colonial documentation practices. For Indigenous peoples whose identities and legal statuses often don't fit within the traditional nation-state structure, citizenship may also mean being forced to accept legal identities from colonisers. The Indian Citizenship Act (ICA) of 1924 unilaterally conferred U.S. citizenship on Indigenous people; although U.S. citizenship was viewed in various ways among Indigenous people, very few saw its conferral as an unambiguously positive development.[3] Indeed, some rejected U.S. citizenship outright in the name of Indigenous sovereignty (Bruyneel, 2007: 97–98). In Commonwealth settler states such as Australia and Canada, state citizenship served to individualise communally held native lands and move communities away from traditional ways of life, while the voting rights of Indigenous citizens – a marker of political membership within the nation – were not protected until the 1960s (Gover, 2017: 458–459).

Setting aside this notion of citizenship-as-empowerment also calls into question the assumption that such status serves as a form of protection. Legal nationality was not enough to thwart harmful constructions of race that posited Mexican Americans as second-class citizens unworthy of full membership in the polity, for instance, while citizenship has been used to strengthen U.S. colonial interests in the Caribbean. Mexican Americans were legally constructed as 'white', yet socially they were viewed as non-white and racially inferior. During the nineteenth-century period of 'Manifest Destiny' (when many believed that white settlers were destined to expand across North America, and when the majority of Mexican American men received U.S. federal citizenship under a 1848 peace treaty), Congress refused to admit New Mexico as a state because of its majority Mexican and Indian population (Gómez, 2018: 5–6). New Mexico became a federal territory in 1850 but its status was different from non-contiguous U.S. colonies such as Puerto Rico, which was not seen as a place where Euro-American 'settler citizens' would eventually predominate – and therefore make the colony a candidate for statehood (Gómez, 2018: 8). Looking towards the Caribbean, Efrén Rivera Ramos (2001) argues that American citizenship was imposed on Puerto Ricans,[4] beginning with the passage of the 1917 Jones Act, as a strategy to further American hegemony as the U.S. faced World War I and growing social and political agitation in the colony. Detached from the right of political participation, including voting in federal elections, this collective naturalisation constructed a form of 'second-class citizens' that also includes citizens in Guam and the U.S. Virgin Islands. 'Citizenship did not efface colonialism. Under the circumstances, it was meant to consolidate it, to make it more palatable, and to make those subject to it more easily governable', Rivera Ramos writes (2001: 156).

Notably, scholarship on statelessness usually posits legal nationality as an essential prerequisite for human rights protection – and that often turns out to be the case. However, there is a difference between the shallow and discriminatory forms of 'citizenship' outlined above and the rights-protective form of truly 'functioning' citizenship that signifies a meaningful relationship between the state and an individual (Kingston, 2019). And while the initial reasons that states granted citizenship and/or issued identity documentation to certain minority groups may have been ill-intentioned, that doesn't mean that those minority citizens (or their descendants) cannot or will not go on to become full members of that political community. The point of this discussion is not to argue that citizenship is a social evil, but rather to highlight that it's not always a social good; this concept is too complicated to be classified as wholly 'good' or 'bad', even as it holds immense value and power in today's world system. Indeed, as the next section illustrates, the very concept of a 'right to a nationality' obscures the realities of how states view their sovereign power to grant – or revoke – citizenship.

Punishment and reward

The revocation of citizenship, almost always accompanied by physical banishment, has long been used as a serious form of punishment. Banishment was appealing in the ancient world because it served as 'a form of punishment and social control that while inflicting a kind of civic death fell short of ending an individual's life', and the legitimacy of banishment to punish and control survived the emergence of the early modern state. It wasn't until the late eighteenth and mid-nineteenth centuries that the practice of deporting citizens became less common (Gibney, 2011: 6–7). In Western states,[5] four distinct phases are identifiable in denationalisation's recent history: 1) denationalisation's emergence with the development of formal immigration controls distinguishing between citizens and aliens, from the late nineteenth century to the end of World War I; 2) denationalisation's apogee, from the early 1920s to the end of World War II in 1945, in which mass denationalisation was undertaken by totalitarian states; 3) denationalisation in retreat from 1945 to 2001; and 4) the more modest revival of denationalisation since the 9/11 terrorist attacks in the United States (Gibney, 2017: 364–366).[6]

Critics argue that the use of denationalisation as punishment is (at best) over-utilised in cases that don't warrant such extreme action, or is (at worst) a human rights violation that devalues citizenship and creates political instability. 'To deprive a person of their citizenship on the grounds of their behavior or opinion is to cast them out of society', explains Colin Yeo (2019). 'It is a modern power of exile or banishment' and should therefore 'be reserved for the most serious cases of crimes against national security', and yet there is a recent trend towards denationalisation in far less serious cases (134). Recent legislation in the UK, Canada, and Australia have expanded the grounds on which nationals can be stripped of their citizenship; supporters invoke symbolic justifications (citizens who engage in certain behaviour don't deserve their citizenship) and security justifications (denationalisation is needed to neutralise threats) (Pillai and Williams, 2017).[7] 'The defining feature of contemporary legal citizenship is that it is secure', writes Macklin (2018). 'Making legal citizenship contingent on performance demotes citizenship to another category of permanent residence. Citizenship revocation thus weakens citizenship itself. It is an illegitimate form of punishment and it serves no practical purpose' (163). Sandra Mantu (2018), in her examination of counter-terrorism strategies in the UK and France, notes that 'political considerations concerning national security have taken center stage in this process rather than human rights and international nationality obligations' (38). Notably, the denationalised are frequently then deported to less powerful countries: 'Rather than confronting the forces that shape these individuals we banish them to states that are often weaker and more fractured than ours', writes Yeo (2019). 'This is to act unjustly towards other states as well as the erstwhile citizens themselves' (135).

In the United States, three intersecting modes of citizenship deprivation have been recently utilised, particularly under the Trump administration. The Open Society Justice Initiative (2019) examines the use of denaturalisation (the revocation of citizenship acquired by foreign nationals or formerly stateless people through naturalisation), the denial and revocation of U.S. passports, and political attacks on citizenship by birth in the United

States as tools of xenophobia and nativism. Studies found a significant rise in denaturalisation compared to previous administrations, for instance, with particular vulnerabilities to visible minorities who are selectively targeted based on national origin. Their analysis shows a lack of procedural safeguards for protecting the rights of naturalised Americans, as well as a strong reason to believe that a significant proportion of such denaturalisation will result in statelessness. 'The power to take away or deny citizenship creates a gaping and unresolved loophole in the protection of human rights', argues Open Society (2019: 6). Further, '[t]he odds are massively stacked against anyone whose citizenship comes under question by the Department of State, the agency responsible for issuing U.S. passports' (12).[8]

On the other side of this coin is the concept of citizenship as something that ought to be earned – and which may serve as a reward for extraordinary behaviour that pleases the state. The 'earning' of citizenship takes many forms and factors into ongoing debates about immigration reform. For instance, naturalisation in several European countries is conditional upon the payment of substantial fees and/or proof of a certain degree of economic self-sufficiency. In his study of nine EU countries from 1985 to 2014, Jeremias Stadlmair (2018) found that naturalisation fees in particular have increased over time. Michael J. Sullivan (2019) argues that long-term undocumented migrants living in the United States should be able to earn legal status and a pathway to citizenship through military service, thereby offering a restitution for violations of immigration law.[9] This expectation of 'earned' citizenship is observable in naturalisation ceremonies; in her study of six Western countries, Bridget Byrne (2014) argues that such ceremonies 'shed light on how the citizen is imagined, and who – or what forms of citizenship – are excluded from this imagining' (2). Similarly, in her analysis of citizenship ceremonies in the United Kingdom and Germany, Elisabeth Badenhoop (2017) argues that such ceremonies can be understood as techniques of subject-formation. They produce a specific subjectivity – the 'Super Citizen' – which 'suggests to migrant citizens that they should think of themselves as a political, economic and cultural asset to the nation-state, thus rendering them responsible for using this potential in the national interest' (421).

More extreme examples of earned citizenship come from exceptional circumstances in which migrants were deemed extraordinary for their survival, heroism, or other features valued by the state. When a boat sank off the island of Lampedusa in October 2013, for instance, the Italian authorities awarded honorary Italian citizenship and a state funeral to more than 350 people who died – yet the 155 Eritrean survivors were charged with illegal entry and detained. 'The symbolic welcome for the dead and criminalization of the living underscored that policies are often motivated by public relations performances aimed at diverse domestic and international audiences', writes David Scott Fitzgerald (2019). 'A message upholding the value of human life, in this case costless because the lives have already been lost, coincides with a message that sovereign borders will be firmly defended' (205–206). Responding to the Wild Boars case noted earlier, Amanda Flaim (2018) argues that 'citizenship is an ordinary right for ordinary people – not a dispensation of the powerful. Stateless people should not have to perform extraordinary feats to have their legal citizenship officially recognized'. In the case of Thailand, she further contends that the Thai government is partially responsible for producing statelessness (because of flawed surveys among minority populations that later make it difficult for stateless people to claim citizenship, for instance) but that the government has the capacity and political support to resolve this matter for hundreds of thousands of people. 'With the global celebrity and moral weight of the Wild Boars, Thailand should use this occasion to be a world leader in statelessness resolution and grant amnesty to its stateless people now', Flaim (2018) writes in the *Bangkok Post*.

Statelessness as a strategy for rights abuse

This perception that citizenship can be granted or taken away in pursuit of state interests, rather than protected as a fundamental human right, fuels the use of statelessness as a strategy for discrimination and further rights abuse. It is well known that statelessness played a key role during World War II, when Nazi Germany denationalised Jewish and other minority citizens under its German Reich Citizenship Law of 1935 (United States Holocaust Museum, n.d.). Yet the years following the Holocaust were also filled with various other examples of statelessness employed as a strategy for rights abuse, including as a method to erase unwanted minorities from national histories and identities. In the 1970s and 1980s, similar discriminatory citizenship laws were used in Bhutan to exclude Bhutanese-Nepali citizens and others outside the new legal category of 'genuine Bhutanese', prompting forced migration to neighbouring Nepal in 1990. The newly stateless who were categorised as 'non-nationals' during a 1988 census were told to leave the country or face imprisonment, and those who protested faced swift retribution (Human Rights Watch, 2007). More recently, in August 2019, around 1.9 million people in the northeastern Indian state of Assam were excluded from the state's National Register of Citizens and threatened with denationalisation. The move coincides with the construction of mass detention camps, which will contain suspected 'illegal' immigrants – many of whom have held Indian citizenship for decades (Rahim, 2019).

One of the most powerful recent examples of statelessness used as a strategy for human rights abuse is the case of Myanmar's Rohingya minority. Their denial of Burmese nationality under the 1982 Citizenship Law has led to pervasive rights violations and processes of erasure, enabled by land theft and mass atrocity crimes such as ethnic cleansing and geno- cide. 'Erasure entails the removal of all traces of something, with obliter- ation as its most extreme form', writes Ken Maclean (2019). 'But erasure is never fully complete... Practices of erasure always leave discernable traces, if only in the form of an absence...' (84). He argues that the erasure of Rohingya in Myanmar has taken two forms: 'lawfare' (the abuse of laws to achieve strategic military or political ends) and 'spacio-cide' (system- atic dispossession and destruction of living space) (MacLean, 2019: 87, 90). Lawfare tactics aimed at transforming Rohingya into stateless persons without rights were achieved years ago, while spacio-cide tactics to destroy Rohingya property and their ability to return home are nearing comple- tion (95). As satellite imagery shows, Rohingya homes were demolished and quickly replaced by new homes occupied primarily by Buddhist citi- zens. State resettlement plans show that the government doesn't intend to return refugees to their original villages, but rather herd them into segre- gated Rohingya-only settlements (McPherson et al., 2018). The Myanmar authorities 'wanted to get everyone out', said Yanghee Lee, the UN spe- cial rapporteur on human rights in Myanmar. 'Now they've got them out, they sure aren't going to give [the land] back to the Rohingya' (quoted in McPherson et al., 2018: para 8).

Furthermore, the case of the Rohingya illustrates how documenta- tion – often seen as a positive good for establishing identity and access- ing services – can be weaponised in the absence of meaningful political membership. Rohingya speak of their documents in ways that reflect con- nections to rights and belonging, but only in relation to documents they held before the first wave of expulsions in 1978. When they describe the documents that came later (including household registration lists and mandatory 'white cards') they recall persecution, extortion, exclusion, and segregation. As a result, the Rohingya associate danger and fear with documentation processes in Myanmar and beyond, including the sharing of biometric and biographic data during their displacement in Bangladesh. Indeed, many are shocked that some international and UN agencies promote nationality verification processes despite the dangers associated with such documentation (Brinham, 2019). Natalie Brinham (2019) writes:

> There is a point at which a human rights approach and a state approach to documents and registration converge. That is the point where universal registration and documentation becomes desirable. Whilst the human rights

approach may draw on a framework that understands documents as providing access to rights, a state government may understand documents and registration as an effective way to govern. Meanwhile, an authoritarian state may understand documents as crucial tools of surveillance and population control that embrace some populations and exclude others. And a genocidal state may consider registration and documentation as an effective way to "cleanse" their nation and erase a population through bureaucratic means (para 10).

Although existing literature on statelessness clearly highlights vital connections between legal nationality and human rights protection within the current world system, it is a mistake to assume that citizenship always represents a social good and operates as a tool for empowerment. The conferral of citizenship and ensuing documentation has been used by governments to exert control and violate rights, while shallow constructions of nationality have often been unable to thwart 'second-class citizenship'. The growing use of denationalisation and denaturalisation, as well as the practice of using citizenship to reward certain deeds (or expecting people to 'earn' citizenship in various ways) highlights how citizenship is often not viewed as a right, but rather as something that can be awarded or taken away at the whim of the government. Indeed, these actions represent the latest phase in a long world history of playing manipulative games with citizenship. This is particularly troubling given the fact that statelessness can be utilised as a strategy for human rights abuse, including discriminatory practices, land-grabbing, ethnic cleansing, and genocide. Careful attention to this weaponisation of citizenship should factor into conversations about statelessness and governance – especially in relation to the international community's efforts to issue documentation within stateless communities and to posit legal nationality alone as a solution to the rights abuses associated with statelessness.

Notes

1 More specifically, 'denationalization is the non-consensual withdrawal of nationality from an individual by his or her own state. The power transforms the individual into an alien (or at least a non-citizen) in the eyes of the law of the state concerned, thus putting an end to the special responsibilities and entitlements which result from citizenship or nationality' (Gibney, 2017: 360).
2 While statelessness is often framed as a sort of invisibility, we should not assume that stateless persons and other noncitizens are devoid of voice or political agency (see Bloom, 2017). It is important to juxtapose discussions of legal erasure with the advocacy accomplished by stateless people, who are becoming more emboldened through global social movement networks (see E, this volume).

3 In the case of Hawai'i and Kanak Maoli (Native Hawaiian) activism, Amy L. Brandzel (2016) illustrates how 'history is mobilized to confirm the colonialist enterprise of the U.S. nation-state by reproducing citizenship as a progressively inclusive and evolutionary paradigm' (103).

4 Rivera Ramos (2001) acknowledges that scholars disagree on whether U.S. citizenship was *imposed* on Puerto Ricans (that is, whether the majority of the population favoured or opposed citizenship), but it's noteworthy that Congress decreed that residents only had six months following the Act's passage to opt out – and the requirements for rejections were burdensome for much of the population at the time (153). Further, he notes that the extension of American citizenship was not a 'negotiated event' that involved codetermination or self-determination (155).

5 Bronwen Manby (2018) reminds us that supposedly 'new' denationalisation policies have been in place throughout sub-Saharan African since the 1960s.

6 Relatedly, see Wadhia (2019) for details on how a variety of noncitizens are 'banned' from the U.S.

7 It is noteworthy that a *de facto* form of denationalisation is sometimes used to quell dissent and punish political rivals. In 2012, the National Police of Rwanda cancelled the passports of 25 Rwandans abroad (and apparently nullified their citizenship statuses). Many of those affected were leaders, or relatives of leaders, of the Rwanda National Congress, an opposition movement (Kingston, 2017a: 434). A number of opposition members have disappeared or been killed in recent years (Human Rights Watch, 2019).

8 Similarly, in the United Kingdom, there are two ways that a British citizen can have their citizenship status taken away: The first is through citizenship deprivation power, which is set out in section 40 of the British Nationality Act 1981, on the grounds that deception was used in acquiring citizenship or on public good grounds. The second is nullification power, where the state declares that a person was never a British citizen at all, even though they were recognised as such before (Yeo, 2019: 135).

9 This stands in stark contrast to recent actions by the American government. Dozens of immigrant recruits who were promised an expedited path to citizenship through a special Defense Department programme were abruptly discharged with little or no explanation in 2018 (Romo, 2018).

References

Arendt, H. (1966) *The Origins of Totalitarianism: New Edition* (New York: Harcourt, Brace & World, Inc).

Badenhoop, E. (2017) 'Calling for the super citizen: Citizenship ceremonies in the UK and Germany as techniques of subject-formation', *Migration Studies*, 5:3, 409–427.

Bloom, T. (2017) *Noncitizenism: Recognising Noncitizen Capabilities in a World of Citizens* (London and New York: Routledge).

Brandzel, A. L. (2016) *Against Citizenship: The Violence of the Normative* (Urbana, Chicago and Springfield, IL: University of Illinois Press).

Brinham, N. (2019) 'When identity documents and registration produce exclusion: Lessons from Rohingya experiences in Myanmar', The London School of Economics and Political Sciences, Middle East Centre Blog, 10 May [Online]. Available at https://blogs.lse.ac.uk/mec/2019/05/10/when-identity-documents-and-registration-produce-exclusion-lessons-from-rohingya-experiences-in-myanmar/ (Accessed 2 April 2020).

Bruyneel, K. (2007) *The Third Space of Sovereignty: The Postcolonial Politics of U.S.-Indigenous Relations* (Minneapolis. MN: University of Minnesota Press).

Byrne, B. (2014) *Making Citizens: Public Rituals and Personal Journeys to Citizenship* (New York: Palgrave Macmillan).

FitzGerald, D. S. (2019) *Refuge Beyond Reach: How Rich Democracies Repel Asylum Seekers* (New York and Oxford: Oxford University Press).

Flaim, A. (2018) 'Stateless "Wild Boars" case shows policy reform need', *Bangkok Post*, 10 August [Online]. Available at www.bangkokpost.com/opinion/opinion/1519050/stateless-wild-boars-case-shows-policy-reform-need (Accessed 2 April 2020).

Gibney, M. J. (2011) 'Should citizenship be conditional? Denationalisation and liberal principles', Working Paper Series No. 75, Refugee Studies Centre, University of Oxford [Online]. Available at www.rsc.ox.ac.uk/files/files-1/wp75-should-citizenship-be-conditional-2011.pdf (Accessed 2 April 2020).

Gibney, M. J. (2017) 'Denationalization', in A. Shachar, R. Bauböck, I. Bloemraad, and M. Vink (eds) *The Oxford Handbook of Citizenship* (Oxford: Oxford University Press): pp. 358–382.

Gómez, L. E. (2018) *Manifest Destinies: The Making of the Mexican American Race*, 2nd edition (New York: New York University Press).

Gover, K. (2017) 'Indigenous citizenship in settler states', in A. Shachar, R. Bauböck, I. Bloemraad, and M. Vink (eds) *The Oxford Handbook of Citizenship* (Oxford: Oxford University Press): pp. 453–477.

Human Rights Watch (2007) 'Discrimination against ethnic Nepali children in Bhutan: Submission from Human Rights Watch to the Committee on the Rights of the Child' [Online]. Available at www.hrw.org/news/2007/10/03/discrimination-against-ethnic-nepali-children-bhutan (Accessed 2 April 2020).

Human Rights Watch (2019) 'Rwanda: Killing is latest attack on opponents' [Online]. Available at www.hrw.org/news/2019/09/24/rwanda-killing-latest-attack-opponents (Accessed 2 April 2020).

Kapoor, N. (2018) *Deport, Deprive, Extradite: 21st Century State Extremism* (New York and London: Verso).

Kingston, L. N. (2017a) 'Bringing Rwandan refugees "home": The cessation clause, statelessness, and forced repatriation', *International Journal of Refugee Law*, 29:3, 417–437.

Kingston, L. N. (2017b) 'Worthy of rights: statelessness as a cause and symptom of marginalization', in T. Bloom, K. Tonkiss, and P. Cole (eds) *Understanding Statelessness* (New York: Routledge): pp. 17–34.

Kingston, L. N. (2019) *Fully Human: Personhood, Citizenship, and Rights* (New York and Oxford: Oxford University Press).

Macklin, A. (2018) 'The return of banishment: Do the new denationalisation policies weaken citizenship?' in R. Bauböck (ed.) *Debating Transformations of National Citizenship* (Cham: Springer): pp. 163–172.

MacLean, K. (2019) 'The Rohingya crisis and the practices of erasure', *Journal of Genocide Research*, 21:1, 83–95.

Manby, B. (2018) 'You can't lose what you haven't got: Citizenship acquisition and loss in Africa', in R. Bauböck (ed.) *Debating Transformations of National Citizenship* (Cham: Springer): pp. 189–196.

Mantu, S. (2018) '"Terrorist" citizens and the human right to nationality', *Journal of Contemporary European Studies*, 26:1, 28–41.

McPherson, P., Lewis, S., Aung, T. T., Naing, S., and Siddiqui, Z. (2018) 'Erasing the Rohingya: Point of no return', Reuters, 18 December [Online]. Available at www.reuters.com/investigates/special-report/myanmar-rohingya-return/ (Accessed 2 April 2020).

Open Society Justice Initiative (2019) 'Unmaking Americans: Insecure citizenship in the United States' [Online]. Available at www.justiceinitiative.org/publications/unmaking-americans (Accessed 2 April 2020).

Pillai, S., and Williams, G. (2017) 'The utility of citizenship stripping laws in the UK, Canada and Australia', *Melbourne University Law Review*, 41:2, 845–889.

Rahim, Z. (2019) 'India builds detention camps for up to 1.9m people "stripped of citizenship" in Assam', *Independent*, 10 September [Online]. Available at www.independent.co.uk/news/world/asia/assam-india-detention-camps-bangladesh-nrc-list-a9099251.html (Accessed 2 April 2020).

Rivera Ramos, E. (2001) *The Legal Construction of Identity: The Judicial and Social Legacy of American Colonialism in Puerto Rico* (Washington, DC: American Psychological Association).

Romo, V. (2018) 'U.S. Army is discharging immigrant recruits who were promised citizenship', *NPR*, 9 July [Online]. Available at www.npr.org/2018/07/09/626773440/u-s-army-is-discharging-immigrant-recruits-who-were-promised-citizenship (Accessed 2 April 2020).

Scott, J. C. (1998) *Seeing Like a State: How Certain Schemes to Improve the Human Condition Have Failed* (New Haven, CT: Yale University Press).

Stadlmair, J. (2018) 'Earning citizenship. Economic criteria for naturalisation in nine EU countries', *Journal of Contemporary European Studies*, 26:1, 42–63.

Sullivan, M. J. (2019) *Earned Citizenship* (Oxford: Oxford University Press).

Torpey, J. (2000) *The Invention of the Passport: Surveillance, Citizenship and the State* (Cambridge: Cambridge University Press).

United States Holocaust Museum (n.d.) 'Nuremberg Race Laws' [Online]. Available at www.ushmm.org/wlc/en/article.php?ModuleId=10007903 (Assessed 2 April 2020).

van Brakel, R., and Van Kerckhoven, X. (2014) 'The emergence of the identity card in Belgium and its colonies', in K. Boersma, R. van Brakel, C. Fonio, and P. Wagenaar (eds) *Histories of State Surveillance in Europe and Beyond* (New York: Routledge): pp. 170–185.

Wadhia, S. S. (2019) *Banned: Immigration Enforcement in the Time of Trump* (New York: New York University Press).

Yeo, C. (2019) 'The rise of modern banishment: Deprivation and nullification of British citizenship', in D. Prabhat (ed.) *Citizenship in Times of Turmoil? Theory, Practice and Policy* (Cheltenham and Northampton: Edward Elgar): pp. 134–150.

8

Statelessness and governance in the absence of recognition: The case of the 'Donetsk People's Republic'

Nataliia Kasianenko

The Euromaidan revolution that engulfed Ukraine in the winter of 2013–2014 marked the beginning of hostilities in the Donbas region. Local rebel groups took over government buildings and made calls for independence from Ukraine. They denounced the Euromaidan revolution and called on local residents of the Donbas to support the creation of two self-proclaimed states, the 'Donetsk People's Republic' (DPR) and the 'Luhansk People's Republic' (LPR).[1] These calls for separatism transformed into a bloody conflict between rebel forces and the Ukrainian military in the spring of 2014 (Zadorozhny and Korotkiy, 2015). At the time of writing, the war in the Donbas continues despite multiple attempts to end the conflict through international agreements and ceasefires. Since 2014, more than 13,000 people have died in the war with over 1.5 million residents of the region displaced (United Nations, 2019). The two 'people's republics' have become politically, economically, and ideologically isolated from Ukraine. According to survey data, most of the residents of the DPR/LPR trust local authorities and hope to be integrated into Russia (Kudelia, 2014; Giuliano, 2018). The Russian government has been supporting the separatist entities without officially recognising them as states or extending promises of future integration (Sasse and Lackner, 2018). Although the leaders of both 'republics' seem to enjoy the internal domestic support of the Donbas residents, they remain heavily dependent on Russian assistance. Therefore, the sources of legitimacy are important, particularly as Ukrainian President Volodymyr Zelensky hopes to end the Donbas conflict and reintegrate the region through a new deal called the 'Steinmeier formula' (BBC, 2019).

This chapter examines the connection between statelessness and governance in the self-proclaimed state of the DPR. Specifically, I highlight how the rebel authorities can contribute to statelessness through their governance in pursuit of internal legitimacy. Using original data from the region – including social media accounts, local newspapers, and official websites for 'state' institutions of the DPR – I identify strategic tools that leaders in self-proclaimed states use to gain domestic support and recognition. These main tools involve the use of citizenship laws, support of an external patron, and provision of public goods. Governance in pursuit of domestic support further exacerbates the issue of statelessness in the 'republic.' While most of the residents of the occupied Donbas have retained their Ukrainian citizenship, many have taken citizenship of the DPR. Adding to this complexity, in April 2019 the Russian government simplified the process of obtaining Russian citizenship for the residents of the 'republic' (President of Russia, 2019).

Legitimacy and statelessness in the absence of recognition

The literature on self-proclaimed states highlights multiple definitions of these political entities. Scholars frequently use terms such as 'quasi-states' (Kolsto, 2006), 'de facto states' (O'Loughlin et al., 2014; Lennon and Adams, 2019), 'unrecognized states' (Markedonov, 2012), 'contested states' (Geldenhyus, 2009), 'informal states' (Isachenko, 2012), and 'separatist states' (Chirikba, 2004).[2] Generally, academic literature views self-proclaimed states as political entities that possess neither sovereignty nor legitimacy. While sovereignty is associated with independence and external recognition, legitimacy is understood as acceptance of political authority (Weber, 1978). In conceptualising legitimacy, the normative approach highlights the moral rightfulness of political authority, while the empirical or descriptive approach is associated with the perceptions and manifestations of public consent to political authority (Duyvesteyn, 2017). Most studies of legitimacy focus on sovereign states with legitimacy being treated as a binary concept.

More recently, scholars started to examine legitimacy in the context of self-proclaimed states and rebel groups and proposed thinking of degrees or types of legitimacy (Clapham, 1998; Caspersen, 2012). In her work, Nina Caspersen (2015) distinguishes between external legitimacy as international recognition, and internal legitimacy as acceptance of the political regime domestically. In the case of self-proclaimed states, a regime might lack external legitimacy yet enjoy internal legitimacy due to domestic support of the local population. This domestic support is essential for rebel leaders and needs to be established early on (Schneckener, 2017).

Legitimacy has also been tied to the ability of a government to provide vital public goods for the population, primarily security and social welfare (Lipset, 1960; Linz and Stepan, 1996; Berg, 2012). Rebel governments may be effective at governance, especially when the state is absent. Rebels can maintain a form of social contract with the public. Beyond effective policy-making, internal legitimacy can also be established through public perception of democratic rule, legitimacy of a rebel group leader, coercion that evolves into the perception of order, and the imitation of state symbols and state performance (Duyvesteyn, 2017). Even in the absence of external recognition, political elites create political institutions, pass legislation, and organise local elections. In addition, every unrecognised entity (e.g., Abkhazia, Northern Cyprus, Somaliland, etc.) relies on political and financial support of an outside state, which might not necessarily translate into statehood, yet contributes to internal legitimacy (Berg and Toomla, 2009; Ker-Lindsay, 2012). This external support also prevents complete isolation of a self-proclaimed state from the international community.

In the case of the two 'republics' in the occupied Donbas, the quest for gaining legitimacy translated into new citizenship policies, which allowed the Donbas residents to obtain passports of the self-proclaimed DPR/LPR. Remaining in the occupied Donbas and taking on citizenship of these de facto states have translated into statelessness. Statelessness of this sort has been widely discussed in the academic literature (Batchelor, 1998; Weissbrodt and Collins, 2006; Tucker, 2014; Fazal, this volume) and largely implies the holding of citizenship that is ineffective to the point that the state is unable or unwilling to provide benefits or protections for its citizens. While the Ukrainian government does not formally strip the newly minted citizens of the 'republics' of their Ukrainian citizenship, the citizens of the DPR/LPR residing in the occupied Donbas are unable to receive protections or public goods from Ukraine.

Citizenship and statelessness in the DPR

Despite the lack of international recognition, the self-proclaimed leaders of the DPR quickly established new government institutions and set up legislative and judicial agencies (Matveeva, 2016). The Ministry of Internal Affairs (MIA) of the DPR began issuing passports of the 'Donetsk People's Republic' in 2016 as a foundation for gaining internal legitimacy and deepening the alienation of Donbas residents from Ukraine. Since 2016, more than 415,000 people have received passports of the DPR (DNR Live, 2020). Yet, no country formally recognises the 'republic' as a state. In essence, having a passport that is not recognised around the world and which blocks any other citizenship from functioning is akin to statelessness. As a result, the conflict in the Donbas has not only led to thousands of people dead, injured, or displaced, it has also contributed to a growing number of stateless persons among the residents of the region (Babko, 2019). The most vulnerable groups for statelessness in the DPR include individuals who have lost their Ukrainian passports and children born in the DPR since 2014.

The residents of the DPR who have lost their Ukrainian passports are often unable to renew them, thus facing the risk of statelessness. In order to reinstate the passport of a Ukrainian citizen, these individuals need to confirm their identity with the Migration Service of Ukraine (MSU). The mere fact that residents of the occupied Donbas who are not migrants have to work with the MSU to regain their citizenship undermines the legitimacy of the Ukrainian government in the region. In addition, the MSU does not have a national electronic database. Thus, to confirm citizenship based on residency, the agency needs to obtain documents located in the territory of the DPR, which the Ukrainian government no longer controls.[3] In rare cases, the Ukrainian government may allow individuals to nominate their family members or neighbours to be interviewed to confirm identity and citizenship (VRU, 2015). However, travelling to Ukraine-controlled territory is difficult and expensive for residents of the DPR. Individuals without passports or other identity documents find it nearly impossible to cross checkpoints between the DPR and Ukraine-controlled territories without the risk of detention. This procedure of regaining citizenship based on residency contradicts the right to Ukrainian citizenship by birth through at least one parent being a Ukrainian citizen (VRU, 2001).

The risk of statelessness is particularly high for children in the DPR. Ukrainian citizenship is formally granted to residents of Ukraine once they are 14 and confirm their residency through a birth certificate issued by the Ukrainian government (VRU, 2016). According to local non-governmental organisations (NGOs), over 40,000 children born in the occupied Donbas from 2015 to 2016 did not receive Ukrainian birth certificates and registration (ADC, 2019). To avoid the prospect of statelessness, some pregnant women temporarily leave the DPR to give birth to their children in Ukraine-controlled territories. This allows the newborns to be registered by the Ukrainian authorities. The children who are born in the DPR and only obtain birth registration from the local authorities are formally stateless since they are only registered with a self-proclaimed state. These children are restricted in their ability to travel outside of the 'republic'. The DPR-issued documents only allow them to travel to Russia and the self-proclaimed states of Abkhazia and South Ossetia (Serdyuk, 2018). The same limitation on travel also technically applies to the residents of the DPR who have obtained new passports issued by the DPR authorities, although many of these individuals have kept their Ukrainian passports as well.

In 2018, the Ukrainian government adopted a law that extended formal recognition to birth certificates and death certificates issued in the occupied Donbas (VRU, 2018). However, the law lacks proper implementation. Thus, to receive a birth certificate issued by the Ukrainian government, the parents of a child who was born in the DPR need to travel to Ukraine-controlled territory and request this document from the civil registration authorities. Once the parents receive a formal written rejection (since the Ukrainian authorities do not recognise birth certificates issued by the self-proclaimed 'republics'), they can initiate a court procedure to register the birth. The complicated nature of the process discourages many families from acquiring birth certificates issued by the Ukrainian government. As a result, only 43% of children born in the occupied Donbas since the start of the conflict in 2014 have received this registration (UNHCR, 2019).

Individuals who have fled the conflict zone and moved out of Ukraine, but then lost their Ukrainian passports, also face legal complications. They cannot return to Ukraine without evidence of their entitlement to Ukrainian citizenship (ADC, 2019). Overall, the attempts of the self-proclaimed government in the DPR to gain legitimacy through new citizenship laws are contributing to statelessness and a growing humanitarian crisis in the region.

Russia as the external patron of the DPR

The internal legitimacy of the DPR largely rests on the external support of the Russian government. Although leaders and residents of the occupied Donbas have long expressed their hope to be integrated into Russia along 'the Crimean scenario', Russia refused to formally annex the 'republic' (Sakwa, 2015). Still, the Russian government has played a major role in supporting the leaders of the DPR politically, militarily, and financially. In April of 2019, a few days after Ukrainians elected President Zelensky, the Russian President signed a new law simplifying the procedures for obtaining Russian citizenship for the residents of the 'republics'. Russian President Vladimir Putin claimed this decision was a necessary solution to a growing humanitarian problem in the Donbas (President of Russia, 2019). He also discussed the possibility of simplifying the acquisition of Russian citizenship for all residents of Ukraine (RIA News, 2019).

Currently, the new procedure for obtaining Russian citizenship involves two decrees. One of them applies to the citizens of Ukraine and stateless people who are residing in the territory of the occupied Donbas. The second decree applies to former residents of the Donbas who fled to Russia as refugees before 27 April 2014. The fact that both decrees apply to either former or current residents of the DPR complicates the application of these rules and enables discrimination against the Donbas refugees who currently reside in Russia. The list of documents required for former residents of the DPR/LPR who have fled to Russia is much longer and includes a medical certificate confirming that an applicant does not have infectious diseases, drug addiction, or HIV/AIDS (Kirillov, 2019). Another group of people excluded from obtaining Russian citizenship is that made up of current residents of the DPR who have not obtained passports from the unrecognised 'republic'. Therefore, the new procedure encourages residents of the occupied Donbas to make a conscious choice of obtaining the passport of a self-proclaimed state and risk losing their Ukrainian citizenship (since Ukraine's Constitution does not allow dual/multiple citizenships) to become citizens of Russia in the future.[4]

The Ukrainian authorities have criticised the new decrees as an act of aggression against Ukraine. The government in Kyiv declared the new Russian passports issued to the residents of the 'republic' as invalid and encouraged other countries to boycott the 'fake documents' (CMU, 2019). According to the Russian government, close to 200,000 residents of the occupied Donbas obtained Russian citizenship in 2019 (TASS, 2020). The process of obtaining citizenship involves paying a substantial fee along with the requirement to travel to the territory of Russia to take the oath of the Russian Federation. Interviews with the Donbas residents who obtained the Russian passports suggest that they prefer to keep all three passports (the Russian, the Ukrainian, and the passport of the 'republic') in order to maximise the opportunities for travel and social benefits (Kohan and Tohmahchi, 2019).

The extension of Russian citizenship to the residents of the Donbas may potentially help alleviate the issue of statelessness in the region, but currently the acquisition of a Russian passport does not translate into entitlements to social benefits for the residents of the DPR. The new citizens of Russia who reside in the DPR do not receive unemployment benefits, child support, or pensions from Russia. There are grounds to suspect that the new decrees provide little benefits for the residents of the DPR and instead primarily serve the interests of the Russian government. The citizenship laws provide an opportunity for Russia to justify a future intervention in the Donbas under the guise of protecting Russian citizens (Peters, 2019). These laws also help delegitimise Ukraine's government in Kyiv (Lennon and Adams, 2019). Beyond the external support from Russia, local political elites in the DPR have made strides to obtain internal legitimacy through different elements of governance in the 'republic'.

Governance in the DPR

Despite the lack of international recognition and substantial dependence on Russian support, the leadership of the DPR used the results of the May

2014 referendum to declare the independence of the 'republic'. Shortly after, the DPR adopted its own constitution (Zadorozhny and Korotkiy, 2015). To enhance their internal legitimacy and centralise political power, rebel leaders organised local elections in late 2014 (Matveeva, 2016). These elections were not transparent and lacked external recognition. Nevertheless, they have helped advance members of local civil society organisations in the DPR to the new legislative body, People's Council of the DPR. Beyond the creation of new political institutions, effective policy-making has been key to maintaining internal legitimacy in the 'republic'.

Maintaining security has been a major priority for rebel leaders in the Donbas since the early spring of 2014. Once the rebels gained control over local government buildings, they set up volunteer paramilitary units to keep rebel-controlled territories secure (Sakwa, 2015). The military of the 'republics' has expanded over the years by recruiting thousands of local residents (Ria News Ukraine, 2017). The rebel leaders have also set up local patrol units to enhance security in areas away from the direct line of conflict (Grigoryuk, 2015). As a result, by 2016, relative peace and stability have returned to the large cities in the Donbas region while the conflict has shifted to the borders of the DPR/LPR (Matveeva, 2016). The ongoing violence contributes to the rally round the flag effect and helps promote the ideological narrative of victimhood and nationalism to further advance the position of local elites in the self-proclaimed state. At the same time, residents of the self-proclaimed DPR increasingly view the Ukrainian government and the Ukrainian state as a foreign adversary and an external enemy responsible for the bloody conflict in the Donbas.

Economic development remains a central concern for the leadership of the 'republic'. The ongoing conflict with Ukraine has led to a significant economic downturn. Many businesses have either left the region or completely shut down. In 2014, the Ukrainian government imposed an economic blockade on the occupied Donbas, which has further exacerbated the region's economic decline (Matveeva, 2016). As major banks closed their branches in the DPR, the residents of the 'republic' were unable to access their accounts and obtain cash (Silchenko, 2015). With the help of the Russian government, local authorities in the DPR made significant efforts to reduce the economic crisis. They created a new electronic banking system and a network of central banks (Beroyeva, 2016). The leadership of the 'republic' also took control over some coal mines in the region and announced rising levels of coal production (DONi News Agency, 2016). Yet significant issues remain. The 2016 nationalisation law allowed the DPR leaders to impose temporary authority over local businesses, which was met with suspicion by Donbas residents (Beroyeva, 2016). Despite the economic blockade, some businesses in the DPR continue paying taxes to the

Ukrainian government (Skorik, 2017). Trade volumes are consistently low since the 'republic' primarily trades with the LPR and Russia. Slow trade contributes to the shortage of consumer goods in the region and reliance on contraband trade with Ukraine (Beroyeva, 2016).

While there is a shortage of reliable data regarding the budget of the DPR, existing estimates suggest that the Russian government covers about 70% of the budget of the 'republic' (Matveeva, 2016). Other estimates point to an even bigger reliance on Moscow (82% of the DPR's budget) (Skorik, 2017). Despite the lack of official data, there is little doubt that the DPR is completely financially dependent on Russia (Donbass News, 2017). Consequently, Russia's political and economic involvement in the region is expanding. The Kremlin is directly involved in policy-making in the republic, while Russian goods are dominating the markets in the DPR (Lennon and Adams, 2019).

In 2014, citing its inability to exercise political control in the DPR/LPR, the Ukrainian government has, for example, ceased sending pension payments to the occupied territories. Pensions are still available for the residents of the 'republic' if they are able to leave the occupied region and register with the government authorities in Ukraine-controlled territory. As such, obtaining pensions from Ukraine requires crossing frequently into Ukraine-controlled territory, which can be both costly and dangerous. However, many retirees are either unwilling or unable to permanently leave their homes and move out of the DPR. As a result, retirees feel abandoned and betrayed by the Ukrainian politicians who claim that 'Donbas is Ukrainian', yet do not support the residents of the Donbas financially (Khomenko, 2014). The inability of the Ukrainian state to provide public goods for the residents of the occupied 'republic' further eroded the legitimacy of the government in Kyiv and contributed to statelessness. The financial dependency of the DPR residents on the self-proclaimed government in the 'republic' and the authorities in Moscow helps promote the idea that the residents of the occupied Donbas are not Ukrainian.

Conclusion

The leadership of the DPR has used a combination of citizenship policies, external support, and the provision of public goods as sources of obtaining internal legitimacy in the 'republic'. Yet, the ability of rebel authorities to maintain this legitimacy is under question as the DPR continues to rely on the government of Russia to maintain the budget of the 'republic' and provide socio-economic benefits for its residents. Until the status of the DPR is formally resolved, the prospect of statelessness looms large over thousands of residents of the occupied Donbas. The financial dependence on Russia presents a growing challenge for cultivating the DPR's legitimacy, particularly as the Russian government started reducing its economic support to the region to encourage the DPR to be more independent (Skorik, 2017). Overall, the 'republic' is currently unable to solve the issue of statelessness and provide social welfare for the residents of the DPR without any external assistance. This weakness could present an opportunity for the Ukrainian government in its efforts to regain influence and legitimacy in the Donbas.

The case of the DPR highlights the powerful link between governance, statelessness, and citizenship. For established states, the inability to govern within a particular territory may contribute to statelessness (both *de jure* and *de facto*). For self-proclaimed states, governance in pursuit of internal legitimacy may involve manipulation of citizenship policies, which enhances the risk of statelessness. The ability of self-proclaimed states to gain internal legitimacy and extend citizenship to residents despite the absence of international recognition has important implications for the future of these political entities. One implication is that resolving separatist conflicts and attempting to reintegrate de facto states using military force or international law could be ineffective and even counterproductive. These conventional tools do not erode the internal legitimacy of de facto states. The second implication attests to the power of citizenship as a tool of geopolitics. The cases of Ukraine's Crimea and the Donbas suggest that violations of state sovereignty and foreign military interventions are increasingly justified on the basis of protecting the citizens of an intervening state or helping a stateless group.

Notes

1 Throughout the chapter, I refer to the occupied regions of the Donbas as 'polities', 'republics', de facto states, and self-proclaimed states.
2 I treat self-proclaimed states as 'separatist entities that display trappings of statehood but lack universal recognition' (Florea, 2014: 789).
3 Ukraine's Migration Service mandates that the residents of the DPR need to reestablish their citizenship by showing evidence of residency in Ukraine in August 1991.
4 Ukraine's government currently has no ability to identify the residents of the Donbas who hold the passport of the 'republic' and/or the passport of the Russian Federation. Therefore, there is no mechanism in place to actively strip the 'citizens' of the DPR of Ukrainian citizenship by confiscating their Ukrainian passports. The threat of statelessness becomes more serious for the residents of the DPR who lose their Ukrainian passports or let them expire.

References

Anti-Discrimination Center (ADC) (2019) 'Statelessness in Russia and Ukraine: Possibilities for solving the problem' [Online]. Available at https://adcmemorial.org/wp-content/uploads/stateless_RU.pdf (Accessed 11 March 2020).

Babko, A. (2019) 'Setting a blueprint for overcoming statelessness in Russia and Ukraine', European Network on Statelessness, 9 July [Online]. Available at www. statelessness.eu/blog/setting-blueprint-overcoming-statelessness-russia-and-ukraine (Accessed 20 June 2020).

Batchelor, C. (1998) 'Statelessness and the problem of resolving nationality status', *International Journal of Refugee Law*, 10, 156–183.

BBC (2019) 'Ukraine conflict: Can peace plan in east finally bring peace?', 29 October [Online]. Available at www.bbc.com/news/world-europe-49986007 (Accessed 11 March 2020).

Berg, E. (2012) 'Parent states versus secessionist entities: Measuring political legitimacy in Cyprus, Moldova and Bosnia and Herzegovina', *Europe-Asia Studies*, 64:7, 1271–1296.

Berg, E., and Toomla, R. (2009) 'Forms of normalisation in the quest for de facto statehood', *The International Spectator*, 44:4, 27–45.

Beroyeva, N. (2016) 'Zhivoy Donetsk, Ukraina' ['Live Donetsk, Ukraine'], *LiveJournal*, 23 August [Online]. Available at https://varlamov.ru/1907750.html (Accessed 11 March 2020).

Cabinet of Ministers of Ukraine (CMU) (2019) 'Volodymyr Groysman: Ukraine will not recognize fake Russian passports issued to residents of the occupied territories', 8 May [Online]. Available at www.kmu.gov.ua/en/news/ukrayina-na-viznavatime-fejkovih-rosijskih-pasportiv-shcho-vidavatimut-zhitelyam-okupovanih-teritorij-volodimir-grojsman (Accessed 11 March 2020).

Caspersen, N. (2012) *Unrecognized States: The Struggle for Sovereignty in the Modern International System* (Cambridge: Polity Press).

Caspersen, N. (2015) 'Degrees of legitimacy: Ensuring internal and external support in the absence of recognition', *Geoforum*, 66, 184–192.

Chirikba, V. (2004) 'Geopolitical aspects of the Abkhazian statehood: Some results and perspectives', *Iran and the Caucasus*, 8:2, 341–349.

Clapham, C. (1998) 'Degrees of statehood', *Review of International Studies*, 24:2, 143–157.

DNR Live (2020) 'Pasport DNR poluchili bolee 415 tysyach chelovek' ['More than 415 thousand people received the passport of DPR'], 11 February [Online]. Available at http://dnr-live.ru/pasport-dnr-poluchili-bolee-415-tyis-chelovek/ (Accessed 11 March 2020).

Donbass News (2017) 'Sekretniy budzhet "DNR" mozhet ostatsya bez rossiyskih vlivaniy?' ['Secret budget of the "DPR" may be left without Russian infusions?'], 6 October [Online]. Available at http://novosti.dn.ua/article/6867-sekretnyy-byudzhet-DPR-mozhet-ostatsya-bez-rossyyskykh-vlyvanyy (Accessed 7 March 2020).

DONi News Agency (2016) 'DPR miners win almost 9 million tons of coal from beginning of year', 3 October [Online]. Available at https://dninews.com/en/news/dpr-miners-win-almost-9-million-tons-of-coal-from-beginning-of-year/ (Accessed 1 June 2020).

Duyvesteyn, I. (2017) 'Rebels & legitimacy; an introduction', *Small Wars & Insurgencies*, 28:4–5, 669–685.

Florea, A. (2014) 'De facto states in international politics (1945–2011): A new dataset', *International Interactions*, 40:5, 788–811.

Geldenhyus, D. (2009) *Contested States in World Politics* (London: Palgrave Macmillan).

Giuliano, E. (2018) 'Who supported separatism in Donbas? Ethnicity and popular opinion at the start of the Ukraine crisis', *Post-Soviet Affairs*, 34:2–3, 158–178.

Grigoryuk, D. (2015) 'Voennaya policiya DNR' ['Military police of the DPR'], *Novorossiya*, 8 July [Online]. Available at https://novorosinform.org/401348 (Accessed 8 March 2020).

Isachenko, D. (2012) *The Making of Informal States: Statebuilding in Northern Cyprus and Transdniestria* (Basingstoke: Palgrave Macmillan).

Ker-Lindsay, J. (2012) *The Foreign Policy of Counter Secession* (Oxford: Oxford University Press).

Khomenko, S. (2014) 'Donbass poteryal pravo na pensii' ['Donbas lost the right to retirements'], *BBC News Ukraine*, 24 November [Online]. Available at www.bbc.com/ukrainian/ukraine_in_russian/2014/11/141124_ru_s_pensions_donbas (Accessed 11 March 2020).

Kirillov, D. (2019) 'Dorogoy Rossiyskiy Pasport' ['Expensive Russian passport'], *Radio Svoboda*, 5 May [Online]. Available at www.svoboda.org/a/29918808.html (Accessed 11 March 2020).

Kohan, A., and Tohmahchi, A. (2019) 'How the residents of the Donbas receive Russian citizenship', *Hromadske*, 21 June [Online]. Available at https://hromadske.ua/ru/posts/dushevno-do-sih-por-slezy-na-glazah-kak-zhiteli-donbassa-poluchayut-rossijskoe-grazhdanstvo (Accessed 11 March 2020).

Kolsto, P. (2006) 'The sustainability and future of unrecognized quasi-states', *Journal of Peace Research*, 43:6, 723–740.

Kudelia, S. (2014) 'Domestic sources of the Donbas insurgency', *PONARS Eurasia Policy Memo*, 351 [Online]. Available at www.ponarseurasia.org/memo/domestic-sources-donbas-insurgency (Accessed 11 March 2020).

Lennon, O., and Adams, G. (2019) 'All is quiet on the Russian front: Ceasefires and the pursuit of legitimacy by self-proclaimed "republics" in Ukraine', *Eurasian Geography and Economics*, 60:6, 656–683.

Lipset, S. M. (1960) *Political Man: The Social Bases of Politics* (Garden City, NY: Doubleday).

Linz, J., and Stepan, A. (1996) *Problems of Democratic Transition and Consolidation: Southern Europe, South America, and Post-Communist Europe* (Baltimore, MD: Johns Hopkins University Press).

Markedonov, S. (2012) 'The unrecognized states of Eurasia as a phenomenon of the USSR's dissolution', *Demokratizatsiya: The Journal of Post-Soviet Democratization*, 20:2, 189–195.

Matveeva, A. (2016) 'No Moscow stooges: identity polarization and guerrilla movements in Donbass', *Southeast European and Black Sea Studies*, 16:1, 25–50.

O'Loughlin, J., Kolossov, V., and Toal, G. (2014) 'Inside the post-Soviet de facto states: A comparison of attitudes in Abkhazia, Nagorny Karabakh, South Ossetia, and Transnistria', *Eurasian Geography and Economics*, 55:5, 423–456.

People's Council of the DPR (n.d.) 'History of DPR People's Council' [Online]. Available at https://dnrsovet.su/history-of-dpr-people-s-council/ (Accessed 1 July 2020).

Peters, A. (2019) 'Passportisation: Risks for international law and stability – Part I', *EJILTalk!* 9 May [Online]. Available at www.ejiltalk.org/passportisation-risks-for-international-law-and-stability-part-one/ (Accessed 14 November 2020).

President of Russia (2019) 'Ukaz Prezidenta Rossiyskoy Federatsii #183' ['Decree of the President of the Russian Federation #183'], 24 April [Online]. Available at www.kremlin.ru/acts/bank/44190 (Accessed 29 June 2020).

RIA News (2019) 'Putin on the simplified Russian citizenship for Ukraine's residents', 27 April [Online]. Available at https://ria.ru/20190427/1553107786.html (Accessed 11 March 2020).

RIA News Ukraine (2017) 'Avakov nazval chislennost voysk DNR i LNR v Donbasse' ['Avakov named the number of troops of the DPR and LPR in the Donbas'], 28 November [Online]. Available at https://rian.com.ua/politics/20171128/1029852333/Avakov-nazval-chislennost-voysk-DNR-LNR-Donbass.html (Accessed 1 June 2020).

Sakwa, R. (2015) *Frontline Ukraine: Crisis in the Borderlands* (London: I.B. Tauris).

Sasse, G., and Lackner, A. (2018) 'War and identity: The case of the Donbas in Ukraine', *Post-Soviet Affairs*, 34:2, 139–157.

Schneckener, U. (2017) 'Militias and the politics of legitimacy', *Small Wars & Insurgencies*, 28:4–5, 799–816.

Serdyuk, A. (2018) 'Neskolko desyatkov tysyach detey na okupirovannoy chasti Donbassa riskuyut ostatsya bez grazhdanstva' ['Tens of thousands of children in the occupied Donbas risk statelessness'], *Vilne Radio* [Free Radio], 21 November [Online]. Available at https://freeradio.com.ua/ru/neskolko-desjatkov-tysjach-detej-v-okkupirovannom-donbasse-ostalis-bez-grazhdanstva/ (Accessed 11 March 2020).

Silchenko, V. (2015) 'Donetsk, chast 1' ['Donetsk, part 1'], *LiveJournal*, 18 February [Online]. Available at https://varlamov.ru/1279197.html (Accessed 11 March 2020).

Skorik, M. (2017) 'Kak dela delayutsya. Na chem derzhatsya ekonomika i finansy DNR i LNR' ['How it is done. What the economy and finance of DRP and LPR rest on'], *SpektrPress*, 8 February [Online]. Available at http://spektr.press/kak-dela-delayutsya-na-chem-derzhatsya-ekonomika-i-finansy-DNR-i-LNR/ (Accessed 11 March 2020).

TASS News Agency (TASS) (2020) 'Okolo 200 tysyach zhiteley Donbassa poluchili rossiyskoye grazhdanstvo v uproshennom poryadke' ['About 200 thousand residents of the Donbas received the Russian citizenship through a simplified procedure'], 1 January [Online]. Available at https://tass.ru/obshchestvo/7457065 (Accessed 11 March 2020).

Tucker, J. (2014) 'Questioning *de facto* statelessness', *Tilburg Law Review*, 19, 276–284.

United Nations (2019) 'Senior officials urge steps to make Eastern Ukraine ceasefire irreversible, telling Security Council Minsk Accords remain largely unimplemented', 12 February [Online]. Available at www.un.org/press/en/2019/sc13698.doc.htm (Accessed 11 March 2020).

United Nations High Commissioner for Refugees (UNHCR) (2019) 'Statelessness update' [Online]. Available at www.unhcr.org/ua/wp-content/uploads/sites/38/2019/10/Statelessness-Update-2019-09-UNHCR-Ukraine-EN-004.pdf (Accessed 11 March 2020).

Verkhovna Rada of Ukraine (VRU) (2001) 'Law #2235', 18 January [Online]. Available at https://zakon.rada.gov.ua/laws/show/2235-14 (Accessed 25 June 2020).

Verkhovna Rada of Ukraine (VRU) (2015) 'Order of the Cabinet of Ministers of Ukraine #302', 25 March [Online]. Available at https://zakon.rada.gov.ua/laws/show/302-2015-%D0%BF (Accessed 25 June 2020).

Verkhovna Rada of Ukraine (VRU) (2016) 'Order of the Cabinet of Ministers of Ukraine #745', 26 October [Online]. Available at https://zakon.rada.gov.ua/laws/show/en/745-2016-п#n2 (Accessed 25 June 2020).

Verkhovna Rada of Ukraine (VRU) (2018) 'Law #2268', 18 January [Online]. Available at https://zakon.rada.gov.ua/laws/show/2268-19#Text (Accessed 25 June 2020).

Weber, M. (1978) *Economy and Society: An Outline of Interpretive Sociology* (Berkeley, CA: University of California Press).

Weissbrodt, D., and Collins, C. (2006) 'The human rights of stateless persons', *Human Rights Quarterly*, 28, 253–264.

Zadorozhny, O., and Korotkyi, T. (2015) 'Legal assessment of the Russian Federation's policy in the context of the establishment and activities of terrorist organizations "Donetsk People's Republic" ("DPR") and "Lugansk People's Republic" ("LPR") in Eastern Ukraine', *European Political and Law Discourse*, 2:1, 8–18.

9

Legal identity and rebel governance: A comparative perspective on lived consequence of contested sovereignty

Katharine Fortin, Bart Klem, and Marika Sosnowski[1]

Arthur: How do you do, good lady. I am Arthur, King of the Britons. [...]
Woman: King of the who?
Arthur: The Britons.
Woman: Who are the Britons?
Arthur: Well, we all are. We are all Britons, and I am your king.
Woman: I didn't know we had a king.
      Monty Python and the Holy Grail (White et al., 1975: Scene 3)

This clip from the British comedy group Monty Python illustratively denaturalises sovereign rule in the above encounter between the mythical figure king Arthur and one of his supposed citizens. The gist of this fragment – the pulling of the rug out from under a self-referential sovereign by his supposed subjects – aptly directs us to the fundamental concerns of this edited volume. Statelessness raises unsettling questions about the established international order of sovereign states and the governance of citizenship. While the manifestations and ramifications of statelessness have received ample attention from scholars and practitioners, there remains a need to pay closer attention to the ways statelessness is produced, the different contexts in which it happens (Institute on Statelessness and Inclusion, 2020), and its relationship to sovereignty.

This chapter, which builds on the analysis of the Donetsk People's Republic (Kasianenko, this volume), explores these issues by studying insurgent movements that confer legal identity, and even forms of citizenship. Such efforts of 'rebel governance' (Arjona et al., 2015) range from the documentation of life cycle events, to the delineation of rights and duties, to citizenship of a de facto (albeit unrecognised) state. These assertions of legal identity may take place both in parallel to and in overlap with the state that the insurgency seeks to supplant.

Our chapter is organised around two questions, addressed in an interdisciplinary way. First, what are the key similarities and differences in how insurgent groups instil legal identity? Second, and based on this comparative mapping, how can legal identity in relation to rebel governance be conceptualised? We address these questions by combining specific elements of political science, anthropology, and international law. In closing, we reflect on the conceptual, empirical, and normative ramifications of these points for legal identity, citizenship, and statelessness.

Through these comparative and conceptual reflections, we hope to help build a research agenda on the topic itself (the production of legal identity by insurgencies) and on its manifold knock-on effects for individuals in armed conflict. These effects engender both theoretical and practical ramifications – including how the rise and fall of insurgent governance may result in people becoming stateless.

Understanding legal identity

The new UN Legal Identity Agenda provides an operational definition of legal identity:

> Legal identity is defined as the basic characteristics of an individual's identity. E.g. name, sex, place and date of birth conferred through registration and the issuance of a certificate by an authorized civil registration authority following the occurrence of birth. In the absence of birth registration, legal identity may be conferred by a legally-recognized identification authority. This system should be linked to the civil registration system to ensure a holistic approach to legal identity from birth to death. Legal identity is retired by the issuance of a death certificate by the civil registration authority upon registration of death.

This identity typically takes material form in identity documentation – a passport, ID card, life cycle documentation (most fundamentally: birth, marital status, and death) – but legal identity is not confined to physical documentation. It comprises personhood in relation to the law and to the governing authority and is the gateway to attaining rights and duties in law. Some of these rights and duties exist at the international level, others are national, and still others relate to more specific personal characteristics like age, gender, or belonging to a racial, ethnic, linguistic, or religious group. Legal identity is arguably more foundational than citizenship, but the concepts are closely linked. In practice, a person's legal identity is typically substantiated with state-authorised documents. A person who does not have such documentation will find it hard to claim citizenship and will face a high risk of statelessness. The connection between a person's legal identity and a state is complicated by the fact that people may have connections with more than one state or a supra-national entity; for example when people are foreign residents, dual, or European citizens (Henrard, 2018). It may also become compromised when armed non-state actors attempt to confer or deny legal personhood in direct contravention of, and often as a challenge to, the legal identity issued by the state. Underpinning all these nuances and variations, however, is the fact that legal identity encompasses a fundamental norm – a recognition of one's existence as a person before the law and not being 'bare life' placed outside of it (Agamben, 2005).

Legal identity comprises a documented relationship between a person, the law, and the governing authority, from which that person derives rights and duties. This governing authority is assumed to be a state. However, as will be shown in this chapter, not only recognised states act as the 'civil registration authority' able to carry out the governance procedures central to legal identity. Within states, legal identity is often tied up with citizenship, producing a relationship between the citizen and the state. And vice versa, this relationship reproduces state authority; a state without citizens is not a state.[2]

The question of legal identity therefore conjures up questions about sovereign fundamentals. On what basis does a state arrogate itself the power to simultaneously confer legal identity on its subjects and position itself as sovereign? There tends to be some friction between the legal answer (the constitutional underpinnings of the state and its international legal obligations as guardian of rights), the political answer (often a narrative of self-determination, nation building, and/or decolonisation), and the historical answer (typically violent subjugation, which then transformed into some kind of social contract) to such a question. In most established states this is a philosophical matter, but this is not the case in contexts where the foundations of the state are contested. This includes: when Indigenous groups reject the state as settler colonial (e.g. Australia; Balint et al., 2014), when people pledge loyalty to a government in exile (e.g. Tibet; McConnell, 2016), when a separatist movement contests the basic legitimacy of the state (e.g. Kurdistan; Watts, 2010), or when such a movement becomes a de facto (e.g. North Cyprus; Navaro-Yashin, 2003) or semi-recognised state (e.g. Palestine; Kelly, 2006).

Legal identity and rebel governance in comparative perspective

To date, there is no robust overview of the ways and extent to which non-state armed groups confer legal identity to the people living under their control. This section maps out some of the variation between civil war contexts. We organise our comparative reflections along three axes, respectively concerning 1) the nature of the insurgency; 2) the nature of the state; and 3) the trajectory of conflict.

First, we suggest that whether and how non-state armed groups register the populations under their control depends on the objectives and ability of the movement. Do they aspire to become sovereign states, and are they able to position themselves as de facto sovereigns? We distinguish three positions on this spectrum. On the extreme end, we find a group like the Islamic State, which was ardent about controlling people and territory in a state-like manner. At the height of its power, the self-declared caliphate re-drew international borders to carve out an unrecognised state with a fine-grained system of civil registration and destroyed what it saw as illegitimate state-issued documentation and civil registration centres. Legal identity among their subject population was thoroughly documented and comprised an elaborate bundle of rights and duties – though arguably more of the latter than the former (Revkin, 2016).

In the middle of the spectrum, we find groups that take a more compromised position. These include movements like the now defeated Liberation Tigers of Tamil Eelam (LTTE), who governed their territories independently but did not issue identity documentation to civilians. Instead, they co-opted the pre-existing structures of the Sri Lankan state. While the LTTE created its own institutions (such as courts, departments, taxes), they allowed the Sri Lankan civil service to work in the areas under their control, though subject to their surveillance. Sri Lanka's detailed civil registration system with the myriad trappings of state welfare (access to education, healthcare, poverty relief, and so on) thus percolated the Tamil state to come. In formal terms, people's legal identity was firmly part of the Sri Lankan state system; they had a Sri Lankan ID card, which entitled them to the remaining trickle of Sri Lankan state services. In actual fact, their bundle of rights and duties was subject to the insurgency because they complied with LTTE rules, they paid LTTE taxes, and their children were forcibly recruited (Klem and Maunaguru, 2017).

At the other end of the spectrum, we find non-state armed groups that either do not have sovereign ambitions or are not able to project the necessary force to control people and territory. This comprises a long list of often lesser-known groups such as insurgencies in Northeast India (Vandekerckhove, 2011), groups that could be classified as 'hit and run' guerrillas (e.g. in El Salvador; Sprenkels, 2018) as well as 'criminal' gangs (e.g. in Brazil, Haiti, or Mexico; Schuberth, 2015). Even in these cases, though, one could argue that the respective movements engage in minimal forms of governance (they impose rules and duties) and civil administration (surveillance of their subject population).

Having outlined this spectrum of insurgent movements, we turn to our second comparative axis: the nature of the state they rebel against. Especially significant, it has been argued, is the degree to which the trappings of state governance have permeated civilian life in the past (Mampilly, 2011). Citizens who have long been surrounded by an array of government institutions (like in Syria) are likely to expect similar forms of governance when a non-state armed group (like the Islamic State) takes over. When the civil service reaches out to the furthest rural ventricles of society (like in Sri Lanka), it presents the insurgency (the LTTE) with the possibility of co-opting them. But when large swathes of a country have witnessed quite feeble and intermittent state presence (like in Myanmar), a different opportunity structure unfolds. The territory of the Kachin Independence Organisation/Army (KIO/A) in Northern Myanmar is right on the border with China. In the absence of Myanmar state institutions capable of issuing identity cards, the KIO/A started issuing its own birth and marriage certificates as well as immigration papers (de la Cour Venning, 2019). Compared to the LTTE, the KIO/A arguably has less thorough control over people and territory and a less elaborate institutional architecture, but given the relative void of state governance, it engages in quintessential matters of legal identity.

The role of 'supporting states' may also affect the picture, especially with regard to movements that do not aspire to an independent state but desire reunification (or closer ties) with a neighbouring state. Relevant cases include the Russian satellite republics mentioned above, including the Donbass in Ukraine (see Kasianenko, this volume), North Cyprus, and the Republican movement in Northern Ireland. In such cases, the provision of legal identity may not be executed only by the non-state armed group, but also – directly or indirectly – by the state to which it seeks allegiance. For example, Russia issues passports to inhabitants of Ukraine's rebellious Donetsk People's Republic (Underwood, 2019), and the Turkish Republic of Northern Cyprus issues passports to its citizens – but these only exist by the grace of their sovereign overlord, Turkey (Kyris, 2018).

Third, we suggest that a major comparative difference is time, or more specifically the temporal stage within the trajectory of conflict. Rebel governance is inherently subject to deferral; it is a political form in the making that derives legitimacy from projections of a state to come. Whether and how legal identity manifests itself as part of an insurgency and what its human consequences are vary enormously depending on the temporal context. This ranges from: armed groups in abeyance (e.g. the KIO/A); the successful transformation to a stable albeit unrecognised state (e.g. North Cyprus) or a semi-recognised sovereign state (e.g. Kosovo); the military defeat of an armed group (e.g. Islamic State); or the group being accommodated into a peace accord (e.g. the Revolutionary Armed Forces of Colombia, FARC). The most significant ramifications for legal identity tend to come up when the insurgency ends. This is currently seen in Iraq and

Syria, where large parts of the population find themselves in deeply precarious positions because their identity documents have been issued by an armed group that has been militarily defeated (i.e. Islamic State).

Legal identity amidst the convoluted landscape of war

The production of legal identity in such contexts where the fundamentals of state sovereignty are contested (or where there are multiple sovereign claimants) is significant because it complicates the notion that the state is the self-evident referent of legal personhood. It is therefore surprising that there is hardly any social and political science scholarship focusing explicitly on this phenomenon. Political scientists have studied insurgent forms of order, but have largely steered clear of legal dimensions (Mampilly, 2011; Arjona et al., 2015). Anthropologists have described the everyday lived realities underpinning such orders but have similarly eschewed legal identity (Lubkemann, 2008; Thiranagama, 2011). Legal scholars have addressed rebel governance through an analysis of human rights law and international humanitarian law, but have not focused on legal identity specifically. To conceptually calibrate the study of insurgent assertions of legal identity, we examine three promising academic strands within this broad interdisciplinary arena: 1) rebel governance and de facto sovereignty; 2) state performance and mimicry; and, 3) legal scholarship in relation to non-state armed groups.

The first strand comprises the burgeoning field of rebel governance. This scholarship shows that many non-state armed groups administer populations, establish state institutions and courts, create systems of taxation and recruitment, and provide (or channel) basic services (Mampilly, 2011; Arjona et al., 2015; Kasfir et al., 2017; Sosnowski, 2018). These practices make tactical sense because they enable resource extraction, recruitment, and legitimation. In more fundamental terms, these practices can be understood as enactments of de facto sovereignty, a nascent form of statehood in aspiration of internationally recognised de jure sovereignty. De facto sovereignty is defined as the ability to exercise 'discipline with impunity' (Hansen and Stepputat, 2006: 296): the power to initiate rules and enforce them without yielding to anyone else (including the de jure sovereign state). However, scholarship on de facto sovereignty puts the emphasis on disciplinary violence and has largely steered clear of legal questions. Though the problem of recognition remains, some armed groups evidently emulate the practices of de jure sovereigns by drafting their own laws, setting up their own courts, and signing up to more onerous international law obligations than the state they are fighting.

The second strand shifts our focus from violent capacities to performative qualities. Of central importance to any political order, seminal authors like Geertz (1980) and Butler (1990) have argued, is the staging of state repertoires. This engenders mimicry. Put simply, states act the way they think states should act, and they do so in such a way that people recognise them as states. From this perspective, the legal and political conduct of states comprises an endless chain of citational practice, where nothing is ever invented afresh – all state conduct is an adaptation of earlier state conduct (Weber, 1995). This perspective sheds light on the practices of non-state armed groups. Very often, the forms of order that they bring into being – the offices, the uniforms, the law books – look a lot like the order they are supposed to replace. These groups engage in a 'dress rehearsal' for sovereign statehood (McConnell, 2016) and this pivots on 'sovereign mimicry' (Klem and Maunaguru, 2017). The analytical merit of such a perspective lies in the fact that mimicry produces a 'duplicate, but not quite' (Bhabha, 1994: 121–123), and this 'not quite' opens up an important space for innovation, for deliberately articulating slightly different (often purportedly superior) forms or order, and even, at times, for mockery. When non-state armed groups instil forms of legal identity on the population under their control, the conceptual lens of mimicry suggests that this has less to do with any desire to comply with legal norms (insurgents studying international law and seeking to honour people's right to legal personhood) than with an effort to act in ways that are recognised as state-like, both by the citizens they are attempting to govern and the international community. This enables them to set up a civil administration and position their group as the guardian and benefactor of the people in ways that largely resemble what the state used to do in the past (or still tries to do).

The third strand comprises two parallel streams of legal literature: one on legal identity, statelessness, and citizenship, and the other on rebel governance in relation to international law. The scholarship on legal identity and statelessness has generally eschewed contexts where armed groups take control and issue legal identity because it is anathema to systems of law where the nation-state is the primary referent (Ladner et al., 2015; Henrard, 2018). Vice versa, legal scholarship on rebel governance tends to overlook the issue of legal identity (Murray, 2016; Fortin, 2017 and 2021). The right to legal identity is intimately connected to human rights law. Article 16 of the International Covenant on Civil and Political Rights (ICCPR) articulates: 'Everyone shall have the right to recognition everywhere as a person before the law'. There are also numerous other legal provisions which are intended to guarantee children are registered at birth (1989 Convention on the Rights of the Child, Article 7; 1966 International Covenant on Civil and Political Rights, Article 24[2]) and that prevent statelessness (1961

Convention on the Reduction of Statelessness, Articles 1–4). This position has gained increased urgency with the Sustainable Development Goals, which set 'legal identity for all' as an explicit target (16:9; Bloom, this volume). This has in turn given rise to a range of technological interventions aimed at optimising the registration of people through biometric means (Gelb and Manby, 2016; World Bank, 2016).

With regard to non-state armed groups, a legal argument can be made that they have an obligation to take on a state's responsibilities regarding legal identity, because they effectively control territory and exercise governmental functions (Murray, 2016; Fortin, 2017). It may also be argued that states faced with an insurgency have an obligation to recognise the information contained within documents registering births, deaths, and marriages issued by non-state armed groups. Case law from the European Court of Human Rights has confirmed that if a state loses control over part of its territory, it does not cease to have jurisdiction over that territory (*Mozer v Moldova* [2016] para 97; *Ilascu and others v Moldova* [2004] para 312). Further support for the idea that civil documentation emerging from rebel-held territory should be recognised by the state against which the armed group is fighting can be found in case law (*Cyprus v Turkey* [2001] para 93–98; *Namibia Advisory Opinion* [1971] para 125). The rationale behind this exception is that if a state adopts a policy of blanket non-recognition of these documents, it will be 'to the detriment of the inhabitants of the territory' (*Cyprus v Turkey* [2001] para 90; *Namibia Advisory Opinion* [1970] para 125). In the *Cyprus v Turkey* case, the court was clearly motivated by the observation that life goes on in the territory of a de facto authority and that life for its inhabitants must be made tolerable (*Cyprus v Turkey* [2001] para 96).

Efforts by non-state armed groups to establish governance structures and run rudimentary civil administrations can thus gain a gloss of legitimacy and legality – not on the basis of the motivations or characteristics of the armed group, but on humanitarian grounds: their efforts embody the fulfilment of a right (*Namibia Advisory Opinion* [1970] para 122).[3] This evidently does not sit easily with the tendency of many states to classify armed groups as terrorists. It also conjures up a whole range of frictions and tensions, both for the state against which the armed group is fighting and for third states. For a person living in a territory controlled by such a group, getting a key life event registered (the birth of a child, a marriage, the death of a spouse) may prove to be essential for securing access to services at home or in a refugee-receiving country. Not having such documents can have severe cascading effects, including losing rights or even becoming stateless (Albarazi and Tucker, 2014). At the same time, in some circumstances such documentation can be taken as evidence of an affiliation with an armed group and may expose the holder to the denial of rights, prosecution, or extra-judicial violence (Amnesty International, 2018; Kao and Revkin, 2018). The dangers of this are currently playing out in Syria and Iraq, where many people who used to live under the Syrian opposition or Islamic State and obtained legal identity documents from these groups have had to weather the change of regime when these de facto sovereigns faltered (Clark et al., 2018; Norwegian Refugee Council, 2019).

We posit that an analysis of the tug of war over legal identity in the context of an armed insurgency must be cognisant of these three perspectives. A study that reduces this phenomenon to 'merely' a matter of violent imposition or places it exclusively in the orbit of legal debate misses the point. To understand how legal identity is produced, contested, and compromised in the context of armed conflict, we must reckon with these three basic elements: It is intricately caught up with the violent assertion of sovereign rule (strand 1); it is shaped by people's everyday understanding of state conduct and the inclination of armed groups to emulate such conduct (strand 2); and it is conjugated with legal principles at various scales, including international law (strand 3).

Conclusion

This chapter opens up a new research agenda by suggesting that the conferral of and contestation over legal identity in the context of civil war comprises a highly significant but vastly understudied field of inquiry. We have reviewed contextual differences related to the nature of the insurgent movement, the nature of the state, and the trajectory of conflict. We have provided suggestions for a methodological lens through which the contested landscape of legal identity in rebel territory can be studied from a comparative and interdisciplinary perspective. We have also argued that the study of legal identity issued by non-state armed movements requires us to combine three conceptual lenses to capture the coercive, the performative, and the legal aspects of this phenomenon.

Our conclusions raise conceptual, empirical, and humanitarian questions that are relevant to both practitioners and academics. The humanitarian significance of the issue of legal identity in rebel-held territory in countries like Ukraine (Norwegian Refugee Council, 2018) and Syria (International Rescue Committee, 2016) has started to gain recognition. People who are confronted with rival sovereign claimants or have personal documentation from a legal referent that ceases to exist (or becomes proof of having been on the wrong side) undergo a Kafkaesque predicament that warrants international attention.

Legal identity is not merely a set of personal characteristics; it concerns a relationship between individuals and governing authorities or states, including a recognition of personhood with a concurrent bundle of rights and duties. The predominant reason someone carrying Islamic State documentation in territory reconquered by Iraq is facing enormous risks lies not with the data contained in the document but with the way this data is couched within the rival sovereign framework of the Islamic State. The North Cypriot government has the capacity and technology to produce passports, but these passports are not effective because of the unrecognised nature of that state. When the wife of a deceased combatant misses out on her pension because his death certificate was not issued by a recognised sovereign government, the main obstacle is probably not the information on the certificate, but instead its form as a referent of the wrong kind of sovereignty. The conceptual and normative challenge with this perspective is that sovereignty is ultimately self-referential. States are sovereign because they are; non-state armed groups are not because they are not. People caught in between can end up without a useful legal identity and without any recognised citizenship.

Notes

1 We gratefully acknowledge funding from the Statelessness Hallmark Research Initiative (University of Melbourne) and the Utrecht Centre for Global Challenges, as well as discussions with contributors at a related workshop (Utrecht, 13–14 June 2019) and the World Conference on Statelessness (The Hague, 26–27 June 2019). We are also thankful for feedback from Haqqi Bahram, Tendayi Bloom, and Nataliia Kasianenko on an earlier draft, and text editing by Lucia van der Meulen.
2 Some states also have non-citizen legal identities, such as that of the Bidoon in Kuwait (Benswait, this volume) or of Russian speakers in Estonia (Vollmer, this volume).
3 For the word 'humanitarian' see *Namibia Advisory Opinion*, para 122.

References

Advisory Opinion: Legal Consequences for States of the Continued Presence of South Africa in Namibia (South West Africa) Notwithstanding Security Council Resolution 276 [1970] ICJ Reports 1971 (*Namibia Advisory Opinion*).
Agamben, G. (2005) *State of Exception* (Chicago, IL: University of Chicago Press).
Albarazi, Z., and Tucker, J. (2014) 'Citizenship as political tool: The recent turmoil in the MENA and the creation and resolution of statelessness', *SSRN*, 8

January [Online]. Available at https://ssrn.com/abstract=2376426 (Accessed 13 March 2020).

Amnesty International (2018) 'The condemned: Women and children isolated, trapped and exploited in Iraq' [Online]. Available at www.amnesty.org/en/documents/mde14/8196/2018/en/ (Accessed 15 April 2020).

Arjona, A., Kasfir, N., and Mampilly, Z. (2015) *Rebel Governance in Civil War* (Cambridge: Cambridge University Press).

Balint, J., Evans, J., and McMillan, N. (2014) 'Rethinking transitional justice, redressing indigenous harm: A new conceptual approach', *International Journal of Transitional Justice*, 8, 194–216.

Bhabha, H. (1994) *The Location of Culture* (Abingdon: Routledge).

Butler, J. (1990) *Gender Trouble* (Abingdon: Routledge).

Clark, J., al-Zarier, B., and Al-Haj Ali, M. (2018) 'Marriage and birth certificates issued in rebel territory pose a "political risk"', *Syria Direct*, 15 January [Online]. Available at https://syriadirect.org/news/marriage-and-birth-certificates-issued-in-rebel-territory-pose-a-political-risk/ (Accessed 13 March 2020).

Cyprus v. Turkey [2001] ECHR Application No. 25781/94.

de la Cour Venning, A. (2019) 'Revolutionary law abidance: Kachin rebel governance and the adoption of IHL as resistance to Myanmar state violence', *International Criminal Law Review*, 19, 872–904.

Fortin, K. (2017) *The Accountability of Armed Groups under Human Rights Law* (Oxford: Oxford University Press).

Fortin, K. (2021) 'To be or not to be? Legal identity in crisis in non-international armed conflicts', *Human Rights Quarterly*, 43:1, 29–69.

Geertz, C. (1980) *Negara: The Theatre State in Nineteenth Century Bali* (Princeton, NJ: Princeton University Press).

Gelb, A., and Manby, B. (2016) 'Has development converged with human rights? Implications for the legal identity SDG', *Center for Global Development*, 3 November [Online]. Available at www.cgdev.org/blog/has-development-converged-human-rights-implications-legal-identity-sdg (Accessed 13 March 2020).

Hansen, T., and Stepputat, F. (2006) 'Sovereignty revisited', *Annual Review of Anthropology*, 35, 295–315.

Henrard, K. (2018) 'The shifting parameters of nationality', *Netherlands International Law Review*, 65:3, 269–97.

Ilascu and others v Moldova [2004] ECHR Application No. 48787/99.

Institute on Statelessness and Inclusion (2020) 'The world's stateless: Deprivation of nationality' [Online]. Available at https://files.institutesi.org/WORLD's_STATELESS_2020.pdf (Accessed 10 June 2020).

International Rescue Committee (2016) 'Identify me: The documentation crisis in northern Syria' [Online]. Available at www.rescue-uk.org/sites/default/files/document/1207/identify-me-july-2016-irc.pdf (Accessed 13 March 2020).

Kao, K., and Revkin, M. (2018) 'To punish or to pardon? Reintegrating rebel collaborators after conflict in Iraq', GLD Working Paper No. 17 [Online]. Available at https://gld.gu.se/media/1503/gld-working-paper-17-final.pdf (Accessed 13 March 2020).

Kasfir, N., Frerks, G., and Terpstra, N. (2017) 'Introduction: Armed groups and multi-layered governance', *Civil Wars*, 19:3, 257–278.

Kelly, T. (2006) *Law, Violence and Sovereignty among West Bank Palestinians* (Cambridge: Cambridge University Press).

Klem, B., and Maunaguru, S. (2017) 'Insurgent rule as sovereign mimicry and mutation: Governance, kingship and violence in civil wars', *Comparative Studies in Society and History*, 59:3, 629–656.

Kyris, G. (2018) 'Sovereignty and engagement without recognition: Explaining the failure of conflict resolution in Cyprus', *Ethnopolitics*, 17:4, 426–442.

Ladner, D., Jensen, E., and Saunders, S. (2015) 'A critical assessment of legal identity: What it promises and what it delivers', *Hague Journal on the Rule of Law*, 6, 47–74.

Lubkemann, S. (2008) *Culture in Chaos: An Anthropology of the Social Condition in War* (Chicago, IL: University of Chicago Press).

Mampilly, Z. (2011) *Rebel Rulers: Insurgent Governance and Civilian Life During War* (Ithaca, NY: Cornell University Press).

McConnell, F. (2016) *Rehearsing the State: The Political Practices of the Tibetan Government-in-Exile* (Chichester: Wiley Blackwell).

Mozer v Moldova [2016] ECHR Application No. 11138/10.

Murray, D. (2016) *Human Rights Obligations of Non-State Armed Groups* (London: Bloomsbury).

Navaro-Yashin, Y. (2003) '"Life is dead here": Sensing the political in "no man's land"', *Anthropological Theory*, 3:1, 107–125.

Norwegian Refugee Council (2018) 'Upholding the rights of conflict-affected population in Ukraine' [Online]. Available at www.nrc.no/globalassets/pdf/briefing-notes/upholding-rights-ukraine/pdf_upholding-the-rights-of-conflict-affected-populations-in-ukraine_eng_final.pdf (Accessed 13 March 2020).

Norwegian Refugee Council (2019) 'Barriers from Birth: Undocumented children in Iraq sentenced to a life on the margins' [Online]. Available at www.nrc.no/resources/reports/barriers-from-birth/ (Accessed 8 April 2020).

Revkin, M. (2016) 'The legal foundations of the Islamic State' [Online]. Available at www.brookings.edu/wp-content/uploads/2016/07/Brookings-Analysis-Paper_Mara-Revkin_Web.pdf (Accessed 8 April 2020).

Schuberth, M. (2015) 'The challenge of community-based armed groups: Towards a conceptualization of militias, gangs, and vigilantes', *Contemporary Security Policy*, 36:2, 296–320.

Sosnowski, M. (2018) 'Violence and order: The February 2016 cease-fire and the development of rebel governance institutions in southern Syria', *Civil Wars*, 20:2, 1–24.

Sprenkels, R. (2018) *After Insurgency: Revolution and Electoral Politics in El Salvador* (Notre Dame: University of Notre Dame Press).

Thiranagama, S. (2011) *In My Mother's House: Civil War in Sri Lanka* (Philadelphia, PA: University of Pennsylvania Press).

Underwood, A. (2019) 'Citizenship without borders: Russian passports for Ukrainian citizens', *Wilson Center*, 3 May [Online]. Available at www.wilsoncenter.org/blog-post/citizenship-without-borders-russian-passports-for-ukrainian-citizens (Accessed 13 March 2020).

United Nations (1961) *Convention on the Reduction of Statelessness* [Online]. Available at https://legal.un.org/ilc/texts/instruments/english/conventions/6_1_1961.pdf (Accessed 13 March 2020).

United Nations (1966) *International Covenant on Civil and Political Rights* [Online]. Available at https://treaties.un.org/doc/publication/unts/volume%20999/volume-999-i-14668-english.pdf (Accessed 13 March 2020).

United Nations Human Rights (1989) *Convention on the Rights of the Child* [Online]. Available at www.ohchr.org/en/professionalinterest/pages/crc.aspx (Accessed 13 March 2020).

Vandekerckhove, N. (2011) 'The state, the rebel and the chief: Public authority and land disputes in Assam, India', *Development and Change*, 42:3, 759–779.

Watts, N. (2010) *Activists in Office: Kurdish Politics and Protest in Turkey* (Seattle: University of Washington Press).

Weber, C. (1995) *Simulating Sovereignty: Intervention, the State and Symbolic Exchange* (Cambridge: Cambridge University Press).

White, M., Chapman, G., Cleese, J., Idle, E., Gilliam, T., Jones, T., and Palin, M. (1975) *Monty Python and the Holy Grail* (Columbia TriStar Home Entertainment).

World Bank (2016) *World Development Report 2016: Digital Dividends* [Online]. Available at www.worldbank.org/en/publication/wdr2016 (Accessed 15 April 2020).

Part II

Living with the problem of citizenship

Figure 3

Obsession

Manal Deeb

Obsession is an empowering artwork to reveal self-identification from beneath layers of originality in an arena of cultural displacement. It provides viewers a chance to peek into the inner statehood of a stateless vision, a delusional gaze, yet a righteous recognition. As one layer, the representation of Arabic calligraphy is a flow of emotions along with the expression of the face. It is not meant to be readable, though viewers may try to insert their own meaning. This is a self-reflection of determination to artistically fight against rejection and stereotype.

Since personality extends itself beyond present existence to what is the past, my self-consciousness to preserve my Palestinian identity made me concerned and accountable for my past, just upon the same ground and for the same reason as I do for the present. A desire for happiness, which is the unavoidable attendance of consciousness of pleasure and pain, my work is an attempt to reach a conscious happiness away from home (in exile).

My artwork presents many identities that are indistinguishable. Each identity has the same apparent memories and perceives identical surroundings, while believing, with evidence, to be representing the real self and the actual memories. My work demands something of the viewer. As one writer has described, I am saying: 'See me, I am not afraid.'

10

Transnational surrogacy, biocitizenship, and statelessness: India's response to the 'ghosts of the republic'

Pragna Paramita Mondal[1]

The conditions that produce statelessness exist in the governance of cross-border reproduction through surrogacy. Transnational commercial surrogacy involves women in the host countries acting as surrogates for foreign homosexual/heterosexual couples or single persons who aspire to parenthood but are unable or unwilling to bear children themselves. In surrogacy, parenthood claims are ridden by ethical complexities, and so is the citizenship claim of the child born to the surrogate woman in the host country and later taken by foreign commissioning parents to their home country. Different legal regimes across various cultures and countries recognise different actors in surrogacy as the bearer of citizenship rights; citizenship can thus be transferred to the newborn through the birth mother, the genetic mother, the genetic father, or the adoptive parents. However, this variance and diversity in laws governing nationality and citizenship attribution in surrogacy can lead to statelessness.

The French Court of Cassation in July 2015, for instance, identified children born through surrogacy abroad as the 'ghosts of the republic' given the illegality of surrogacy in France. The Court thereby hinted at the obscured, ghosted status of individuals whose right to citizenship is held questionable by law. This chapter thus addresses the problematic of 'citizenship' in the context of transnational surrogate births by probing how doctrines of moral and political legitimacy determine the ascriptive value and legality of these 'biocitizens'. In countries where surrogacy is not permissible, extra-contractual considerations may control the outcome of the arrangement even though the surrogacy contract is labelled invalid. The implication of many such judgments acknowledging the 'negative obligations' generated in the context of transnational surrogacy is vital because it relates to questions on the ideology of citizenship, nationhood, identity, and belonging.

The Indian experience of transnational commercial surrogacy presents an interesting case. It operated in a legal void across several draft bills and amendments although the parenthood rights of the commissioning parents and the foreign citizenship rights of the surrogate child were clearly spelled out. The ban on international surrogacy in 2014 by the Indian government, and later its sole provisioning for married infertile Indian couples, was neatly outlined by a desire to legalise a certain category of domestic surrogate children who could inherit Indian nationality and Indian citizenship beyond any admissible doubt. The Surrogacy Regulation Bill (SRB) of 2016 invokes the idea of the 'legitimate' citizen and plays out the politics of non-engagement of an authoritarian state that apparently regards 'infertile' people as a monolithic category and surrogate babies as the problematic surplus. The SRB has thus consolidated anxieties about the non-legality of newborns resulting from transnational commercial surrogacy and redefined the parameters of 'legality' of surrogate babies in a broader sense.

Transnational surrogacy, biological citizenship, and statelessness

Gestational surrogacy is a form of Assisted Reproductive Technology (ART) in which a woman receives the genetic embryo of a commissioning party and carries the pregnancy to term on its behalf, either commercially or altruistically. The development of New Reproductive Technologies has been discussed critically as a fallout of capitalist globalisation (Rudrappa, 2016; DasGupta and Das Dasgupta, 2014; Sarojini and Marwah, 2014) with emphases on the effects of the *geneticisation* of women's bodies, or the need of a feminist politics to redefine risk and information in reproductive bio-markets (Hartmann, 2014). Transnational commercial surrogacy became popular in the past two decades as a part of the 'reproductive tourism' of the 'developed world' to the countries of the global South. This reproductive travel became rampant due to the absence of strict legal regimes in the countries of the global South, the affordability and accessibility of reproductive services, and the easy availability of women acting as surrogates there (Pande, 2014; Deomampo, 2017; Majumdar, 2017). However, the law's administration of transnational and domestic surrogacy varies widely across nations and transborder surrogacy thus yields its own set of complexities and contradictions.

The literature on transnational surrogacy highlights that it poses serious challenges to principles underlying the determination of citizenship among different nations (Nichol, 2016; Deomampo, 2017). Transnational surrogacy has resulted in the statelessness or 'not belonging' of the surrogate child, making them the most vulnerable stakeholder in the arrangement. This dilemma generates a counterpoint to the commodification argument on transnational surrogacy (Vora, 2009), however; had the surrogate baby been merely a 'product' bearing commodity status, the question of its belonging or ownership could have been resolved without engaging in legal and biopolitical complexities. The surrogate baby as a human subject with socio-political claims, needs, and rights thus busts the myth of its commodified origin and most certainly defeats its own commoditisation and moralistic appropriation.

While several thinkers have linked nationalism and citizenship to ideas of kinship (Anderson, 1983; Alonso, 1994) or regarded the commonality of racial origin and political history as conclusive (Balibar, 1991), transnational surrogacy redefines 'parents', 'kins', and 'citizens' and dismantles the *jus soli* ('right of the soil') or *jus sanguinis* ('right of blood') principles of determining citizenship. In the case of ARTs and transnational surrogacy, embryo creation sometimes requires genetic material from donors; the sperm or egg may have been provided by different individuals (having different nationalities) while the foetus is carried by another woman in a different country. This gives rise to several possibilities of ascertaining citizenship and each possibility, in fact, undercuts the spirit of the others. In Israel, for instance, the law upholds the right of the womb because Jewishness (in religious terms) is traditionally understood as being matrilineal and the gendered nature of citizenship stipulates that all children borne by Israeli surrogate women acquire Jewish citizenship following the line of gestational motherhood (Ministry of Health State of Israel, 1996).

Ethnographer Elly Teman (2010) reveals how the state made the Israeli surrogates recreate the notion of nation building based on ethnic lineage. Israel maintains a strictly regulated state-sponsored commercial surrogacy programme that was previously available only for infertile heterosexual Israeli couples, but was later extended to single women and in 2020, after much mobilisation and legal review, to homosexual Israeli citizens. The statute requires that the surrogate be an Israeli woman unrelated to the intended parent and mandates that the couple, the surrogate, and the donors (if required) share the same religion so that assigning citizenship to the child does not assume extra-constitutional dimensions.

Comparative research on Indian transnational surrogacy in American and European contexts suggests differential understandings of citizenship (Deomampo, 2015). In the United States, citizenship involves both the principles of *jus soli* and *jus sanguinis* and in the case of transnational surrogacy may be transferred from an American citizen to the genetic child. The Consular Report of Birth Abroad (CRBA) prescribes specific guidelines for U.S. citizens to produce clear and convincing evidence (sometimes in the form of DNA testing) of the child's biological relationship to the transmitting U.S. citizen parent. The 'birth certificate' procured from Indian infertility clinics as the vital legal document validating the transmission of U.S. citizenship is also open to diverse interpretations because it hinges on contextual meanings of biogenetic parenthood (see also Buterman, this volume). The U.S. statute thus requires one of the commissioning parents to initiate an adoption procedure back home if he/she is not genetically related to the surrogate child and refrains from being named as the parent in the Indian birth certificate. Recent studies have pointed out the perils of relying on the traditional biological approach of identifying legal parentage and have proposed the 'intent' clause as a tool to prevent statelessness among surrogate children (Nichol, 2016).

Most European countries (EU and non-EU) adhere to limited notions of biological citizenship within a rigorous moral and religious framework (Pennings, 2002; Rigon and Chateau, 2016). In March 2004, for example, in Italy – stronghold of the Roman Catholic Church – the government banned all gamete donation, embryo cryopreservation, and surrogacy procedures (Blyth and Farrand, 2005). In December 2011, the Holy Synod of the Bulgarian Orthodox Church issued a statement against assisted reproduction and surrogacy and labelled surrogate children 'impure' and commissioning parents 'infidels' (Brunet, 2013). There are also restrictions imposed in several other countries – including the ban on assisted reproduction for lesbians and single women in France, prohibition on oocyte donation and surrogacy in Norway and Germany, and sanctions on commercial surrogacy in Greece and the United Kingdom (Pennings et al., 2008).

ART laws present additional complexity in countries such as Norway. Norway bans commercial surrogacy, egg donation, and anonymous sperm donation on its soil in opposition to commodification and exploitation, and also as a means of prioritising genetic citizenship (Howell and Melhuus, 2007). In the case of surrogacy, nationality is constituted either by the commissioning Norwegian father who contributes his semen or by the birthing mother who lends her womb to gestate the child. Distinct from the American law on transnational surrogacy, however, citizenship cannot be transmitted from a Norwegian commissioning mother who has used her eggs to form the embryo because nationality is embedded not in the Norwegian egg but in the womb (Kr:løkke, 2012). The legal compass of transnational surrogacy thus drastically shifts across nations and has a direct bearing on the fate of surrogate children, who may become 'stateless' due to juridical or institutional contingencies.

Legal disputes around the citizenship rights of surrogate children may be understood by referring to two important cases of domestic surrogacy in the U.S. First, the 1987 *Baby M* case in New Jersey had a momentous influence on later interpretations of surrogacy contracts (Markens, 2007; Younger, 1988). This watershed case involved Mary Beth Whitehead, who was hired by the commissioning couple William and Elizabeth Stern to act as their surrogate. Whitehead subsequently changed her mind and, upon birth, refused to hand over the child to the couple. The Baby M case was a case of traditional surrogacy. Whitehead was inseminated with Stern's sperm and was the genetic mother of the child. Her claim was thus founded upon a much more complex biological, ethical, and legal paradigm; the case was conceived as a custody battle and was not specifically based on a violation pertaining to a breach of contract. Nonetheless, the two consecutive rulings on the case considered the enforceability of the surrogacy contract to settle the custody issue of the child and accepted the custodianship of the Sterns on the ground of protecting the best interests of the child while granting visitation rights to Whitehead (In the Matter of Baby M, 1988).

Second, in the 1993 *Johnson v. Calvert* case, the contract was cited by the Supreme Court of California as proof of intent and the ruling was set in favour of the plaintiffs Mark and Crispina Calvert. In this case, the surrogate was impregnated with the embryo created by the sperm and egg of the commissioning parents, who filed a petition seeking a declaration that they were the legal parents of the unborn child when the surrogate allegedly demanded that the payments were due in order for her to release the child. The judgment enforced the surrogacy contract and was based on the law stating that the natural mother is the one who *intended* to bring about the birth of the child and *intended* to raise it as her own. In fact, the surrogate, according to the jury, would not have been given the opportunity to become pregnant or deliver the child had she expressed her own *intent* to be the child's mother prior to implantation of the fertilised egg.

Transnational surrogacy litigations also are based on parentage claims and custody disputes that drive similar legal petitions for domestic surrogacy, but here the outstanding agenda behind settling legal parenthood is the determination of citizenship of children born in foreign countries through artificial reproduction. The 'ghosting' effect that laws in certain prohibitive countries have on defining the socio-legal status of these 'stateless' surrogate children is generally countered by statutes on provisioning the right to social and family life. Consider the 2014 *Mennesson v. France* and the 2014 *Labassee v. France* cases, for instance, in which babies born via U.S. surrogates to French intended parents were rendered stateless. French law denied citizenship rights under the pretext of implicitly validating a surrogacy contract by acknowledging 'certain negative obligations'. The European Court of Human Rights intervened and pronounced that no legal arrangement regarding the surrogate babies should result in the infringement of their right to respect for family and private life (Puppinck and Hougue, 2014). Although surrogacy remains prohibited in France, the French Court of Cassation in July 2015 repealed the earlier decree and ruled that these 'ghosts of the republic' would be granted civil status and allowed to share their parents' nationality.

The 2015 *Paradiso and Campanelli v. Italy* case presents a counterpoint to this argument on the validity of the contract and the birth certificate, bypassing statelessness while generating negative externalities for non-biological parenthood. An Italian couple utilised surrogacy in Russia but had no genetic link to the child because it was conceived through a donor programme and gestated by a Russian surrogate woman. The Russian birth certificate named the commissioning couple as the parents in view of the *intention* clause and because non-genetic parenting is legally permissible there. The Italian state prohibits surrogacy and assisted reproduction; it accused the commissioning parents of fraud when the genetic testing yielded negative results and dismissed the Russian birth certificate as invalid. In an extreme move, state authorities took the child from the Campanellis, opened proceedings for adoption on ground of abandonment, and later placed it with a foster family. While the Italian state recognised that the child had Italian citizenship through the Campanellis, it refused to bestow Mr. Campanelli with parental rights to prevent violation of national law – in disregard of rights to family and private life.

Across these judgments, whether sanctioned by law or not, the surrogacy contract within international legal premises seems to be a dubious reference point. It remains unacknowledged in many cases and overtly functional in others, while being irrevocably related to an assertion of the national and legal identity of the surrogate child. Despite its manifest unenforceability in complex and diverse ethico-legal situations, the contract continues to function as the irrefutable evidence of a negotiated exchange between consenting parties. This approach to understanding citizenship and statelessness in surrogacy is also useful as we deliberate on its implication in the Indian context.

Surrogate citizenship and statelessness within India's legal regime

The pre-legislation phase

In connection with international litigations, statelessness issues that surfaced in Indian commercial surrogacy pertained to legal sanctions in other countries. It was not the fallout of the lacuna that existed in the Indian lawmaking on assisted reproduction, and therefore does not justify the government-imposed ban on commercial surrogacy. Over the past three decades, India has witnessed myriad developments in the legal situation on surrogacy and has received consecutive drafts and revisions of the ART (Regulation) Bill (Government of India, 2008, 2010, 2014, 2016, 2019). The legislative process has shifted from a liberal to a carceral model (Kotiswaran, 2018) and has ended in a ban, first on transnational surrogacy, and later on all commercial surrogacy in 2016. Surrogacy and artificial reproduction began in India in the late 1990s and continued without legal or medical directives until 2005, when the Indian Council of Medical Research (ICMR) drafted the 'National Guidelines for Accreditation, Supervision and Regulation of ART Clinics in India'. These guidelines were framed as a general catalogue of prescriptive techniques for infertility treatment in India. However, it was not until 2008 that the ICMR began working on the recommendations for the ART (Regulation) Bill. Legal interventions on surrogacy in India began thereafter. Two major trials over citizenship rights in transnational surrogacy made global headlines during this period of legal ambiguity and shaped the motive and direction of future ART legislations in the country.

The much-publicised *Baby Manji* case involving a Japanese commissioning parent undergoing transnational surrogacy in India surfaced in 2008 (Mahapatra, 2008; Press Trust of India, 2008). Japanese law does not allow surrogacy and Manji Yamada, the surrogate baby, was thus caught in a legal flux and became stateless as the first 'surrogate orphan' (Pande, 2014). This citizenship row happened because of the incompatible legal frameworks in the two countries and the ex-post contractual alterations that changed the terms of custodial relations between the concerned parties. The commissioning couple got divorced before the baby was born and the commissioning mother refused to take custody of the child. The commissioning father failed to adopt the baby because the Indian Guardians and Wards Act (1890) prohibits a single man from adopting a girl. The Japanese Civil Code associates motherhood with birthing and in this case considered the surrogate as the legal mother. However, the surrogate had already handed over the baby and was not interested in having custody, thus eliminating the possibility of Indian citizenship. In the absence of an Indian passport, the baby was denied a Japanese passport or visa and was thus rendered stateless without claims to either Indian or Japanese nationality. The baby only had a 'certificate of identity' that is granted to stateless people in India. Mediations at the Rajasthan High Court and the Supreme Court of India eventually ensured that Mr. Yamada procured a birth certificate listing only the father's name and a one-year visa from the Japanese Embassy in India to allow the baby to travel to Japan with her grandmother as the female guardian (*Baby Manji Yamada vs Union of India*, 2008).

The 2009 *Jan Balaz v. Anand Municipality* case was another significant piece of litigation on citizenship crisis in cross-border surrogacy. The surrogate twins Nikolas and Leonard remained stateless for two years, deprived of both German and Indian citizenships (Mahapatra, 2010). The babies were not entitled to German citizenship because Germany did not yet recognise surrogacy. The Indian municipal birth certificate recorded the surrogate as the legal mother of the twins, but the Regional Passport Office (RPO) revoked Indian citizenship documents because legal provisions of surrogate citizenship in India were not yet spelled out clearly. The commissioning father moved the Gujarat High Court to secure Indian citizenship for the babies and facilitate inter-country adoption so that the process of applying for German citizenship could be initiated. The Court ruled in favour of the twins but made pronouncements on the gravity of the 'legal, moral and ethical issues, which have no precedents in this country' and invoked the debate on whether surrogate babies born in India were to be treated as Indian citizens (Mail Today Bureau, 2009).

The post-legislation phase

When the ART (Regulation) Draft Bills were drawn up, the onus of the legislators was to ensure that surrogate babies born to foreign commissioning couples in India were not subjected to statelessness. There was also the need to protect the rights of the child and to absolve the Indian state of ethical criticisms and diplomatic catastrophes due to inter-country citizenship litigations. Thus, the Draft Bills of 2008 and 2010 introduced the idea of local guardianship for cases of transnational surrogacy. The 2010 version additionally required foreigners to acquire documentation from their home country as proof that the baby would be allowed entry and granted their citizenship. The Draft Bills formulated the statute that the birth certificate of the surrogate child would bear the names of the commissioning couple as parents, thereby attesting the primacy of the legal contract in determining surrogate citizenship. This implied that under the Indian law, the surrogate child would naturally acquire the nationality of the commissioning (or the *intended*) parent.

Both Draft Bills penalised the act of abandoning the surrogate child under all circumstances, including when it is born with congenital anomalies. Statelessness induced by abandonment had been reported in 2012, for instance, when an Australian couple undergoing surrogacy in India had preferentially left behind one of their twins in a clinic in New Delhi. The surrogate baby boy was supposedly put up for adoption, but his whereabouts remain unknown (Doherty et al., 2014). In the controversial Baby Gammy case in Thailand in 2014, Australian parents allegedly took the healthy twin sister Pipah but abandoned the boy, Gammy, who was born with Down's Syndrome. The Thai surrogate mother eventually filed for custody of Pipah after the commissioning father was found to be a convicted child sex offender. Yet the Family Court of Western Australia allowed Pipah to remain with the Farnells under regular supervision by child protection authorities. The judgment also cleared the commissioning parents of abandoning Gammy, stating that they were forced to leave him because it was the surrogate mother's wish to keep the boy with her in Thailand. This ruling emphasised the need to recognise the ethical and emotional dilemmas that arise when the contractuality of a surrogacy procedure is overridden (Pearlman, 2016).

In 2012, the Indian Ministry of Home Affairs (Foreigners Division) mandated the 'surrogacy visa' for foreigners and dictated that only heterosexual married couples would be allowed to engage in surrogacy in India. This was followed by the 2014 Draft Bill prohibiting foreigners from seeking commercial surrogacy services in India while still including NRIs (Non-Resident Indian), OCIs (Overseas Citizen of India), PIOs (Person of Indian Origin), and foreigners married to Indian citizens on the list. The Surrogacy (Regulation) Bill of 2016 and 2019 changed the rhetoric of artificial reproduction in India and banned all commercial surrogacy. Altruistic surrogacy (with a 'close female relative' acting as the surrogate) was restricted to married Indian couples experiencing at least five years of proven infertility and excluded NRIs, OCIs, PIOs, and foreigners – even while NRIs and OCIs enjoy certain citizenship privileges.[2]

My field research on Indian surrogacy in the cities of Kolkata, Mumbai, Pune, Anand, and Howrah between 2014 and 2017 revealed underlying tensions that stakeholders faced during the extended period of surrogacy legislation. One of the strongest criticisms against the ban on commercial transnational surrogacy was voiced by Indians based abroad (the NRIs, OCIs, and PIOs) who were completely phased out of the list of eligible recipients of surrogacy services in India. Their perceived sense of discrimination followed from a neoliberal critique of market restrictions, and some of them considered this prohibition and their generalisation with other foreign nationals as a case of selective victimisation. According to some of my respondents, the ban compromised the investment and accrual rights that their partial citizenship in India offered in terms of entitlements. An OCI commissioning parent in Kolkata, who had undergone a successful surrogacy in 2014 and had intended to repeat the procedure for a second child, responded to their exclusion in 2016: 'This is a betrayal on the Indian government's part… There is such a hue and cry about diaspora outreach and investments in "Make in India" projects… I do not understand how there can be citizenship issues or ethical dilemmas if they think of us as their own people…'

An IVF specialist in a reputed clinic in Mumbai expressed dissatisfaction with the 'systemic failure' argument that the Ministry of External Affairs brought to the table (personal interview, 2017). The notion of 'legality' that the SRB 2016 was realigning thus encompassed the citizenship claims of the 'infertile' (as defined in the Bill) who sought surrogacy, the citizenship rights of surrogate children, and the field of professional medical ethics that practitioners were responsible for. The SRB also validated the prescriptive model of citizenship that the Indian state was gravitating towards and there was a deliberate reconstruction of the status of a 'citizen' and what defines citizenship in the particular context of reproduction.

Conclusion

Indian laws on surrogacy (as they evolved until 2014) assumed a liberal and scientific approach towards surrogacy with a focus on issues such as: the compensation and insurance privileges of the surrogate women, the custodial rights of commissioning parents secured through the designated surrogacy birth certificates, IVF clinics' accountability in medical negligence, anti-abandonment clause and citizenship rights of the child, and the monitoring and supervision by surrogacy boards. The blanket ban on foreigners and on commercial surrogacy involving cross-border citizenship issues undercut the spirit of previous legislation and was the first step towards promoting a model of non-transactive, non-market, kinship-based altruistic surrogacy in the subsequent phases. A rational, non-interventionist protocol in the Indian case could certainly resolve ethical and legal dilemmas in international surrogacy and forge a just and inclusive form of biocitizenship.

Denial of citizenship in cross-border surrogacy could create 'domino effects' for the surrogate child's inheritance and civil rights, and its rights to identity and private life. Some recommended legal reforms on transnational surrogacy use the existing 1993 Hague Convention on Intercountry Adoption and develop 'soft law measures' through international judicial convergence and collaboration to preserve the best interests of the surrogate child (Wells-Greco, 2015; Thomale, 2017). Some have also suggested an international legal instrument or a global convention on surrogacy that ratifies the commercial, remunerative nature of surrogacy procedures and is based on standard legal practices and common strategies of supervision, and is also able to protect the child's right to access private genetic information (Trimmings and Beaumont, 2011).

A significant effort in designing a global Protocol on legal parentage pertaining to international surrogacy agreement (ISA) and surrogate citizenship has been underway as part of the Hague Conference on Private International Law's (HCCH) Parentage / Surrogacy Project (HCCH, 2020). Seven meetings of the Council on General Affairs and Policy (CGAP) have so far been convened since 2012 to discuss the conditions of determining parental legality in international adoption and surrogacy cases. The latest report submitted by the CGAP in October 2020 suggests that the ad-hoc remedies offered by judicial and administrative authorities in international surrogacy disputes need to be replaced with either a more robust 'recognition approach' based on the method of certification or with a 'traditional private international law approach' of ascertaining legal parentage in diverse contexts (Project, 2020). The Experts' Group is keen on outlining the obligatory nature of provisions following the recognition method and maps an 'a posteriori', an 'a priori', or a combination of both approaches to execute verification and safeguard measures before the certification mechanism is deployed by states. The initiative is still in the consultation phase and is working towards building consensus on major issues in legalising surrogate parenthood at the international and domestic levels. It attests to the fact that the future directions in recognising the factuality of non-biological parenthood and in framing accommodative policies on citizenship demand a more unified, progressive and responsible lawmaking on surrogacy across countries and regimes.

Notes

1 I would like to thank my PhD supervisor, Prof. Achin Chakraborty, for his valuable comments and insights. Thanks are also due to the editors and the anonymous reviewer for their critical inputs in preparing the final draft.
2 In response to this blanket ban, OCIs submitted a plea of intervention to the Supreme Court of India in 2015. The ban has not been lifted, though there are now some recommendations in their favour made by the Select Committee in its latest Report presented at the Rajya Sabha (Upper House) on 5 February 2020.

References

Alonso, A. M. (1994) 'The politics of space, time and substance: State formation, nationalism, and ethnicity', *Annual Review of Anthropology*, 23, 379–405.

Anderson, B. (1983) *Imagined Communities: Reflections on the Origin and Spread of Nationalism* (London: Verso).

Balibar, É. (1991) 'Racism and nationalism', in É. Balibar and I. Wallerstein (eds) *Race, Nation and Class: Ambiguous Identities* (London: Verso): pp. 37–67.

Blyth, E., and Farrand, A. (2005) 'Reproductive tourism – A price worth paying for reproductive autonomy?', *Critical Social Policy*, 25:1, 91–114.

Brunet, L. (2013) *A Comparative Study in the Regime of Surrogacy in EU Member States. A Study, Directorate General for Internal Policies, Policies Department C: Citizens' Rights and Constitutional Affairs* (Brussels: Legal and Parliamentary Affairs, European Parliament).

DasGupta, S., and Das Dasgupta, S. (eds) (2014) *Globalization and Transnational Surrogacy in India* (Lanham, MD: Lexington Books).

Deomampo, D. (2015) 'Defining parents, making citizens: Nationality and citizenship in transnational surrogacy', *Medical Anthropology*, 34, 210–225.

Deomampo, D. (2017) *Transnational Surrogacy Race, Kinship, and Commercial Surrogacy in India* (New York: New York University Press).

Doherty, B., Davey, M., and Hurst, D. (2014) 'Surrogate baby left in India by Australian couple was not trafficked, investigation finds', *The Guardian*, 9 October [Online]. Available at www.theguardian.com/australia-news/2014/oct/09/surrogate-baby-left-in-india-by-australian-couple-was-not-trafficked-investigation-finds (Accessed 5 June 2020).

European Court of Human Rights (2014a) *Labassee v. France*, Application No. 65941/11.

European Court of Human Rights (2014b) *Mennesson v. France*, Application no 65192/11.

European Court of Human Rights (2015) *Paradiso and Campanelli v. Italy*, Application No. 25358/12.

Government of India (2008) *The Assisted Reproductive Technology (Regulation) Bill, 2008* [Online]. Available at www.prsindia.org/uploads/media/vikas_doc/docs/1241500084~~DraftARTBill.pdf (Accessed 20 July 2020).

Government of India (2010) *The Assisted Reproductive Technologies (Regulation) Bill, 2010* [Online]. Available at https://main.icmr.nic.in/sites/default/files/guidelines/ART%20REGULATION%20Draft%20Bill1.pdf (Accessed 22 July 2020).

Government of India (2014) *Assisted Reproductive Technology (Regulation) Bill, 2014* [Online]. Available at https://www.prsindia.org/uploads/media/draft/Draft%20Assisted%20Reproductive%20Technology%20(Regulation)%20Bill,%202014.pdf (Accessed 20 July 2020).

Government of India (2016) *The Surrogacy (Regulation) Bill, 2016* [Online]. Available at www.prsindia.org/sites/default/files/bill_files/Surrogacy%20%28Regulation%29%20Bill%2C%202016.pdf (Accessed 20 July 2020).

Government of India (2019) *The Surrogacy (Regulation) Bill 2019* [Online]. Available at www.prsindia.org/sites/default/files/bill_files/Surrogacy%20(Regulation)%20Bill,%202019.pdf (Accessed 20 July 2020).

Gujarat High Court (2009) *Jan Balaz v. Anand Municipality and Others*, Special Civil Application No. 3020 of 2008.

Hartmann, B. (2014) 'The gene express; speeding towards what future?', in N. Sarojini and V. Marwah (eds) *Reconfiguring Reproduction Feminist Health Perspectives on Assisted Reproductive Technologies* (New Delhi: Zubaan): pp. 22–31.

Hague Conference on Private International Law (HCCH). (2020). *The Parentage / Surrogacy Project*. Available at www.hcch.net/en/projects/legislative-projects/parentage-surrogacy (Accessed 16 November 2020).

Howell, S., and Melhuus, M. (2007) 'Race, biology and culture in contemporary Norway: Identity and belonging in adoption, donor gametes and immigration', in P. Wade (ed.) *Race, Ethnicity and Nation: Perspectives from Kinship and Genetics* (New York: Berghahn Books): pp. 53–71.

Indian Council of Medical Research (2005) *National Guidelines for Accreditation, Supervision and Regulation of ART Clinics in India* (New Delhi: Ministry of Health and Family Welfare, Government of India).

Kotiswaran, P. (2018) 'Law's paradoxes: Governing surrogacy in India', in S. Mitra, S. Schicktanz, and T. Patel (eds) *Cross-Cultural Comparisons on Surrogacy and Egg Donation Interdisciplinary Perspectives from India, Germany and Israel* (Cham: Palgrave Macmillan): pp. 127–151.

Kroløkke, C. (2012) 'From India with love: Troublesome citizens of fertility travel', *Cultural Politics*, 8:2, 307–325.

Mahapatra, D. (2008) 'Baby Manji's case throws up need for law on surrogacy', *The Times of India*, 25 August [Online]. Available at https://timesofindia.indiatimes.com/india/Baby-Manjis-case-throws-up-need-for-law-on-surrogacy/articleshow/3400842.cms (Accessed 3 June 2020).

Mahapatra, D. (2010) 'German surrogate twins to go home', *The Times of India*, 27 May [Online]. Available at https://timesofindia.indiatimes.com/india/German-surrogate-twins-to-go-home/articleshow/5978925.cms (Accessed 3 June 2020).

Majumdar, A. (2017) *Transnational Commercial Surrogacy and the (Un)Making of Kin in India* (New Delhi: Oxford University Press).

Markens, S. (2007) *Surrogate Motherhood and the Politics of Reproduction* (Berkeley, CA: University of California Press).

Mail Today Bureau (2009) 'Surrogate babies born in India are Indians', *India Today*, 13 November [Online]. Available at www.indiatoday.in/india/story/surrogate-babies-born-in-india-are-indians-60734-2009-11-13 (Accessed 3 June 2020).

Ministry of Health State of Israel (1996) *Agreements to Carry a Fetus Law (Agreement Approval and Status of the Infant)* [Online]. Available at www.health.gov.il/English/Topics/fertility/Surrogacy/Pages/default.aspx (Accessed 10 December 2019).

New Jersey Supreme Court (1988) *In the Matter of Baby M*, 537 A.2d 1227, 109 N.J. 396.

Nichol, B. M. (2016) 'A child without a country: Dissolving the statelessness of children born through surrogacy', *Michigan State Law Review*, 907, 907–945.

Pande, A. (2014) *Wombs in Labor: Transnational Commercial Surrogacy in India* (New York: Columbia University Press).

Pearlman, J. (2016) '"Baby Gammy" was not abandoned in Thailand, court rules', *The Telegraph*, 14 April [Online]. Available at www.telegraph.co.uk/news/2016/04/14/baby-gammy-was-not-abandoned-in-thailand-court-rules/ (Accessed 3 June 2020).

Pennings, G. (2002) 'Reproductive tourism as moral pluralism in motion', *Journal of Medical Ethics*, 28, 337–341.

Pennings, G., de Wert, G., Shenfield, F., Cohen, J., Tarlatzis, B., and Devroey, P. (2008) 'ESHRE taskforceonethics and law 15: Cross-border reproductive care', *Human Reproduction*, 23:10, 2182–2184.

Press Trust of India (2008) 'Baby Manji to unite with dad in Japan', *India Today*, 31 October [Online]. Available at www.indiatoday.in/latest-headlines/story/baby-manji-to-unite-with-dad-in-japan-32578-2008-10-31 (Accessed 3 June 2020).

Project, E. G. (2020, October) 'Report of the Experts' Group on the Parentage / Surrogacy Project (meeting from 12 to 16 October 2020)'. Available at https://assets.hcch.net/docs/a6aa2fd2-5aef-44fa-8088-514e93ae251d.pdf (Accessed 15 November 2020).

Puppinck, G., and Hougue, C. (2014) 'ECHR: Towards the liberalisation of surrogacy: Regarding the *Mennesson v. France* and *Labassee v. France Cases* (N°65192/11 & N°65941/11)' *Revue Lamy Droit Civil*, 118.

Rigon, A., and Chateau, C. (2016) 'Regulating international surrogacy arrangements – state of play', European Parliament [Online]. Available at www.europarl.europa. eu/RegData/etudes/BRIE/2016/571368/IPOL_BRI(2016)571368_EN.pdf (Accessed 3 June 2020).

Rudrappa, S. (2016) *Discounted Life: The Price of Global Surrogacy in India* (New Delhi: Orient Blackswan).

Sarojini, N., and Marwah, V. (2014) *Reconfiguring Reproduction: Feminist Health Perspectives on Assisted Reproductive Technologies* (New Delhi: Zubaan).

Supreme Court of California (1993) *Johnson v. Calvert*, 851 P.2d 776.

Supreme Court of India (2008) *Baby Manji Yamada vs Union of India*, Writ Petition (C) No. 369.

Teman, E. (2010) *Birthing a Mother: The Surrogate Body and the Pregnant Self* (Berkeley, CA: University of California Press).

Thomale, C. (2017) 'State of play of cross-border surrogacy arrangements – Is there a case for regulatory intervention by the EU?', *Journal of Private International Law*, 13:2, 463–473.

Trimmings, K., and Beaumont, P. (2011) 'International surrogacy arrangements: An urgent need for legal regulation at the international level', *Journal of Private International Law*, 7:3, 627–647.

Vora, K. (2009) 'Indian transnational surrogacy and the commodification of vital energy', *Subjectivity*, 28, 266–78.

Wells-Greco, M. (2015) *The Status of Children Arising from Inter-Country Surrogacy Arrangements* (The Hague: Eleven International Publishing).

Younger, J. T. (1988) 'What the Baby M case is really all about', *Law & Inequality: A Journal of Theory and Practice*, 6:2, 75–82.

11

The birth certificate as fetish object in the governance of citizenship and its presumed sex and gender norms

Jan Lukas Buterman

Identification documentation such as birth certificates authenticate an individual's right to access privileges associated with citizenship. This means that in jurisdictions where a birth certificate requires a person to be located, from birth, within one and only one of two classifications: male or female, such location is also made necessary for citizenship (Monro, 2003; Spade, 2008; Currah, 2009; Amnesty International, 2014). Where the technology of the birth certificate, an administrative tool, is revered above that of the person in the allocation of membership and rights, it arguably reaches the status of 'fetish'. This chapter examines some of the ways that birth certificates afford a particular type of citizenship, predicated on cisheterosexual norms as an unquestioned imaginarium of the 'good' citizen. It finds that this may exclude trans and queer persons within a state's borders from enjoying the benefits of citizenship, in addition to constructing stateless persons by excluding some people from accessing birth certificates.

Identification technologies as technologies of the state

States rely upon the ability to recognise a citizen through proxies like identification documents such as the birth certificate. However, individuals are not born fully formed citizens. Even in jurisdictions where citizenship is conferred by birth, the birth itself must first be recognised through the formal administrative process of birth registration (problems with this are identified in Mondal, this volume). Birth registration is a key part of establishing legal identity and citizenship, and official documentation arising from that registration – such as the birth certificate – is required subsequently to prove that any given individual is a citizen (United Nations Children's Fund, 2019). Being incapable of presenting this identification documentation means that an individual is incapable of proving that they have a relationship with a state, and may thus not be considered a national under its law.

My concerns about identification documents as technology were sparked by my experiences – then and even now – of transitioning from one sex to another. Even as someone who has not relocated across a jurisdictional border, processes to amend my documentation were not straightforward. Amending my documents revealed the need to engage in complex, sometimes even conflicting, statutory and regulatory processes, problems that transcend any particular jurisdiction (Couch et al., 2008). It became clear that any problems with a foundational document, such as a birth certificate, resulted in (or at least contributed to) many other significant problems, such as access to housing, employment, education, and so forth (Grant et al., 2011). Beyond being often a frustratingly difficult document to amend for trans people, what is a birth certificate? What does it do?

Birth certificates

A birth certificate is a foundational identification technology. It underpins the ability to acquire further identification documents necessary for work, study, or other activities (Watkins, 2007). This physical document is used by many jurisdictions and administrative bodies to determine citizenship and identity by establishing a legal name and codifying family relations. It establishes 'the existence of a person under law, and lays the foundation for safeguarding civil, political, economic, social and cultural rights' (UNHRC, 2014: 3).

The birth certificate is comprised of a number of technologies intended to serve administrative needs. Drawing on data enmeshed within a larger birth registration process, birth certificates are documents rendered physically on some form of substrate, often paper or polymer, standardised throughout any given issuing jurisdiction. Other conventions such as calendar reckoning, geographical descriptions, naming practices, and familial lineage are all technologies incorporated into and expressed through the birth certificate. Any specifications, conventions, or standards employed in the birth registration process, as well as any resulting artefacts such as birth certificates, are administered by each issuing jurisdiction.

Normative conventions

Birth certificates extend the ability of the state to impose its norms on its population. As a technology of state, the birth certificate is a powerful regulator of sex and gender norms (Buterman, 2017). These norms form an imaginarium of the good or suitable citizen from birth onwards. States express this desired imaginarium through a wide assemblage of technologies, including laws, regulations, and policies, as well as data-gathering and management systems, and any attendant extrusions of those systems in the form of physical artefacts such as the birth certificate.

Male or female

Societies with rigid notions of male and female pose documentary problems for trans people that may be impossible to overcome without 'fundamental changes to the current system of sex and gender categorization' (Monro, 2003: 449). The legal determination of sex has varied throughout history, a determination made not by the individual in question but instead by 'a range of people from judges to physicians' (Whittle and Turner, 2007: 8.6). Paisley Currah (2009) underscores two key problems for trans people, both centred on the state: 'inconsistency between jurisdictions on the question of legal definition of sex for the purposes of sex designation or the applicability of sex discrimination laws' (249) and 'inconsistency within jurisdictions in the legal definition of sex for different social functions (such as driver's licences, birth certificates, marriages, passports, veterans benefits)' (249–250). While socially, individuals may express many different identities that go beyond rigid classifications of male or female, state identification practices erase or even exclude such persons from recognition or participation as citizens. Sally Hines (2007) notes that people who 'construct identities outside the gender binary remain on the margins of citizenship: residing as non-citizens' (14).

Even for trans people who transition within a gender binary, accessing citizenship rights remains difficult. Case law reifies 'theories of the normal' (Lloyd, 2005: 153) that are used to exclude trans people from basic civil rights protections, even to the point of facing 'systemic dismissal... as legal subjects' (Lloyd, 2005: 154). The very existence of trans people, 'with their conflicting identity documentation and binary-defying bodies, resist the state-constructed notion that possessing and living a single, static, easily categorisable identity individualise each citizen' (Herman, 2015: 88). Even in jurisdictions that allow for the amendment of documents such as birth certificates, individuals are typically still required to conform to a strict male–female binary (De Mauro Rucovsky, 2019). As B Camminga (2017) notes, 'there is a connection here between the performance of gender, its use as an administrative tool, nationhood, and citizenship' (69).

Language

The state's imaginarium of a good citizen may include rigid notions of what is a suitable name for an infant assigned to a particular gender (Josephson and Einarsdóttir, 2016), a practice that ossifies both gender and cultural norms into birth documentation. Similar issues arise from norms governing the specific language or orthography allowed in birth registrations. An obvious issue is the problem posed by disallowing people to name their children according to their own language. Related issues arise when such norms also force people to use orthography that does not correctly reflect the spelling nor meaning of a name, compounded further by claims of technological limitations that would prevent the inclusion of broader orthography for official documentation purposes (Gullberg, 2016). These are examples of birth certificates obsolescing or nullifying personal narratives of kinship and belonging, as that might otherwise be expressed through traditional names or even languages of cultures that may be passively or actively disallowed by the state.

Family status

Family status is yet another expression of the imaginarium of the state enmeshed within the birth certificate. These norms are deployed against parents (whether cis or trans) who may be prevented from obtaining birth certificates for their offspring. For example, one state's imaginarium of the good citizen includes being a heterocitizenly-married citizen, thus creating barriers for single mothers, or mothers married to non-citizen fathers, to obtain foundation documents such as citizenship certificates for their children (Mulmi and Shneiderman, 2017). Birth registration and certification may be denied for many reasons, including one's family status (see Paramita Mondal, this book). The newborn infant, though supposedly entitled to full civil and human rights protection by virtue of being human, finds instead that its rights are contingent upon factors delimited by an authoritative sphere that does not necessarily contemplate diverse expressions of gender, sexuality, or parentage (see Schnyder, this volume). Gender alone may play a critical role in preventing birth registration. Approximately twenty nations do not allow women to pass citizenship to their children (UNHCR, n.d.). In jurisdictions where a child can only be registered by its father, single female-identified parents, same-sex parents who identify as female, or even mixed-sex parents with a noncitizen father would not be able to ensure their offspring have citizenship.

For trans people specifically, additional complexities arise regarding the meaning and use of certain data fields on birth certificates. For example, an individual who is legally a man, but who subsequently becomes pregnant and gives birth, may be refused the right to be labelled as the child's father on the birth certificate (Booth, 2020). In my own experience, I was able to change both name and sex, but discovered that newly ordered birth certificates for my children listed my prior legal name as the mother, meaning that I had no formal document establishing my legal relationship to my own minor children. Any claims that I may make regarding who I am, or who my offspring are, cannot be substantiated and authenticated without formal identification artefacts (Lyon and Bennett, 2008). This means that I cannot narrate the fact of my own existence and that of my children; only formal identification artefacts can do so.

How did we get here?

Historically, birth certificates as we understand them today in many states – a centralised process administered by an authoritative sphere as opposed to records kept by families or religious organisations – began in Britain as a response to public health concerns when increased epidemic mortality swept through ever-growing urban centres (Brumberg et al., 2012). Birth certificates do not certify an individual's birth, but represent a certified abstract from a larger record, the birth registration. Birth registration records may include a wide variety of information, such as the length of gestation, birth weight, and so forth, most of which is not included in the certified abstract later used as an identification document for an individual. Birth registrations provide useful data for public health surveillance, including monitoring infant mortality and maternal health (Phillips et al., 2018), a key aspect of their invention and adoption across many jurisdictions.

Over time, this public-health oriented document has been incorporated into the schema of citizenship, becoming an essential technology of state that supposedly renders citizens intelligible to their state through formal identification systems. Birth certificates are so essential to the project of intelligibility that today two international treaty instruments recognise birth registration as a fundamental human right: the International Covenant on Civil and Political Rights (United Nations, 1966) and the Convention on the Rights of the Child (United Nations, 1989). The importance of this right is 'closely linked to the realization of many other rights; socioeconomic rights, such as the right to health and the right to education, are at particular risk where birth registration is not systematically carried out, and the protection of children is jeopardized' (UNHRC, 2014: 3).

Technology as a medium

A technology that becomes so enmeshed within our societies that we no longer take notice of it has become a 'medium'. A medium 'employs a particular symbolic code, as it finds its place in a particular social setting, as it insinuates itself into economic and political contexts' (Postman, 1985: 84). As in the examples above, we see the medium of the birth certificate employs a particular symbolic code, classifying and structuring individuals into administrative categories that may not reflect the lived experiences or realities of those it purports to represent. Similarly, the birth certificate has fully insinuated itself into both economic and political contexts; politically, the birth certificate is expected for citizenship to be determined, and economically, state-issued identification documents generally are expected for one to be able to participate in economic life.

One who has never faced challenges with obtaining a birth certificate may never consider the importance of that particular foundation document in their life. Yet as a medium, it is essential to understand that the technological effects produced by the birth certificate carry on into other identification documents (McLuhan, 1994). Birth certificates beget drivers' licences, passports, and a host of other formal documentation progeny that are increasingly expected for one to be able to participate fully in social and economic life.

The effects of a medium

Under Marshall and Eric McLuhan's (2007) notion of the laws of media, every medium has a fourfold effect. These laws frame these effects as enhancing, obsolescing, retrieving, and (when pushed to an extreme) reversing into something else. The discussion above provides numerous examples of birth certificates enhancing the power of the state through classifying its citizens according to rigid, predetermined categories such as sex and orthographies permitted for naming a child (in addition to other powers that may include limiting what a child might be named). Similarly, these examples show that the state's reliance on birth certificates obsolesces or nullifies individual agency to determine kinship, to attest that one belongs or is related to one who belongs, or to express a family status that does not meet the normative imaginarium of the state.

Retrieving dominion by the state

The remaining two effects are also salient to this analysis. First, a brief look at a medium's retrieval of something that was previously obsolesced is useful. In my own life, I was raised within a cultural imaginarium of freedoms that included the ability to pursue my interests and skills through education and employment opportunities. I was born and reside in Canada, a constitutional monarchy governed by a democratically elected parliament. Transitioning sex uncovered a myth of the state; I realised that the freedoms supposedly assured through democracy were not, in fact, available equally to all. Instead, I discovered that the birth certificate retrieved dominion over the individual by the state in a way that obliterated any freedoms I assumed I might fundamentally claim for myself, such as the freedom to identify myself correctly. If the state chose to ignore my request for amendments on my birth certificate, then any identification begat from the birth certificate would similarly challenge my ability to participate in economic and social life. Amending the birth certificate is thus 'not a personal matter, but one that involves the state' (Appell, 2014: 387). For a trans person, this involvement typically spans many different agencies and levels of government, even if the individual is not in the process of actively crossing a jurisdictional border (Koenig, 2011).

Sovereign states each maintain statutory instruments for determining citizenship. Such laws vary widely. Citizenship may be determined by location, that one is born within a particular territory. It may also be determined by lineage, that one is born of parents who are able to confer that citizenship to their offspring. Sometimes, citizenship is attainable through marriage to a citizen. Citizenship may also depend upon the period, such as in the case of a post-colonial state establishing different citizenship criteria than its colonial administration previously required.

Birth certificates establish a particular aggregation of technologies as a fact matrix that citizenship depends upon. Yet this matrix is an uneven yoke; while phrases such as 'birth registration' and 'birth certificates' are stated as a universal good and, indeed, a universal goal (UNHRC, 2014), such universality belies the fact that the assemblages – the laws, policies, regulations, norms and assumptions, and so forth – forming birth registration in any given jurisdiction vary widely, meaning that birth registration is not available to everyone at all times in all places (e.g. see Liew, this volume). 'Birth certificate' is a label that seemingly refers to a singular arte-fact, yet the implementation of birth registration and certification is far from cohesive.

This lack of cohesiveness matters a great deal. For one, it means that the treaty definition of a stateless person as 'a person who is not considered as a national by any State under the operation of its law' (United Nations General Assembly, 1954: Article 1.1) may well include persons one might assume easily qualified for citizenship within a state. Second, the expect-ation that '[e]very stateless person has duties to the country in which he finds himself, which require in particular that he conform to its laws and regulations as well as to measures taken for the maintenance of public order' (United Nations General Assembly, 1954: Article 2.1) is overtly impossible for those whose existence is considered contrary to the state's imaginarium of the 'good citizen' and expectations of public order. This includes, as per examples discussed above, trans people, queer people, unmarried people, people married to noncitizens, and so forth.

Even if not legally recognised as stateless, trans and queer individuals face barriers for obtaining birth certificates and the rights of citizenship within their home states, rendering them stateless in the sense of a lack of functioning citizenship (Kingston, 2019), a condition of noncitizenship (Bloom, 2018). Noncitizenship presents complications for crossing bor-ders, whether for temporary purposes such as work or travel, or permanent migration. International travel documentation standards are established by the International Civil Aviation Organisation. While these standards per-tain to documents such as passports, it is important to remember that pass-ports are not stand-alone documents; passports are begat from foundation documents such as birth certificates. Accordingly, trans people who cannot access correct foundation documents, or cis people who are prevented from obtaining these same documents, are effectively bound to the jurisdiction they find themselves within, as they cannot meet the preconditionary docu-mentary proofs required to obtain international travel documents such as passports. Again, while identification documents following from the birth certificate may not be identical, the effects of one medium always carry for-ward into its progeny (McLuhan, 1994), so the fourfold effects of the tech-nology of the birth certificate will also be expressed by other documents such as the passport.

With regard to migration, some jurisdictions will only recognise the sex identified in official state-issued documents, meaning that a trans per-son's immigration documents may not correctly reflect their identity and may not be amendable under that jurisdiction's existing legal, policy, and regulatory frameworks. Similarly, trans and queer refugees often cannot meet a burden of proof about their transness or queerness (Bachmann, 2017; Immigration and Refugee Board of Canada, 2017; UKLGIG, 2018). Immigration administrators basing their understanding of trans and queer lives on stereotypes or other culturally embedded stereotypes can get in the way of recognising and understanding the refugee's needs. Rather than being recognised for who they are, trans and queer people instead must rely upon identity categories imposed by authorities representing divergent norms and expectations, and may experience adverse effects from a prior jurisdiction imposed upon and expressed through the frameworks of a new jurisdiction.

When certainty reverses into a fetish

What happens when a medium is pushed to its extreme? The birth certificate, with its modern origins as part of an assemblage of public health surveillance practices, has changed to a foundational identification document. For clarity, the birth certificate was never intended to be an identification document, nor is it particularly well suited for this purpose. Regardless of its fitness for purpose, the birth certificate has come to be understood as essential for an individual to obtain citizenship. The desired universality of birth certificates has established them as a cultural fetish object. Bruno Latour (2010) directs us to the history, development, and deployment of the notion of a fetish, a term that refers to 'something irrationally reverenced' (Oxford English Dictionary, 2016), which applies here to the artefact of the birth certificate. Despite the many components that form a birth certificate having some degree of fluidity and instability – birth dates might be estimated, parentage may be incorrect, and so forth – once fixed in the artefact's structure, the birth certificate is itself irrationally reverenced as a source of pure, unalterable truth – a source of fact.

Yet, Latour (2010) disputes what a fact might be, noting that 'the word "fact" seems to point to an external reality, and the word "fetish" seems to designate the foolish beliefs of the subject' (21). The socio-cultural conditions in which the birth certificate exists maintain that the artefact is objectively factual, while the beliefs or understanding of the individual about their own identity are brushed aside in favour of the 'factishness' (Latour, 2010) of the fetish object. The fetishishation of the birth certificate allows for 'bureaucratic claims of our own official registers to know us to be ourselves alone, and no one else' (Groebner, 2001: 27). Ultimately, only the state may determine who we are, as we are rendered incapable of attesting to our identity, no matter how few facts the fetish object truly conveys.

Conclusion

The fourfold effects of the technology of the birth certificate are powerful and, in the expressed desire for universal implementation, affect every person. Even in circumstances where one has been unable to obtain a birth certificate (for whatever reason), states' expectation that every individual can produce such a document – and that such a document represents some sort of factual attestation about the person – means that the birth certificate still operates as a cultural fetish object. Through assemblages of law and technologies, exemplified in the birth certificate, states express and enforce norms that form a particular imaginarium of the 'good' citizen.

This imaginarium, however, is not shared; each jurisdiction has control over many different elements commonly found on the birth certificate. Consequently, the norms of one jurisdiction may be imposed on another, such as when a trans person is unable to migrate under their amended identity due to cisheteronormative barriers that remain in their originating jurisdiction. As the state demands intelligibility of its citizens through presenting a coherent birth certificate to establish citizenship and identity, those who are unable to do so remain unintelligible and incoherent to the state. The role that the technology of the birth certificate plays in reproducing both citizenship and statelessness must not be overlooked.

To ensure that technologies of state like the birth certificate do not function to exclude trans or queer people, it is crucial that such technologies are separated from normative presumptions or agendas relating to sex or to gender. Unnecessary categorisation should be removed from core identification tools. Where some form of sex or gender categorisation is required, it should be inclusive. This is relevant on the state level, but must also play out on the level of global data collection and analysis which also still presumes everyone can be neatly fitted into the categories of 'male' or 'female'. The focus of this chapter has been on implications of birth certificate technologies for transgender individuals. However, interrogating this fetishisation is crucial for understanding the role of the birth certificate much more widely.

References

Amnesty International (2014) 'The state decides who I am: Lack of legal gender recognition of transgender people in Europe' [Online]. Available at www.amnesty. org/en/documents/EUR01/001/2014/en/ (Accessed 30 April 2020).

Appell, A. R. (2014) 'Certifying identity', *Capital University Law Review*, 42:2, 361–405.

Bachmann, C. L. (2017) 'No safe refuge: experiences of LGBT asylum seekers in detention', Stonewall and UK Lesbian & Gay Immigration Group [Online]. Available at https://uklgig.org.uk/wp-content/uploads/2017/03/no_safe_refuge. pdf (Accessed 30 April 2020).

Bloom, T. (2018) *Noncitizenship: Recognising Noncitizen Capabilities in a World of Citizens* (Abingdon and New York: Routledge).

Booth, R. (2020) 'Transgender man loses appeal court battle to be registered as father', *The Guardian*, 29 April [Online]. Available at www.theguardian.com/ society/2020/apr/29/transgender-man-loses-appeal-court-battle-registered-father-freddy-mcconnell (Accessed 30 April 2020).

Brumberg, H. L., Dozor, D., and Golombek, S. G. (2012) 'History of the birth certificate: From inception to the future of electronic data', *Journal of Perinatology*, 32:6, 407–411.

Buterman, J. L. (2017) 'The question concerning identification: A tetradic analysis of the Alberta birth certificate' (unpublished Master's thesis, University of Alberta). doi.org/10.7939/R3ZC7S644.

Camminga, B. (2017) 'Categories and queues: The structural realities of gender and the South African asylum system', *TSQ: Transgender Studies Quarterly*, 4:1, 61–77.

Couch, M., Pitts, M., Croy, S., Mulcare, H., and Mitchell, A. (2008) 'Transgender people and the amendment of formal documentation: Matters of recognition and citizenship', *Health Sociology Review*, 17:3, 280–299.

Currah, P. (2009) 'The transgender rights imaginary', in M. Albertson Fineman, J. E. Jackson, and A. P. Romero (eds) *Feminist and Queer Legal Theory: Intimate Encounters, Uncomfortable Conversations* (Farnham, Surrey: Ashgate Publishing): pp. 245–257.

De Mauro Rucovsky, M. (2019) 'The travesti critique of the gender identity law in Argentina' (translated by I. Russell), *TSQ: Transgender Studies Quarterly*, 6:2, 223–238.

Grant, J. M., Mottet, L. A., Tanis, J., Harrison, J., Herman, J. L., and Keisling, M. (2011) 'Injustice at every turn: A report of the National Transgender Discrimination Survey', National Center for Transgender Equality and National Gay and Lesbian Task Force [Online]. Available at www.transequality.org/sites/ default/files/docs/resources/NTDS_Report.pdf (Accessed 30 April 2020).

Groebner, V. (2001) 'Describing the person, reading the signs in late medieval and renaissance Europe: Identity papers, vested figures, and the limits of identification, 1400–1600', in J. Caplan and J. Torpey (eds) *Documenting Individual Identity: The Development of State Practices in the Modern World* (Princeton, NJ: Princeton University Press): pp. 15–27.

Gullberg, S. (2016) 'Annual report 2015–2016', Office of the Languages Commissioner for the Northwest Territories [Online]. Available at https://olc-nt.ca/wp-content/uploads/2017/11/OLC-Annual-Report-for-2015-2016.pdf (Accessed 30 April 2020).

Herman, E. L. (2015) 'Tranarchism: Transgender embodiment and destabilization of the state', *Contemporary Justice Review*, 18:1, 76–92.

Hines, S. (2007) '(Trans)Forming gender: Social change and transgender citizenship', *Sociological Research Online*, 12:1, 1–18.

Immigration and Refugee Board of Canada (2017) 'Chairperson's guideline 9: Proceedings before the IRB involving sexual orientation and gender identity and expression' [Online]. Available at www.irb-cisr.gc.ca/en/legal-policy/policies/Pages/GuideDir09.aspx (Accessed 30 April 2020).

Josephson, J., and Einarsdóttir, Þ. (2016) 'Language purism and gender: Icelandic trans* activists and the Icelandic gender binary', *TSQ: Transgender Studies Quarterly*, 3:4, 376–387.

Kingston, L. N. (2019) *Fully Human: Personhood, Citizenship, and Rights* (Oxford: Oxford University Press).

Koenig, J. L. (2011) 'Distributive consequences of the medical model', *Harvard Civil Rights-Civil Liberties Law Review*, 46, 619–645.

Latour, B. (2010) *On the Modern Cult of the Factish Gods* (Durham, NC: Duke University Press).

Lloyd, A. W. (2005) 'Defining the human: Are transgender people strangers to the law?', *Berkeley Journal of Gender, Law & Justice*, 20:1, 150–195.

Lyon, D., and Bennett, C. J. (2008) 'Playing the ID card: Understanding the significance of identity card systems', in C. J. Bennett and D. Lyon (eds) *Playing the Identity Card: Surveillance, Security and Identification in Global Perspective* (Abingdon: Routledge): pp. 3–20.

McLuhan, M. (1994) *Understanding Media: The Extensions of Man* (Cambridge: MIT Press).

McLuhan, M., and McLuhan, E. (2007) *Laws of Media: The New Science* (Toronto: University of Toronto Press).

Monro, S. (2003) 'Transgender politics in the UK', *Critical Social Policy*, 23:4, 433–452.

Mulmi, S., and Shneiderman, S. (2017) 'Citizenship, gender and statelessness in Nepal: Before and after the 2015 constitution', in T. Bloom, K. Tonkiss, and P. Cole (eds) *Understanding Statelessness* (Abingdon: Routledge): pp. 135–152.

Oxford English Dictionary (2016) (Oxford: Oxford University Press).

Phillips, D. E., Adair, T., and Lopez, A. D. (2018) 'How useful are registered birth statistics for health and social policy? A global systematic assessment of the availability and quality of birth registration data', *Population Health Metrics*, 16:21, 1–13.

Postman, N. (1985) *Amusing Ourselves to Death: Public Discourse in the Age of Show Business* (New York: Penguin).

Spade, D. (2008) 'Documenting gender', *Hastings Law Journal*, 59, 731–841.

UK Lesbian & Gay Immigration Group (UKLGIG) (2018) 'Still falling short: The standard of Home Office decision-making in asylum claims based on sexual orientation and gender identity' [Online]. Available at https://uklgig.org.uk/wp-content/uploads/2018/07/Still-Falling-Short.pdf (Accessed 30 April 2020).

United Nations (1966) *International Covenant on Civil and Political Rights* [Online]. Available at www.ohchr.org/Documents/ProfessionalInterest/ccpr.pdf (Accessed 30 April 2020).

United Nations (1989) *Convention on the Rights of the Child*, Treaty Series, 1577, 3 (entered into force 2 September 1990). Available at www.ohchr.org/Documents/ProfessionalInterest/crc.pdf (Accessed 30 April 2020).

United Nations Children's Fund (UNICEF) (2019) 'Birth registration for every child by 2030: Are we on track?' [Online]. Available at https://data.unicef.org/resources/birth-registration-for-every-child-by-2030/ (Accessed 19 June 2020).

United Nations General Assembly (1954) *Convention Relating to the Status of Stateless Persons*, 28 September 1954, United Nations, Treaty Series, vol. 360, p. 117 [Online]. Available at www.refworld.org/docid/3ae6b3840.html (Accessed 30 April 2020).

United Nations High Commissioner for Refugees (UNHCR) (n.d.) 'Gender discrimination and childhood statelessness' [Online]. Available at www.unhcr.org/ibelong/wp-content/uploads/Gender-discrimination-childhood-statelessness-web.pdf (Accessed 30 April 2020).

United Nations Human Rights Council (UNHRC) (2014) 'Birth registration and the right of everyone to recognition everywhere as a person before the law' [Online]. Available at www.ohchr.org/Documents/Issues/Children/BirthRegistration/Report BirthRegistration.pdf (Accessed 30 April 2020).

Watkins, M. (2007) 'National ID cards', University of Ottawa, Canadian Internet Policy and Public Interest Clinic [Online]. Available at https://cippic.ca/en/national-id-cards (Accessed 30 April 2020).

Whittle, S., and Turner, L. (2007) 'Sex changes? Paradigm shifts in "sex" and "gender" following the Gender Recognition Act', *Sociological Research Online*, 12:1.

12

Seeking 'a right to belong': A stateless Shan youth's journey to citizenship in northern Thailand

Janepicha Cheva-Isarakul[1]

I am sitting opposite Muay,[2] a 20-year-old stateless Shan youth in her second year of a nursing degree. My right hand moves quickly to keep up with the long list of scholarships and loan services that she is citing to me. Even though Muay has spent all her life since the age of two in Thailand, is fluent in Thai, and has emotional attachment to the country, she is legally considered an 'alien' – a term used for a non-Thai and/or a stateless person. This status means that Muay has to pay an exorbitant fee as a foreign student at her university and has no access to financial aid from the Thai government. External scholarships and loans, therefore, are her lifelines to higher education. Ironically, one scholarship requires that a recipient promise to return to his/her 'home country' to develop their career. It is unclear whether a stateless person like Muay and the organisation administering the scholarship share the same definition of a 'home country'. What is clear is that the Thai state does not grant her the legal right to call Thailand 'home'.

Muay belongs to one of the groups of children and youth that Jacqueline Bhabha calls 'Arendt's children' (Bhabha, 2009: 413). One of the defining characteristics of this category includes not having a country to call their own because they are either non-citizens or children of non-citizens. Included within this term are citizen or migrant children living in so-called 'mixed status', or 'undocumented families, and unregistered or stateless children living in the country of their birth with their immigrant parents' (Bhabha, 2009: 413).[3] The term encompasses a child who may be qualified for a nationality of another country, but is not legally allowed to be present in their current location, as well as a citizen child who is at risk of being separated from their non-citizen parents.

That Bhabha's formulation focuses on children's *de facto* experience of insecurity, as opposed to their *de jure* qualification for a nationality in another country, is critical because it recognises statelessness as an emotional experience beyond a legal status.[4] The complex belonging of 'Arendt's children' also highlights the difficulties in distinguishing between the two contexts of statelessness – 'statelessness *in situ*' and 'statelessness in the migratory context' (see Vleiks, 2017). While legal scholars articulate the difference between the two contexts in terms of attachments to the state (through birth, long-term residence, family ties), the practical challenge remains that for many states, 'significant and stable ties' are narrowly legally interpreted by possessing a birth certificate from that country, rather than their lived experience (see Buterman, this volume). Even though long-term residence is considered a form of attachment to a country in which one lives according to international norms (UNHCR, 2014), children of 'temporary' labour migrants in many countries such as Thailand do not receive acknowledgement of their genuine connection to the state due to their parents' legal classification.

While it is widely acknowledged that statelessness is complex and multifaceted with 'no singular appropriate way to respond' (Bloom et al., 2017: 2; see also Bhabha, 2011; Lawrance and Stevens, 2017), identity documents occupy a central role in the United Nations High Commissioner for Refugees' (UNHCR) #IBelong Campaign to End Statelessness by 2024 as an important tool for statelessness identification, prevention, and reduction. As argued by Caroline Vandenabeele (2011), legal identity is in theory 'a primary right that exists regardless of whether one has a document to prove this citizenship' and '[o]fficial, government-issued and recognized documents… do not confer legal identity; they merely confirm it' (307). Despite this, in reality state-issued identity documents are seen as crucial to establishing a person's legal personhood (Lopez et al., 2012) in order to receive entitled rights and social protection. Some scholars, however, have noted this emphasis on identity documents as an 'end game' or as a means to unlock rights and reduce statelessness could inadvertently strengthen exclusion, undermine universal human rights, and place evidentiary burdens on those who are stateless (Reddy, 2015; Kingston, 2017; see also Lawrance and Stevens, 2017). The campaign acknowledges neither the instability of the regime of documentation issuance nor the fact that identity documents can be a commodity with a market of its own (see Sadiq, 2008). Instead, identity documents 'are often conflated with 'true' identity and belonging.

This chapter describes and examines the narrative of seeking documentation and legality of an 'Arendt's child', Muay, who was born in the Shan state and migrated to Thailand with her parents at the age of two. Material proof of identity, particularly a birth certificate, has become imperative in claiming 'a right to belong' in Thailand (*A Right to Belong*, 2002; see also Flaim, 2015 and 2017). Muay's inability to prove her birth in Thailand means that she lacks what the Thai laws consider 'meaningful connections'[5] with the Thai state, where she has been raised and educated. In order to obtain full legal status as a citizen, the option available to a child of migrants such as Muay is to recognise Myanmar as their official state. In other words, they can only resolve their *de facto* statelessness by getting citizenship from the state from which they fled.

By focusing on Muay's journey of seeking legality from Myanmar, this chapter provides two important insights. First, it sheds ethnographic light upon a common phenomenon Catherine Allerton calls 'documentary pragmatism' – a flexible attitude of stateless persons to the tactical acquisition or borrowing of identity documents (Allerton, 2017: 258). Allerton also warns that such pragmatism may have unintended or potentially problematic future consequences for children. Second, Muay's story helps us understand both the practical and emotional implications of narrowly interpreting legal ties to a particular type of documentation. Caught in the rhetoric of documentation as identity and legality, many stateless persons such as Muay are in search of a documentary solution not only to address their lack of legal status, but also to feel a sense of recognition and belonging. While on the surface the narrative in this chapter seems to suggest that acquisition of citizenship confers instantaneous belonging and puts statelessness to rest, it also reveals the violence of 'evidentiary burdens' on the stateless.

Muay: How a lifetime of statelessness ended in ten days

Muay is one of the first stateless youth I met when I started my PhD ethnographic fieldwork in 2015.[6] I was instantly intrigued by her life story, since at the time she was one of the few stateless youth in Chiang Mai enrolled in tertiary education. The truncated version of her life narrative below is based on four in-depth interviews I conducted with her between 2015 and 2018. As the language of these interviews was Thai, her words in this chapter are my translation.

The beginning of Muay's life story was a fate all too common among migrants from the Shan state – escaping from violence and oppression by Myanmar's military junta to search for better livelihoods in the more prosperous Thailand. The movements between present-day Myanmar's Shan state and Thailand's northern city of Chiang Mai, though historically regular and common, have increasingly been politicised, policed, and monitored in the last two decades.[7] At the time of her family's migration in the mid-1990s, however, Thailand was still transitioning from being a labour-exporting to a labour-importing country; its labour migration policies and management were ad-hoc (Chantavanich et al., 2007). As a result, the family was not classified as labour migrants, but instead as part of the 'Highland community (but not hill tribe)'.[8] Each family member was issued a card with a thirteen-digit-identification number beginning with the number six (commonly referred to as the 'Number Six Card'). This card allows its holder to reside in Thailand at the discretion of the Thai state and is renewed every ten years. However, a holder of a Number Six Card can, theoretically, be eligible for Thai citizenship if they were born in the country during a specific window of years. The fact that Muay was born outside of Thailand ruled out the possibility of her obtaining Thai citizenship despite her long-term residence in the country.

Muay had no recollection of her first two years in Myanmar. When her first memories were formed, she was already living in a rural district in Chiang Mai, where her parents settled and still reside. After completing grade nine at a Thai school in rural Chiang Mai, Muay faced a common dilemma among stateless youth: whether or not to continue her education. Further education was deemed pointless by adults around her, given the occupational restrictions imposed on stateless persons in Thailand. Until 2016, long-term stateless aliens in Thailand were legally restricted to twenty-seven occupations (UNHCR, n.d.). Muay described the decision to quit school as 'the most difficult period' in her life. Through a friend, she learned about the School for Shan State Nationalities Youth (SSSNY), which aims at educating Shan youth to become 'active citizens participating in social and political change in Burma' (SSSNY, n.d.). After completing the programme, Muay worked part-time as a teacher for a Shan-led organisation, providing evening classes to children of Shan migrants at construction sites around Chiang Mai. She studied part-time at a Burmese/Shan NGO that offered evening classes to adult migrant learners. These classes were taught in English by foreign volunteers to help prepare for the General Educational Development (GED) tests.[9] Muay used this American equivalent of a high school degree to enrol in a nursing programme. Informal education she received from the Shan activist groups increased her identification with Shan identity and its political struggle. Although her parents spoke to her in the Shan language while growing up, they did not tell her much about their lives in the Shan state. It was only through her later engagement with the Shan activist community that her Shan consciousness was born. Muay learned to read and write in Shan with the organisation. She describes the freedom she feels when with her Shan activist friends: 'There is no barrier. [Being with them] frees my thinking'.

In our meetings in the first year of my PhD fieldwork in 2015, Muay viewed her statelessness as transformative instead of limiting, as it provided her with an opportunity to learn about and embrace her Shan heritage. Given the determination displayed by the Thai state to address statelessness, she was still hopeful that change would come to children of migrants like her. However, Muay soon realised that as someone born outside of Thailand, she was not considered a priority group. In our subsequent meetings and interviews a few years afterwards, she grew increasingly frustrated by her inability to publicly claim any place 'home'. Despite her pride in her Shan identity, Muay also felt she could not convey her Shan identity to outsiders due to their lack of understanding. For example, when she had to introduce herself in front of her international peers at university, she said she was from 'Burma' to avoid further questions. 'Other people can say which country they are from but I don't feel that I could say I was from Thailand. Anyway, if I say I am from the Shan state, they will say: "The Shan state is in Burma. So, you are Burmese." ' To simplify things and minimise questions, she situationally adopted Burmese as her identity at university although she admitted feeling uneasy doing so, especially knowing the long history of oppression experienced by Shan people at the hands of the Myanmar military junta (Grundy-Warr and Wong Siew Yin, 2002; Laungaramsri, 2006; Quintana, 2010). In her words, 'Stateless children are confused about where they belong'. Statelessness, once seen by Muay as a source of empowerment and self-awareness, started to become increasingly burdensome and limiting.

The deadline of university graduation prompted Muay's determination to resolve her legal status. When she inquired with the Nursing and Midwifery Council whether she would be eligible to take a licensing exam as a Number Six Card holder, she received a negative response. They told her that a proof of citizenship was a requirement for sitting the exam.[10] Muay consulted with an NGO network on statelessness, who insisted that she was eligible and advised her to take the Council to court. Having little faith in the Thai judicial system, she did not want to dispute the case and instead sought the alternative option – returning to Myanmar to get citizenship so she could sit for the licensing exam and practise as a nurse in Thailand.

Muay prepared for her solo trip with much fear and anxiety, as this would only be the second time in her life that she went back to Myanmar after migrating to Thailand. 'I felt so nervous. There was also huge time pressure. I didn't have much time to spend there because there was an important scholarship ceremony I had to attend. If I missed that, they would not renew my scholarship. Also the final semester was about to start. It all had to happen quickly', Muay explained. Even in the van to go to the border, she was still 'undecided' as to whether to go through with her plan.

To get to Myanmar, Muay used an agent who arranged the necessary documents to circumvent bureaucratic requirements and who organised the transport from Chiang Mai to the village in Myanmar where some of Muay's relatives still reside. At the border, Muay performed her perfect Thai speech and demeanour when interacting with the border guards, who easily let her leave. After arriving in the Shan state, she received help from a Shan friend whom she had known from the Shan youth group in Chiang Mai. As Muay cannot speak or write in the Burmese language, the friend completed all the administrative tasks at the local registration office on her behalf. Similar to some of my other participants, Muay's parents came back to Myanmar a few years ago to add her to the house registration under her Shan name, as a safety net for their children.[11] After presenting required documents and witnesses, Muay was told to wait for a passport without knowing how long it would take. When I asked how she spent her time while there, she laughed and replied 'I was feeling so lost! I didn't know what to do with myself because there was nothing to do there. I just spent days helping my relatives peel onions and garlic'.

Ten days and less than $20 USD in passport fees later, Muay was a Myanmar citizen. She was handed a passport and a national ID card under her Shan name. She hid these documents and returned to Thailand using the same Number Six Card issued by the Thai state under her Thai name. However, on her way back she was able to use the newly acquired Myanmar identity while still within Myanmar, which gave her a newfound sense of belonging. 'At the hotel or when buying the bus ticket, they asked for my ID card. [When I presented it], I felt like "I'm here". It was like I didn't feel any different from others around me… even though I have never lived in Myanmar. I grew up here [in Thailand], but the first feeling I had [when presenting the Myanmar ID card] is that I existed.'

The challenge for Muay became how to reconcile the Myanmar identity with the Thai one, as Muay was registered at her university under her Thai name. She had already asked the university administration whether her name could be changed and, unsurprisingly, found out they had no idea how to deal with a situation like hers. At the same time, they did not seem resistant to her wish. She realised that exploiting the grey area was possible. Muay plans to change her name within the university system to the same name as on her newly acquired Myanmar passport. She also plans to use the passport for the licensing exam. She rests her hopes on the ASEAN Economic Community (AEC), which claims to open borders for high-skilled occupations including nursing. 'Hopefully I can work within the region and no longer be bound.' The NGO network, however, was not pleased with her decision because they wanted her to fight the Council and be the 'case study' to inspire other stateless persons. Muay was disappointed by their reaction but insisted that she made the right decision for herself: 'It's my life. I cannot keep waiting for things to change… In the past, I was sad because I tried to stay here. I was not flexible. Now I let go of the idea of having to stay and open my heart. There is no need to stay if they don't want me'.

Seeking a 'right to belong' as an Arendt's child:
Legal identity and documentary pragmatism

Muay's journey exposes how 'documentary pragmatism' is sometimes adopted in search of legal recognition and belonging from a place some stateless persons may have no social ties with, as the place they call home fail to acknowledge their lived experiences as 'meaningful connections' to the state. Legal documentation becomes a commodity, and to an extent a legal fiction (see Kuzmova, this volume). Even when a stateless person is entitled to a legal identity as part of an official policy, it might still not be straightforward to claim that right without various forms of capital. Inga Gruß (2017) reports her informants' view that '[a]nyone could get a Burmese passport' with the right amount of money (25). While some of my Shan informants expressed how they viewed the rules in both Thailand and Myanmar as 'inconsistent' and 'corrupt', they similarly feel that Myanmar's bureaucracy allows more room to obtain citizenship if financial resources are available.[12] Lack of confidence in the authorities on both sides means migrants will seek legality through documentation in any way they can. Although Muay seems to have received her Myanmar passport by paying a standard fee, her total journey involved paying a broker (to arrange paperwork for her travel) and her parents' preparation (by adding her name to the house registration a few years prior to create her documentary connection to a territory from which they had escaped).

Whether it was because Myanmar's registration system was less robust, the corruption was widespread, or the officials were more inclusive, it is obvious that adopting documentary pragmatism allowed Muay to obtain 'instantaneous' legal citizenship. However, this has come at a cost of abandoning the hope of becoming a Thai citizen by slotting herself into the 'other' category. Upon realising that the degree she had fought hard to attain may leave her unable to practise as a nurse in the country she called her own, Muay reinterpreted her identity and created a new one through paperwork. In other words, she had to reinterpret her identity as Burmese, which is not her home country, in order to work in Thailand, which is. That is, to stay in her 'home' country, she needed to claim membership somewhere else.

Documentary pragmatism demonstrated by Muay reiterates how identities are always in flux and strategic, and always attuned to the broader dynamics of power (Ríos-Rojas, 2011: 89). Documentary pragmatism forces people's hands to choose a nationality that is made available to them, rather than one that may correspond with their lived experiences and belonging. Yet Muay sees her action as liberating and meaningful because this gives her a tangible sense of existence and belonging. Between having a citizenship, ill-fitting as it might be, and none at all, Muay chose what was available to her. The newfound legal status as a citizen of Myanmar does not mean that Muay now leads a life free of burden and worries – she still has to deal with the administrative and practical complications of having had (and continuing to have) a double identity.

Throughout my fieldwork, I have also observed how emphasis on identity documents places the evidentiary burdens and blame on stateless people. As I have argued elsewhere (Cheva-Isarakul, 2019, 2020), giving insufficient consideration to both the instability of the regime of documentation issuance and its commoditisation results in statelessness being framed as an individual's failure to prove their identity or follow bureaucratic steps, rather than a systemic violence against certain minority groups. That 'a right to belong' is made conditional upon an identity document is internalised so deeply by many stateless youth that they themselves feel only documents, not social relationships in the everyday, can offer them belonging and validation of existence. The narrative of conflating a legal document with belonging carries various implications, one of which brings us back to the question of who can be considered stateless. How are we to classify youth such as Muay, who is now officially a citizen of Myanmar and thus is no longer *de jure* stateless, if she cannot reside legally and rightfully as a citizen in the country where she has spent most of her life, speaks the language, participates in society, and has social networks and relationships?

Conclusion

This chapter illustrates the implications of the narrow legal interpretation that 'significant and stable ties' and 'a right to belong' rest on identity documents such as a birth certificate, rather than one's lived experiences and social ties. By focusing on the journey to legal citizenship of stateless youth Muay, a Shan youth of migrant parents, this chapter contributes insight into the evidentiary burden placed upon, and documentary pragmatism commonly practised by, 'Arendt's children'. This chapter also sheds light on how *de jure* statelessness can be resolved through a documentary solution, but *de facto* and effective statelessness may still endure.

The burdens of not possessing the required material proof of belonging have prompted educated youth such as Muay to seek necessary documentation from the state they had previously escaped, in order to improve their life chances in the state they consider 'home'. Their decisions to practise documentary pragmatism point to the power of documents in providing a sense of belonging by materialising and confirming their membership. While their life stories are at present an exception rather than a norm, this unexpectedly flexible and strategic belonging may become more common among educated stateless youth in Thailand. Given Myanmar's economic growth and Thailand's declining fertility rate, educated stateless youth offer potential as a critical 'human resource' to be sought after by the two countries that have previously denied them membership. In the name of 'human rights', we may soon observe a legal trend to make room for the educated stateless population to obtain legal citizenship. However, the question remains whether a legal identity can substitute belonging accumulated through lived experience. Can legal citizenship truly give stateless people a place to call 'home'?

Notes

1 This chapter draws on the author's PhD thesis titled 'Navigating the illegible state: Everyday experiences of statelessness among Shan youth in Northern Thailand', completed in 2020.

2 Pseudonym.

3 Other characteristics of 'Arendt's children,' according to Bhabha, are that 'they are minors; they are, or they risk being, separated from their parents or customary guardians' (Bhabha, 2009: 413).

4 The debates on defining and theorising various types of statelessness are rich and on-going. In this chapter, I use *de jure* statelessness to refer to the situation of those who are not considered a national by the law of any State. I use *de facto* statelessness to refer to the lived experience of deprivation of rights and security attached to a nationality in a place a person calls home, regardless of whether they are qualified for and/or hold a nationality elsewhere. For further discussion on the challenges of defining statelessness, see Van Waas and de Chickera (2017).

5 Thai nationality laws emphasize a 'meaningful connection' to the country (จุดเกาะเกี่ยว), which is often interpreted as being born in the country or having Thai parentage.

6 For my research, I employed a wide range of ethnographic methods, including participant observation, various types of interviews (structured, semi-structured, informal, focus-group), and photo elicitation. In total, I conducted over 100 interviews and meetings with stateless youth, parents, NGO workers, and state officials.

7 The Shan exemplify the complexity of statelessness in a migratory transit and destination country such as Thailand and the unstable geopolitics of the border zone. Although identified as a unified social group by the Thai public, the legal categorisation of the Shan by the Thai state is diverse due to the different waves of migration from the Shan state of Myanmar to northern Thailand and the Thai state's erratic registration practices. This politics of classification, while unstable and arbitrary, can profoundly affect the life chances of the children. It is not within the scope of this chapter to provide a thorough historical and political context. See Jirattikorn (2012) for background on the various waves of the Shan

migrants, and Laungaramsri (2003 and 2014) for the Thai state's complex classification of aliens.

8 The Shan are not included among the nine recognised 'hill tribes' by the Thai state. Instead, they are classified as a 'highland community'. Despite their cohabitation at times with other highlanders, the Shan have never been considered a 'hill tribe' in the Thai national imagination. Jirattikorn attributes the reasons as being their tendency to reside in lowland valleys and their socio-cultural practices of wet rice cultivation and Theravada Buddhists, which they share with the Thai (Jirattikorn, 2012: 218–219).

9 GED tests are a group of subject tests which, when passed, provide certification that the test taker has United States or Canadian high school-level academic skills. It is an alternative to the U.S. high school diploma.

10 Muay was told that a holder of a foreign passport could sit the exam, if she/he is able to complete the exam in the Thai language.

11 My fieldwork reveals that many migrant parents followed this practice of secretly adding the names of their children to a relative's household in the Shan state.

12 This comment does not apply for everyone. Natalie Brinham's chapter (this volume) discusses the Rohingyas' difficulties in obtaining Myanmar citizenship.

References

A Right to Belong (2002), Directed by David Feingold [Film] (Philadelphia, PA: Ophidian Films Ltd).

Allerton, C. (2017) 'Contested statelessness in Sabah, Malaysia: Irregularity and the politics of recognition', *Journal of Immigrant & Refugee Studies*, 15:3, 250–268.

Bhabha, J. (2009) 'Arendt's children: Do today's migrant children have a right to have rights?', *Human Rights Quarterly*, 31:2, 410–451.

Bhabha, J. (ed.) (2011) *Children Without a State: A Global Human Rights Challenge* (Cambridge, MA: MIT University Press).

Bloom, T., Tonkiss K., and Cole, P. (eds) (2017) *Understanding Statelessness* (New York: Routledge).

Chantavanich, S., Vungsiriphisal P., and Laodumrongchai, S. (2007) *Thailand Policies Towards Migrant Workers from Myanmar* (Bangkok: Asian Research Centre for Migration).

Cheva-Isarakul, J. (2019) 'Diagnosing statelessness and everyday state illegibility in Northern Thailand', *The Statelessness and Citizenship Review*, 1:2, 214–238 [Online]. Available at https://statelessnessandcitizenshipreview.com/index.php/journal/article/view/53 (Accessed 31 December 2019).

Cheva-Isarakul, J. (2020) 'Navigating the illegible state: Everyday experiences of statelessness among Shan youth in Northern Thailand' (PhD thesis, Victoria University of Wellington).

Flaim, A. (2015) 'No land's man: Sovereignty, legal status, and the production of statelessness among highlanders in Northern Thailand' (PhD thesis, Cornell University).

Flaim, A. (2017). 'Problems of evidence, evidence of problems: Expanding citizenship and reproducing statelessness among Highlanders in Northern Thailand', in B. Lawrance and J. Stevens (eds) *Citizenship in Question: Evidentiary Birthright and Statelessness* (Durham, NC: Duke University Press): pp. 147–164.

Grundy-Warr, C., and Wong Siew Yin, E. (2002) 'Geographies of displacement: The Karenni and the Shan across the Myanmar-Thailand border', *Singapore Journal of Tropical Geography*, 23:1, 93–122.

Gruβ, I. (2017) 'The emergence of the temporary migrant: Bureaucracies, legality and Myanmar migrants in Thailand', *Sojourn*, 32:1, 1–35.

Jirattikorn, A. (2012) 'Brokers of nostalgia: Shan migrant public spheres in Chiang Mai, Thailand', in C. Plüss and C. Kwok-bun (eds) *Living Intersections: Transnational Migrant Identifications in Asia* (Dordrecht: Springer Netherlands): pp. 213–234.

Kingston, L. N. (2017) 'Worthy of rights: Statelessness as a cause and symptom of marginalisation', in T. Bloom, K. Tonkiss, and P. Cole (eds) *Understanding Statelessness* (New York: Routledge): pp. 17–34.

Laungaramsri, P. (2003) 'Ethnicity and the politics of ethnic classification in Thailand', in C. Mackerras (ed.) *Ethnicity in Asia* (London: Routledge): pp. 157–173.

Laungaramsri, P. (2006) 'Imagining nation: Women's rights and the transnational movement of Shan women in Thailand and Burma', *Focaal – European Journal of Anthropology*, 47, 48–61.

Laungaramsri, P. (2014) 'Contested citizenship: Cards, colors, and the culture of identification', in J. Marston J. (ed.) *Ethnicity, Borders and the Grassroots Interface with the State* (Chiang Mai: Silkworm Books): pp. 143–162.

Lawrance, B., and Stevens, J. (eds) (2017) *Citizenship in Question: Evidentiary Birthright and Statelessness* (Durham, NC: Duke University Press).

Lopez, L. G., Sejersen, T. B., Oakeshott, N., Fajth, G., Khilji, T., and Panta, N. (2012) 'Civil registration, human rights and social protection in Asia and the Pacific', *Asia Pacific Population Journal*, 29:1, 75–98 [Online]. Available at https://doi.org/10.18356/ba046677-en (Accessed 22 April 2020).

Quintana, T. (2010) 'Progress report of the Special Rapporteur on the situation of human rights in Myanmar', *Human Rights Council Thirteenth Session A/HRC/ 13/48* [Online]. Available at www2.ohchr.org/english/bodies/hrcouncil/docs/ 13session/A-HRC-13-48.pdf (Accessed 22 April 2020).

Reddy, M. (2015) 'Response to the Global Action Plan to End Statelessness', unpublished paper. Presented at Symposium on Statelessness, Kenan Institute for Ethics, Duke University.

Ríos-Rojas, A. (2011) 'Beyond delinquent citizenships: Immigrant youth's (re)visions of citizenship and belonging in a globalized world', *Harvard Educational Review*, 81:1, 64–94.

Sadiq, K. (2008) *Paper Citizens: How Illegal Immigrants Acquire Citizenship in Developing Countries* (Oxford: Oxford University Press).

School for Shan State Nationalities Youth (SSSNY). n.d. 'About us' [Online]. Available at https://sssny.org/about-us/ (Accessed 31 December 2019).

United Nations High Commissioner for Refugees (UNHCR) (n.d.) 'Thailand' [Online]. Available at www.unhcr.org/ibelong/imvisible-thailand/ (Accessed 03 January 2020).

United Nations High Commissioner for Refugees (UNHCR) (2014) *Handbook on the Protection of Stateless Persons under the 1954 Convention relating to the Status of Stateless Persons* (Geneva: UNHCR) [Online]. Available at www.unhcr.org/dach/wp-content/uploads/sites/27/2017/04/CH-UNHCR_Handbook-on-Protection-of-Stateless-Persons.pdf (Accessed 3 June 2020).

Van Waas, L., and de Chickera, A. (2017) 'Unpacking statelessness', in T. Bloom, K. Tonkiss, and P. Cole (eds) *Understanding Statelessness* (New York: Routledge), pp. 53–69.

Vandenabeele, C. (2011) 'To register or not to register? Legal identity, birth registration, and inclusive development', in J. Bhabha (ed.) *Children Without a State: A Global Human Rights Challenge* (Cambridge, MA: MIT Press), pp. 307–330.

Vleiks, C. (2017) 'The concepts of "statelessness *in situ*" and "statelessness in the migratory context"', in T. Bloom, K. Tonkiss, and P. Cole (eds) *Understanding Statelessness* (New York: Routledge): pp. 35–52.

13

Being excluded or excluding yourself?: Citizenship choices among the stateless youth in Estonia

Maarja Vollmer

In 1991, just after the re-independence of Estonia from the Soviet Union, people who had held Soviet citizenship – and were rendered stateless – constituted 32% of the total population. In 2018, the proportion was 6%, meaning that approximately 77,000 individuals had not naturalised in twenty-eight years. An additional 18,000 young stateless persons had been born and raised in Estonian territory in the same period. This is remarkable, since these people had (and continue to have) the possibility to acquire Estonian citizenship through a naturalisation process. Rejecting Estonian nationality means living with an undetermined citizenship. Such status sets some restrictions (such as lack of free movement within the European Union and lack of voting rights), but does not substantially limit everyday life.

The aim of this chapter is to explore the motivations of young stateless people in acquiring (or not acquiring) Estonian citizenship in the face of continued statelessness. It aims to show that attitudes towards citizenship acquisition are more complicated than they sometimes seem. Citizenship is not simply about a rational pursuit of state rights and benefits, but involves questions about belonging, nationalism, and legitimacy. The focus here is on the often-overlooked perspective of young people. It is based on secondary data analysis of previous studies and literature, and in-depth interviews with stateless youth in Estonia, aged 20–35. This chapter focuses on the narratives of five young people: Andrei, Elena, Viktor, Irina, and Viktoria.[1] They were selected for this analysis because they were born and raised in Estonia and do not plan to leave Estonia in the near future. They have taken steps towards acquiring citizenship but are, for different reasons, still not citizens of Estonia. They were interviewed in Estonian and their words are translated into English by the author.

The chapter begins with an overview of statelessness and naturalisation in Estonia. It introduces previous literature on changing meanings of membership, followed by an overview on young people and statelessness in Estonia – including their barriers to citizenship and what kind of self-perceptions being stateless brings for them. The chapter ends with discussion of whether there are grounds for a change.

Statelessness and naturalisation in Estonia

After the collapse of the Soviet Union, Estonia gained its re-independence in August 1991. In the following year, after a public referendum, Estonia got a new constitution that established the basis of citizenship and outlined a list of fundamental rights for people living in the country. Although the constitution does not use the term 'nation-state', the preamble states that the constitution 'must guarantee the preservation of the Estonian people, the Estonian language and the Estonian culture through the ages' (The Constitution of Estonia, 1992).

With the re-enactment of the Citizenship Act in 1991, the basis for obtaining Estonian citizenship was reasserted. The law specifies that citizenship is based on an ethnic rather than a territorial connection to Estonia. This means that people have to prove their Estonian ethnic origin to obtain Estonian citizenship, or else go through a full naturalisation process. This is the case regardless of how long they have lived in the country or whether they support an independent Estonia.

As noted, people who had a Soviet citizenship and became stateless[2] constituted 32% of the Estonian population in 1991, almost all of them Russian-speaking (Estonian Integration Monitoring, 2008). They were given a chance to get Estonian citizenship on easier terms until 1995, and by the end of that year around 65,000 stateless people had naturalised (Police and Border Guard Board, 2019). Around the same time, another 65,000 people had decided to leave for Russia. This immediate mobility demonstrated the perceived belonging of the person. By 1998, another 35,000 left for Russia (Danjoux, 2002: 240; Vetik, 2011), whereas 41,000 naturalised at the same time in Estonia (PBGB, 2019).

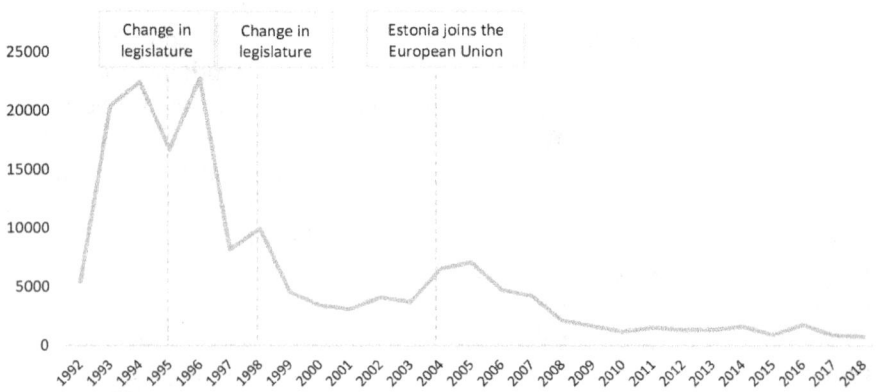

Figure 1. Yearly naturalisation rates in Estonia 1992–2018 (PBGB, 2019)

Changes in naturalisation rates can be tied to changes in legislation. They dropped significantly after amendments to the Citizenship Act in 1995, which made the criteria for naturalisation more complex. The subsequent rise in 1998 relates to a change in legislation making the application for underage stateless persons easier. The following rise in naturalisation rates is connected to Estonia's entrance into the European Union in 2004. Since then, naturalisation rates have dropped and have been at a steady low with an average of 1,200 people with unidentified citizenship naturalising yearly (PBGB, 2019). In 2018, the population of stateless people in Estonia was slightly below 80,000, which constitutes around 6% of the Estonian population.

Changing meanings of membership

Research in the field has shown a transformation in the meaning of membership and citizenship in contemporary European societies. Since the mid-1980s, many scholars (e.g. Schuck & Smith, 1985; Hammar, 1990; Brubaker, 1992a; Soysal, 1994) have argued in various ways that citizenship – as once described by T. H. Marshall (1992) – has been devalued, and alien rights have been exerted to the point where having (or not having) citizenship in the country of residence makes no substantial difference. Yet in this case, it is important to distinguish between stateless people in Estonia and people with an alternative citizenship. Without any citizenship, their decision not to naturalise in the country of residence has different implications.

Estonia has not signed or ratified the 1954 Convention relating to the Status of Stateless Persons, nor the 1961 Convention on the Reduction of Statelessness. Allowing people to remain stateless is not only violating a person's right to nationality, first asserted as a human right in the Universal Declaration of Human Rights (United Nations, 1948), but it may also weaken a person's sense of identity or limit their full participation in society. Furthermore, stateless people are often excluded from political processes and stopped from fulfilling their potential, which may have repercussions for social cohesion (UNHCR, 2010). Therefore, being without citizenship may have a major impact on people's lives and leave many feeling rejected, causing tensions in their everyday interactions with the majority population.

However, the Estonian unofficial motto is that 'citizenship cannot be forced on anyone' (Ruutsoo, 1998: 152). Its large population of stateless people seems to be a result of a nexus of different factors. These people have lived in Estonia for more than twenty years and have not found enough possibilities or reasons to naturalise within this period. The ongoing high number of stateless people indicates a contradiction between the needs and realities of stateless people and Estonian citizenship policies. Conceptions of state membership are based on the idea of a bounded community in which rules of legal citizenship set the parameters for exclusion (Gonzales and Sigona, 2017). Such a large stateless population may be unusual and exceptional in the global context, but it has a particularly critical influence for a country with a population of just 1.3 million.

Young people and statelessness in Estonia

According to the 2011 Estonian public census, 19,231 people aged up to 39 years had unidentified citizenship, while that number was 18,439 for people aged 15–39 (Statistics Estonia, 2011); the gap between these categories shows 792 stateless children under the age of 15. Altogether, there were approximately 1,500 stateless minors in 2011 – with those numbers decreasing steadily over time (Statistics Estonia, 2011). The population of children born in already independent Estonia points to a direct 'heritage' of the Soviet Union. It is important to consider how the reasons why elderly people avoid the naturalisation process may differ from those of young people (the focus of elder persons is the focus of Benson et al., this volume). The younger generation is more open to different options, and their citizenship decisions have bigger impacts on their future lives. This is why the empirical part of this chapter focuses mainly on stateless youth in Estonia.

Secondary data analysis and interviews show that there is a range of reasons for people staying stateless. First, the primary reason for not naturalising relates to difficulties with learning the Estonian language and passing the citizenship test. These challenges were cited as the biggest obstacle for 61% of stateless respondents in 2002 and for 34% in 2008 (EIM, 2002 and 2008). In 2017, 86% of stateless people cited language problems as one of the reasons for not acquiring citizenship (EIM, 2017). Language can be linked to personal choice of belonging (Vihalemm, 1998 and 1999); studies have found (e.g. Võõbus, 2009) that people who do not speak Estonian feel they experience discriminatory attitudes from nationals, which further prevents them from practising the language on a daily basis. This might imply cultural differentiation and the re-production of the symbolic power relations between non-nationals and citizens.

The issue of language appeared in some of my interviews with young stateless people. Most respondents interact almost only with Russians and do not move out of their circle. For one interviewee, the refusal to communicate in Estonian and with Estonians derived from his strong feelings against Estonia and its exclusionary citizenship policies. For another, it was because she has only ever lived in a city where most people speak only Russian and she has developed prejudices regarding how Estonians see her when she cannot speak Estonian fluently.

This leads to the second reason why some youth remain stateless: there has been a strong emotional unwillingness to acquire Estonian citizenship, as people believe this is something they should have been granted automatically. In 2008, 23% of stateless people indicated that they felt the naturalisation process was humiliating (EIM, 2008). This feeling was also confirmed by all the stateless youth I interviewed. Even though my respondents had taken steps towards naturalising, they feel they are left without something that should be theirs by birth. For example, Andrei's application was denied and he developed strong feelings about everything related to citizenship and being a Russian-speaking person in Estonia. When asked whether he would try again, he replied:

> I mean, why? Either you give it to me as given and as it should be or I'm not going [expletive]. Cause you know I have my own pride... I don't see the way I should be begging for the thing I see is mine by birth. If this government and this nation, if they do not want me to be part of it, then I'm not, I'm not going to [starts laughing]. In Russian we say you can be lovely without the other person loving you.

This example shows that denial of citizenship, despite being born and raised in Estonia and taking the necessary steps to naturalise, creates strong emotions. These may make a person unwilling to apply again, particularly if someone believes they are being denied something they already have a birthright to.

Third, some people prefer Russian or another citizenship over Estonian nationality. The desire for Russian citizenship rose from 5% in 2000 to 19% in 2008 (EIM, 2000, 2008: 141). Remarkably, the preference among stateless people to acquire Estonian citizenship was the highest in 2000 at 74%, but by 2008 the percentage had dropped down to 51% (EIM, 2000, 2008). Elena, for example, feels that she does not need any kind of citizenship. At times she has been satisfied with the grey passport held by non-citizen Estonians, since it makes travelling to visit her relatives easier for her: 'I was in Russia earlier [this year]. Then, a visa, you don't need one. As soon as I want, I'll go to St. Petersburg, then I'll take my passport [waves her grey passport], my ticket and off I'll go.' Irina had a similar response, yet her opinion changes when she talks about travelling to other countries without national protection: 'What would change in my life is firstly, you know, I would have the confidence that if something happens to me somewhere on the other side of the border and I need to turn to some place, they wouldn't tell me that "hehe you don't have the citizenship, goodbye, it's not our problem."' Other studies have found that ease of travel to Russia or other former Soviet Union states have been important factors for stateless people under 35 years of age (Võõbus, 2009: 64). In 2015, 40% of stateless respondents cited this concern as a reason to remain stateless (EIM, 2015: 9).

Lastly, lacking Estonian citizenship does not affect a person's daily life (Vetik, 2011: 163). In 2015, 39% of stateless respondents cited this as a reason for remaining stateless (EIM, 2015), compared to 19% in 2008 (EIM, 2008). Notably, social security in Estonia as a non-resident is higher than in Russia (Vetik, 2011). In 2008, 16% of stateless respondents did not want to change their status (EIM, 2008), and by 2010 already 40% wanted to remain stateless (IISS, 2010). This percentage has dropped significantly in recent years back to previous rates; however, in 2017, 18% of respondents stated that they do not want any citizenship (EIM, 2017).

Barriers to citizenship

One previously unidentified reason for remaining stateless that was revealed in several interviews is the stiffness of Estonian citizenship policies. Viktor compared the current system to someone continuously 'putting spokes in their wheels'. He felt that necessary information is withheld by the government and only given out little by little. In his words, this results in the person being 'breathless from running around', losing motivation, and finally giving up. His 'journey of naturalisation' is almost unbelievable, since he has been trying to acquire Estonian citizenship for more than twelve years. He was going regularly to the migration board every two to three years but encountered various obstacles. For example, after passing the exams and waiting the one-year waiting time, the officer could not see he had submitted an application and so he was forced to wait another year. Then, he could not show the required years of legal income, since he had not been working. Later, he could not show permanent residence in Estonia because he had been an international student in another country. All this resulted in frustration with the system and made him unwilling to invest time in re-applying. It also echoes experiences in other countries, such as Malaysia (Liew, this volume) and Thailand (Cheva-Isarakul, this volume).

My interview with Viktoria highlights how people's reasons for remaining stateless in Estonia is a mixture of emotional unwillingness, reactions to stiff citizenship policies, and financial concerns. Her example shows that you can be a talented person and Estonian in every way, but it is just not enough because of your non-Estonian origin. Viktoria notes:

I've always wanted to have a citizenship but I had a little problem with how I should get it. For me it is very odd that I have to take an exam for it... I was born here, I went to all Estonian institutions, 95% of my friends are Estonian. My parents are the only Russian-speaking people I communicate with and so... I see no greater possibility to integrate into Estonian society as I have. And they still don't give it to me.

I was awarded with a gold medal at my graduation from my high school. And my teachers wrote a letter to the president. They collected forty signatures to it and wrote that "she was awarded with a gold medal upon graduation. She is a very good student; she represents us in Olympiads and so on and please reward her with the citizenship." And what he [the president] replied: "No, she still needs to take the exam but I will invite her to the presidential reception". I was like, hello, I can go there anyway because I was the best student in my class. This is no gift because I would get it anyway and so he just said no. And then all the teachers were confused too that why do I need to take the exam and pay money and all this when really... I don't know...

Even though Viktoria gave different reasons for not having a citizenship, she focused on her current financial status and explained:

Well basically my only reason now is that I don't have money. It costs a lot. The exam costs money and then making a new ID-card costs money, making a new passport costs money. And I am a student, I count every cent. I really need to. It will cost me more than 100 euros. And at the moment I really do not have such money. I have other things, important things, that I postpone because I do not have money. And then a thing like some documents, papers, it really isn't such a priority for me that I would spend money on it.

Postponing applying for a citizenship may be related to an emotional unwillingness to acquire one, as well as material constraints. Viktoria's story shows that remaining without citizenship does not hinder her life to a significant extent.

'But who am I?'

The citizenship situation among young people may be seen from a different angle compared to that of older persons. Many young people have been born and raised in Estonian territory and they meet all the preconditions to be fully integrated into the society. It can be difficult to understand how even though one may have the same course of life as their Estonian peers, sometimes incomprehensible steps need to be taken to prove belonging to Estonia. It was clear from several interviews that you can be perfectly proficient in Estonian, live all your life in Estonia, but it is still not enough. Extra effort has to be taken and loyalty proven over and over again. Estonia's reason for exclusionary citizenship policy was to avoid becoming 'nationally extinct' (Brubaker, 1992b), which helps to explain the many barriers placed on access to citizenship.

The interviewed stateless young people have made efforts to overcome these negative messages, but at times the citizenship policy impacts their self-perceptions. For example, when asked what it means to be without a citizenship, this is how they replied:

> 'So, at the moment I am a UFO. An alien.'

> 'Do I have a tail or horns or something, what's so different?'

> 'I am at the moment like a homeless. Well, who am I? Estonian? No. Russian? No. But who am I?'

The answers carried over to having troubles identifying themselves, especially in the presence of friends or other people:

> 'Well, people's reaction is like, "Why don't you have a passport already?", "Why are you such undefined? What? Grey?" Ah I don't know. Those small things...'

> 'When I was studying in the Netherlands, there people were like "Alien's passport, what the hell is this?" And I had to explain to people what it is. They were holding to their heads – "What's the matter with you that you don't even exist?" (laughs). You are like a million people and then you have such citizenship policy.'

The perceived symbolic power invested in the Estonian non-citizen identity documents is found also in other contexts (Benswait, this volume, argues that the Kuwaiti 'security card' should be seen as a semiotic tool in a wider project of political discourse).

Grounds for a change

Until now, the Estonian state's reluctance to change its citizenship policies has been connected to uncertainty about peoples' reaction and allegiances after obtaining citizenship – which may result in potential security threats (Park, 1995; Safran, 1997). However, research shows that young people choose statelessness for a variety of reasons, not limited to their possible lack of perceived connection with Estonia. All of the interviewees in this study viewed the criteria for obtaining citizenship as generally justified, but they felt it was unfair towards people like themselves who were born and have lived in Estonia. At the same time, they generally believed that the criteria are achievable if a person wants to gain citizenship. This belief is connected to having a certain attitude towards the citizenship, proving that a state of readiness shapes the actions taken (see also Blumer, 1969). In 2017, around one in five stateless people in Estonia indicated that they did not want any country's citizenship (EIM, 2017). Yet, the young interviewees' responses showed that, while citizenship is not 'worth' taking immediate action for, it is nevertheless something that they thought worth obtaining in the long term.

Modern policies contain an array of rites that give content and meaning to the imagined community (Danjoux, 2002: 113), and young people do not get significant confirmation that they are part of this community. For example, stateless youth take notice of Estonians' general warm and welcoming attitudes towards other nationalities – but when a Russian-speaking person does not speak Estonian, people's reactions often go cold. Viktoria explained that this pushes people away even further because the perceived message is 'We don't want you here'. The boundaries of membership are enforced and challenged in everyday situations (see also Glenn, 2011), and with this attitude the Soviet descendants do not see themselves being included in the society.

It is impossible to say for sure whether the citizenship choices of these stateless youth are voluntary or involuntary. Their answers showed clearly that they do not wish to be in their current situation and they would like to be full members of the society they live in, but there are factors other than citizenship hindering them. While they do have the possibility to naturalise if they put in extra effort, by doing this they would play a role they disagree with and let go of a specific power that lets them act on the basis of what they believe is rightfully theirs. From the stateless people's unwillingness to become full members of the Estonian society by naturalising, it can be assumed that they have partly self-excluded themselves as a way to more easily tolerate the situation (see also Bourdieu, 2002; Grygiel, 2009).

When asked their opinions on Estonia's approach to the descendants of former Soviet citizens, respondents agreed that they should have been granted citizenship if they were born in Estonian territory. Their opinions were not so uniform when asked if the state is doing enough, or if the state should do more for stateless people. Elena contends that citizenship cannot be forced on people: 'If a person doesn't want to speak [Estonian] then what is the state supposed to do? "Go! Go! Do it!" Well if the person doesn't want to do it then s/he doesn't want to do it… citizenship is only citizenship and that's it.' Irina focused the issue on personal choice for stateless people, implying that if she personally wants to, she would do everything to get citizenship – and if she does not take that action, she simply does not want citizenship enough to take the needed steps.

Conclusion

The stories presented in this chapter show that these young people in Estonia with undetermined citizenship have at times been highly motivated to become citizens. However, they have experienced difficulties applying for citizenship – sometimes despite their full integration into the society. They have often made real effort, but citizenship policies are uncompromising and therefore many young stateless people cannot fulfil their potential as full members of Estonian society. Respondents noted that even though they feel a sense of belonging to Estonia, they do not feel wanted. Furthermore, they have problems with their self-identification due to the grey non-citizen passport, as well as categorisation as 'aliens'. This is connected to their perceived status and reinforced by negative interactions with the majority population. This suggests that citizenship is not just a matter of formal legal status, but rather it is also a matter of belonging, which requires recognition from all members of the community.

This chapter shows that even if citizenship may seem like a rational pursuit of state rights and benefits, it can be much more complex and charged with questions about belonging, nationalism, legitimacy, and acceptance. The young people interviewed for this study were defined as 'foreigners' despite their long-standing connection to Estonia, and this labelling stood in the way of their access to citizenship. Finding a satisfactory solution requires compromises from the government and stateless persons, but both could benefit from increasing the social cohesion in Estonia. This opposition has developed and taken new forms within a period of nearly thirty years. As such, it may seem like a challenging gap to overcome. However, the young people born and raised in Estonia after its independence in 1991 should be granted Estonian citizenship retrospectively. This would help to end the exclusion of these young people from Estonian society, and thereby also end statelessness in the country. This policy shift would not only help to increase social inclusion, but also show the currently stateless youth in a clear manner that they belong and are accepted in Estonia.

Notes

1 Names have been changed to protect the identities of participants.
2 A stateless person in this chapter is defined as in Article 1 in the Convention relating to the Status of Stateless Persons, i.e. a person 'who is not considered as a national by any state under the operation of its law' (UNHCR, 1954). Terms relating to people with 'unidentified citizenship' and who are 'stateless' are used interchangeably. Referring to a person holding a grey passport will be also used with the same meaning as the 'grey passport/alien's passport' is the official identification document of people with no citizenship in Estonia.

References

Blumer, H. (1969) *Symbolic Interactionism: Perspective and Method* (Englewood Cliffs, NJ: Prentice Hall).

Bourdieu, P. (ed.) (2002) *The Weight of the World: Social Suffering in Contemporary Society* (Cambridge: Polity Press).

Brubaker, R. (1992a) *Citizenship and Nationhood in France and Germany* (Cambridge, MA: Harvard University Press).

Brubaker, R. (1992b) 'Citizenship struggles in Soviet successor states', *International Migration Review*, 26, 269–291.

Constitution of the Republic of Estonia (1992) [Online]. Available at www.riigiteataja.ee/en/eli/521052015001/consolide (Accessed 12 June 2020).

Danjoux, O. (2002) *L'etat, c'est pas moi: Reframing Citizenship(s) in the Baltic Republics* (Lund University: ProQuest, UMI Dissertations Publishing).

Estonian Integration Monitoring (EIM) (2000) *Integration Monitoring* (Tallinn: Tallinn University Institute of International and Social Studies).

Estonian Integration Monitoring (EIM) (2002) *Integration Monitoring* (Tallinn: Tallinn University Institute of International and Social Studies).

Estonian Integration Monitoring (EIM) (2008) *Integration Monitoring* (Tallinn: Integration Foundation and the Office of the Minister of Population, Government of the Republic of Estonia).

Estonian Integration Monitoring (EIM) (2015) *Integration Monitoring* (Tartu: Praxis and Institute of Baltic Studies).

Estonian Integration Monitoring (EIM) (2017) *Integration Monitoring* (Tartu: Institute of Baltic Studies and Praxis).

Glenn, E. N. (2011) 'Constructing citizenship: Exclusion, subordination and resistance', *American Sociological Review*, 1:76, 1–24.

Gonzales, R. G., and Sigona, N. (eds) (2017) *Within and Beyond Citizenship: Borders, Membership and Belonging* (Abingdon: Routledge).

Grygiel, J. (2009) 'The power of statelessness', *Policy Review*, 154, 35–50.

Hammar, T. (1990) *Democracy and the Nation State: Aliens, Denizens and Citizens in a World of International Migration* (Abingdon and New York: Ashgate).

Institute of International and Social Studies (IISS) (2010) 'Uuringu "Eesti lõimumiskava eesmärkide saavutamise monitooring 2010" kokkuvõte' ['The monitoring of fulfilling the Estonian Integration Plan 2010'], study summary, Tallinn University.

Marshall, T. H. (1992) *Citizenship and Social Class* (London: Pluto Press).

Park, A. (1995) 'Russia and Estonian security dilemmas', *Europe-Asia Studies*, 47:1, 27–45.

Police and Border Guard Board (PBGB) (2019) 'Statistics on citizenship: Naturalized persons 1992–2019'.

Ruutsoo, R. (1998) 'Eesti kodakondsuspoliitika ja rahvusriigi kujunemise piirjooned' ['Estonian citizenship policy in a context of emerging nation-state'], in M. Heidmets (ed.) *The Russian Question and Estonia's Choices* (Tallinn: Tallinn University Press): pp. 139–202.

Safran, W. (1997) 'Citizenship and nationality in democratic systems: Approaches to defining and acquiring membership in the political community', *International Political Science Review*, 18:3, 313–335.

Schuck, P. H., and Smith, R. M. (1985) *Citizenship Without Consent: The Illegal Alien in American Polity* (New Haven, CT: Yale University Press).

Soysal, Y. N. (1994) *Limits of Citizenship: Migrants and Postnational Membership in Europe* (Chicago, IL: The University of Chicago Press).

Statistics Estonia (2011) 'Population census 2011 by gender, county, age group, citizenship status and native and foreign-origin' [Online]. Available at https://andmed.stat.ee/et/stat/rahvaloendus__rel2011__pelisus-ja-ranne__polis-ja-valis-rahvastik/RL0529 (Accessed 16 November 2020).

United Nations (1948) *The Universal Declaration of Human Rights*.

United Nations High Commissioner for Refugees (UNHCR) (1954) *Convention relating to the Status of Stateless Persons*.

United Nations High Commissioner for Refugees (UNHCR) (1961) *Convention on the Reduction of Statelessness*.

United Nations High Commissioner for Refugees (UNHCR) (2010) 'Preventing and reducing statelessness' [Online]. Available at www.unhcr.org/en-us/about-us/background/4ca5937d9/preventing-reducing-statelessness-1961-convention-reduction-statelessness.html (Accessed 10 June 2020).

Vetik, R. (2011) 'Statelessness, citizenship and belonging in Estonia', in B. Blitz (ed.) *Statelessness and Citizenship: A Comparative Study on the Benefits of Nationality* (Cheltenham: Edward Elgar Publishing): pp. 160–171.

Vihalemm, T. (1998) 'Eesti kool kui vene laste võimalik sotsialiseerumiskeskkond' ['Language school as a possible socialising agent for Russian pupils'] in M. Lauristin, S. Vare, T. Pedastsaar, and M. Pavelson (eds) *Mitmekultuuriline Eesti: Väljakutse Haridusele* [*Multicultural Estonia: Challenge to education*] (Tartu: Vali Press): pp. 337–399.

Vihalemm, T. (1999) 'Group identity formation processes among Russian-speaking settlers of Estonia: A linguistic perspective', *Journal of Baltic Studies*, 1:30, 18–39.

Võõbus, V. (2009) 'Hinnangud Eesti kodakondsuspoliitikale' ['Opinions on the Estonian citizenship policies'], The Ministry of Internal Affairs of Estonia [Online]. Available at www.siseministeerium.ee/sites/default/files/dokumendid/Uuringud/Kodakondsus_ja_r2nne/2009_hinnangud_eesti_kodakondsuspoliitikale.pdf (Accessed 12 June 2020).

When I was 14 years old, my family discovered that we are stateless when we were denied political asylum in the United States after 6 years of shuffling between court hearings and the lawyer's office. The country that we were born in no longer exists, the country that replaced it does not recognize our birth certificates and the country that we were living in does not want us either. ● We felt unwanted, unprotected and a fear settled in as we watched the news reporting on ICE raids of undocumented immigrants all around the country, I saw children herded into police cars and I was scared that would happen to us. ● The following year I developed an eating disorder, internalizing deportation fears, societal pressures and out of desperation to focus on anything else, something I could control. The realities of being stateless and undocumented in the United States did not fully reveal themselves until I became an adult; at 18 years old I would discover that I was not able to get a driver's license, a bank account, a mobile account and without the means for a work permit, I had to turn to manual labor for income. ● In the midst of this, I discovered I was not eligible for Federal Student Aid nor was I eligible for grants to pursue higher education. Heartbroken, I piled more hours into my restaurant job. Within months, I was diagnosed with Type 1 Diabetes, a chronic illness in which my pancreas discontinued insulin production creating a life long dependency on synthetic insulin, monitoring my blood sugar and doctors visits. When I was released from the ICU, I was luckily given supplies to last several weeks. At home, I was so confused about my body, it felt foreign and I developed insomnia during the first several months. I felt like my body aged overnight, I did not feel like myself and I felt like I came out of the ICU broken. ● When my hospital supplies ran out I went to pick up my first prescription, a single vile of insulin. I remember being stunned, ignorant and innocent as I watched the pharmacist processed the payment consisting my whole paycheck, $400 I walked home wide-eyed, in shock and I remember collapsing at the entranceway of my home breaking down and for the first time feeling anger. Feeling like my body betrayed me, hating myself for it because I was even in a worse predicament than before. It dawned on me that I was diseased with no means to an education, valid employment or the tools that I needed to survive; that I could die because of my status. ● After a week of depression and panic, survival kicked in. I went to the public health department of my city, lied about my status and was able to register for a program that allowed me to purchase at a sliding scale based on my income the prescriptions I needed to take care of my health to manage this disease . . .

Figure 4

Letter

Karina Gareginovna Ambartsoumian-Clough

Transcription:

When I was 14 years old [correction: this should read '13 years old'], my family discovered that we are stateless when we were denied political asylum in the United States after 6 years of shuffling between court hearings and the lawyer's office. The country that we were born in no longer exists. The country that replaced it does not recognise our birth certificates and the country that we were living in does not want us either. We felt unwanted, unprotected, and a fear settled in as we watched the news reporting on ICE raids of undocumented immigrants all around the country. I saw children herded into police cars and I was scared that would happen to us. The following year I developed an eating disorder, internalising deportation fears, societal pressures, and out of desperation to focus on anything else, something I could control. The realities of being stateless and undocumented in the United States did not fully reveal themselves until I became an adult: at 18 years old I would discover that I was not able to get a driver's licence, a bank account, a mobile account, and without the means for a work permit, I had to turn to manual labour for income. In the midst of this, I discovered I was not eligible for Federal Student Aid nor was I eligible for grants to pursue higher education. Heartbroken, I piled more hours into my restaurant job. Within months, I was diagnosed with Type 1 Diabetes, a chronic illness in which my pancreas discontinued insulin production creating a lifelong dependency on synthetic insulin, monitoring my blood sugar and doctors' visits. When I was released from the ICU, I was luckily given supplies to last several weeks. At home, I was so confused about my body, it felt foreign and I developed insomnia during the first several months. I felt like my body aged overnight. I did not feel like myself and I felt like I came out of the ICU broken. When my hospital supplies ran out, I went to pick up my first prescription, a single vial of insulin. I remember being stunned, ignorant and innocent as I watched the pharmacist processed the payment consisting my whole paycheck, $400. I walked home wide-eyed, in shock and I remember collapsing at the entranceway of my home, breaking down and for the first time feeling anger. Feeling like my body betrayed me, hating myself for it because I was even in a worse predicament than before. It dawned on me that I was diseased with no means to an education, valid employment, or the tools that I needed to survive: that I could die because of my status. After a week of depression and panic, survival kicked in. I went to the public health department of my city, lied about my status, and was able to register for a programme that allowed me to purchase at a sliding scale based on my income the prescriptions I needed to take care of my health to manage this disease...

14

Statelessness and governance at the periphery: 'Nomadic' populations and the modern state in Thailand, Côte d'Ivoire, and Lebanon

Christoph Sperfeldt

The figure of the 'nomad' is typified by a mobile and self-reliant lifestyle (often across borders), a lack of permanent residence, communal land use, and traditions of self-government. This representation seems antithetical to the idea of the modern nation-state with its settled population, private land ownership, and centralised governance structures operating within fixed boundaries. As a result, populations identified as 'nomadic' are variously romanticised or presented as a governance 'problem' that needs to be resolved. This chapter examines what this means for state-based citizenship and governance practices.

The chapter is based on the findings of a project focused on access to citizenship and other proof of legal identity by populations identified as 'nomadic', and the challenges these groups face when lacking such proof. This research comprised desk research and qualitative fieldwork,[1] and the literature review uncovered a striking disconnect. On the one hand, there is a considerable volume of mostly anthropological studies with deep insights into the lifestyles and cultures of 'nomadic peoples' based on long-term field observations, but little consideration of matters of legal identity. On the other hand, governance literature stipulates solutions to development and citizenship concerning 'nomadic populations' that often evidence limited knowledge about the concerns of affected populations (Alexander, 2019).

This disconnect creates barriers to evidence-based policy-making, as well as participatory and local ownership-driven development. The qualitative field research involved three geographically distributed case studies of current or former 'nomadic' groups who are stateless or at risk of statelessness, namely mobile marine Moken populations in Thailand, Fulbe pastoralists in Northern Côte d'Ivoire, and Bedouin populations in Lebanon.[2] This chapter summarises some of the findings of this research with a focus on how these populations are considered in states' legal identity regimes. In particular, it provides a critical discussion of the practices relating to citizenship and legal identity that states employ and the difficulties they encounter in including populations with current or former mobile lifestyles.

Labelling the 'nomad'

Behind the reductionism associated with the figure of the 'nomad' is a complex and dynamic reality comprising a great variety of populations and lifestyles with different degrees of mobility.[3] Generally speaking,

> nomadism denotes a mobile way of life organised around cyclical or seasonal patterns. Nomadism refers to groups of people who practice spatial mobility to enhance their well-being and survival... Mobility is both a distinctive source of cultural identity and a management strategy for sustainable land use and conservation.
>
> (Gilbert, 2014: 3)

Yet, no commonly agreed-upon definition of the term 'nomad' exists. The spectrum of mobility ranges from fully mobile, to semi-mobile (often seasonal), to more sedentarised ways of living, with great differences both between and within groups labelled as 'nomadic'. There exists a great fluidity in these mobility practices, and the degrees of mobility may vary over time. Hence, there is no consensus as to where nomadism starts and where it ends. Moreover, self-identification rarely corresponds with the labels imposed on groups designated as 'nomadic'. None of the case study groups in our research would self-identify as 'nomads'. At times, the term was actively rejected by individuals, as it carried negative connotations in the countries concerned. The word is used here keeping in mind the complexities associated with its meaning and use in different contexts.

Importantly, many communities who have practised mobile lifestyles in the past and have moved to more sedentary ways of living are still *perceived* by surrounding populations and authorities as 'nomadic' and labelled as such (Alexander, 2019). Such perceptions might be more pronounced when different mobility practices exist within the same ethnic, linguistic, or cultural group, such as when some parts of a group still pursue mobile lifestyles and others have settled, sometimes decades ago. This phenomenon of the continued use of the term 'nomadic' for previously mobile but now sedentary populations is widespread, including in our three case studies which stretch across three global regions. It reveals a certain stickiness of the label of 'nomad', with often negative implications for the citizenship status of (formerly) mobile communities.

Encountering the 'nomad': Expansion of
state governance into peripheries

The literature on mobile peoples is filled with explicit or implicit biases against their lifestyles and subsistence strategies (see also Benswait, this volume). Their ways of living have been portrayed in various contexts as less economically productive and inferior to the economy of the modern state, as well as environmentally destructive and culturally backwards. These assumptions have informed policy-making and state-sponsored sedentarisation programmes. The received wisdom seems to be that the only way 'nomadic' peoples can take part in modern society and benefit from state-distributed welfare is by ending their mobile lifestyles and becoming settled (Scott, 2009). While these assumptions have been challenged by scholarly research, many myths continue to be reproduced in contemporary development discourses.

Yet external pressures on their lifestyles have forced many mobile populations to consider more sedentary ways of living (Salzman, 1980; Khazanov and Wink, 2001). Such pressures include population growth; expansion of private land holdings and conservation efforts into their territories; climate change and the changing conditions of pasture and water sources; and expanding state regulation in previously neglected peripheries. These problems are compounded by the fact that these communities are marginalised in most states' policy-making, which favours the sedentary economy. Thus, it is not necessarily a choice or a perceived superiority of sedentarised lifestyles that make mobile communities settle, but rather a reflection of these external pressures. This does not mean that such peoples are passive victims to these developments. They have historically shown great capacity for adaptation, resilience, and resistance to external pressures. Their lives are not static, but constantly evolving in the context of changing environments.

Progressive expansion of state governance into the lives of mobile peoples, and the oftentimes long-lasting consequences, are visible in all three case studies, albeit during different time periods. For instance, the ancestors of Bedouins interviewed for this study moved freely and grazed their livestock in what is today Syria and Lebanon. Since the nineteenth century, policies and land reforms have forced them to settle. After the establishment of a French mandate over Lebanon, the colonial government set out regulations to limit Bedouins' migration, reduce herd sizes, and encourage the building of houses. Today, most Bedouin in Lebanon live in settled communities (Chatty et al., 2013a).

In the 1970s, the Ivorian government sought to encourage cattle raising by establishing the *Société pour le développement des productions animales*

(SODEPRA) with the goal of securing self-sufficiency in beef production (Diallo, 2008). Fulbe pastoralists were encouraged to relocate from other countries to Côte d'Ivoire. SODEPRA incentivised them to become more sedentary and convert to herding as a wage-earning activity. Many Fulbe began working for local Ivorian 'tutors', raising cattle owned by settled Ivorian groups. Today, even those practising transhumance (moving livestock from one grazing ground to another in a seasonal cycle) often have a fixed base that is attributed to a landowner or 'tutor'. The end of SODEPRA in 1995 and the outbreak of civil war in 2002 impacted Fulbe pastoralists. Pastoral routes were not maintained; cattle vaccination programmes were discontinued, and much grazing land was privatised. While cattle-raising remains an economic activity in Côte d'Ivoire, most Fulbe interviewed reported that lack of space means that their herd sizes have decreased.

The Moken in Thailand have historically lived a mobile hunter-gatherer lifestyle based on the seas and migrating on houseboats, known as *kabang* (Arunotai, 2017). The 2004 tsunami was a catalyst for accelerating their sedentarisation. Following post-tsunami reconstruction efforts, the Moken were settled in communities on islands off the Thai coast. Driven by supposedly humanitarian objectives, new houses were built by NGOs and government agencies – the traditional *kabang* have largely disappeared. Although most Moken still go out to the sea to fish, those interviewed expressed how their livelihoods have changed. Many reported a noticeable decrease in the ecological abundance of sea resources as well as external restrictions on fishing for their daily needs. The Moken's traditional livelihoods have increasingly been replaced by wage earning linked with tourism and fishing industries.

The three case studies show that 'nomadic' populations have experienced drastic changes in their traditional ways of life over the past decades. Governance interventions have shaped these developments. In this process, all three case study populations have gradually adopted more sedentary lifestyles, albeit to different degrees and at different times. Only in Côte d'Ivoire do some smaller cross-border Fulbe groups continue to practise more traditional nomadic mobility. Yet, in all case studies the legacies of former mobile lifestyles remain alive and have significantly affected the peoples' legal and citizenship status in countries to which they have historical ties.

State law, citizenship, and mobile peoples

In many ways, current state-based laws are not designed to include mobile populations (Alexander, 2019; Gilbert, 2014). The way matters of nationality – and by extension statelessness – are conceived reveals a continuous reliance on a system of fixed territorial links. Bronwen Manby (2018) notes that '[t]he entire system of international and most domestic law on citizenship (and other) issues has grown up around the idea that individuals have their "home" in one fixed place and that states have a sovereign right to know where that place is' (339). The figure of the mobile 'nomad' therefore sits at odds with how state-based nationality laws conceive of the requisite links to the state territory. Further complexities arise from the fact that the traditional territories and waters of such populations may straddle multiple borders. Present-day states continue to grapple with borders that were arbitrarily drawn during colonial periods and cut across these areas.

In order to prove their belonging to a state-based polity, (formerly) mobile populations are often required to prove their historical presence on the territory. For instance, Côte d'Ivoire amended its nationality law in 1972, introducing one of the most restrictive nationality laws in the region. Many Fulbe pastoralists who were in Côte d'Ivoire before that date do not have proof of their presence in the country (UNHCR, 2016). Similarly, many stateless persons in Lebanon trace the origins of their problems back to the formation of the modern state of Lebanon. A French census, conducted in 1932, has played an instrumental role in determining who would later be considered to be Lebanese citizens (Frontiers Ruwad, 2011). Many Bedouin were excluded or refused to participate in the colonial census.

Field research highlights widespread challenges to establishing proof of a nationality, including instances of statelessness. Only a few Fulbe in Côte d'Ivoire reported having proof of Ivorian nationality, most of whom had settled in the country prior to colonial independence. There was a difference between the older generation of Fulbe born abroad in countries like Mali and Burkina Faso, who often had some documentation from those countries, and the younger generation born in Côte d'Ivoire, who frequently had no documentation at all. All Fulbe participants were interested in Ivorian nationality. Less than half of Bedouin research participants in Lebanon had national identification documents, most of whom had benefited from a 'naturalisation' law passed in 1994. Many of those who are 'undocumented' have held such status across generations and can be considered stateless. Out of a total Bedouin population in Lebanon of approximately 150,000, Dawn Chatty and colleagues estimate that some 100,000 lack citizenship, of which approximately 50,000 are 'undocumented' (*maktumeen al-qayd*) (Chatty et al., 2013b). Finally, it is estimated that there are still around 600 stateless Moken living in Thailand out of an estimated population of more than 1,000.[4]

Counting and registering (formerly) 'nomadic' populations

A central feature of state governance is the numerical accounting and administrative registration of populations under its control. Yet despite expanding state regulations into territories and maritime zones inhabited by 'nomadic' peoples, we know little about how many such people exist worldwide. The few existing estimates – ranging between tens to hundreds of millions, often limited to pastoralists – are speculative. Country-level data rely on censuses or household surveys that capture mobile peoples with great inconsistency. Roy Carr-Hill (2015) argues that such surveying tools omit by design populations that are mobile and hard to reach. Similarly, Sara Randall (2015) shows that while many censuses and household surveys make an effort to include 'nomadic' populations, many groups are still significantly undercounted in demographic data. As a consequence, mobile populations and their concerns often remain invisible to policy makers.

Registering populations is another governance practice foundational to accessing proof of nationality. The most common challenges raised by participants during fieldwork relate to acquiring proof of birth on the state's territory; proof of descent from a citizen or otherwise recorded individual; and proof of historical ties to the territory (such as proof of residence). For the purposes of establishing nationality, birth and other civil registration is particularly relevant. Yet civil registration schemes struggle to include mobile populations (African Union Commission, 2017). Due to mobile lifestyles, remoteness, illiteracy, and other factors, immediate birth registration is not always possible, and late birth registration requires overcoming significant obstacles. In Lebanon, births need to be declared within 30 days, and formal registration must occur within a year. Otherwise a judicial proceeding is required, which is both costly and lengthy. Likewise, Côte d'Ivoire requires families to register their children's births during the first three months of life.[5] Individuals whose births have not been declared within three months must go through a time-consuming and expensive judicial process to obtain a so-called *jugement supplétif* from the local courts (UNHCR, 2016). Our research therefore found that many Fulbe children born in Côte d'Ivoire do not have birth certificates.

Moken's mobility practices and life on remote islands mean that proof of birth remains a challenge across many communities in Thailand. A lack of awareness and physical distance to registration offices – coupled with weather conditions during the rainy season and costly travel – emerge from interviews as obstacles to birth registration. Most older Moken cannot provide their own or their children's date of birth, as their understanding of time differs from the information required by state officials. Although in Thailand a birth must be registered within fifteen days in order to avoid complications, some children remain unregistered for years after their birth. The arrival of a Thai health officer on the Surin Islands improved registration rates among the Moken community there. By recording and reporting the births in Moken communities to the Ministry, this scheme has provided an efficient way to increase birth registration rates in communities visited for this research.

In a context of complex nationality laws, widespread non- or underregistration of (formerly) mobile groups, and inaccessible corresponding institutions, individuals belonging to these groups struggle to meet the evidentiary requirements for claiming or acquiring a nationality as stipulated by state laws and regulations – despite their long, often historical ties to a state's territory.

'Nomads' as the perpetual foreigner

A host of other bureaucratic obstacles pose barriers for (formerly) 'nomadic' populations to access proof of nationality. While some problems are more structural in nature – including physical distances, logistical difficulties, and lack of resources – others can be described as discriminatory practices. Research found an often-prevalent presumption that populations labelled as 'nomadic' are not nationals of the states in which they live. This creates an assumption of foreign status that is difficult to overcome, even if individuals can produce documentary evidence to the contrary. Field research confirmed widespread stereotypes and negative attitudes among majority populations and local officials towards 'nomadic' populations. Often these populations were framed as a 'problem'. These perceptions rarely disappear and, at times, remain present decades after these populations have settled.

In Côte d'Ivoire, research found a lack of sympathy and support among authorities for Fulbe pastoral communities, most of whom were framed as members of a foreign population (UNHCR, 2016). Negative comments included claims that the Fulbe do not pay taxes, that they are a threat to farming, that they have fraudulent documents, and that they cross the border illegally. The Fulbe were also linked to security threats. Fulbe participants struggled with the fact that they were treated as outsiders in Côte d'Ivoire. Similar stereotyping has been found in Thailand, where the Moken were often described as being backward, uneducated, and 'uncivilised'. This research found a correlation between challenges faced by Moken communities in Thailand to accessing proof of legal identity and their proximity to the Thai–Myanmar border. Government officials expressed their mistrust of Moken populations in communities near the border, generally considering them to be immigrants. However, the extent to which the legacies of mobile lifestyles are a ground for discrimination in themselves and how this intersects with the treatment of broader minority groups to which affected populations may belong (ethnically, linguistically, or religiously) is not always clear.

As for the consequences of lack of nationality or other proof of legal identity, (formerly) 'nomadic' people highlighted at least three challenges in interviews: 1) regulation and restrictions of freedom of (cross-border) movements; 2) access to territories and waters; and 3) access to rights and services, especially in education and health.

Regulating the freedom of (cross-border) movement

Mobile peoples have moved through their traditional lands and waters for generations. Colonial border-drawing turned many mobility practices into an act of cross-border movement, subject to immigration regimes. Government-imposed restrictions and movement control often go hand-in-hand with protections for development projects and conservation efforts, strengthened migration controls, and security operations. These measures have foreclosed traditional migratory routes for nomadic peoples. While some borders remain porous, others have become impenetrable. The large number of nomadic peoples affected by restrictions on cross-border movements contrasts with the dearth of bilateral or multilateral arrangements to facilitate their movement (Davis et al., 2018). The region with the most advanced cross-border policies of relevance to nomadic groups is Africa.[6]

Restriction of freedom of movement, both within countries and across borders, due to a lack of proof of legal identity was raised in all three case studies. In fact, it was the primary concern raised in interviews with Fulbe pastoralists in Côte d'Ivoire and with Moken in Thailand. Undocumented Fulbe frequently report being harassed at checkpoints by police and asked to pay fines. Similarly, Moken have traditionally travelled across the archipelagos of the Andaman Sea, frequently crossing the Thai–Myanmar border and have relatives on both sides of the border. Prior to the tsunami, the Moken's lack of legal documentation was tolerated in practice, and most participants stated that they could visit relatives on both sides of the border. Since the tsunami, initiatives to expand state control and register inhabitants have increased, although many Moken remain unregistered. Even Moken holding non-Thai citizen identification documents cannot travel outside of the province where they are registered without permission from district officials. Due to practical and financial obstacles, few non-citizen Moken participants seek such permission, living in constant fear when travelling to neighbouring islands. According to interviewees, overcoming the movement restriction is one of the key motivators for getting Thai citizenship.

Restricting access to traditional territories and waters

'Nomadic' peoples' access to their lands, forests, and waters is critical to their subsistence strategies and culture. Most of these strategies are based on collective and seasonal use of territories. This approach has been challenged by regulatory systems of land use and ownership, which favour sedentary lifestyles (Gilbert, 2007). Mobile peoples' access to their traditional lands and waters has been shrinking rapidly. Reasons include the expansion of crop agriculture and private land ownership onto 'unoccupied' land traditionally used by nomadic peoples, the creation of protected areas for conservation and tourism purposes, resource extraction on hitherto remote lands and water areas, and the securitisation of borderlands. In the ensuing struggle over use and ownership of land and waters, undocumented or stateless populations frequently lose out.

None of the communities interviewed for our study who lacked a proof of nationality had ownership over the land on which they resided. Especially within Côte d'Ivoire and Thailand, there was a visible trend away from customary use of land and waters, traditionally frequented by mobile populations, to an expansion of private or state-controlled property regimes. One such trend is the incorporation of Moken's traditional maritime areas into new conservation zones (UNESCO, 2007). In 1982, with the expansion of tourism development, the Surin Islands in Thailand became a national marine park. This was accompanied by regulations imposing fishing restrictions and limiting Moken's access to certain maritime areas. Nowadays, most Moken men on the Surin Islands are hired to work on the tourist boats, whereas the women sell handicrafts to tourists. While the park management has made efforts to increase livelihood opportunities, not all Moken are happy with their dependent lifestyles. This example illustrates how well-meaning conservation efforts can transform the lives of mobile populations, especially if they are carried out without sufficient involvement of these populations and due regard to their rights (Chatty and Colchester, 2002).

Access to land was reported as a major problem by Fulbe research participants in Côte d'Ivoire. Even sedentary herd owners often do not own the land their herds graze. Under SODEPRA, land was owned by the state, but much of the land now appears to be under private ownership for agriculture. Fulbe participants were concerned about a lack of grazing space due to the shrinking amount of communal land and the disappearance of pastoral corridors. Across Northern Côte d'Ivoire, the land under agricultural cultivation has increased. The primary concern for both the Fulbe and the local authorities was the resultant tensions between farmers and pastoralists. Considering these developments, many Fulbe evidenced a great deal of frustration and fear about the future viability of their way of life. Many seemed resigned to the idea that transhumance might have to end; others demanded that the government take a more active role in providing space for transhumance.

Providing state services to the periphery

Another interconnection exists between the legal status and citizenship of (formerly) mobile peoples and the level of access to fundamental socio-economic rights and public services. There can be friction between development-focused service provision and the ability of such groups to maintain a mobile lifestyle and protect their culture. Most discussions in communities interviewed during our research centred on education and health services, though the importance assigned to such services varied with the level of integration in the surrounding sedentary society.

The education sector has generally been concerned about how to reach out to children in mobile communities through campaigns aimed at achieving universal primary education (Krätli, 2001). This research found that access to primary education has improved for the populations under study, including those without proof of legal identity, while secondary school education remains a challenge without a more robust proof of legal identity. However, challenges remain with providing culturally sensitive education. In Thailand, for instance, it was not until 2005 that all children, regardless of their legal status, had the right to free education. These previous access restrictions, combined with the more mobile lifestyles of the past, mean that the educational experience of older Moken generations was uneven. Although most can communicate in the Thai language, their literacy is low, making it difficult for them to engage with state laws that impact on their lives. Moken children nowadays have some access to primary education. Yet dropout rates remain high with various reasons cited by participants , including occupational restrictions for non-nationals and a lack of incentives to pursue further education. Children who would like to continue their education beyond primary school must move to the mainland. One theme emerging from interviews with Moken parents was a concern about their language and culture, and the effects of state education on their children when it is taught exclusively in majority-languages.

Access to education was not reported as a major problem in interviews with Fulbe communities in Côte d'Ivoire, although awareness and enrolment rates seem to be lower than in the other case studies. Many Fulbe parents practising transhumance expressed a preference for sending their male children to Koranic schools, which are usually boarding schools, as they otherwise struggle to find a place where their male children can live. Yet, youth often have few options for employment once they finish at these schools as they learn neither herding nor skills to work in the wage economy. Many girls, especially in mobile communities, do not attend school.

During the 1990s, governments and development agencies tended to ignore 'nomadic' populations when developing healthcare systems, so these populations lagged behind their settled counterparts in most health indicators (Omar, 1992). This research found that the relevance of access to health services for (formerly) mobile populations increased with their integration into sedentary society. For instance, access to health services was a great concern among 'undocumented' Bedouin in Lebanon, where the healthcare system is highly privatised and most expenditures come from out-of-pocket payments. Research participants considered lack of nationality as the main barrier to accessing subsidised health services, which are restricted to Lebanese citizens (Chatty et al., 2013b). The challenge for women accessing hospitals to give birth was a prominent issue in interviews. This perpetuates the risk of statelessness, since children are less likely to receive birth notifications from medical professionals if they are born at home.

Conclusion

This chapter shows the challenges faced by state-based nationality laws and associated governance practices to include 'nomadic' populations and their mobile lifestyles. The 'nomad' makes us see the degree to which existing systems of citizenship take fixed territorial links, such as residence and birth on the territory, for granted. (Formerly) 'nomadic' populations around the globe therefore frequently struggle to establish proof of nationality – many remain undocumented or even stateless – despite their long-established ties to a state's territory. While mobile peoples may have historically avoided state governance, the ever-expanding reach of the state into its peripheries has changed many peoples' traditional ways of life and created new realities. In particular, the state's reliance on legal identity regimes for administration and regulation has increasingly restricted (formerly) mobile populations' access to the common good, especially free movement and traditionally shared territories and waters.

This research highlights the importance of acknowledging and considering in state policies and citizenship regimes the agency and choices of these communities under rapidly changing ecological, economic, and socio-political conditions. Possible entry points for action include: more consideration of the rights of 'nomadic' peoples which sit uncomfortably at the intersection of the human rights regimes for the protection of minorities and indigenous peoples – none of which fully captures the unique circumstances of their lifestyles (Gilbert, 2014); enhancing bilateral or multilateral cross-border regimes that accommodate traditional mobility practices; promoting in international and national legal instruments an understanding of 'habitual residence' capable of considering periodic but regular presence on a state's territory, while keeping in mind the right to maintain a mobile lifestyle;[7] and more pro-active and possibly collective approaches to nationality determination that counter discrimination and address the predicaments shared by entire groups with similar characteristics (rather than relying on individualised approaches that apply general policies and laws without considering current or former mobility practices). The goal must not be to make 'nomadic' peoples fit into the constraints of nationality laws that often date back to colonial eras, but rather to find flexible legal and administrative solutions that consider the specificity of their lifestyles. These findings have relevance for global campaigns, such as the Sustainable Development Goals' 'no-one-left-behind' agenda and the #IBelong Campaign. They will need to avoid falling into the same traps as the many colonial and post-colonial initiatives that explicitly or implicitly promoted sedentarisation among mobile peoples to incorporate them into state structures.

Notes

1 The author acknowledges the contributions from the project's research consultants – Janepicha Cheva-Isarakul (Thailand), Heather Alexander (Côte d'Ivoire), and Thomas McGee and Walaa Kayyal (Lebanon) – as well as the support from our research partners, including the Chulalongkorn Social Research Institute, the Association Femmes Juristes, Frontiers Ruwad, and the American University of Beirut.

2 Fieldwork was carried out in 2018–2019 and involved 296 individuals across the three case studies through focus group discussions, individual community interviews, and key informant interviews. Our findings are not representative of the broader populations to which the participants belong.

3 This study is limited to 'nomadic' populations in the traditional sense and does not address more popular notions of the term 'nomad', including digital nomads or other migratory lifestyles in the globalised world.

4 Another up to 3,000 Moken are estimated to live in Myanmar (Human Rights Watch, 2015).

5 In 2018, Côte d'Ivoire amended its civil status laws to improve registration rates in the country.

6 Among others, the African Union's (2010) Policy Framework for Pastoralism in Africa and the ECOWAS (1998) Transhumance Protocol.
7 The Draft Protocol to the African Charter on Human and Peoples' Rights on the Specific Aspects of the Right to a Nationality and the Eradication of Statelessness in Africa (version May 2017) could serve as a model for an interpretation of residence in the context of mobile lifestyles, including by considering factors such as the use of water points, seasonal grazing sites, the burial sites of ancestors, and testimony of community members.

References

African Commission on Human and Peoples' Rights (2017) *Draft Protocol to the African Charter on Human and Peoples' Rights on the Specific Aspects of the Right to a Nationality and the Eradication of Statelessness in Africa* [Online]. Available at www.achpr.org/public/Document/file/English/draft_citizenship_ protocol_en_may2017.pdf (Accessed 11 November 2020).

African Union (2010) 'Policy framework for pastoralism in Africa: Securing, protecting and improving the lives, livelihoods and rights of pastoralist communities' [Online]. Available at https://au.int/sites/default/files/documents/ 30240-doc-policy_framework_for_pastoralism.pdf (Accessed 17 June 2020).

African Union Commission (2017) 'Migrants, refugees, internally displaced persons and stateless persons in civil registration and vital statistic systems in Africa', ECA Fourth Conference of African Ministers responsible for Civil Registration Experts Meeting, Nouakchott, 4–8 December [Online]. Available at http://apai-crvs.org/ sites/default/files/public/EN-CRVS%20AND%20STATELESSNESS-CRMS5.pdf (Accessed 20 July 2020).

Alexander, H. (2019) 'The nationality and statelessness of nomads under international law' (PhD thesis, Tilburg University).

Arunotai, N. (2017) '"Hopeless at sea, landless on shore": Contextualising the sea nomads dilemma in Thailand', *AAS Working Papers in Social Anthropology*, 31, 1–27.

Carr-Hill, R. (2015) 'Non-household populations: Implications for measurements of poverty globally and in the UK', *Journal of Social Policy*, 44:2, 255–275.

Chatty, D., and Colchester, M. (eds) (2002) *Conservation and Mobile Indigenous Peoples: Displacement, Forced Settlement, and Sustainable Development* (New York: Berghahn Books).

Chatty, D., Mansour, N., and Yassin, N. (2013a) 'Statelessness and tribal identity on Lebanon's eastern borders', *Mediterranean Politics*, 18:3, 411–426.

Chatty, D., Mansour, N., and Yassin, N. (2013b) 'Bedouin in Lebanon: Social discrimination, political exclusion, and compromised health care', *Social Science & Medicine*, 82, 43–50.

Davis, J., Ogali, C., Slobodian, L., Roba, G., and Ouedraogo, R. (2018) 'Crossing boundaries: Legal and policy arrangements for cross-border pastoralism', Food and Agriculture Organization of the United Nations and International Union for Conservation of Nature [Online]. Available at www.fao.org/3/ca2383en/ CA2383EN.pdf (Accessed 30 March 2020).

Diallo, Y. (2008) *Nomades des Espaces Interstitiels: Pastoralisme, Identité, Migrations (Burkina Faso – Côte d'Ivoire)* (Köln: Rüdiger Köppe Verlag).

Economic Community of West African States (ECOWAS) (1998) *Decision A/DEC.5/ 10/98 Relating to the Regulations on Transhumance Between ECOWAS Member States*. Abuja: Twenty-first Conference of Heads of States [Online]. Available at http://extwprlegs1.fao.org/docs/pdf/eco147525.pdf (Accessed 20 July 2020).

Frontiers Ruwad (2011) *Invisible Citizens: Humiliation and a Life in the Shadows: A Legal and Policy Study on Statelessness in Lebanon* (Beirut: Ruwad Frontiers Association).

Gilbert, J. (2007) 'Nomadic territories: A human rights approach to nomadic peoples' land rights', *Human Rights Law Review*, 7:4, 681–716.

Gilbert, J. (2014) *Nomadic Peoples and Human Rights* (New York: Routledge).

Human Rights Watch (2015) 'Stateless at sea: The Moken of Burma and Thailand' [Online]. Available at www.hrw.org/report/2015/06/25/stateless-sea/moken-burma-and-thailand (Accessed 17 June 2020).

Khazanov, A. M., and Wink, A. (eds) (2001) *Nomads in the Sedentary World* (Richmond: Curzon Press).

Krätli, S. (2001) *Education Provision to Nomadic Pastoralists: A Literature Review*, Institute of Development Studies, Working Paper 126 [Online]. Available at www. ids.ac.uk/publications/education-provision-to-nomadic-pastoralists-a-literature-review/ (Accessed 30 March 2020).

Manby, B. (2018) *Citizenship in Africa* (London: Hart Publishing).

Omar, M. A. (1992) 'Health care for nomads too, please', *World Health Forum*, 13:4, 307–310 [Online]. Available at https://apps.who.int/iris/handle/10665/ 52277 (Accessed 30 March 2020).

Randall, S. (2015) 'Where have all the nomads gone? Fifty years of statistical and demographic invisibilities of African mobile pastoralists', *Pastoralism*, 5:1, 1–22.

Salzman, P. C. (1980) *When Nomads Settle: Processes of Sedentarization as Adaptation and Response* (New York: Praeger).

Scott, J. (2009) *The Art of Not Being Governed: An Anarchist History of Upland Southeast Asia* (New Haven, CT: Yale University Press).

United Nations Educational, Scientific and Cultural Organization (UNESCO) (2007) *Bridging the Gap between the Rights and Needs of Indigenous Communities and the Management of Protected Areas: Case Studies from Thailand* (Bangkok: UNESCO Bangkok) [Online]. Available at https://unesdoc.unesco.org/ ark:/48223/pf0000155745 (Accessed 20 March 2020).

United Nations High Commissioner for Refugees (UNHCR) (2016) 'Statelessness and nationality in Côte d'Ivoire' [Online]. Available at www.refworld.org/docid/ 58594d114.html (Accessed 30 March 2020).

15

Ageing and stateless: Non-decisionism and state violence across temporal and geopolitical space from Bhutan to the United States

Odessa Gonzalez Benson, Yoosun Park,
Francis Tom Temprosa, and Dilli Gautam[1]

Statelessness of refugees in old age is rarely examined, even though the profound implications of such socio-political exclusion are particularly severe at the end of life. Resettlement with a path to citizenship is the conventional 'durable solution' for stateless refugees. But as this chapter illustrates, there is no viable path to citizenship for a specific group of resettled refugees who are older. Drawing on previous and current work using contextual and empirical field data, we examine the case of older Bhutanese refugees who were denationalised by the state of Bhutan and resettled in the United States. Despite their eligibility for naturalisation as resettled refugees in the United States according to the Refugee Act of 1980, this population remains stateless because the English-language requirement of the naturalisation process structurally bars them from attaining U.S. citizenship (USCIS, 2019c and 2020a). For this aged, often non-literate population, learning English is a functional impossibility. They are trapped in a paradox; they remain permanent noncitizens in their place of resettlement, but they do not qualify for resettlement elsewhere because they have been granted legal status as permanent residents in the United States. U.S. citizenship laws and international refugee policies work in conjunction here to render them permanently stateless (Gonzalez Benson and Park, 2018). Moreover, being resettled-yet-stateless holds profound material and symbolic implications, such as losing eligibility for social security entitlements without gaining citizenship (USSSA, 2016). This is compounded by increasing precarity in recent years – for instance, the Trump Administration's threat to revoke permanent residency status and deport immigrants who use public assistance (Kilgore, 2018; Hauslohner et al., 2019).

From a theoretical standpoint, we examine this phenomenon using the concepts of 'state of exception', developed by the Italian moral philosopher

Giorgio Agamben (2005), and 'state decisionism' (Nyers, 2006), or the idea that state power is enacted through the state's capacity to decide and to act in moments outside legally defined parameters. We apply here its conceptual flipside – non-decisionism, or the idea that state violence is enacted not only through action and decision, but in some cases through the state's refusal to act and decide (Gonzalez Benson and Park, 2018). State violence must be understood to include not only what states do but also what states choose not to do.

Furthermore, we extend these discussions by exploring the linking of state violence across temporal and geographic distances, specifically the linking of the non-decisionism of the American state in the current moment with the exclusionary decisionist acts done by the Bhutanese state thirty years ago. We join others in evidencing that the state of exception is not an exception but the norm, and we further argue for recognition of a network, system, or continuum of state violence and exceptionalism across time and national boundaries. We draw from interviews and focus groups with older Bhutanese men in order to call attention to the voices of older resettled refugees in their struggle for American citizenship, thus revealing heightened anxieties and feelings of hopelessness.[2]

Bhutanese refugees

Bhutan is a small constitutional monarchy in the Himalayas, abutting India to its south, China to its north, and Nepal to its west. It is a historically Buddhist nation, in which Tibetan and Indian subsects of Buddhism have competed for religious domination and political power. Towards the turn of the twentieth century, the Drukpa Buddhist subsect of the Ngalung (an ethnic group of Tibetan origin) emerged as dominant and established an absolute monarchy in 1907. The Ngalung culture and Drukpa religious practices thus became the dominant way of life into which all others were assimilated.

One group, the Lhotshampa – Hindus of Nepali origin who had immigrated, with government permission, into Bhutan's southern region in the late 1800s – resisted this assimilation. In the mid-twentieth century, this small minority group began to organise, demanding political representation and social and economic equity. Acquiescing to this demand, Bhutan passed the Nationality Act of 1958, bestowing legal Bhutanese citizenship to persons of Nepalese origin, including the Lhotshampa. This legal inclusion was short-lived, however; the ruling Drukpa later assailed the move as anti-nationalist (Rizal, 2004) and instituted increasingly oppressive and violent policies of assimilation and exclusion.

Thirty years after its passage, the 1958 law was essentially reversed under Bhutan's 1985 Citizenship Act. Called 'One Nation, One People', the Act aimed to create a homogenous national identity. Bhutan established compulsory assimilation policies, thereby banning Hindu culture, language, and religion (Rizal, 2004; Ferraro, 2012). Further, Bhutanese citizenship was made valid only with documentary proof of registration of permanent domicile filed with the Ministry of Home Affairs on or before 31 December 1958 – an impossible requirement for most of the Lhotshampa (Ferraro, 2012). The Citizenship Act also allowed for the denationalisation of anyone who exhibited any manner of 'disloyalty' to the 'King, Country and People of Bhutan' (Ferraro, 2012: 414), such as protesting the new citizenship policies, or refusing to comply with the new mandates to convert to Buddhism and adopt the Drukpa dress and language. It was the start of a series of legal acts and state actions that resulted in mass denationalisation and religious, cultural, and ethnic persecution.

In the final accounting, more than 100,000 Lhotshampa fled to Nepal (Ferraro, 2012; Rizal, 2004) and resided in refugee camps provided by the United Nations High Commissioner for Refugees (UNHCR) (Muggah, 2005) for more than two decades. During that time, the impacts of statelessness compounded with challenges of displacement, such as threats to education and livelihood rights (Kingston and Stam, 2017). In 2008, the UNHCR began resettling Bhutanese refugees to the United States, Australia, Canada, Denmark, the Netherlands, New Zealand, Norway, and other countries, with the large majority of about 85,000 refugees resettled to the United States (UNHCR, 2009; White House Initiative, 2016).

The legal landscape: U.S. naturalisation, refugee law, and the Bhutanese case

Generally, resettlement in the United States is a path to citizenship. A year after arrival in the United States, resettled refugees become legal permanent residents (USCIS, 2017) who are endowed with the right to work. Legal permanent residents become eligible for naturalisation after five years of living continuously in the country under that status (USCIS, 2015). However, applicants must pass English language and civics tests in order to qualify for naturalisation. In the language test, they must show English reading, writing, and speaking abilities. In the civics test, they must correctly answer, at the minimum, six out of ten questions about U.S. government, history, and geography (USCIS, 2019c and 2020a).

Many Bhutanese refugees in the U.S. have gained citizenship, yet some of the older cohort are unable to learn English (Kingston and Stam, 2017), and so many are unable to pass English language requirements for American citizenship and thus must remain stateless (Gonzalez Benson and Park, 2018). Most older people within the Bhutanese refugee community never had formal schooling in Bhutan or in the refugee camps in Nepal. 'Many of [the older adults] just learned how to write their name', according to one community leader who noted that some elders of the Bhutanese community are non-literate and cannot read and write even in Nepali, their first language, thus making learning English nearly impossible. One elder expressed his difficulty in learning English in this manner: 'Because of the torture I suffered in Bhutan and my hardship in the refugee camp to provide for the family, I never got a chance to learn English. I regret it now for not being able to comprehend and memorize enough English to get my U.S. citizenship'. Similarly, another poignantly explained the challenge of cognitive functioning and decline. 'Because of how I left Bhutan, I felt only half of my brain was functional, and our situation in the refugee camp was not suitable for me go to school and learn because I had to take care of my family', he said.

There are exemptions to the language test. Applicants who are at least 50 years old and have lived with permanent resident status for at least twenty years (fifteen years for people who are age 55 or older) are exempt from the language test and allowed interpreters for the civics test (USCIS, 2019a). Alternatively, immigrants can seek a waiver by showing a certificate attesting that they suffer from a physical or mental impairment (USCIS, 2019a). This would allow them to be assigned language interpreters and extended test times, or be allowed to take the exam off-site (USCIS, 2020b). The older Bhutanese refugees in our study do not, for the most part, qualify for these exemptions. Many have met the age requirement for exemption, but not the residency requirement. Naturalisation remains a functional impossibility for this population.

Given that denationalisation was the cause of their exile in the first place, the inability to obtain citizenship upon resettlement represents a deep symbolic injury for this group. There are, moreover, significant material consequences. For many of these older refugees, who are excluded from social and economic participation in the larger society due to their lack of English language proficiency, social security is their sole source of income. However, this resource is slated to be revoked, unless they soon gain citizenship. The Social Security insurance entitlement time limit, known as the 'seven-year rule', was instituted as part of sweeping welfare policy reforms in 1996. It dictates that resettled refugees' eligibility for entitlements or benefits expires within seven years of arrival if they do not become American citizens within that timeframe (USSSA, 2016). In 2017, the seven-year rule began to be applicable for the first large cohorts of older

Bhutanese refugees who began arriving in 2009 and gaining permanent residency status in 2010.

The 'right to have rights'

Third-country resettlement is a 'durable solution' to the problem of statelessness, reflecting ideals of human rights, humanitarianism, and ethical considerations (Carens, 1991; Boswell, 2005). As Hannah Arendt (1950) famously argued, within the modern schema of nation-states, the 'right to have rights' hinges upon attachment to a state. The resettled-yet-stateless Bhutanese refugees represent a limit case. Their exceptional circumstances illustrate the bounds or limits to Arendt's argument. As legal permanent residents, older monoglot Bhutanese refugees resettled in the United States are attached to a state. Yet simultaneously, with no hope of ever attaining citizenship rights, they also remain permanently unattached to any state.

In Agamben's (2005) terminology, the liminal status of the individuals in our limit case represent the 'bare life', embodying that ultimate human 'nakedness' that can exist only outside the modern political sphere (see also Somers, 2008). Those in our limit case have moved towards such possibilities, stepping out of the 'zone of indistinction' (Agamben, 2005) that is the refugee camp, into a political community where 'the good life', indicating full membership in society and the polity (Neal, 2007: 3), is theoretically possible but functionally impossible.

U.S. refugee law is the legal structure that allows resettled refugees to be lawfully admitted into the country and mandated services for housing and provision of basic needs in the first months of arrival (Adelman, 1991; Haines, 2010). They are thus distinguished from undocumented migrants – who are rendered 'illegal' and deportable because of their mode of entry and whose residence is not legally recognised by the state. Yet, these refugees are not fully within the national–juridical framework. The reinstatement of basic rights and economic rights (and perhaps even social rights) notwithstanding, their political rights remain beyond reach. The status and protections – the right to have rights – provided by U.S. refugee law is contradicted by its citizenship law. While claims for political membership of stateless refugees under UN jurisdiction in refugee camps compel action and attention from the international community, the stateless refugees who have been resettled in the United States – who are considered to have been granted state membership – do not garner such attention. They are no longer the charge of the international community.

Older Bhutanese people are thus legal subjects of the United States, accountable to its laws but with no voice or representation in its processes

(Gibney, 2009). Bhutan, with its restrictive citizenship policies – as well as Myanmar, which excluded about 1.3 million members of the Muslim Rohingya from citizenship (Al Jazeera, 2014; Brinham, this volume) – exemplify such tyrannical rule. While the U.S. democracy differentiates itself from those countries with discriminatory and persecutory citizenship laws, our limit case contests that distinction.

Not an exception, but a continuum and a system of exceptions: Geographic and temporal links of state violence in Bhutan and the United States

Agamben's (1995 and 2005) 'state of exception' denotes the power of the state to go beyond legal boundaries to manage life by determining membership in (or exclusion from) the polity, thereby exerting and making visible its authority. The state is powerful and exceptional in its capacity to go beyond the limits of law while simultaneously remaining bound by it. A constitutive element of state power is state decisionism, the executive capacity to decide to transgress its law. It is precisely this decisionism and capacity to decide on the exception to the rule of law that marks the very power of the state (Nyers, 2006). State decisionism, thus, is understood to be an inherently violent act made through an absence or suspension of law, or by reconstituting the boundaries of law (Agamben, 1995 and 2005; Mills, 2008).

The state's constitutive power is not limited to decisionism, however, but resides also in non-decisionism (Gonzalez Benson and Park, 2018). Most applications of the state of exception consider when subjects are in a situation in which a violent and extrajuridical, decisionist act of sovereignty is imposed upon them in order to *exclude* them. We argue that our limit case presents the flip side to that: the older, non-English-speaking Bhutanese refugees present the state with an opportunity to make a decision to transgress the law in order to *include* them. But precisely at this rare moment when the state could use its decisionist powers of sovereignty not to exclude but to include, the United States has made no decisions and has taken no actions.

Social membership prefigures a political one, 'at least until they are codified into a new national identity' (Fresia and von Kanel, 2015: 4). As an ethno-religious minority group, the Lhotsampa were outside of the national imaginary the ruling elites of Bhutan promoted as authentically Bhutanese. Resettled thirty years later in the United States, they are yet again aliens outside the social imaginary of the American nation. Socially excluded from the American national identity, they are also left to remain economically, legally, and politically so. The state could amend existing naturalisation laws to waive English language requirements that are tied to additional residency requirements in the United States, but it does not do so. Other legal accommodations could be pursued, but are not.

As such, the initiating or 'original' statelessness created by decisionist violence by the Bhutanese state over three decades ago is perpetuated and supported by non-decision of the U.S. state currently. The older, non-English-speaking Bhutanese refugee – solitary and banished – is nevertheless able to speak about state power. She illustrates the interlinking of state violence across temporal and geopolitical space, and evidences how the 'state of exception' is *not an exception, but the norm.* In this case study, the state of exception is not an exception, but part of a continuum or system of exceptions. Bhutan in the 1980s and the United States of today may seem worlds apart, but the non-decisionism of the U.S. state has not only forged permanent statelessness within its legal borders, but it also condones and upholds the state violence of denaturalisation and ethnic persecution perpetrated by Bhutan in that era. While the actions of Bhutan were condemned by the international community, the non-actions of the United States are not. Both, we argue, are forms of state violence. Therefore, the U.S.'s non-decision, its refusal to act to make an exception to include, is a sin of omission that is not alone, but acts within a continuum or network of sovereign acts of exclusion.

Implications, symbolic and material

The American imagining of the 'citizen', while symbolic, is also utterly material. The state's failure to provide a rights-based process for older refugees to acquire citizenship in due time has consequential material – social and economic – repercussions. Most urgent, as mentioned earlier, is their eligibility for social security; if they do not become U.S. citizens, eligibility for this public benefit expires within seven years of arrival (USSSA, 2016). Those who do not acquire citizenship are deprived of entitlements to a pension, upon which many of them depend for living, access to healthcare, and other services that are crucial in old age.

The elders in our case share a collective fear of abandonment. The practice of the Bhutanese community has been intergenerational living; adult children living together with older parents and providing and caring for them in all necessary ways. But some elders are worried about their future in their children's homes. The culture shift from parents being the head of the family to parents being dependent on their children – because of a lack of language and cultural understanding – has been difficult. One respondent worried that he is 'old and cannot get a job', and does not know 'how long [he] can live'. Another elder shared this collective concern:

I don't know how long my children can take care of me. Also, I take ten pills a day. Without my Medicare, I won't be able to afford to buy my medicines. My children have their own financial problems. I feel like I will die not long after not being able to afford to buy medicine.

As non-citizens, their status in the country is precarious. Permanent residency status could be revoked. U.S. President Donald Trump's administration drafted an executive order in 2018 to deport immigrants who were accessing public benefits (Kilgore, 2018; Hauslohner et al., 2019). In 2019, the Trump administration expanded the definition for 'inadmissibility on public charge grounds', making the use of many of the public benefits – for which legal immigrants have long been eligible without penalty – a cause for deportation and exclusion from entry, permanent residency, and naturalisation (Park, 2019; USCIS, 2019b).

These issues are particularly troubling for older refugees who have vulnerabilities that lie at the intersection of age, language, and immigration status/statelessness. The older persons in this study had been farmers who were stripped of citizenship and livelihood upon refugeehood. As older monoglots who speak only one language (in this case Hindi), unlike their younger counterparts, they are also less able to acquire skills for employment purposes in the United States. They are also vulnerable because they depend on other family members once their entitlements to public welfare expire. One community leader who was interviewed expressed 'fear that they will be deported... [i]nsecurity is rising... Without [citizenship], there is frustration and insecurity'. Whether or not such new immigrant policy-restriction measures are pushed forward, their threat highlights rising anti-immigrant sentiments that affect resettled refugees in various ways. Fear, anxiety, and precarity are invoked for the older stateless monoglots, strengthening the case that 'state violence' occurs even inside sovereign borders and established communities (see Agamben, 2005).

Viewed in the light of having the effect of a *suspension of inclusion*, rather than merely an *effect of exclusion*, older stateless monoglots are caught in a violent cyclical suspension of hope, belief, and despair that they would be accommodated into a polity. This is especially so because they are already presumed to be en route to a 'durable solution', but their situation of statelessness is perpetuated from statelessness to statelessness. State non-decisionism in the United States, understood in this sense, sustains and perpetuates the original state of statelessness in Bhutan. The older stateless monoglots are systematically treated as bodies at the mercy of the state.

A feeling of resignation and hopelessness 'about coming to the United States' now grips the community. 'They are just waiting to die', reflected one man about others in this community. Offering a simple but profound insight, one older Bhutanese man expressed how language ability, as trivial as it may seem to those who speak English as their native tongue, is what is causing him to die a stateless man: 'Now, I am scared how the end of my life looks like for not being able to speak enough English'.

Others recall how Bhutan did not accept them as citizens, despite living in Bhutan for generations, and now after a decade in the U.S., they 'don't even have citizenship and don't know how the US government will treat [them]'. While they have family and food to eat in the United States, they do not feel that the United States is their home. Neither is Bhutan home, for returning to Bhutan might cost them their lives. It is the memory of a distant past. Some shared that they regret resettlement to the U.S., reflecting the notion that being stateless in the refugee camps nevertheless offered the possibility for citizenship one day, no matter how unlikely. Today there is no such possibility. For older stateless monoglots, some of whom are sickly and face the last moments of life, having citizenship and dying in the land where one is a citizen is about more than eluding statelessness. It is about evading an undignified death. One respondent reflected on the cultural tradition in which a handful of soil is thrown over bodies after death, 'signifying that homeland as part of the rites from life to death… the assurance that the departed will have a space somewhere in heaven or paradise'. But with no such 'homeland', the state precludes even this dignity upon death.

The weight of state violence notwithstanding, some have focused on contested processes and 'indeterminacy' on the ground (Ajana, 2013; Fresia and von Kanel, 2015; Holian, 2012; Nyers, 2006). Contestations materialise in localised community efforts for redress and resistance (Gonzalez Benson and Park, 2018). Resettled Bhutanese communities across the country conduct legal advocacy and call for allowing translators in citizenship testing – thus, a waiving of English language requirements for citizenship – specifically for monoglot elders who are stateless in the United States. More broadly, there are international efforts, such as UNHCR's #IBelong Campaign to End Statelessness, to which the United States is a signatory (UNHCR, 2013 and 2017). Also, a global treaty for older persons is under discussion and, if successful, would be a significant development in international human rights law. In 2018, the document 'The Rights of Older Persons in the Global Compact on Refugees', submitted by the NGO Committee on Ageing to the UNHCR, included references noting that older refugees have rights and specific age-related needs that the law ought to accommodate (UNHCR, 2018). That document recognises heterogeneity and intersectionality among older persons, and the importance of upholding their autonomy and participation in decision making. It recognises the vulnerability of older persons, but also values their experiences, skills, and capacities. Regarding older refugees who resettle, the report calls for community-based support mechanisms; for housing, land, and property rights; and for family reunification. However, this document overlooks statelessness upon resettlement for older persons, illustrating the invisibility of this issue.

Referring to their statelessness, two older Bhutanese men lamented a suspended sense of hope:

> I just want to belong to a nation before I die. I want my grandchildren to visit my grave and be proud of me as an American.

> I am Bhutanese by birth, practice Nepali culture and traditions, and currently live in the U.S., but I don't belong to any of these countries. If I obtain U.S. citizenship, I can announce proudly that I am a U.S. citizen, that I belong to a nation. It will be my proudest accomplishment.

Notes

1 Portions of this chapter are adapted from a previously published article; see Gonzalez Benson and Park (2018).
2 Interviews were conducted in Nepali. Where respondents are quoted, they have been translated into English by the authors.

References

Adelman, H. (ed.) (1991) *Refugee Policy: Canada and the United States* (Toronto: Yorks Lane Press).

Agamben, G. (1995) *Homo Sacer: Sovereign Power and Bare Life* (Stanford, CA: Stanford University Press).

Agamben, G. (2005) *State of Exception* (Chicago, IL: University of Chicago Press).

Ajana, B. (2013) 'Asylum, identity management, and biometric control', *Journal of Refugee Studies*, 26:4, 576–595.

Al Jazeera (2014) 'UN calls for "full Rohingya citizenship"', 30 December [Online]. Available at www.aljazeera.com/news/americas/2014/12/un-calls-full-rohingya-citizenship-myanmar-monks-rakhin-2014123044246726211.html (Accessed 22 November 2018).

Arendt, H. (1950) *The Origins of Totalitarianism* (New York: Harcourt Brace).

Boswell, C. (2005) *The Ethics of Refugee Policy* (Burlington, VT: Ashgate).

Carens, J. (1991) 'States and refugees: A normative analysis', in H. Adelman (ed.) *Refugee Policy: Canada and the United States* (Toronto: Yorks Lane Press): pp. 18–29.

Ferraro, M. F. (2012) 'Stateless in Shangri-La: Minority rights, citizenship, and belonging in Bhutan', *Stanford Journal of International Law*, 48:2, 405–435.

Fresia, M., and von Kanel, A. (2015) 'Beyond space of exception? Reflections on the camp through the prism of refugee schools', *Journal of Refugee Studies*, 29:2, 250–272.

Gibney, M. (2009) 'Statelessness and the right to citizenship', *Forced Migration Review*, 32, 50–51.

Gonzalez Benson, O. G, and Park, Y. (2018) 'Resettled yet stateless: Elderly monoglot refugees in the United States as a limit case to citizenship', *Journal of Human Rights Practice*, 10:3, 423–438.

Haines, D. (2010) *Safe Haven: A History of Refugees in America* (Sterling, VA: Kumarian Press).

Hauslohner, A., Miroff, N., Sacchetti, M., and Jan, T. (2019) 'Trump officials move to deny green cards, path to citizenship for poor immigrants', *The Washington Post*, 12 August [Online]. Available at www.washingtonpost.com/immigration/trump-administration-aims-to-make-citizenship-more-difficult-for-immigrants-who-rely-on-public-assistance/2019/08/12/fe3f8162-b565-11e9-8949-5f36ff92706e_story.html (Accessed 8 July 2020).

Holian, A. (2012) 'The ambivalent exception: American occupation policy in postwar Germany and formation of Jewish refugee spaces', *Journal of Refugee Studies*, 25:3, 452–473.

Kilgore, E. (2018) 'Trump could try to deport legal immigrants who get federal benefits', *New York Magazine*, 8 February [Online]. Available at http://nymag.com/daily/intelligencer/2018/02/trump-may-try-to-deport-legal-immigrants-who-get-benefits.html (Accessed 8 July 2020).

Kingston, L. N., and Stam, K. (2017) 'Recovering from statelessness: Resettled Bhutanese-Nepali and Karen refugees reflect on the lack of legal nationality', *Journal of Human Rights*, 16:4, 389–406.

Mills, C. (2008) *The Philosophy of Agamben* (Montreal: McGill-Queen's University Press).

Muggah, R. (2005) 'Distinguishing means and ends: The counterintuitive effects of UNHCR's community development approach in Nepal', *Journal of Refugee Studies*, 18:2, 151–164.

Neal, A. (2007) 'Georgio Agamben and the politics of the exception', conference paper, Sixth Pan-European International Relations Conference of the 2016 ECPR General Conference Standing Group on International Relations, 12–15 September (Turin, Italy).

Nyers, P. (2006) 'The accidental citizen: Acts of sovereignty and (un)making citizenship', *Economy and Society*, 35:1, 22–41.

Park, Y. (2019) 'Our house is on fire: Social work and the crisis of immigration', *Affilia: Journal of Women and Social Work*, 34:4, 413–420.

Refugee Act 1980. Pub. L. No. 96–212, 94 Stat. 102 (1980) [Online]. Available at www.govinfo.gov/content/pkg/STATUTE-94/pdf/STATUTE-94-Pg102.pdf (Accessed 16 July 2020).

Rizal, D. (2004) 'The unknown refugee crisis: Expulsion of ethnic Lhotsampa from Bhutan', *Asian Ethnicity*, 5:2, 151–177.

Somers, M. (2008) *Genealogies of Citizenship: Markets, Statelessness, and the Right to Have Rights* (Cambridge: Cambridge University Press).

United Nations High Commissioner for Refugees (UNHCR) (2009) 'Over 20,000 Bhutanese refugees resettled from Nepal' [Online]. Available at www.unhcr.org/4aa641446.html (Accessed 1 October 2017).

United Nations High Commissioner for Refugees (UNHCR) (2013) 'Draft overview of implementation of pledges' [Online]. Available at www.unhcr.org/52023f289. pdf (accessed 8 July 2020).

United Nations High Commissioner for Refugees (UNHCR) (2017) '#IBelong Campaign' [Online]. Available at www.unhcr.org/ibelong/ (Accessed 8 July 2020).

United Nations High Commissioner for Refugees (UNHCR) (2018) *The Rights of Older Persons on the Global Compact on Refugees* [Online]. Available at www.unhcr.org/en-us/events/conferences/5a6703357/rights-older-persons-global-compact-refugees.html?query= (Accessed 16 July 2020).

U.S. Citizenship and Immigration Services (USCIS) (2015) 'Rights and responsibilities of a green card holder (permanent resident)' [Online]. Available at www.uscis.gov/green-card/after-green-card-granted/rights-and-responsibilities-permanent-resident/rights-and-responsibilities-green-card-holder-permanent-resident (Accessed 16 July 2020).

U.S. Citizenship and Immigration Services (USCIS) (2017) 'Green card for refugees' [Online]. Available at www.uscis.gov/green-card/green-card-through-refugee-or-asylee-status/green-card-refugee (Accessed 16 July 2020).

U.S. Citizenship and Immigration Services (USCIS) (2019a) 'Exceptions and accommodations' [Online]. Available at www.uscis.gov/us-citizenship/citizenship-through-naturalization/exceptions-accommodations (Accessed 16 July 2020).

U.S. Citizenship and Immigration Services (USCIS) (2019b) 'Final rule on public charge ground of inadmissibility' [Online]. Available at www.uscis.gov/archive/archive-news/final-rule-public-charge-ground-inadmissibility (Accessed 16 July 2020).

U.S. Citizenship and Immigration Services (USCIS) (2019c) 'The naturalization test' [Online]. Available at www.uscis.gov/us-citizenship/naturalization-test (Accessed 16 July 2020).

U.S. Citizenship and Immigration Services (USCIS) (2020a) 'A guide to naturalization' [Online]. Available at www.uscis.gov/us-citizenship/citizenship-through-naturalization/guide-naturalization (Accessed 16 July 2020).

U.S. Citizenship and Immigration Services (USCIS) (2020b) *USCIS Policy Manual: Volume 12, Citizenship and Naturalization* [Online]. Available at www.uscis.gov/policymanual/HTML/PolicyManual-Volume12.html (Accessed 16 July 2020).

U.S. Social Security Administration (USSSA) (2016) 'Program operations manual system: Time-limited eligibility for certain aliens' [Online]. Available at https://secure.ssa.gov/poms.nsf/lnx/0500502106#e (Accessed 1 October 2017).

White House Initiative on Asian Americans and Pacific Islanders (2016) 'Bhutanese refugees find home in America' [Online]. Available at https://obamawhitehouse.archives.gov/blog/2016/03/11/bhutanese-refugees-find-home-america (Accessed 16 July 2020).

16

Asking the 'other questions': Applying intersectionality to understand statelessness in Europe

Deirdre Brennan, Nina Murray, and Allison J. Petrozziello[1]

This chapter is an invitation to join the conversation on how to bring intersectional feminist analyses to statelessness work. It presents an introductory analysis of how a complex web of power, socio-cultural, disciplinary, interpersonal, hegemonic, and structural relations impact those affected by statelessness. The discussion is grounded in the experiences of multiply marginalised populations in Europe, such as Romani women and same-sex parents. The authors contribute theoretical and practical expertise to move the sector towards a more nuanced understanding of the lived experiences of people affected by statelessness, and what this means for policy advocacy in the short and longer term.

A brief history of intersectionality

> 'There is no such thing as a single-issue struggle because we do not live single-issue lives.'
>
> Audre Lorde (1982)

Intersectionality is a concept that, although first used by Kimberlé Crenshaw in the 1980s, stems from a long history of U.S. Black feminism, both theoretically and through embodied experiences. In Crenshaw's seminal piece, she used the term to critique anti-discrimination law which, through its single-axis framework as she described it, was erasing the multidimensionality of Black women's experiences (Crenshaw, 1989: 139). Crenshaw gives examples of a number of U.S. court cases in which the courts insisted claims by Black women plaintiffs were treated as a cause of action for race discrimination or sex discrimination, but not both (1989: 141). As she succinctly puts it, the tendency was to 'treat race and gender as mutually exclusive categories of experience and analysis' (Crenshaw, 1989: 139). In treating categories as such, cases were dismissed because neither sex discrimination nor race-based discrimination could be proved. For example, in the case Crenshaw describes, of the unfair dismissal of Black women, there was no evidence of sex discrimination because the company in question was employing white women. Any grounds for race-based discrimination were also rejected because Black men were not being dismissed. This was a refusal to see the overlapping consequences of discrimination for Black women, specifically, and therefore 'the employment experiences of white women obscured the distinct discrimination that Black women experienced' (Crenshaw, 1989: 148).

As mentioned, while the term intersectionality is pinpointed to Crenshaw in 1989, this call to 'reject additive models of oppression, race, class and gender studies' (Hill Collins, 2008: 21) began in the early 1980s by several other prominent African-American women scholar-activists, including Angela Davis and Audre Lorde. Further back, the actual meaning of the term intersectionality, and its articulation, has its roots in the slavery period in the United States. Patricia Hill Collins notes how Sojourner Truth, an emancipated slave who never learned to read or write, rejected the blanket term 'woman' in her now infamous speech 'Ain't I a woman?' (Hill Collins, 2008: 18). In doing so, she was challenging the privileges afforded to white women during this period that were not extended to Black women. Now again, and at the start of another decade in 2020, the need for this term's value has not dissipated. Crenshaw's article has tens of thousands of online citations, not to mention the numerous conferences, special editions, and even government web pages dedicated to examining and explaining the term 'intersectionality'. It has been heralded as 'one of the most important contributions to feminist scholarship' (Davis, 2008: 67). This chapter promotes and explores the ways intersectionality can be further incorporated into the field of statelessness research and practice in order to understand the multidimensionality of the lives of people affected by statelessness (Brennan, 2019: 177).

Avoiding pitfalls

Before illustrating how intersectionality can be applied to statelessness research, this section briefly touches on potential implementation pitfalls and how to avoid them. The concept of intersectionality was, and continues to be, a critique of how gender was prioritised (specifically in white feminist activism and research)[2] as the central oppressive force in women's lives, whitewashing over the role of class and race and so on. This history of intersectionality is essential for conceptualising its application to statelessness research and activism today. While it is important to bring into focus the specific experience of stateless women (Brennan has pointed out this lack of research thus far), this chapter is not a call to simply 'ask the question of women' (2019: 171). Prioritising gender risks ignoring the other forces of oppression in stateless people's lives, like national or economic circumstances, that may impact both stateless men and women at different times or places. Intersectionality is a way of looking at the interconnectedness of forms of oppression, not necessarily to organise them hierarchically.

Moreover, a key caution to consider in the application of intersectionality is to avoid further victimisation. Our aim in redressing the omission of intersectionality from statelessness research is not to add further othering to the specific experiences of stateless women, older stateless people, or stateless people from minority ethnic groups. In seeking to understand how their experiences may be unique and multidimensional, we can recognise stateless people's independence, agency, and leadership rather than seeing them through a single lens of victimhood.

Applying intersectionality

Just as intersectionality challenged the idea that there is a universal truth to women's experiences, it too can be used to debunk the myth that stateless people are a coherent group. A categorisation of 'stateless people' that focuses on the commonalities of their experiences, rather than the intersecting modes of oppression they may experience, can 'blunt rather than sharpen our analysis of oppression' (Kapur, 2002: 9). An intersectional approach therefore forces interrogation of the socio-political context of a stateless person's experience. Using Crenshaw's influential work on the treatment of Black women in the U.S. court system, intersectionality is also valuable in our conception of legal remedies to statelessness. In addition to the violation of one's right to citizenship, what is their whole experience of discrimination?

Exactly how has intersectionality, as an analytical research (or legal) tool been applied in cases of Black women's discrimination, and what lessons can be drawn for statelessness work? Crenshaw uses the analogy of traffic at an intersection 'coming and going in all four directions' and that discrimination, like traffic, may flow in different directions (1989: 149). She says an accident at this intersection may be caused by a car coming from one direction or from all. This means that if a Black woman is harmed, her injury could be a result of sex discrimination or race discrimination, or both (Crenshaw, 1989). Crenshaw moves away from the metaphorical level to state that 'Black women can experience discrimination in ways that are both similar to and different from those experienced by white women and Black men' (1989: 149).

In statelessness work, it is worth examining how a stateless person who is a cis woman or who is queer, for example, may experience discrimination in ways that are both similar to and different from those experienced by, for instance, a stateless cis man or a woman with citizenship. Questions one can ask include: How does a stateless person who is a woman experience disadvantage, or discrimination, in her access to reproductive healthcare? How does her class, age, and/or ethnicity play a role in her treatment or access to such healthcare? In the latter question, we can use Crenshaw's insight to gauge how a stateless woman may, or may not, have negative experiences in her reproductive choices similar to a woman with citizenship in her community. These are not the only dimensions to consider. For example, how might someone's ethnicity make them vulnerable to discrimination and abuse, regardless of their citizenship status? We may use Crenshaw's example of the intersecting road to examine how, like a stateless man, a woman's *status* as a stateless person may impede her access to healthcare through, for example, financial difficulties or lack of insurance. The investigation into healthcare access is important and highlights the way those involved in advocacy or policy work are familiar with the consequences of statelessness. What intersectionality asks, however, is to investigate what *other* roads of experience lead to the intersection of a stateless person's life.

A simple technique for applying an intersectional approach to one's work is offered by Mari Matsuda: 'ask the other question' (1996: 123). For example, when she sees something that looks racist, she asks, 'Where is the patriarchy in this?' When she sees something that looks homophobic, she asks, 'Where are the class interests in this?' Of course, this merely marks the beginning of analysis and the hard work of making sense of these connections. As Sara Ahmed puts it, 'intersectionality is a *starting point*, the point from which we must proceed if we are to offer an account of how power works' (2017: 3, emphasis added).

With these instructions for application, it is worth noting that the term 'intersectionality' remains elusive even within gender studies. Davis writes that there is a vagueness to the term, including whether intersectionality is a theory, a concept, or a reading strategy for doing feminist analysis (2008: 68). She says the term's lack of specific parameters has been interpreted optimistically by scholars in the field, since it enables the term to be drawn upon in nearly any context of inquiry. This provides exciting opportunities for statelessness research; as Davis notes, the ambiguity with the term's definition allows 'endless constellations of intersecting lines of difference to be explored' (2008: 77). Using Matsuda's simple formula to ask the other question, Davis says one's research will take on new and surprising turns and provide endless opportunities to interrogate one's blind spots (2008: 77).

Applying intersectionality to address statelessness in Europe

Any stateless person may experience negative consequences, including in access to fundamental rights such as civil documentation, health, education, and employment. However, scholars and practitioners often fall into the trap of examining the causes and consequences of the exclusion experienced by stateless people as if they were a homogenous group, or (at best) groups defined by a common perceived cause of their statelessness (for example, exclusion of a particular minority from citizenship). Yet, as explained above, within these groups there will be a multiplicity of lived experiences and factors at play related to gender, race, age, disability, sexuality, religion, and other aspects of identities. To get to a more nuanced understanding of the causes and consequences of statelessness, and therefore to reach more appropriate and relevant solutions to the difficulties faced by stateless persons, it is necessary to 'ask the other questions'.

In its work with stateless people and their allies across Europe, the European Network on Statelessness (ENS) has begun to ask some of these 'other questions'. By introducing feminist analyses into its work, ENS has started to unpick some of the assumptions about the causes and consequences of statelessness. Based on what is known (and well documented) about issues such as women's unequal access to resources, gender segregation in labour markets and education systems, violence against women and girls, reproductive rights, and gendered social norms, ENS is working towards unpicking crucial layers. For example, how might stateless women experience these inequalities? What about stateless Romani women and stateless disabled Romani women? It is also important to reverse the question to focus on causes: how might gendered, racialised, and other inequalities heighten the risk of statelessness?

While some of the answers may seem obvious, they are under-researched and often invisible in current statelessness debates, and therefore go unaddressed by policy makers and service providers. A stateless woman is likely to be even further from the labour market and have even less ability to make choices about her (and her family's) life than a woman national. Her precarious legal status puts her at greater risk of trafficking, forced marriage, sexual exploitation, or domestic abuse, and her lack of legal identity may be used as a tool to exert power over her in abusive or exploitative situations.

ENS's work on Romani statelessness in the western Balkans and Ukraine has demonstrated that the nationality problems faced by Romani people in the region have not 'just' come about as a result of state succession or displacement (European Roma Rights Centre et al., 2017). Individual experiences of (and risk of) statelessness are rooted in a toxic combination of post-conflict state succession, displacement, entrenched antigypsyism, patriarchy, and other factors. Many Romani women fear stigma and discrimination at the hands of state service providers, as Roma women or as undocumented or stateless Roma women without health insurance, leading many to decide to give birth at home. Complex bureaucratic procedures for birth registration (which often require mothers to be documented and have a permanent place of residence), lack of access to legal aid, and officials' discriminatory attitudes all combine to make the registration of children very difficult (Praxis et al., 2018). Statelessness is therefore passed on to the next generation and the cycle continues (European Roma Rights Centre et al., 2017).

Heteronormative and gendered social norms can also impact individuals' ability to resolve or prevent statelessness (see Benswait, this volume; Buterman, this volume). Expectations placed on women in different contexts range from being primary caregivers and leaving administrative tasks to men in the family, to marrying in order to be monogamous and have children in wedlock. When women do not conform to these norms, they can face immense social and familial pressures. If a child is born (or perceived to be born) out of wedlock and only the mother is listed on the birth certificate, for example, she might face barriers to registering the birth, thereby heightening the risk of statelessness for the child (European Network on Statelessness, 2020b).

Although there is no longer direct gender discrimination in European nationality laws, the ways many of these laws are drafted and procedures implemented reflect and exacerbate heteronormative and gendered social norms. These indirect forms of gender discrimination increase the risk of statelessness (European Network on Statelessness, 2020c; Petrozziello, 2019a). For example, in many cases the man married to the mother is legally the father of the child. Birth certificates must contain the names of a 'birth mother' and a 'father', or unmarried fathers must take additional steps to prove their paternity (European Network on Statelessness, 2020a; see also Buterman, this volume). This can cause difficulties for the children of unmarried and same-sex parents, particularly if women cannot confer their own nationality to their children. For example, discriminatory limitations exclude children born abroad to an unmarried Maltese father from acquiring Maltese nationality (European Network on Statelessness, 2020d), and unmarried Austrian fathers must take steps to prove their paternity within a limited timeframe for their children born abroad to acquire Austrian nationality (European Network on Statelessness, 2020a). Recent cases have been reported of Polish authorities refusing to transcribe birth certificates and recognise the nationality of children born to same-sex parents abroad (European Network on Statelessness, 2020e; Sieverding, 2019). Such examples illustrate how multiple forms of discrimination on the basis of sex, marital status, and sexual orientation intersect and persist in the drafting and implementation of nationality laws, at worst creating new cases of statelessness in Europe, and at best hindering prevention and reduction. The examples also demonstrate how what may appear to be straightforward and 'universal' civil documentation procedures may be instrumentalised to become exclusionary and discriminatory in practice, turning birth registration, for example, into what Petrozziello calls a 'bordering practice' (Petrozziello, 2019b; see also Buterman, this volume; Abuya, this volume).

What these examples begin to illustrate is that racism and patriarchy, among other factors, need to be unpicked in order to sharpen our analysis and nuance our understanding of the causes and consequences of statelessness. Without this nuance, proposed solutions will not work. Viewing a high rate of home births or the young average age of Romani mothers as 'cultural practices', or perceiving the solution to Romani statelessness to be for 'the community to take an interest in being documented' (as ENS found were common beliefs held by policy makers and officials in the region) not only denies the agency of affected individuals and communities, but also ignores the underlying, intersecting oppressions. Such blunt analysis therefore prevents effective approaches.

To get to a sharper analysis of the root causes and consequences of statelessness, we have to engage with and listen to stateless people (see various chapters in this volume: Bloom; Benswait; Wooding; E). Any tendency towards essentialist categories cannot reflect people's lived reality. To get to that reality, it is necessary to ask those 'other questions' and listen to the answers. Intersectionality helps us to look inside categories, such as a minority group, to understand differences in lived experiences and stitch together new understandings, greater awareness, and more effective coalitions for change.

Transformative potential of feminist global governance

Not only does the feminist theory of intersectionality help to unpack the complexity of statelessness, it also has implications for transforming governance. Feminist scholarship on governance highlights the historic and ongoing struggles of multiply marginalised peoples for a series of R's – recognition, redistribution, regulation, rights, representation (Rai and Waylen, 2008; Fraser, 2010). The first of these, recognition, is paramount to achieving citizenship, which has not always been a given for women and/or racialised people(s), including ethnic and religious minorities, during and after nation-state formation. This is why diverse feminists around the world have long engaged in a politics of recognition. For there to be redistribution and rights, first one has to be recognised as a subject – or in Lindsey Kingston's terms, 'fully human' (Kingston, 2019). In other words, political subjectivity precedes legal recognition of citizen-subjects (Nyers, 2015). Once legal citizenship is achieved, efforts to enhance the quality and substance of that citizenship on an equitable basis for all peoples must continue. In short, power and struggles to shift how it is wielded within (and beyond) state institutions are central to feminist theories of governance.

There are two ways in which such an approach can be potentially transformative. First, it is sometimes assumed that on a state level, non-citizenship of that state and citizenship of that state are binary opposites; and so that there is a binary on the international level between statelessness (non-citizenship of every state) and citizenship (citizenship of some state). Feminist scholarship makes it possible to look beyond this, to see citizenship as a multi-layered construct mediated by social difference (Yuval-Davis, 1999). A person may both be a citizen and at the same time find themselves excluded or discriminated against in ways that prevent them from fully realising their citizenship in some or all dimensions (Bloom, 2018). The intersectional lens in this chapter does not deny that there may be experiences that are shared between citizens and those without citizenship in virtue of their sex, gender, or ethnicity, for example. It adds that someone who is both a non-citizen and a woman, for example, may experience *additional* forms of discrimination that are peculiar to the experience at the intersection.

Second, by recognising and engaging with people's intersecting identities, those working in advocacy and policy development relating to statelessness can identify new allies and build new coalitions with activists centred on (among others) women's rights, domestic workers' rights, LGBTIQ* rights, and disability rights, as well as anti-trafficking campaigners and youth organisations. Feminist global governance scholars (Rai and Waylen, 2008) recognise many potential fields of contestation and coalitional politics (including supra-national human rights mechanisms, transnational advocacy networks, and development initiatives). Feminist statelessness scholars and advocates have already begun searching for common ground and new channels for advocacy, while avoiding the pitfall of collapsing differences in lived experiences among the stateless. This includes work being done to bring statelessness and nationality rights to the forefront of debates around Beijing +25, the Sustainable Development Goals, the Global Compacts on Migration and Refugees, and the work of treaty bodies such as the Committees on the Elimination of Discrimination Against Women (CEDAW), the Rights of the Child (CRC), the Rights of Persons with Disabilities (CRPD), Migrant Workers (CMW), or the Elimination of Racial Discrimination (CERD). While some of these channels often fall into the trap of being siloed, intersectional analysis helps to connect the dots and to think strategically about how and where to make rights claims at the supra-national level.

Adopting an intersectional lens re-politicises the issue of statelessness, bringing into view multiple axes of power. It offers a radical alternative to depoliticised discussions of statelessness as if it were a legal anomaly or the result of cultural practices. Seeing citizenship and statelessness not (only) as a matter of individual relationship to a given nation-state, but as an integral part of global system(s) of governance – with all of their inherent legacies of colonialism, including racism, patriarchy, and heteronormativity – horizons of genuine transformation come into view.

Conclusion

Just as intersectionality has shown there is no one universal truth about women's experiences, nor is there one universal experience of statelessness. This chapter argues for the usefulness of intersectionality as an analytical tool to help unpack the complexity surrounding statelessness, and specifically the ways in which multiple forms of discrimination (including but not limited to gender discrimination) can be both cause and consequence of statelessness. In short, stateless populations are created and maintained according to varying structures of power; within each structure, stateless people's experiences of exclusion also differ.

For brevity's sake, the chapter focused mostly on the consequences or lived experiences of multiple marginalisations. Structural causes of statelessness are examined elsewhere, including how power structures including patriarchy shape ideas about belonging.[3] Such assumptions continue to underpin nationality laws on the books since colonial times, as well as contemporary migration regimes determining who can move regularly, who can bring or form families, and ultimately, who has a path to citizenship. Where pathways are blocked, the systems for doing so follow established hierarchies based on race and gender, among others.

The chapter has also shown that intersectionality sharpens our understanding of the ways in which stateless people's experiences of exclusion differ. Such insights are crucial for those working to develop and advocate for policy solutions, which necessarily must go beyond legal remedies to statelessness. Asking questions about lived experiences seems to lend itself to more practical humanitarian intervention and protection, whereas asking questions about causes remits us to questions of social justice and fundamental rights. In either case, recognising the multiplicity of marginalisations and rights violations points to the potential for coalition building among actors working on seemingly disparate issue areas, such as women's rights (to sexual and reproductive health) and statelessness, as part of a continuum of rights protection and fulfilment.

In the long term, if construction of citizenship is linked to the maintenance of normative power structures like patriarchy and institutionalised racism, then combatting statelessness and building inclusive societies requires a dismantling of those forms of governance. This is the long game; seeing it as such helps us think historically and progressively about struggles for personhood and citizenship. In the meantime, we contend that starting from the lived experiences of stateless people, and asking the other question(s), can make a promising starting point in the political project of fulfilling multiply marginalised people's human right to a nationality.

Notes

1 Authors are listed in alphabetical order to reflect the collaborative and equally substantive contributions made by each.
2 For further reading on feminist epistemologies, see Ramazanoğlu and Holland (2002).
3 Deirdre Brennan and Allison Petrozziello's respective ongoing feminist statelessness research seeks to contribute in this regard, following Brennan's call for feminist statelessness research (2019), while Nina Murray has called for feminist analysis to inform the work of the statelessness sector (2019). Brennan's work theorises patriarchy as a cause of statelessness and feminist activism as a solution, while Petrozziello focuses on the intimate realm of (mostly racialised/othered) women's bodies, childbirth, and birth registration as a site of migration control and production of statelessness. ENS has set out to mainstream intersectional analysis through its work, setting out its vision for this in its five-year strategic plan (European Network on Statelessness, 2020e).

References

Ahmed, S. (2017) *Living a Feminist Life* (Durham, NC: Duke University Press).

Bloom, T. (2018) *Noncitizenism: Recognising Noncitizen Capabilities in a World of Citizens* (Abingdon: Routledge).

Brennan, D. (2019) 'Statelessness and the feminist toolbox: Another man-made problem with a feminist solution?' *Tilburg Law Review*, 24, 170–181.

Crenshaw, K. (1989) 'Demarginalizing the intersection of race and sex: A black feminist critique of antidiscrimination doctrine, feminist theory and antiracist politics', *University of Chicago Legal Forum*, 8, 138–167.

Davis, K. (2008) 'Intersectionality as buzzword: A sociology of science perspective on what makes a feminist theory successful', *Feminist Theory*, 9, 67–85.

European Network on Statelessness (2019) 'Solving statelessness in Europe: Our strategic plan 2019–23' [Online]. Available at www.statelessness.eu/sites/www. statelessness.eu/files/attachments/resources/ENS-Strategic-Plan-2019-23.pdf (Accessed 28 May 2020).

European Network on Statelessness (2020a) 'ENS Statelessness Index Survey: Austria' [Online]. Available at https://index.statelessness.eu/country/austria (Accessed 28 May 2020).

European Network on Statelessness (2020b) 'ENS Statelessness Index Survey: Germany' [Online]. Available at https://index.statelessness.eu/country/germany (Accessed 12 June 2020).

European Network on Statelessness (2020c) 'ENS Statelessness Index Survey: Italy' [Online]. Available at https://index.statelessness.eu/country/italy (Accessed 12 June 2020).

European Network on Statelessness (2020d) 'ENS Statelessness Index Survey: Malta' [Online]. Available at https://index.statelessness.eu/country/malta (Accessed 12 June 2020).

European Network on Statelessness (2020e) 'ENS Statelessness Index Survey: Poland' [Online]. Available at https://index.statelessness.eu/country/poland (Accessed 12 June 2020).

European Roma Rights Centre, European Network on Statelessness, and Institute on Statelessness and Inclusion (2017) 'Roma belong: Statelessness, discrimination and marginalisation of Roma in the Western Balkans and Ukraine' [Online]. Available at www.statelessness.eu/sites/www.statelessness.eu/files/attachments/resources/roma-belong.pdf (Accessed 28 May 2020).

Fraser, N. (2010) 'Who counts? Dilemmas of justice in a postwestphalian world', *Antipode*, 41, 281–297.

Hill Collins, P. (2008) *Black Feminist Thought: Knowledge, Consciousness, and the Politics of Empowerment* (New York, Routledge).

Kapur, R. (2002) 'The tragedy of victimization rhetoric: Resurrecting the 'native' subject in international/post-colonial feminist legal politics', *Harvard Human Rights*, 15.

Kingston, L. N. (2019) *Fully Human: Personhood, Citizenship, and Rights* (New York: Oxford University Press).

Lorde, A. (1982) 'Learning from the 60s', in *Sister Outsider: Essays and Speeches by Audre Lorde* (Berkeley, CA: Crossing Press): pp. 126–137.

Matsuda, M. J. (1996) *Where is Your Body? And Other Essays on Race, Gender, and the Law* (Boston, MA: Beacon Press).

Murray, N. (2019). 'Join the feminist revolution in work to address statelessness', European Network on Statelessness blog. 18 July 18 [Online]. Available at www.statelessness.eu/blog/join-feminist-revolution-work-address-statelessness (Accessed 28 May 2020).

Nyers, P. (2015) 'Migrant citizenships and autonomous mobilities', *Migration, Mobility & Displacement*, 1, 23–39.

Petrozziello, A. J. (2019a) '(Re)producing statelessness via indirect gender discrimination: Descendants of Haitian migrants in the Dominican Republic', *International Migration*, 57, 213–228.

Petrozziello, A. J. (2019b) 'Bringing the border to baby: Birth registration as bordering practice for migrant women's children', *Gender & Development*, 1, 31–47.

Praxis, European Network on Statelessness, European Roma Rights Centre, Institute on Statelessness and Inclusion (2018) 'Alternative report concerning Serbia to the Committee on the Elimination of All Forms of Discrimination against Women (CEDAW) (72 Pre-Sessional Working Group)' [Online]. Available at www.statelessness.eu/sites/www.statelessness.eu/files/attachments/resources/ Alternative%20Report%20concerning%20Serbia%20for%20cosideration%20 at%20the%20CEDAW%20%20Pre-Sessional%20Working%20Group%20 72%20prepared%20by%20NGO%20Praxis%20ISI%20ENS%20and%20 ERRC_July%202018.pdf (Accessed 28 May 2020).

Rai, S., and Waylen, G. (eds) (2008) *Global Governance: Feminist Perspectives* (Houndmills: Palgrave Macmillan).

Ramazanoğlu, C., and Holland, J. (2002) *Feminist Methodology: Challenges and Choices* (London, Thousand Oaks, CA, and New Delhi: Sage).

Sieverding, B. (2019) 'Even where countries in Europe recognise marriage equality, children born to same-sex families remain at risk of statelessness', European Network on Statelessness blog, 7 November [Online]. Available at www. statelessness.eu/blog/even-where-countries-europe-recognise-marriage-equality- children-born-same-sex-families-remain (Accessed 29 November 2019).

Yuval-Davis, N. (1999) 'The "multi-layered citizen"', *International Feminist Journal of Politics*, 1:1, 119–136.

Part III

Rethinking governance

Staatloos

Figure 5

I don't recognize me in the shadows

Thana Faroq

This photograph was taken in 2018, when the lady pictured wrote this note.

أنا أعيش في هولندا منذ ثلاث سنوات ونصف تحت اسم Staatloos يعني لا أنتمي لوطن أو بلا وطن.

من الصعب عدم الإعتراف بجنسيتك أو وطنك، والأصعب عدم الإعتراف بها من قبل الدول العربية الشقيقة أكثر صعوبة من عدم الإعتراف بهما من قبل الغرب ولكن رغم هذا الشعور السيء هناك شيء جيد وهو أنني استطعت السفر إلى دولة عربية شقيقة لم أكن أستطيع أن أسافر اليها عندما كنت في سوريا لأنني فلسطينية.

كنت أريد أن أذهب لأرى أمي وإخوتي ولكن هذا البلد العربي الشقيق رفض أن يعطيني فيزا أكثر من مرة وعندما أصبح عندي إقامة في هولندا أخذت الفيزا من أول مرة وسافرت ورأيت أمي وإخوتي والحمدلله رب العالمين.

مجرد إقامة في دولة أوروبية كانت كفيلة بأن آخذ فيزا الى دولة عربية شقيقة.

Translation:
I have been living in Holland for three years as *Staatloos*, which means I do not belong to a country or I am without a country. It is hard not to have your citizenship or state recognised, and harder to have them denied by neighbouring Arab countries and recognised by the West. Despite this feeling, it is something good. I was able to travel to an Arab country that I was not able to go to before when I was in Syria because I am Palestinian. I wanted to see my mother and siblings, but this Arab country kept rejecting my visa application. When I became a resident of Holland, I was granted a visa immediately and travelled and saw my mother and siblings, thanks to God Almighty. A simple residency permit in a European country was enough to grant me a visit visa to a fellow Arab country.

17

The ethics of quantifying statelessness

Heather Alexander

Over the last few years, the United Nations High Commissioner for Refugees (UNHCR) has launched a series of statelessness mapping projects to identify and, in some cases, quantify statelessness in countries around the world. The population of a country is surveyed during a statelessness mapping project, along with its legal framework and civil identity systems, to determine if statelessness exists in that country and, if possible, what types of people are at risk (including their location and numbers). To date, UNHCR has completed mapping projects in multiple countries in Africa, the Americas, and Europe.[1]

Though many of these projects have been carried out by partner organisations and governments, there is no question that UNHCR is a major player driving these initiatives. UNHCR's intense involvement in statelessness mapping makes sense; the agency is mandated by the United Nations General Assembly to identify, prevent, and reduce statelessness, as well as to protect stateless people. In 2014, UNHCR launched the Global Action Plan to End Statelessness: 2014–2024.[2] The identification of statelessness is a major part of this initiative. Action 10 of the Global Action Plan is to improve both qualitative and quantitative data on stateless populations around the world.

Yet while mapping statelessness may sound straightforward, in practice it poses a number of serious ethical concerns that are unique in UNHCR's history of gathering data on populations of concern. In particular, this chapter focuses on mapping projects that employ statistics. It does this in order to explore some of the ethical problems with quantifying statelessness.[3] It draws on the personal experiences of the author in quantifying statelessness, as well as a review of the published results of mapping projects that employed quantitative statistics.[4] For reasons of confidentiality, this chapter will mostly refrain from citing specific mapping studies, but will instead highlight general observations.[5]

Statistical mapping projects employing quantitative methods present unique challenges for UNHCR.[6] Broadly speaking, these challenges can be divided into three categories: 1) conceptual/methodological challenges; 2) logistical challenges; and 3) ethical concerns. While UNHCR has acknowledged many of these challenges in its statistical reporting on statelessness (UNHCR, 2019c), the agency has not addressed them in an in-depth way and their impact on statelessness statistics remains poorly understood. Importantly, in ways that are not always well understood or acknowledged, conceptual/methodological and logistical challenges frequently become ethical concerns. For example, when a methodology is not rigorous, it can give incorrect and non-representative outcomes. Thus, the study can be easily altered, or persons may be improperly included or excluded, violating their rights. Likewise, logistical challenges can impact the feasibility of the methodology, affecting the outcome and leading to a non-representative result.

The ethics guidelines set forth by the Centre for Humanitarian Data identifies ethical concerns relating to the collection of humanitarian data. These include: 1) validity; the data is not representative; 2) bias; the data is skewed; 3) ossification; the data reinforces existing problems; 4) transparency; the process is not clear, explainable, or visible; 5) privacy; and 6) ownership and consent (United Nations Office for the Coordination of Humanitarian Affairs, 2020). Each of these issues are addressed in this chapter.

Statelessness exists on a spectrum

One challenge of quantifying statelessness is that it comes in degrees and, therefore, exists on a spectrum (Massey, 2010; Tucker, 2014).[7] This makes it vague.[8] Examples abound of concepts that are vague because they exist on a spectrum. For example, baldness exists on a spectrum. At what point has a particular person lost enough hair to count as bald for the purposes of a quantitative study on baldness? Contrast this with a study to quantify the number of hairs on a particular man's head. Each hair is a discrete unit. This makes hairs very easy to count.

Some stateless people may lack all human rights and be subject to detention, deportation, and even death, while others may lack only the right to vote or the right to hold public office (contrast, for example: Benwait, this volume; and Vollmer, this volume). Some classes of nationality may be inferior to others. Some nationalities may actually confer inferior rights to those held by stateless persons in another country (see Swider, 2017). Such nationalities are sometimes labelled 'non-functioning' (Kingston, 2014; see also Kuzmova, this volume). Some states may contain persons who have a nationality but are non-deportable and who lack state protection. Such nationalities are often labelled 'ineffective' (UNHCR, 2010).

UNHCR (2010) has stressed that '[t]he issue... is not whether or not the individual has a nationality that is effective, but whether or not the individual has a nationality at all'. This conclusion makes it sound as if there is a clear dividing line between stateless persons and persons with a nationality, but in practice there is not. This methodological challenge becomes an ethical problem if the study is not transparent about what levels of statelessness are being included and why.

There is no agreement on what key terms mean

The definition of statelessness relies on key terms and concepts about which there is no agreement. It is easy to count things that are defined using precise, agreed-upon terms – and this does not mean that the terms need to be simplistic (Chalmers, 2009). For example, it is easy to count apples because the meaning of the term apple is precise and widely agreed upon. There may be red apples and green apples, but few people would argue that some oranges should be included in a study on apples.

The international definition of a stateless person is 'a person who is not considered as a national by any State under the operation of its law' (United Nations, 1954). While this definition is only one sentence long, it contains two key concepts that are not clearly defined: 'not considered' and 'operation of law.' There is disagreement over what these concepts mean. As the statelessness mapping project in the UK put it in 2011, '[t]he definition [of statelessness]... presents difficulties in interpretation and, consequently, application' (UNHCR, 2011). As a result, the definition is the subject of disagreement among experts and open to manipulation. This is a poor foundation on which to build a quantitative study and a serious ethical problem because, once again, it is not clear which classes of persons are to be included or excluded.

First, it is not obvious what it means for a state to 'not consider' someone a national. 'Not considered' implies some sort of affirmative action on the part of the state. UNHCR (2014: 12) has this to say: 'Establishing whether an individual is not considered as a national under the operation of its law requires a careful analysis of how a State *applies* its nationality laws in an individual's case...' The word 'apply' strongly suggests an affirmative, wilful action. Yet not all statelessness is caused by an affirmative, wilful action by a state (for instance: Benson et al., this volume, refers to 'non-decisionism'). For example, it is not clear if the definition of statelessness intends to distinguish between purposeful discrimination and bureaucratic ineptitude (see Liew, this volume). Someone may be unable to register as a national because there is no consulate in their country of residence (see Cheva-Isarakul, this volume). What of cases where individuals have refused or renounced nationality? In which of these cases has the state *applied* its nationality law? Are such individuals *not considered* nationals by the state?

Likewise, the phrase 'under the operation of its law' is also vague. It clearly includes not only the nationality laws of the state, but their implementation by a wide array of government agencies and offices, not all of which may agree with one another or work together. If one government agency accepts an individual as a national, but another does not, which agency represents 'the operation of law'? UNHCR (2014: 13) offers this advice:

> A state may not in practice follow the letter of the law, even going so far as to ignore its substance. The reference to 'law' in the definition of statelessness in Article 1(1) therefore covers situations where the written law is substantially modified when it comes to its implementation in practice.

Once again, this definition of 'operation of law' implies purposeful action on the part of the state. In essence, the state operates its law the way a driver operates a car. Statelessness is caused when the state does 'not follow', 'ignores', or 'modifies' the law. But is a state 'operating' its law when an individual cannot obtain an identity document because the relevant office is closed, or too far away, or the price is too high (see Vollmer, this volume)? What if the individual cannot fill out the necessary forms because he or she cannot read (see Sperfeldt, this volume)?

Certain factors – such as poverty, disability, and illiteracy – can increase the difficulties of registration, but do not, on their own, mean that the individual is stateless. In some cases, conflict and instability can mean that government does not function (see Fortin et al., this volume; Kasianenko, this volume; Bahram, this volume). This fact must be taken into account by any mapping methodology, but does not necessarily mean that the state 'does not consider' the person to be a national.

Each country has different procedures for establishing nationality under the law and each issues its own identification. In some cases, the courts may be involved. In others, documentation may provide evidence of nationality without proving nationality. Importantly, as UNHCR has stressed, the mere failure to register or the lack of ID documents does not create statelessness (Manly, 2012), so it is not possible for a mapping study to simply count the number of people without documents. Developing a methodology to capture these nuances and different actors is extremely difficult.

UNHCR's (2014) advice is to define statelessness as broadly as possible, but in a quantitative study, this is not desirable.[9] Being purposefully over-inclusive in a quantitative study is to admit, from the outset, that the data is not valid – that it does not represent what it is purported to represent.

Mapping statelessness requires identifying a negative

Statelessness is defined by a negative: the absence of nationality. While it is relatively easy to count who has been granted refugee status or those registered as the nationals of a country, counting the lack of nationality requires establishing a negative. In some countries, stateless populations have statelessness-confirming identity documents. This is the case in Kuwait (see Benswait, this volume) and Estonia (see Vollmer, this volume), for example. Elsewhere, stateless persons do not have access to any identity documents. Even in countries where stateless identity cards exist, we cannot assume that every stateless person holds one.

Statelessness is sometimes established, at least in part, by an inability to obtain identity documents or to register as a national. Such cases might require proving a series of negatives by showing both the inability to obtain a number of different documents and the level of difficulty the person has experienced in trying to obtain these documents.[10] At what point does the absence of evidence of nationality, including the absence of civil registration and identity documents, become sufficient to establish statelessness? If an individual has certain identity documents but cannot obtain others, how should this person be classified? Some identity documents, such as national ID cards, are clear evidence of nationality, but is their absence sufficient to prove statelessness? What if the person has not exhausted all avenues to obtain these documents? How can an agent of a mapping study be sure that existing ID cards are not fraudulent, or if they are, in practice, respected by the authorities? Proving a negative requires a complex methodology that may be difficult to explain or justify, calling into question the validity of the results.

Identifying statelessness is often a complex, individualised process that is difficult to scale

In many cases, establishing that someone is stateless requires building a profile of the individual and an analysis of their status under the laws of multiple countries. This inquiry can be narrowed by reference to the common ways of establishing nationality via a 'link' between the individual and the state such as birth, long-term residence, descent from a national, education, marriage, military service, financial investment, or other qualifying factors. This process is time consuming and requires a high level of expertise. It may require identifying, evaluating, and comparing identity documents and instances of civil registration from multiple countries. Nationality laws also change over time, meaning that reference must often be made to multiple laws enacted at different periods.

In individual cases, UNHCR or a government may build a profile of an individual from multiple data points, including: the nationality laws of various relevant countries, any ID cards the individual may have, court procedures they have undergone, statements they may have obtained from relevant authorities such as embassies, evidence of discrimination against groups of which they are members, and other factors (UNHCR, 2014). Two factors must be considered: First, it is necessary to examine the nationality laws and procedures of various relevant countries, including whether or not nationality is applied automatically or non-automatically. Second, the extent to which various documents issued by those countries prove nationality or simply bolster a claim to nationality must also be considered. There is an important difference in how birth certificates are used to establish nationality between countries that practice *jus soli* (based on birth on the territory) and countries that practice *jus sanguinis* (based on birth to citizen parents), for example.

This process is extremely difficult to scale for a statelessness survey. All relevant data points must be gathered, then assigned a weight based on the extent to which they establish nationality. There is no way to account for the possibility of fraudulent documents. Persons may claim to have a document but be unable to produce it.

In one UNHCR-funded mapping project, the survey questionnaire ran to over thirty questions, including lists of over ten types of documents for not only the individuals being questioned, but also for their parents and grandparents. Synthesising this complex questionnaire into a single statistic was extremely difficult. One flow chart had over twenty steps and required multiple cross-referencing to various annexes. Complexity and the need for a high level of expertise greatly increases the risk that such a study will be inaccurate. These methodological challenges quickly become ethical problems because they have a huge impact on the study's validity and transparency.

Logistical challenges can violate ethics

A host of logistical challenges further raise the possibility of error in a mapping study. While an individual statelessness determination procedure is usually conducted by trained experts, such as government or UNHCR lawyers, a survey usually relies on minimally trained staff who may not understand the questionnaire or be qualified to identify documents properly.

Individuals questioned may not understand or have relevant information. Some individuals may fear interacting with any authorities or sharing personal information.

In many countries, collecting data is not done through a dedicated survey, but is derived from existing government databases, such as census and immigration data. Such data may be unavailable, incomplete, or unreliable. It was collected for other purposes and must be adapted for statelessness mapping. For example, one country collects data on immigrants with 'no nationality', but since border agents are not trained to identify such people and to fill in the form properly, it is impossible to know if this statistic is accurate. Another country does not collect this data at all. One government survey segregates information from European immigrants differently from African immigrants, producing a skewed result.

In a closely related problem, there is little uniformity in the data collected by different mapping projects, meaning that different mapping projects cannot be compared. The accuracy of various studies may vary widely, but with several mapping studies coming out at once, it is inevitable that the statistics on statelessness in one country will be compared to those in another. These logistical problems affect the validity of mapping projects.

Conceptual, methodological, and logistical challenges: 'Double invisibility' or branding groups as stateless

The various conceptual, methodological, and logistical challenges mentioned above mean that mapping studies suffer from a high risk of either excluding stateless people or over-counting them. In many cases, the risks for over-estimation or under-estimation are not made clear in the final mapping report. These exercises in over- or under-counting have serious ethical consequences. Excluding classes of people from the study risks creating what I term 'double invisibility', where stateless groups are rendered further invisible by being excluded from the official mapping study (see E, this volume). Including groups who may not be stateless, however, risks branding them as stateless and opening them up to danger or abuse.[11]

In some cases, governments have already labelled certain persons as stateless. A clearly defined class of persons may be excluded from nationality by law, such as the exclusion of the Rohingya from nationality in Myanmar (see Brinham, this volume). In other cases, stateless persons may hold identity documents labelling them as stateless, such as with some *Bidoon* communities in the Middle East (see Benswait, this volume). In such contexts, counting statelessness can be accomplished with relatively little cost to

UNHCR by counting the number of people who are members of an ethnic community or who hold ID labelling them as stateless. Yet while the labelling of persons as officially stateless by the government makes them easier to count, this way of compiling statistics on statelessness is dangerous. Relying on government data of those who are already labelled as officially stateless risks legitimising and ossifying this illegal status, reinforcing and validating it by a United Nations agency (see Bloom, this volume).

Many populations in the world are of undetermined nationality (Massey, 2010) occupying a grey zone between statelessness and nationality. Until recent decades, they may have been treated as nationals or have not needed documents. The mapping project itself can be used to brand such individuals as stateless, with serious ethical consequences (see Abuya, this volume). Doing so risks ossification, or the reinforcement of existing, and often negative, stereotypes. Labelling such individuals may incentivise the government to formalise their lack of a nationality, for example, or remove them from the country.

An over-reliance on predetermined categories risks perpetuating false assumptions about who is stateless

UNHCR sometimes relies on predetermined categories of persons who are at risk of statelessness based on assumptions. Such mapping projects often rely on government data, such as the census, collected for other purposes. This raises the issue of consent (Solove, 2013), where individuals may have offered up data to UNHCR or the government for one purpose, only to later have UNHCR use that data without their further consent to label them stateless, or not stateless, as part of a mapping project.

It also raises the problem of ossification, whereby mapping studies reinforce existing false assumptions about who is stateless. Such mapping studies are conclusory, as assumptions made by UNHCR on who is at risk are reinforced by a mapping project built around those categories. Such conclusory studies risk hiding the true nature of a situation. For example, there might be considerable evidence that an ethnic group who migrated to a country before colonial independence is stateless. A mapping project may simply count the number of members in that ethnic group. Yet this is not really a statelessness mapping study, but rather a census of a particular ethnic group believed to be at-risk of statelessness.

UNHCR often employs its own, vague categories when counting stateless people. For example, UNHCR draws a distinction between stateless persons in a migratory context and those *in situ*, or within their 'own countries' (developed in Vlieks, 2017).[12] Once again, however, the definition of 'own country' remains confusing and under-articulated, while *in situ* statelessness is defined nowhere under international law. For example, how many years, or generations, must a population live in a country before they are in their 'own country' or before they become *in situ*? The use of such undefined terms makes the study less transparent.

Yet this does not mean that the distinction UNHCR is attempting to develop between stateless migrants and *in situ* stateless populations is meaningless or useless; quite the contrary. The distinction matters greatly in the sources of information used to compile statistics of potentially stateless persons. Mapping projects done in countries presumed to have only migratory populations may avoid looking for *in situ* statelessness entirely and focus instead only on statistics from immigration agencies. Once again, as the methodologies are radically different for statelessness mapping in countries with primarily *in situ* populations, versus those with primarily migratory populations, it is difficult to compare them.

Mapping statelessness and pressures on UNHCR

UNHCR had funded many statelessness mapping projects around the world and, as a result, has often played a large role in creating the policies, methodologies, and procedures for such studies. This has added a number of additional ethical concerns because of the unique pressures faced by UNHCR in achieving its mandate. It should be noted that UNHCR has recently rolled out a data ethics strategy (UNHCR, 2019a), but its protocols for mapping statelessness should be much more robust. UNHCR has an agency-wide Data Protection Policy (UNHCR, 2015), enacted in 2015. However, responsibility for implementing this policy at the country level rests with existing UNHCR staff who may not be properly trained on the policy.

Often, individual field offices are expected to draft their own Standard Operating Procedures – including, for example, the length of time the field office can retain data on its server (UNHCR, 2019a). UNHCR should address more robustly the ethics of mapping statelessness, as well as approach statelessness mapping not only through the lens of data privacy, but from multiple ethical perspectives – some of which are summarised in this section.

UNHCR's experiences working closely with governments on refugee issues do not translate well to statelessness mapping, where the government may be an unreliable or dangerous partner. Statistics are closely tied to UNHCR fundraising. The amount of money spent on beneficiaries is used to calculate appeals for donor governments to give funds. This means that it may be inappropriate in some cases for UNHCR to be carrying out the study. There are serious ethical concerns with sharing personal information with governments or other actors. In some cases, the results of mapping studies have not been released to the public due to political concerns. These facts argue in favour of more independent mapping studies.

The expertise of UNHCR matters greatly to the effectiveness of statelessness mapping since the agency dominates the field. Yet UNHCR is not used to undertaking complex statistical surveys. The agency usually quantifies its beneficiary populations (such as refugees, internally displaced persons, and asylum-seekers) based on their registration with UNHCR or partners. Engagement with the agency is often voluntary on the part of individuals and may bring substantial benefits, such as refugee status or food rations. By contrast, engagement with UNHCR on mapping statelessness is often done involuntarily through large-scale surveys with weak consent procedures. Taking part in a mapping study brings few to no immediate benefits and may cause serious harm.

UNHCR is used to keeping sensitive refugee data confidential and has a thorough process in place. The process for keeping stateless persons' information confidential is less established in most, if not all, field offices. This is a critical issue, because much of the data collected to map statelessness is highly personal and invasive, touching on not only the stateless person themselves, but also their families.

Data protection should be included in agreements with implementing partners and the government, but in practice this may not occur. Implementing partners are often crucial to the success of mapping projects. Gaps in UNHCR's expertise mean that there is an urgent need for specific protocols on data protection for partners. There is also no independent ethics review of statelessness mapping projects, such as might take place under a university system. There is often a lack of clarity as to whether or not the implementing partner, UNHCR headquarters, field offices, or the government have the right to maintain their own copies of the data.

Finally, many UNHCR mapping studies rely heavily on key informant interviews and qualitative studies. Such studies may rely overly on 'gatekeeper' individuals to identify possible stateless communities for quantitative studies, raising the risk of skewed results.

Conclusion

Statelessness mapping may play a critical role in the identification and quantifying of statelessness, serving as a powerful advocacy tool and helping to identify at-risk populations. Yet, as this chapter has shown, statelessness mapping is no easy undertaking. The conceptual and methodological challenges are immense. Meanwhile, logistical challenges also complicate mapping studies. All of these challenges have ethical implications, as they can result in the under-counting of statelessness, 'double invisibility', and the over-counting of statelessness, as well as risk branding populations as stateless to governments.

UNHCR lacks robust privacy and data management protocols that are tailored to mapping statelessness. Any agency carrying out statelessness mapping should take into account various existing ethical frameworks for data collection from vulnerable populations, particularly when it comes to agency over data and retention and sharing policies (Greenwood et al., 2017). This must involve developing agency-wide ethics guidelines for statelessness mapping that include impact assessments, especially when information is being shared with governments.

Statelessness mapping is a recent innovation and is still in the experimental phase. This greatly raises the ethical stakes. The agency's experience in counting refugees and other beneficiaries means that it is reliant on methods of data collection that may not be appropriate for stateless people. As UNHCR rushes to map statelessness worldwide by 2024 in compliance with the Global Action Plan, ethics should be at the centre of every mapping project.

Notes

1 Mapping projects have been completed in the United Kingdom, the Netherlands, Belgium, Malta, Norway, Austria, Iceland, Lithuania, Sweden, Estonia, Portugal, Finland, Poland, Albania, the United States, and several other countries – some unpublished. Additional statelessness studies have been completed in Japan, Ghana, South Sudan, Slovenia, Italy, Romania, Latvia, Macedonia, Côte d'Ivoire, Kuwait, Brazil, Chile, Colombia, and in various regions such as East and West Africa, Central Asia, and others.

2 Some UNHCR statelessness mapping projects pre-date the Global Action Plan, such as the UK mapping project, which was completed in 2011 (UNHCR, 2011).

3 This chapter adopts the definition and guidelines for data ethics from the Centre for Humanitarian Data (see United Nations Office for the Coordination of Humanitarian Affairs, 2020).

4 The author was personally involved in two of these mapping projects and has studied the results of two others that employed statistics. The views expressed in this chapter are entirely the author's own.

5 It should be noted that many mapping projects do not employ statistics. Some of the ethical concerns discussed in this chapter, however, might also apply to these projects.

6 For a summary of some of the issues discussed in this chapter, see Institute on Statelessness and Inclusion (2013).

7 While in the past, UNHCR and other experts frequently categorised stateless-ness as being either *de jure* (by operation of law) or *de facto*, many experts are moving away from these categorisations.

8 There is a large philosophical literature on vagueness. See, for example: Alston (1964); Chalmers (2009).

9 The UK mapping project encountered the problem with vague definitions; see UNHCR (2011).

10 This type of vagueness constitutes 'combinatorial vagueness' (see Alston, 1964).

11 Other chapters in this volume consider the roles of censuses in these challenges. See Fazal; Benswait; Sperfeldt.

12 The phrase 'own country' comes from Article 12(4) of the International Covenant on Civil and Political Rights (ICCPR) and its interpretation by the UN Human Rights Committee (UNHCR, 2014).

References

Alston, W. P. (1964) *The Philosophy of Language* (Hoboken, NJ: Prentice-Hall).

Chalmers, D. (2009) 'Verbal disputes', *Philosophical Review*, 120, 515–566.

Greenwood, F., Howarth, C., Escudero Poole, D., Raymond, N. A., and Scarnecchia, D. P. (2017) *The Signal Code: A Human Rights Approach to Information During Crisis* (Cambridge, MA: Harvard Humanitarian Initiative) [Online]. Available at https://hhi.harvard.edu/publications/signal-code-human-rights-approach-information-during-crisis (Accessed 21 June 2020).

Kingston, L. N. (2014) 'Statelessness as a lack of functioning citizenship', *Tilburg Law Review*, 19, 127–135.

Manly, M. (2012) 'UNHCR's mandate and activities to address statelessness in Europe', *European Journal of Migration and Law*, 14:3, 261–267.

Massey, H. (2010) 'UNHCR and de facto statelessness', UNHCR Division of International Protection [Online]. Available at www.unhcr.org/4bc2ddeb9.pdf (Accessed 21 June 2020).

Solove, D. (2013) 'Privacy self-management and the consent dilemma', *Harvard Law Review*, 126, 1880–1903.

Swider, K. (2017) 'Why end statelessness?', in T. Bloom, K. Tonkiss, and P. Cole (eds) *Understanding Statelessness* (Abingdon: Routledge): pp. 191–209.

Tucker, J. (2014) 'Questioning de facto statelessness by looking at de facto citizenship', *Tilburg Law Review*, 19, 276.

United Nations (1954) *Convention Relating to the Status of Stateless Persons*.

United Nations High Commissioner for Refugees (UNHCR) (2010) 'Expert Meeting, The Concept of Stateless Persons Under International Law: Summary conclusions (Prato conclusions)' [Online]. Available at www.unhcr.org/en-us/protection/statelessness/4cb2fe326/expert-meeting-concept-stateless-persons-under-international-law-summary.html (Accessed 21 June 2020).

United Nations High Commissioner for Refugees (UNHCR) (2011) 'Mapping statelessness in the United Kingdom' [Online]. Available at www.unhcr.org/en-us/protection/basic/578dffae7/unhcr-mapping-statelessness-in-the-united-kingdom.html (Accessed 21 June 2020).

United Nations High Commissioner for Refugees (UNHCR) (2014) *Handbook on the Protection of Stateless Persons* [Online]. Available at www.unhcr.org/en-us/protection/statelessness/53b698ab9/handbook-protection-stateless-persons.html (Accessed 21 June 2020).

United Nations High Commissioner for Refugees (UNHCR) (2015) 'Data protection policy' [Online]. Available at https://cms.emergency.unhcr.org/documents/11982/52542/Data+Protection+Policy/06bc03cf-e969-4329-a52b-161ae1eb42d7 (Accessed 21 June 2020).

United Nations High Commissioner for Refugees (UNHCR) (2019a) 'Data Transformation Strategy 2020–2025: Supporting protection and solutions' [Online]. Available at www.unhcr.org/5dc2e4734.pdf (Accessed 21 June 2020).

United Nations High Commissioner for Refugees (UNHCR) (2019b) 'Guidance on registration and identity management' [Online]. Available at www.unhcr.org/registration-guidance/ (Accessed 21 June 2020).

United Nations High Commissioner for Refugees (UNHCR) (2019c) 'UNHCR statistical reporting on statelessness' [Online]. Available at www.unhcr.org/5d9e182e7.pdf (Accessed 21 June 2020).

United Nations Office for the Coordination of Humanitarian Affairs (2020) 'Note 4: Humanitarian data ethics', Centre for Humanitarian Data [Online]. Available at https://reliefweb.int/report/world/centre-humanitarian-data-guidance-note-series-data-responsibility-humanitarian-action-1 (Accessed 21 June 2020).

Vlieks, C. (2017) 'Contexts of statelessness: The concepts "statelessness *in situ*" and "statelessness in the migratory context"', in T. Bloom, K. Tonkiss, and P. Cole (eds) *Understanding Statelessness* (Abingdon: Routledge): pp. 35–52.

18

Registering persons at risk of statelessness in Kenya: Solutions or further problems?

Edwin O. Abuya

In December 2018, the government of Kenya sought to amend several pieces of legislation using The Statute Law (Miscellaneous Amendments) Act, 2018 (No. 18 of 2018). Among the statutes targeted was the Registration of Persons Act (Cap 107 of the Laws of Kenya). These amendments, which came into operation in January 2019, introduced the National Integrated Identity Management System (NIIMS) programme. Under the terms of this programme, all citizens and non-citizens residing in the country are required to register their details in a central database. Once entered on the official roll, a person is given a unique number – commonly referred to as 'Huduma Namba'. According to the government, those who fail to register will be disallowed from accessing any government service (Musyoki, 2019).

Three human rights organisations challenged the compulsory registration requirement in the High Court (*Nubian Rights Forum and Others v The Hon. Attorney General and Others*; see Republic of Kenya, 2019a). They argued that the system was discriminatory against persons at risk of statelessness (para 307). Lacking documentation, persons in this category were likely to be excluded from the system and its accompanying benefits. The government denied this allegation (para 347). A High Court decision on 1 April 2019 suspended the requirement for compulsory registration, pending hearing and determination of the case. This made citizens and non-citizens free to register for a Huduma Namba. However, the final decision on 30 January 2020 dismissed the case. While it allowed the government to proceed with the NIIMS programme, the court underlined that comprehensive legislation must be passed to govern this regime (para 1047).

Persons at risk of statelessness experience several hurdles accessing the NIIMS programme, yet it was reported in April 2019 that members of the Shona Community – a group of persons at risk of statelessness descended from Zimbabwean immigrants – living in the Kinoo area of Nairobi had registered for the Huduma Namba (Mugo, 2019).[1] This chapter reviews this process and its outcomes. Was it beneficial to persons at risk of statelessness or did it end up creating more problems? To help answer this question, I conducted fieldwork in January 2020 with members of the Shona Community living in the Kinoo area of Nairobi, including a focus group discussion (N=7) with representatives of the community. All participants were male adults who worked in the informal sector. Discussions covered four key issues: why people applied for the Huduma Namba, the registration process, expectations from the process (particularly for those with disabilities or seeking labour integration), and what could improve the situation.[2]

This chapter is divided into four sections. First, it considers why Shona individuals applied for the Huduma Namba. It then evaluates the registration regime, highlighting some of the concerns this framework presented. The chapter then explores the impact of the Huduma Namba on the ground. It focuses on issues surrounding access to the job market, as well as the rights of persons with disabilities (PWDs). The chapter concludes by arguing that the government should do more to meet the needs of persons at risk of statelessness in Kenya.

Reasons for registration

Clause 9A of The Statute Law (Miscellaneous Amendments) Act 2018 introduced the legal framework for the Huduma Namba. This clause amended the Registration of Persons Act. These amendments came into operation on 18 January 2019 and created the NIIMS platform. Among others, this project was designed to:

(a) create, manage, maintain, and operate a national population register as a single source of personal information of all Kenyan citizens and registered foreigners resident in Kenya;
(b) assign a unique national identification number to every person registered in the register;
(c) harmonise, incorporate, and collate into the register information from other databases in government agencies relating to registration of persons;
(d) support the printing and distribution for collection of all national identification cards, refugee cards, foreigner certificates, birth and death certificates, driving licenses, work permits, passport and foreign travel documentation, and student identification cards;
(e) prescribe, in consultation with the various relevant issuing authorities, a format of identification document to capture the various forms of information contained in the identification documents in paragraph (d) for purposes of issuance of a single document where applicable; and
(f) verify and authenticate information relating to the registration and identification of persons.

(Republic of Kenya, 2019b)

Research suggests two reasons why members of the Shona Community registered for the Huduma Namba. The first reason lies in their historical experience. The community had learned the value of complying with official directives.[3] In early 2000, the Kenyan government called all foreigners to present themselves to designated areas to be register and, thereafter, be issued with identification documentation. According to focus group participants, this was seen as an opportunity to acquire government-issued documents. Many hoped this would address problems associated with lack of documentation. Members of the community presented themselves promptly for registration and state officials collected their personal data. All applicants were then issued a Waiting Card – a document acknowledging one had applied for an identification document and was awaiting its issuance. Tonderai, a member of the Shona Community, explains why he registered for the Huduma Namba:

> I remember clearly the call by the Kenyan government in early 2000 for all foreigners to register. Because we did not have any official documentation, we were very excited. We hoped that the problems we have faced all along would soon come to an end. I, together with my colleague, left for the registration centre very early in the morning. The officials took our details. My fingerprints were also taken. They then gave us a paper with a number written on it. We have been waiting since then for the official documentation to be issued. To date it has not come through. When we asked, we were told that we were not the individuals the government targeted in this exercise. We wonder why they took our details. However, I used this number when I applied for a SIM card. I still have this paper to date.

The second reason why members of the Shona Community responded was that they wanted the state to formally recognise them. Any form of documentation issued by the government was sufficient to realise this goal, thus removing them from their hidden spaces propelling them to the forefront. The fact that the government would eventually store their details on a central database was seen as an advantage. According to participants, the government would affirm their presence in the country through this initiative. The Huduma Namba, which was state based, provided a window for members of the Shona Community to obtain formal paperwork. Consequently, many members of this community clasped this opportunity with both hands. Consider the words of Masimba:

> When I heard the government had launched a programme aimed at issuing all those who resided in the country with a document, I was thrilled. For the first time, members of our community would receive an official paper. Taking our details meant that the government was finally recognizing us as residents of this country. We would also be on the government records. Previously we were hidden. This number was going to remove us from the cold. It would make us at least have a status in this county.

Members of the community had high hopes for the Huduma Namba. The question is whether this document met expectations.

The registration process

To obtain a Huduma Namba, one is required to fill out a free form – the Digital Data Capture Form.[4] Among other details, applicants are required to indicate their birth certificate and National Identity Card number (for nationals) or passport number and nationality or refugee or alien card number (for non-citizens). The form requires those in the latter category to indicate their status in the country. 'Stateless' persons are included by the form in the category of 'non-citizens'. Upon completion of this administrative process, successful applicants are issued with an Acknowledgement Slip (see Republic of Kenya, n.d.). Once the data is verified, an applicant is issued with the Hudama Namba document.

The requirements for identification documentation are a huge hurdle for members of the Shona Community. When the Huduma Namba system was rolled out, the first individuals who came to register with the local authorities were unsuccessful. This created a lot of anxiety for members of the community who were already stressed. Fortunately, this first hurdle was overcome. Makamu, an official at a human rights organisation, noted that the system would not initially allow Shonas to register – but system reconfigurations allowed their details to be processed so they could acquire an Acknowledgement Slip. Tonderai, a member of the Shona Community, recalls:

> The first time I tried to register, I was unsuccessful. The officials tried several times to make the system work. It just could not take my details. Other members of my community tried, but could not get through. With the help of the local administration, however, we were able to cross this bridge. They worked it out in a way that the machine accepted those of us who are [at risk of becoming] stateless, like others, to register. I was thrilled to complete the process. I tell you it was a huge relief. Other members of the community also went through successfully.

However, the reach of the registration machine was seriously limited. While one would expect the system to be deployed uniformly, it functioned only in the Kinoo area of Nairobi City County. Attempts by members of the Shona Community to register in other parts of the county were unsuccessful. According to Rudo, those who lived in other parts of the Nairobi County had to travel to Kinoo in order to be registered:

> We got word from relatives and friends living in other parts of Nairobi [City] County that they were unable to be registered. Kinoo is our initial home.

This is where our parents settled initially when they arrived in the country. We grew up and started our families in this area. Having grown up here, we are familiar with all local government officials. Those who migrated elsewhere, unlike us, are not so familiar with the local Administration. So when the system refused to accept them, they had to look for alternatives. We advised them to come to Kinoo. Here we are known. Eventually, many travelled to Kinoo. A good number of members of our community now hold Acknowledgement Slips.

While some members of the Shona Community received Acknowledgement Slips, the problem lay in the fact that they had to travel to Kinoo to obtain this document. Those living elsewhere faced serious challenges. Unlike nationals and other non-nationals who were able to register in any part of the country, members of the Shona Community outside the Kinoo area had to travel long distances to be registered. The fact that there was also only one working machine, unlike in other data collection centres, was quite problematic at several levels. This process can be challenged for being discriminatory, for instance. The Kenyan Constitution has several provisions that prohibit discrimination. Article 10(2)(b) declares 'non-discrimination and protection of the marginalized' as one of the national values and principles of governance in the country. Additionally, Article 27 contains a substantive equality provision and anti-discrimination prohibition. It is doubtful whether having only one working machine for a community of about 2,000 individuals accords its members the dignity and respect that are due to them under the terms of Article 28 of the Constitution and international human rights frameworks, as reflected by Article 5 of the African (Banjul) Charter on Human and Peoples' Rights. One of the key objectives of the Huduma Namba was creation of a database of 'all Kenyan citizens and registered foreigners' residing in the country. For this goal to be met, it was imperative that the state facilitate access to registration centres by every person – citizen or non-citizen, regardless of where they resided. Towards this end, the government must ensure that every person who wants to enjoy the service can access it with relative ease (Samuel, 2014: 94–95). In other words, one need not spend substantial resources to gain access to the facility. Meeting the negative obligation requires government to remove any barriers to accessing the amenity (Akande and Sekoi, 2005: 59).

Scholars debate the challenges associated with documentation and citizenship provision. In his work on birth registration, Jonathan Todres (2003: 35) contends that there is a connection between access to registration centres and availability of resources. According to Todres, this would explain the low enrolment rate in rural areas compared to their urban counterparts. The author alleges that it is 'expensive' for those in the rural areas to 'travel' to the registration points. This claim is a bit weak;

like rural dwellers, those residing in the urban areas must also travel in order to be registered. Granted, resources many be considerably greater in urban areas compared to rural parts of a country. This is not to mean, however, that all urban dwellers are wealthy. Generally speaking, persons at risk of statelessness, irrespective of whether they live in urban or rural settings, have very modest resources (Hussein, 2009: 19). Lack of documentation is a major barrier to accessing the formal labour market (as discussed below), and gaining documentation is challenging due to expensive travel costs – as well as lack of other official documentation, which may require people to travel during the day to avoid harassment or detection by police. Bureaucracy in the national registration office is also a major impediment for those seeking to register as citizens in Kenya (Kimotho and Oluoch, 2016: 70)

To realise the objectives of the Hudama Namba project requires government to remove these barriers. This calls for two undertakings. First, all eligible members within its territory should be able to access the registration points with relative ease. Second, the registration process must run smoothly, from start to finish. Against the preceding analysis, could one say that the government of Kenya met its obligations to the Shona Community? The response must be in the negative.

Tangible benefits from the Huduma Namba?

Existing scholarship underscores the connection between documentation and legal entitlements (Tien-Shi, 2012; Buterman, this volume; Liew, this volume). When the Shona applied for the Huduma Namba, they expected it to address some difficulties caused by lack of documentation. Using entitlements due to PWDs[5] and the right of access to the labour market as examples, this section examines issues surrounding the outcome of this exercise.

Entitlements to persons with disabilities

The intersection between the rights of PWDs and claims to nationality is critical. According to the World Bank (2019), one billion people – 15% of the world's population – experience some form of disability. Consequently, there is need for research in order to understand and respond to the specific needs of PWDs whose nationality is under threat. This approach is consistent with the UNHCR's (2006: para c) call for engagement in under-researched areas as a way towards 'crafting strategies to [address] the problem' facing those at risk of statelessness'.

Despite the apparent need for data, literature has yet to explore the intersections between disability and individuals at risk of statelessness (see also Brennan et al., this volume). Granted, some authors have conducted research on PWDs within known stateless populations. Landry and Tupetz (2018), for instance, examine needs of Rohingyas with disabilities living as refugees in Bangladesh. Notably, this work focuses on those individuals who have fled to other states in search of protection. Consequently, their protection obligations lie with the host state, not their home country. Overall, studies in the area of statelessness have failed to give sufficient attention to persons at risk of statelessness living with disabilities (Blitz and Lynch, 2011; Manby, 2015; Belton, 2017). PWDs within any statelessness community are disadvantaged twice: suffering from the impacts of statelessness, while also dealing with difficulties arising from their physical environment – including spaces that often exacerbate unique challenges.

In Kenya, the rights of PWDs are protected by law. Article 260 of the Constitution contains provisions that seek to protect PWDs.[6] Article 27 outlaws discrimination on grounds of, among others, 'disability', and outlines entitlements due to PWDs. These entitlements are fleshed out by domestic law via the 2003 Persons with Disabilities Act (PDA). Kenya has also ratified the 2008 Convention on the Rights of Persons with Disabilities (CRPD). It is thus obligated to observe the provisions of this treaty, which it has since domesticated. This protection regime does not discriminate between nationals and non-nationals. In other words, Kenya has legally recognised its obligations to PWDs within the stateless community. Applicants for the Huduma Namba are required to indicate whether or not they live with any disability. If someone's response is 'yes', they are required to indicate the nature of their disability, as well as their disability registration number (DRN).[7]

Government responsibilities to PWDs in the Shona Community are set out in Section 20 of the PDA (including early identification of disability, rehabilitation, free or affordable health services), while Article 25 of the CRPD guarantees the 'highest attainable standard of health without discrimination on the basis of disability'. Despite these commitments, the Kenyan government's record shows that it does not always comply with its legal obligations. Empirical data affirm that the state has violated PWDs' rights to health in a number of case (Muga, 2003; Tanabe et al., 2015) – and those at risk of statelessness are often worse off. Study participants confirmed that the government was hardly involved in safeguarding their health in general, and PWDs in the community were particularly vulnerable. In spite of securing Acknowledgement Slips, the community had to support PWD members in the absence of state action and protection. In the words of Runako:

> There are a number of disabled persons in our community. Would you expect
> the government to offer them any assistance, yet it does not come to our aid?
> These folks are really suffering. Many times the community has to chip in
> and assist. But this is not enough, as we ourselves are struggling to make ends
> meet. When we go to any government facility we are asked to produce an ID.
> If you say you don't have one, you are treated as a foreigner. The effect of this
> is horrible – we have to pay double for any service. The Acknowledgement Slip
> has not been of any use in this regard. Why did we bother to take it?

The requirement that persons at risk of statelessness and living with disabilities produce a DRN is also very problematic. Part A02 of the DRN registration form requires an applicant to indicate their ID or Birth Certificate
number. Securing these documents is challenging for persons at risk of statelessness because most do not hold official documentation. Among other
particulars, an applicant is required to indicate their nationality and mobile
phone number. In Kenya, however, a person must supply a service provider
with a copy of their ID or passport to gain a mobile number – making this
difficult for those at risk of statelessness. Simply put, it is unlikely that a
PWD from the Shona Community will successfully complete this form and
obtain a DRN. Eventually, they will likely be excluded from state benefits
granted to other PWDs.

Access to employment

Employment, either in the formal or informal sectors, is fundamental to
the life of any individual. International and domestic laws protect this
right. Pursuant to Article 6 of the International Covenant on Economic,
Social and Cultural Rights (ICESCR), state parties 'recognize the right to
work, which includes the right of everyone to the opportunity to gain his
living by work which he freely chooses or accepts, and will take appropriate steps to safeguard this right'. Article 15 of the 1981 African (Banjul)
Charter on Human and Peoples' Rights guarantees every person the 'right
to work under equitable and satisfactory conditions'. Article 41 of the 2010
Constitution of Kenya and the 2007 Employment Act, Cap 226, reinforces
Kenya's international obligations. The right to work places both a positive
and a negative obligation on states. The former requires them to undertake
measures that will promote and protect the realisation of this entitlement
by every person in the country. States are also prohibited from unjustified
interference with this right.

Despite these legal requirements, lived experiences for members of
the Shona Community reflect obstacles to employment rights. Those
who applied for the Huduma Namba expected this document to, among
other things, guarantee their work rights; that is, they anticipated that

documents would facilitate their access to the regular labour market. Members of this community have been unable to gain formal employment following years of marginalisation, forcing many to run their own informal businesses to make ends meet. Lack of documents meant they were unable to access financial services offered by banks, to obtain relevant permits, or to utilise services offered by mobile phone providers. The Huduma Namba was seen as an avenue for facilitating access to these facilities, and, thereby, improve their livelihoods. However, these services were still out of reach for some of the members of this community in January 2020, despite the fact that they had a Huduma Namba. Masimba made the following comments:

> When I registered for the Huduma Namba, I expected it to enable me to improve my business. As you can see, I ran my business. But it has been quite difficult to get a permit. I have to use a proxy, with an ID card, to run my business in this room. It is not easy. Getting a SIM card is still not possible. So, too, is opening a bank account. Yet I have a number of clients who would like to pay me by cheque. When they hear I don't have a bank account, that's the end of our conversation. They look for other traders. To receive and withdraw money using a phone, one has to rely on Kenyans with ID. The person has to be reliable. If you find one who is untrustworthy, they can run away with your money. In a nutshell, you are at the mercy of others. It is very stressing.

The Huduma Namba therefore failed to facilitate access to the regular labour market for persons at risk of statelessness, just as it had failed to protect many fundamental rights for PWDs.

Conclusion: Towards rendering *huduma*

Huduma is a Swahili word meaning 'service'. Yet it is apparent that the Huduma Namba has failed to meet the needs of the Shona Community and created further problems. Some steps could be taken to improve the current state of affairs, however. For instance, it is important first to establish the number of persons at risk of statelessness living with disabilities within this community. The United Nations High Commissioner for Refugees (2006) underlines the value of states identifying persons at risk of statelessness in their territories, noting that this exercise is a vital first step in protecting basic human rights. Previous research shows that the number of persons at risk of stateless in Kenya is yet to be established (Kenya National Commission on Human Rights and United Nation High Commissioner for Refugees, 2010). Consequently, the National Task Force for the Identification and Registration of Eligible Stateless Persons as Kenya Citizens ('Statelessness Taskforce'), which was established in August 2019 via Gazette Notice No.

7881 (see Kenya Gazette, 2019), needs to embark immediately on this task. These data, which should be updated regularly, are useful in formulation of programmes designed to improve the lives and livehoods of individuals at risk of statelessness. (Furaha, an official working with a human rights agency in Nairobi, affirmed this statement.) The number of persons at risk of statelessness living with disabilities must be also be captured in the national census.

Kenyan law requires the Huduma Namba system to be available to everyone in all parts of the country. Accordingly, the government must take steps to address exclusion of any category of members within its population. As noted earlier, the Kenyan High Court directed the government to pass comprehensive legislation to regulate operation of the Huduma Namba system. Limitations highlighted in this chapter must be addressed comprehensively by operational law. This legislation must comply with basic due process standards. Monitoring the implementation process is crucial if genuine results are to be attained.

Programmes such as the Huduma Namba are short-term initiatives. Yoda, a government official, argued persuasively that provision of official documentation is the 'real solution' to the plight facing persons at risk of statelessness. Through these documents, persons at risk of statelessness can gain citizenship and the bundle of rights and obligations that come with this status. This is not an easy task. All human rights defenders must join hands in this quest – as asserted by Tembo, an official of an NGO in Nairobi. Affected people such as the Shona Community must be at the forefront of these efforts, not in the background, and action must be sustained in order to bear fruit. Otherwise, there a high chance that the human rights of this vulnerable population will continue to be severely restricted.

Notes

1 This community is largely descended from Shona migrants who settled in Kenya from what is now Zimbabwe in the 1960s in order to establish the Gospel of God Church. Today, members of this community are unable to establish a sufficient pre-1963 connection to Kenya for the purposes of citizenship and do not have any connection to Zimbabwe either, thus leaving them stateless.

2 The discussion was carried out in Swahili and translated to English by the author. Interviews with government (n=1) and non-state (n=3) officials were conducted in English via telephone. These officials were selected because of their expertise in nationality/citizenship matters. To protect the identity of interviewees, pseudonyms have been used. The small sample size means that the research findings are

indicative, not conclusive. That said, the chapter offers an empirical lens through which we can explore the Huduma Namba registration regime and begin an evaluation of recommendations for reform.

3 Research with communities at risk of statelessness suggests that past experience plays a central role in their decision-making process (Rurup, 2011; Vollmer, this volume). These lessons contribute a great deal in determining the level of future engagement with government officials.

4 For a sample of this form, visit www.hudumanamba.go.ke/wp-content/uploads/ 2019/05/Huduma-nanba-form.pdf (Accessed 12 November 2019).

5 In Kenya, the Persons with Disabilities Act defines 'disability' as 'a physical, sensory, mental or other impairment, including any visual, hearing, learning or physical incapability, which impacts adversely on social, economic or environmental participation'.

6 Article 260 of the Constitution defines 'disability' to include 'any physical, sensory, mental, psychological or other impairment, condition or illness that has, or is perceived by significant sectors of the community to have, a substantial or long-term effect on an individual's ability to carry out ordinary day-to-day activities'.

7 The applicable form is available from the National Council for Persons with Disabilities.

References

Akande, T. M., and Sekoi, O. O. (2005) 'A survey of birth and death registration in semi-urban settlement in middle-belt Nigeria', *European Journal of Scientific Research*, 8, 56–61.

Belton, K. (2017) *Statelessness in the Caribbean: The Paradox of Belonging in a Postnational World* (Philadelphia, PA: University of Pennsylvania Press).

Blitz, B., and Lynch, M. (2011) *Statelessness and Citizenship: A Comparative Study of the Benefits of Nationality* (Northampton, MA: Edward Elgar).

Constitution of Kenya (2010) [Online]. Available at http://kenyalaw.org/kl/index. php?id=398 (Accessed 24 July 2020).

Hussein, A. (2009) 'Kenyan Nubians: Standing up to statelessness', *Forced Migration Review*, 32, 19–20.

Kenya Gazette (2019) 'Gazette Notice No. 7881: The National Taskforce for the Identification and Registration of Eligible Stateless Persons as Kenya Citizens', CXXI:10, 3554 [Online]. Available at http://kenyalaw.org/kenya_gazette/gazette/ volume/MTk5MA--/Vol.CXXI-No.110/ (Accessed 29 July 2020).

Kenya National Commission on Human Rights and United Nation High Commissioner for Refugees (2010) 'Out of the shadows: Towards ensuring the rights of stateless persons and persons at risk of statelessness in Kenya' [Online]. Available at www.unhcr.org/4e8338d49.pdf (Accessed 20 November 2019).

Kimotho, R., and Oluoch, K. (2016) 'Assessment of effectiveness of citizen registration systems in Kenya', *Journal of Public Policy and Administration*, 1, 58–75.

Landry, M., and Tupetz, A. (2018) 'Disability and the Rohingya displacement crisis: A humanitarian policy', *Archives of Physical Medicine and Rehabilitation*, 99, 2122–2124.

Manby, B. (2015) 'Nationality, migration and statelessness in West Africa: A study for UNHCR and IOM' [Online]. Available at https://humantraffickingsearch.org/wp-content/uploads/2017/07/Nationality-Migration-and-Statelessness-in-West-Africa-REPORT-EN.pdf (Accessed 1 April 2020).

Muga, E. (2003) 'Screening for disability in a community: The "ten questions" screen for children in Bondo, Kenya', *African Health Services*, 3, 33–39.

Mugo, G. (2019) 'Stateless community in Kinoo Lists for Huduma Namba', *Star*, 23 April [Online]. Available at www.the-star.co.ke/news/2019-04-23-stateless-community-in-kinoo-lists-for-huduma-namba/ (Accessed 2 December 2019).

Musyoki, W. (2019) 'Consequences of not getting the Huduma Namba – Gov't spokesman Kiraithe', *Citizen Digital*, 25 April [Online]. Available at https://citizentv.co.ke/news/consequences-not-getting-huduma-namba-govt-spokesman-kiraithe-242570/ (Accessed 1 December 2019).

Organization of African Unity (1981) *African (Banjul) Charter on Human and Peoples Rights* [Online]. Available at www.refworld.org/docid/3ae6b3630.html (Accessed 24 July 2020).

Persons with Disabilities Act (Kenya) (2003) [Online]. Available at www.un.org/development/desa/disabilities/wp-content/uploads/sites/15/2019/11/Kenya_Persons-with-Disability-Act.pdf (Accessed 24 July 2020).

Republic of Kenya (n.d.) 'Huduma Namba: FAQs' [Online]. Available at www.hudumanamba.go.ke/faqs/ (Accessed 5 April 2020).

Republic of Kenya (2019a) *Nubian Rights Forum and Others v The Hon. Attorney General and Others* [Online]. Available at http://kenyalaw.org/caselaw/cases/view/172447/ (Accessed 29 July 2020).

Republic of Kenya (2019b) *The Statute Law (Miscellaneous Amendments) Act, 2018, No. 18 of 2018*, Kenya Gazette Supplement No. 161 (Acts No. 18) [Online]. Available at http://kenyalaw.org/kl/fileadmin/pdfdownloads/AmendmentActs/2018/StatuteLaw_MiscellaneousAmendments_Act_2018.pdf (Accessed 29 July 2020).

Rurup, M. (2011) 'Lives in limbo: Statelessness after two world wars', *Bulletin of the German Historical Institute*, 49, 113–134.

Samuel, O. A. (2014) 'Human factor issues in the use of e-government services among Ghanaian middle age population: Improving usability of existing and future government virtual interactive systems design', *Journal of Information Engineering and Applications*, 4, 85–106.

Tanabe, M., Nagujjah, Y., Rimal, N., Bukania, F., and Krause, S. (2015) 'Intersecting sexual and reproductive health and disability in humanitarian settings: Risks, needs, and capacities of refugees with disabilities in Kenya, Nepal, and Uganda', *Sexuality and Disability*, 33, 411–427.

Tien-Shi, C. (2012) 'Statelessness in Japan: Management and challenges', *Journal of Population and Social Studies*, 21, 70–81.

Todres, T. (2003) 'Birth registration: An essential first step toward ensuring the rights of all children', *Human Rights Brief*, 10:3, 32–35.

United Nations Department of Economic and Social Affairs (2006) *Convention on the Rights of Persons with Disabilities* [Online]. Available at www.un.org/development/desa/disabilities/convention-on-the-rights-of-persons-with-disabilities.html (Accessed 24 July 2020).

United Nations High Commissioner for Refugees (2006) *Conclusion on Identification, Prevention and Reduction of Statelessness and Protection of Stateless Persons,* 106 (LVII)-2006.

United Nations Human Rights (1966) *International Covenant on Economic, Social and Cultural Rights* [Online]. Available at www.ohchr.org/en/professionalinterest/pages/cescr.aspx (Accessed 24 July 2020).

World Bank (2019) 'Disability inclusion' [Online]. Available at www.worldbank.org/en/topic/disability (Accessed 10 December 2019).

19

Too little too late? Naturalisation of stateless Kurds and transitional justice in Syria

Haqqi Bahram[1]

Falling outside the constellation of nation states, Kurds in Syria and other Middle Eastern states have long endured severe treatment.[2] As part of a stateless nation (Vali, 1998), Syrian Kurds became the subject of double statelessness when a discriminatory and exceptional census in 1962 stripped about 120,000 individuals of Syrian nationality in a systematic denationalisation – comprising 20% of the total Kurdish population at the time (Human Rights Watch, 1996; Tejel, 2009). As described by Human Rights Watch (1996), '[t]he census served, in effect, as a sweeping mechanism to disenfranchise large numbers of Syrian Kurds and their descendants' (12). This was within a comprehensive plan of demographic change including the Arabisation of the Kurdish northeast of Syria in what is known as 'the Arab belt' scheme (Human Rights Watch, 1996 and 2009). While official numbers were concealed by the Syrian state, the organisation Syrians for Truth and Justice (2019) revealed that there were more than 500,000 stateless Syrian Kurds by 2011, as newer generations inherited statelessness and the issue remained unresolved.[3]

The immediate outcome of the census was the invention of the two stateless sub-categories of *ajanib* and *maktoumeen* among Syrian Kurds (Human Rights Watch, 1996; Montgomery, 2005; Yildiz, 2005; Tejel, 2009). The Arabic word *ajanib* (plural; singular *ajnabi* [m], *ajnabiyya* [f]) means 'aliens/foreigners' and *maktoumeen* (plural; singular *maktoum* [m], *maktouma* [f]) means 'unregistered' or literally 'concealed/hidden' (see Human Rights Watch, 1996: 16–23). *Ajanib* Kurds were given special red identity cards that explicitly marked them as 'foreigners' after their nationality was removed through the 1962 census (Montgomery, 2005). The Syrian state claimed that *maktoumeen* Kurds were 'alien infiltrators' who reside 'illegally' and without documents in the country (Human Rights Watch, 1996). This translated into severe restrictions on fundamental human rights for both groups (Lynch and Ali, 2006) – including the right to legal identity, birth certificates, education, employment, property ownership, travel, and political participation – to such a degree that 'the stateless Kurds, for all practical purposes, were rendered nonexistent' (Tejel, 2009: 51). With the intensifying exclusion and lack of access to rights, this situation turned into an existential dilemma for many stateless Syrian Kurds.

Forty-nine years after the census and parallel to the pressure of expanding protests against the repressive Syrian regime, a Presidential Decree No. 49 (re)granted Syrian nationality to *ajanib* on 7 April 2011. This came within a package of several other decrees, presented by the Syrian state as the 'comprehensive reform programme' in a bid to curb the growing demands of protestors during the first year of the public unrest. Regaining nationality at this very challenging socio-political moment, Syrian Kurds found themselves faced with a 'solution' to their statelessness that came with lots of uncertainties. At the time of writing, nine years after the naturalisation and a time marked by armed conflict, the situation is still unclear for Syrian Kurds in terms of their access to rights, reparation, inclusion, and belonging, as well as the recognition of their identity in Syria.

By engaging a transitional justice perspective, this chapter interrogates the naturalisation of Syrian Kurds and the implications of the Syrian state policy of 'solving' this case of *in-situ* statelessness. Through a critical analysis of the so-called 'reform' and the legal transition of Syrian Kurds from *ajanib* category to national, the chapter engages with a discussion of human rights, justice, and the legacy of statelessness while uncovering the incoherence of the Syrian state's policy. Given the role that identity-based discrimination has played in producing statelessness in Syria, the discussion highlights the identity conflict that has intensively materialised in the naturalisation process when Syrian Kurds are documented as Arab nationals of Syria. The chapter further demonstrates the challenges relating to 'solving statelessness' within the currently limited transitional justice process for Syria and concludes by suggesting potential ways of responding to statelessness based on an intersectional and non-hierarchical understanding of human rights.

Naturalisation and transitional justice?

While statelessness is not conventionally a problem addressed by transitional justice, it is an issue that is intrinsically connected to *lack of justice* and violations of human rights. Looking back in history, statelessness has never been a sole legal problem. In her critical analysis of the function of human rights and the right to have rights, Hannah Arendt (1973) identified statelessness as a human condition beyond legal rights, a condition that drastically affects people's lives, identities, and choices. When some people are denied membership or deemed unworthy of rights, it is imperative to see the systems of discrimination that produce statelessness as it 'does not occur in vacuum' (Kingston, 2017: 25). Article 15 of the Universal Declaration of Human Rights explicitly states that 'everyone has the right to a nationality' and 'no one shall be arbitrarily deprived of his nationality nor denied the right to change his nationality' (United Nations, 1948). The violation of the human right to a nationality is particularly severe when it takes the form of denationalisation; when communities of people are deprived of nationality in their 'own countries' through discriminatory and exclusionary practices (see also Gyulai, 2014; Vlieks, 2017). The international community has crafted instruments that aim to protect stateless persons and measures to reduce statelessness; for example, the 1954 Convention Relating to the Status of Stateless Persons and the 1961 Convention on the Reduction of Statelessness. Despite this, discriminatory laws and state policies have not stopped offering new ways to deny belonging and equal membership to groups of people and individuals who consequently become stateless (see UNHCR, 2014a; Fazal, this volume).

The exceptional 1962 census that targeted Syrian Kurds with denationalisation occurred one year after the 1961 Convention came into being. Syria is not a signatory or party to either of the two conventions. The statelessness of Syrian Kurds should be treated as a question of violation of human rights based in discrimination, requiring justice more than a symbolic change in legislation. When the naturalisation decree was issued, questions about the status of justice, inclusion, and reparations immediately became central. The real problem as seen by affected people was not only the revocation and denial of legal nationality for forty-nine years; it was rather the injustice that made the denationalisation and the human rights consequences possible (McGee, 2014; Syrians for Truth and Justice, 2019). The day after the decree was issued, demonstrations broke out across Kurdish areas in Syria demanding that violations of human rights be addressed and reparations be made for victims of denationalisation (Welateme, 2011). For many persons, receiving nationality was indeed celebrated, yet it was clear that the injustices associated with statelessness would not disappear altogether. The transition from stateless to national would be meaningless if not combined with mechanisms fostering inclusion and belonging in just and transparent ways, as made evident throughout the demonstrations.

In the current transitional context of Syria – where major elements of the political regime, governance, and the state itself are all contested, and the demands for justice are increasing – denationalisation and statelessness appear as fundamental issues that seek a place in the transitional justice paradigm pursued for the country. In theory, transitional justice as a practice has witnessed a proliferation of institutional and judicial application around the globe for the last three decades or so. Nevertheless, there seems to be no clear scholarly or practical consensus on the definition, scope, and application of transitional justice (Nagy, 2008; Gready and Robins, 2014). This is evident in historical example of cases of transitional justice and responses and discourses in various contexts (Elster, 2004; Zunino, 2019), as well as in the idea, theory, and subject of justice itself (Rawls, 1999). In any case, the guiding principle for any intervention taken under the nomenclature of transitional justice is often built on a general understanding that it is about 'reckoning with the past, attending to the needs of victims, and setting the foundations for democracy, human rights and the rule of law' (Nagy, 2008: 275). Accepting the above holistic understanding of transitional justice, as I do in this chapter, it is manifest that human rights occupy the centre of any approach to transitional justice, and statelessness as a violation of human rights should therefore be part of transitional justice work.

Looking through the transitional justice lens, no elements of justice as highlighted above are evidently present in what happened in the 2011 naturalisation action by the Syrian state. Moreover, this action does not conform to any of the United Nations' guiding principles of transitional justice, especially the requirement of the centrality of victims in design and implementation and the comprehensiveness of approach to address the violation of rights, including the right to a nationality (United Nations, 2010). In the absence of a basis for democracy, human rights, and the rule of law, 'solving' statelessness has been carried out in total obscuration of the past and failure to attend to the needs of the victims. Not only was granting Syrian nationality depicted as an 'administrative reform', the Syrian state did not aim to bring justice to the affected people. The 'reform', as such, overlooked the historical injustice inflicted on Syrian Kurds and presented the act of granting nationality as a generous endowment by the Syrian president. The text of the decree itself was so brief, composed of only three sentences, that for an external observer it might resemble a mere bureaucratic and a 'normal' response to a small-scale issue.

The legacy of statelessness

Naturalisation and access to legal nationality are often seen as solutions that potentially end the problems associated with statelessness, but the legacy of statelessness afterwards is rarely discussed. This is reflected, for example, in the UNHCR's Global Action Plan to End Statelessness in 10 years (UNHCR, 2014a and 2014b) and the ongoing 'I Belong' Campaign (UNHCR, 2014c; Schnyder, this volume). While such work is vital and should be praised, from a justice and human rights point of view more needs to be done. This is mainly because statelessness is not a mere technical problem that can be fixed by a change in the law. Moreover, such concentration on the legalistic solutions risks 'ignor[ing] important, subtle realities about the nature of marginalisation and rights abuses' (Kingston, 2017: 17). Therefore, while solutions to statelessness involve engagement with legal reform, they need to expand to include other missing elements of establishing justice afterwards.

Statelessness scholarship has increasingly focused on exploring ways of understanding, theorising, and solving statelessness with the assumption that legal nationality acquisition 'is the principal appropriate remedy' for statelessness (Bloom et al., 2017: 2). The consequence is that less attention is given to the experiences of those who are directly impacted by 'solutions' to their statelessness. In other words, the whole host of outstanding issues in post-statelessness tend to be ignored when (re)gaining nationality is celebrated as a 'premature declaration of triumph' (Balaton-Chrimes, 2014: 16). Nationality is celebrated with the assumption that inclusion and access to basic human rights follow naturally.

However, once a person is able to change legal status from stateless to national, a long-lasting legacy of statelessness unfolds. Stateless Syrian Kurds who went through naturalisation provide strong evidence for this legacy. It represents a barrier that turns their rights into 'rights on hold'. In a recent study conducted by Syrians for Truth and Justice (2019) on the detrimental effects of the 1962 census, several testimonies by Syrian Kurds are given on outstanding issues after the naturalisation. These include the exclusionary process of naturalisation and the distinctive identity documents. Testimonies further refer to the social stigma and complex problems of property and land ownership in addition to lost opportunities for a dignified life.

As the 'reform' decree only targeted *ajanib* and purposefully excluded *maktoumeen* from the naturalisation, it offered an unequal 'solution' to statelessness. While *ajanib* had been registered in civil records and thus had a claim to a certain restricted form of documentation, *maktoumeen*, as the name itself suggests, were basically unregistered. Although some *maktoumeen* did manage to change categories and become *ajanib* with the hope of benefitting from the decree, many are still struggling with exclusion and their status as *maktoumeen* (Albarazi, 2013; McGee, 2016; McGee and Albarazi, 2020). In fact, the 'reform' rather sustained a stratified statelessness among stateless Syrian Kurds; a stateless *maktoum* would aspire and likely work hard to be recognised as a stateless *ajnabi* in order to be considered for naturalisation.

Another problem that explains the exclusionary process of naturalisation is that of the identity documents issued for *ajanib*, which are exclusively distinguished with placing a number '8' after the registration number (Syrians for Truth and Justice, 2019). This distinctive mark drives a persistent fear on the part of the naturalised who thus remain particularly branded and not similarly registered as other Syrian nationals. This also raises concerns about being a target of a future re-denationalisation amidst the growing lack of trust in the procedures of the Syrian state.

In addition to distinctive documentation, the legacy of statelessness emanates from the arbitrariness through which (non)registration of stateless Syrian Kurds had been carried out in the past. This was manifested, for example, in the denial of birth certificates, arbitrary age estimation, and other instances of the state's 'biopower' over the existence of the stateless person.

Beyond documents and registration, the statelessness legacy developed also as a stigma haunting individuals in their social environments when many stateless individuals could not marry or form families legally in the past. Adding to this is the 'pressure of passing on that stigma to children and future generations' (Türk, 2014: 46). Similarly, problems of land and property ownership also continue. A Syrian Kurdish stateless person could not inherit anything, but he/she *would* inherit statelessness. As such, statelessness has basically created a condition where individuals have been deprived of most of the basic opportunities of life, including the right to a dignified life that a naturalisation process has failed to address.

This legacy – and the absence of access to equal human rights and inclusion through naturalisation – indicate that the legal solution, although very much needed and vital for this case of statelessness, could not on its own produce justice. This is particularly important given that statelessness is not a stand-alone issue, but rather is part of an intersecting net of problems including discrimination and marginalisation (Brennan et al., this volume). As such, the reality of stateless Syrian Kurds suggests that their denationalisation and later naturalisation require a subtle and profound understanding. This must include considering the struggle for Kurdish identity and recognition.

Naturalisation as identity subjugation

Recognising that Syrian Kurds were targeted with denationalisation and the later distinctive naturalisation because of their ethnic identity as Kurds, this naturalisation represents another layer of the long-standing discrimination practised by the Syrian state and its Arabisation schemes (Tejel, 2009; Gunes, 2019). The non-recognition of the ethnic identity of Kurds and the denial of any other non-Arab identity as inscribed in the Syrian Constitution calls the Syrian state's intentions into question. In addition, the naturalisation followed the popular protests, suggesting it was also as a policy to distance the Kurds from taking part in the opposition.

In a field study conducted in 2014, Thomas McGee (2014) questions the identity politics of this naturalisation, highlighting the 'widespread suspicion of the motivations behind the April 2011 decree' (178). Article 1 of this decree explicitly states that individuals registered in the Hasakah *ajanib* records shall be granted Syrian *Arab* nationality. As such, the decree avoids recognising those who are included under this provision as Syrian *Kurds*, instead forcing Arab identity on anyone that consequently becomes a Syrian national.

Seen in the context of conflict between the Syrian state ideology and Kurdish non-conformity, denationalisation and the later selective naturalisation thus expose issues that are not limited to the *ajanib* and *maktoumeen*, but that impact the entire Kurdish population in Syria (McGee, 2014). Therefore, any solution that aims to 'solve' statelessness in this context needs to be built on the understanding that injustice has been experienced on both the personal level as denationalised persons and on the collective level as the unrecognised and oppressed Kurdish ethnic minority in Syria.

Putting this into a broader context of ways of understanding and responding to statelessness, it is imperative to note that denationalisation, deprivation of nationality-based rights, and selective naturalisation are all issues that can happen because of the state's systemic racism and hence such issues develop as symptoms of 'existing discrimination and marginalisation' (Kingston, 2017: 23). Any attempt therefore to address statelessness will need to re-examine the structures within which such problems are created and aggravated (Bloom et al., 2017). Failing to do so in general would mean that naturalisation is only tapping on the surface of the problems. In the Syrian context, it would mean that naturalisation has been but a pseudo-justice that covers up a system of ethnic discrimination and subjugation of the Kurdish identity within the country.

Statelessness and challenges in transitional justice

Noticing the complexity of statelessness and the simplistic approach taken by the Syrian state in addressing it, it is evident that a set of challenges blocks the way for Syrian Kurds to realise equal nationality rights and other essential human rights, from which a process of transitional justice and reconciliation could potentially commence. While some of these challenges directly relate to the Syrian context *per se*, others are inherent in the developing global constellations of transitional justice more generally.

In her genealogy of transitional justice, Ruti G. Teitel (2017) argues that today's global rule of law appears to be more dependent on the expansion of the law of war, incorporated as international humanitarian law that 'enables the international community to hold a regime's leadership accountable and condemn a systematic persecutory policy, even outside the relevant state' (91). As such, transitional justice is shifting from a legal phenomenon related to conflict resolution, post-conflict conditions, and establishment of democracy to become a normalised and globalised practice for intervention under the campaigns against terrorism. Such a constellation proves problematic as it attempts to focus on present exceptional status to guide future politics while transitional justice requires a look backward to the past to respond to the conflict (Teitel, 2017). In fact, it is through these retrospective models that transitional justice can initiate critical responses.

In the Syrian case, the limited international judicial arrangement seems to narrowly focus on war crimes and campaigns against terrorism. To this end, humanitarian dilemmas, including the deprivation of nationality and statelessness, have fallen outside the legal agenda for transitional justice. Equal nationality rights, for example, is rendered a minority issue and other basic human rights become secondary to the need to replace the current repressive regime with a democratic one. Even this later attempt is placed secondary to the rhetoric of 'war on terrorism' and the need to eradicate extremism in the country. This hierarchal and non-intersectional approach to the value of fundamental human rights as pillars of transitional justice indicates a problem in the global human rights discourse as a whole.

This further raises the question of why some issues make it into the international human rights agenda, while others (like statelessness) do not. In this regard, Lindsey N. Kingston (2013) notes that despite the 'global pervasiveness and negative ramifications' of statelessness, there are still obstacles that hinder its emergence as an issue onto the global agenda (74). According to Kingston, factors including the heterogeneity of the issue, the lack of understanding of statelessness, and the lack of both global solutions and political will all contribute to this gap. Seen within the global transitional justice perspective highlighted above, the statelessness gap means that the lives of some people are put on hold when other issues related to war crimes and combatting terrorism top the agenda for international action. This translates in practice into prolonged peace processes and consequently some rights, such as the right to a nationality, could fall in the category of 'rights that can wait' if not distorted or rejected altogether as unlawful claims in certain contexts.

While the violence continues, further challenges impede a meaningful transitional justice and a 'solution' to statelessness in Syria. These are represented by the absence of basic mechanisms of transitional justice and the lack of political will, not only by the Syrian state but also by the formal political opposition. Nine years after the emergence of the initial inclusive slogan of the public protests, 'Syria for all Syrians', the Syrian political opposition does not seem to be able to ensure a meaningful inclusion for Kurds, at present or in post-conflict Syria. Indeed, opposition leaders have failed the Syrian Kurdish community on several occasions (McGee, 2014). In both camps, the Kurdish question (including the problem of statelessness and its legacy, exclusion, and reparations) appear to be postponed as minor issues until other major issues – the crisis or the conspiracy (as the Syrian regime calls it), and the fall of the dictatorship regime (as the opposition demands) – are resolved.

Conclusion

The full realisation of transitional justice is always challenging, and the Syrian situation is no exception. The approach and vision that guides any process of transitional justice often plays a crucial part in how inclusive and just it can be. This chapter demonstrates how the nationality 'reform' lacks the foundational premises of transitional justice. This is evidenced by exclusionary naturalisation, the unfolding legacy of statelessness, and discriminatory identity politics. Issues such as the denial of nationality still fall outside the humanitarian and international agenda when weighed against other issues, such as war crimes and war on terrorism.

For statelessness to be prevented and addressed justly and humanely, this method of ranking problems needs to be re-addressed. The human right to a nationality needs to be equally emphasised in transitional justice undertakings. This further suggests that the practice of transitional justice must claim a *transformative* role that allows for intersectional and non-hierarchical responses (Gready and Robins, 2014). In the Syrian context, this could inform responses to statelessness in four ways.

First, international legal frameworks must be adhered to by ensuring that no one is left behind and that no one is denied their Syrian nationality (see also Bloom, this volume). The ratification of both the 1954 and 1961 Statelessness Conventions by any future Syrian government can be a first step in this regard.

Second, the rule of law and legal empowerment should be ensured by providing access to legal assistance and developing anti-discriminatory laws. This also includes developing domestic legislation and monitoring mechanisms for nationality laws so that future denationalisation and/or statelessness are prevented.

Third, the statelessness legacy must be addressed by ensuring that all the detrimental and accumulative effects of denationalisation and statelessness are acknowledged and mitigated. This includes addressing the exclusionary powers of the Decree No. 49 by including *maktoumeen* and other Syrian Kurds in the diaspora in naturalisation processes, as well as establishing effective mechanisms for reparations in relation to all forms of expropriation, especially of agricultural lands.

Finally, a constitutional recognition of Kurdish identity is essential to set the foundation for a multi-ethnic and democratic future Syrian society where Syrian nationality is not imposed as mono-ethnically and culturally Arab as it is today. These responses are crucial for any process of reconciliation, peace, and transitional justice and are equally fundamental for informing any future social contract among the population of Syria.

While this case has highlighted governance failings in response to statelessness in the Syrian context, it also forces more wide-ranging considerations about the relationship between statelessness and governance. Crucially, human rights, including the right to a nationality, are not 'rights that can wait' in processes of transitional justice. This further implies the need to expand lenses to look at statelessness and its legacy as global political and structural issues that demand comprehensive solutions, including transitional justice undertakings, which should primarily operate within a framework of universal human rights.

Notes

1 An early draft of this chapter was presented at the 2019 General Conference of the *European Consortium for Political Research* (ECPR) at the University of Wrocław, Poland.
2 Mainly living in Turkey, Iran, Iraq, Syria, and some parts of the former Soviet Union, the Kurdish population is estimated to currently be between 40 to 50 million. See, for example, McDowall (2004) for a history of the Kurds.
3 Syrians for Truth and Justice (STJ) is an independent non-governmental organisation of human rights defenders, advocates, and academics working to uncover human rights violations and promote inclusiveness in Syria.

References

Albarazi, Z. (2013) 'The stateless Syrians', Tilburg Law School Research Paper No. 011/2013 [Online]. Available at https://papers.ssrn.com/sol3/papers.cfm?abstract_id=2269700 (Accessed 14 June 2019).
Arendt, H. (1973) *The Origins of Totalitarianism* (New York: Harcourt Brace Jovanovich).

Balaton-Chrimes, S. (2014) 'Statelessness, identity cards and citizenship as status in the case of the Nubians of Kenya', *Citizenship Studies*, 18:1, 15–28.

Bloom, T., Tonkiss, K., and Cole, P. (eds) (2017) *Understanding Statelessness* (Abingdon: Routledge).

Edwards, A., and van Waas, L. (eds) (2014) *Nationality and Statelessness under International Law* (Cambridge: Cambridge University Press).

Elster, J. (2004) *Closing the Books: Transitional Justice in Historical Perspective* (Cambridge: Cambridge University Press).

Gready, P., and Robins, S. (2014) 'From transitional to transformative justice: A new agenda for practice', *International Journal of Transitional Justice*, 8:3, 339–361.

Gunes, C. (2019) *Kurds in a New Middle East. The Changing Geopolitics of a Regional Conflict* (Cham: Palgrave Macmillan).

Gyulai, G. (2014) 'The determination of statelessness and the establishment of a statelessness-specific protection regime', in A. Edwards and L. van Waas (eds) *Nationality and Statelessness under International Law* (Cambridge: Cambridge University Press): pp. 116–143.

Human Rights Watch (1996) 'Syria: The silenced Kurds' [Online]. Available at www.hrw.org/sites/default/files/reports/SYRIA96.pdf (Accessed 14 June 2019).

Human Rights Watch (2009) 'Group denial: Repression of Kurdish political and cultural rights in Syria' [Online]. Available at www.hrw.org/sites/default/files/reports/syria1109webwcover_0.pdf (Accessed 14 June 2019).

Kingston, L. N. (2013) '"A forgotten human rights crisis": Statelessness and issue (non)emergence', *Human Rights Review*, 14:2, 73–87.

Kingston, L. N. (2017) 'Worthy of rights: statelessness as a cause and symptom of marginalisation', in T. Bloom, K. Tonkiss, and P. Cole (eds) *Understanding Statelessness* (Abingdon: Routledge): pp. 17–34.

Lynch, M., and Ali, P. (2006) 'Buried alive: Stateless Kurds in Syria', *Refugees International* [Online]. Available at www.refworld.org/pdfid/47a6eba80.pdf (Accessed 10 June 2019).

McDowall, D. (2004) *A Modern History of the Kurds*, 3rd edition (London: Tauris).

McGee, T. (2014) 'The stateless Kurds of Syria: Ethnic identity and national ID', *Tilburg Law Review*, 19:1–2, 171–181.

McGee, T. (2016) 'Statelessness displaced: Update on Syria's stateless Kurds', Statelessness Working Paper Series No. 2016/02 [Online]. Available at https://files.institutesi.org/WP2016_02.pdf (Accessed 14 June 2019).

McGee, T., and Albarazi, Z. (2020) 'Eight years of displacement: Syria's statelessness still unidentified', *Oxford Monitor of Forced Migration*, 8:2, 39–44.

Montgomery, H. (2005) *The Kurds of Syria: An Existence Denied* (Berlin: Europäisches Zentrum für Kurdische Studien).

Nagy, R. (2008) 'Transitional justice as global project: critical reflections', *Third World Quarterly*, 29:2, 275–289.

Rawls, J. (1999) *A Theory of Justice*, revised edition (Cambridge, MA: Harvard University Press).

Syrians for Truth and Justice (2019) 'Syrian citizenship disappeared: How the 1962 census destroyed stateless Kurds' lives and identities' [Online]. Available at https://stj-sy.org/en/745/ (Accessed 10 June 2019).

Teitel, R. G. (2017) 'Transitional justice genealogy', in R. Jamieson (ed.) *The Criminology of War* (London: Routledge): pp. 489–514.

Tejel, J. (2009) *Syria's Kurds: History, Politics and Society* (London: Routledge).

Türk, V. (2014) 'The status of statelessness 60 years on', *Forced Migration Review*, 1:46, 46–48.

United Nations (1948) *Universal Declaration of Human Rights* [Online]. Available at www.ohchr.org/EN/UDHR/Documents/UDHR_Translations/eng.pdf (Accessed 10 May 2019).

United Nations (2010) 'Guidance note of the Secretary-General: United Nations approach to transitional justice' [Online]. Available at www.un.org/ruleoflaw/files/TJ_Guidance_Note_March_2010FINAL.pdf (Accessed 1 March 2020).

United Nations High Commissioner for Refugees (UNHCR) (2014a) 'Ending statelessness within 10 years', UNHCR Special Report. Geneva: UNHRC [Online]. Available at www.unhcr.org/protection/statelessness/546217229/special-report-ending-statelessness-10-years.html (Accessed 10 May 2019).

United Nations High Commissioner for Refugees (UNHCR) (2014b) 'Global Action Plan to End Statelessness' [Online]. Available at www.refworld.org/docid/545b47d64.html (Accessed 10 May 2019).

United Nations High Commissioner for Refugees (UNHCR) (2014c) 'I Belong Campaign to End Statelessness' [Online]. Available at www.unhcr.org/ibelong-campaign-to-end-statelessness.html (Accessed 10 May 2019).

Vali, A. (1998) 'The Kurds and their "others": Fragmented identity and fragmented politics', *Comparative Studies of South Asia, Africa and the Middle East*, 18:2, 82–95.

Vlieks, C. (2017) 'Contexts of statelessness: The concepts "stateless *in situ*" and "stateless in the migratory context"', in T. Bloom, K. Tonkiss, and P. Cole (eds) *Understanding Statelessness* (Abingdon: Routledge): pp. 35–52.

Welateme (2011) 'Demonstrations in Kurdish areas' [Online, Arabic]. Available at http://welateme.info/erebi/modules.php?name=News&file=print&sid=8210 (Accessed 10 October 2019).

Yildiz, K. (2005) *The Kurds in Syria: The Forgotten People* (London: Pluto Press).

Zunino, M. (2019) *Justice Framed: A Genealogy of Transitional Justice* (Cambridge: Cambridge University Press).

20

Statelessness elimination through legal fiction: The United Arab Emirates' Comorian minority

Yoana Kuzmova[1]

Since the early 2000s, the government of the United Arab Emirates (U.A.E.) first elevated and then eliminated statelessness as a policy issue through a series of unconventional population management policies. The centrepiece of this effort was the U.A.E.'s mass purchase of so-called 'economic citizenship' passports from the African country of Comoros for at least 50,000 stateless residents (Union of Comoros National Assembly, 2017: 44). In keeping with the authorities' narrative about statelessness as a spurious status, the stateless were allowed to 'reveal' their 'true' nationality first.[2] For those who failed to claim one, the U.A.E. assigned Comoros nationality. Through exhaustive interviews, application forms, compilations of documentary evidence, and DNA sample collections over the course of two months in the fall of 2008, the U.A.E. vetted the future 'Comorians' (Lynch, 2010). Were it not for its exclusionary outcomes, the process could be termed a statelessness determination procedure or even a mapping exercise (for more on mapping statelessness, see Alexander, this volume). Having concluded that the registrants were indeed without access to documentary proof of citizenship, the U.A.E. proceeded to provide this diverse grouping of residents with a form of citizenship documentation, a passport, issued by the Union of Comoros. Thus, through a transactional mass 'naturalisation' the U.A.E. convened a new Comorian 'minority'. After presenting the historical and political context of how this happened, this chapter discusses the process as an example of governance of statelessness through 'legal fiction'.

The historical context of U.A.E. citizenship policy

The U.A.E. is a federation of seven emirates founded in 1971. Abu Dhabi, the largest emirate and seat of the federal government, holds most of the U.A.E.'s oil reserves and economic power. The federation formed following a century-long period of loose association with the British Empire, when it was known as the Trucial States or Trucial Oman (the relevant truces being between the British Empire and rulers of the emirates). The emirates had the status of 'protected states', rather than being colonies of the British Empire.

The British governance of the emirates' foreign affairs as protected states until 1968 was instrumental in unifying the emirates by first entrenching treaties with individual rulers and then creating the Trucial States Council (Jamal, 2015). Through its political agents and representatives, Britain had made itself an indispensable mediator between Abu Dhabi's ambitions for a centralised union built around its superiority in size and oil reserves, and the remaining emirates' will to retain control over their internal affairs (Hawley, 1970: 23).

Prior to their departure from the Trucial States, the British were concerned with the possibility of leaving behind a sizeable stateless population (Hall, 1969; McCarthy, 1969a). Britain's concern with statelessness was evident in an early nationality law draft proposed to the Sheikhs in 1953, which provided for automatic naturalisation of the non-Arabs that had come with the British (Political Agency Trucial States, Dubai, 1961). The preoccupation was to avoid responsibility for the protection of British subjects who had come from India and Pakistan and were now settled in the U.A.E. (McCarthy, 1969b). However, the Sheikhs were not in favour of this approach and relied primarily on their Arab advisers to draft the federal nationality law in 1969 (Hall, 1969). Already by their independence, each of the oil-producing states of the Gulf had attracted significant proportions of migrant workers, many of whom were also Arabs from elsewhere in the Middle East. The rulers' reliance on these workers, as well as on the counsel of Arab jurists, had to be balanced against locals' concern for limiting the scope of rightful recipients of the state's oil rents to a group of 'original' citizens. The exact way of determining who counted as an original citizen was far from clear and was influenced by earlier population surveys. For example, British officials had entirely excluded nomadic tribes from the first census in 1968.

The U.A.E. nationality law emerged, somewhat counterintuitively, after the first passport laws were put in place with the aid of Britain in the individual emirates prior to independence (Jamal, 2015). Thus, at the time of the union's creation each emirate could document its citizens but a process of inter-emirate recognition of such citizenship did not exist. The competing visions of citizenship among the different emirates prior to independence were not fully resolved during the formation of the federation (Lori, 2019). Prior to independence, each emirate's ruler issued his own passports. The ruler of Abu Dhabi continually resisted the introduction of unified passports across the emirates out of suspicion of the other rulers' practice of selling passports to persons not entitled to them (Political Agency Trucial States,

1967). At state formation, this created an unknown set of 'contested' citizens, consisting primarily of ethnic minorities whose citizenship was only recognised by emirates other than Abu Dhabi.

Abu Dhabi's foundational 'suspicion' towards the integrity of other emirates' citizenship-granting practices was reinforced through the passage of a federal nationality law that employed an ethnonational definition of citizenship. As a result, and just as the British political agents feared, the population of non-Arab British subjects who had been in the region for generations did not gain a right to naturalise under the new nationality laws for at least twenty years after the Union was formed (U.A.E., 1975, Article 8). The terms of the nationality law and uncertainty surrounding its application resulted in a restricted access to naturalisation post-independence. Consensus around the role of the federal government was absent in promulgating immigration policies until 1976. That year, a formal agreement around the supremacy of federal policy was reached, but its application varied widely from emirate to emirate (Nyrop et al., 1977). As a result, many of the pre-independence residents and formerly nomadic groups remained in an ambiguous position recognised at the local level but not at the federal level. Until a few years after the U.A.E. constitution was officially adopted in 1996, each emirate retained control over the nominally federal passport office on its territory. In this way, for the first two decades since its founding in 1971, the U.A.E.'s constituent emirates implemented provisional practices of incorporation that kept statelessness from surfacing (United Nations Human Rights Council, 2010). While aware of a significant population of undetermined nationality, federal authorities did not initially treat this as problematic. Rather, policy choices at the federal level were made to narrowly control access to full citizenship, while turning a blind eye to individual emirate rulers' practices of informal and partial incorporation. The public acknowledgement of a 'statelessness problem' arose in the early 2000s (see Lori, 2019). Thereafter, a process of solution seeking was set in motion, culminating with the 'conversion' of stateless residents into 'economic citizens' of the Union of Comoros.

The U.A.E.'s unincorporated minorities and the construction of a 'statelessness problem'

Emirati society is characterised by the highest non-citizen population worldwide (>80%) (World Bank, n.d.). Although this was not applied for decades, U.A.E. federal law and institutions presume a 'non-Emirati-citizen' status for those who lack or are not inscribed in a family book (*khulasat-al-qaid*, a booklet containing a summary of one's ancestry). This recourse to ancestry is embedded in the nationality statute, under which a citizen by law is someone who can trace their lineage to a citizen of one of the emirates in 1925 (U.A.E., 1975).

The size of the U.A.E.'s population has grown dramatically in the last fifty years. Its structure, however, has not changed as dramatically; populations belonging to the constitutive tribes have been living side-by-side with non-Arabs for over a century (Potter, 2017). The non-Arabs have traditionally come from across the Persian Gulf and the Indian Ocean littoral (Seccombe, 1983). During the period of Empire, Britain brought significant populations from the Indian sub-continent to the region. Slavery also contributed to diversifying the local population and was not officially abolished until the early 1960s. After 1971, practically all migration has been conceptualised as the inflow of temporary labour. The new federation created no clear avenues for gaining citizenship for the significant numbers of settled non-citizens on its territory, whose presence is attested to in 1960s diplomatic communiques in the British Archives of the Emirates (Hall, 1969; McCarthy, 1969a). Dubai's ruler from independence until 1990, Sheikh Rashid, favoured the incorporation of migrants, a policy in line with Dubai's long-standing role as a global trade hub. A group of more than 2,000 Zanzibaris of Omani origin who fled to Dubai in the 1960s were, for example, issued decrees of naturalisation by the Dubai ruler by the late 1990s. Members of the Zanzibari community in Dubai have waited for official 'ratification' of these decrees by Abu Dhabi for over two decades. Frustrated by such provisional practices, the federal government, through the Ministry of Interior, occasionally set out regulations initially invalidating then reinstating local (individual emirate) passports (U.A.E. Minister of Interior, 1974a and 1974b; U.A.E. Minister of State, 1989).

By the early 1990s, labour market 'Emiratisation' was being introduced. 'Emiratisation' refers to a set of policies meant to increase the proportion of citizens' employment in the public and private sectors. In practice, this required hardening the requirements for valid proof of citizenship to secure employment, and imposing a penalty on the private sector for not employing nationals. Devising a process to apply for Emirati citizenship only became a real policy concern in 1992, when adherence to the 1972 Nationality Law would have allowed non-Arabs to apply for naturalisation (U.A.E., 1975; under Article 8 non-Arabs could apply for Emirati citizenship after having resided in the U.A.E. for 'not less than thirty years, of which twenty years... after this law enters into force'). A committee was created to tackle naturalisation but there is no indication that it took any steps towards demystifying naturalisation. Once the provisional U.A.E. constitution was adopted as permanent in 1996, the federal government claimed its constitutionally bestowed right to control matters of citizenship, and the individual emirates' provisional citizenship practices were phased out. The resulting loss of status for thousands of 'presumed nationals' created a governance puzzle for Abu Dhabi, which gradually started to emerge in public discourse.

An attempt to preserve Dubai's informal control over citizen incorporation can be seen in an August 2003 order by the Dubai ruler Mohammad bin Rashid, insisting that only a passport is required to treat someone who meets naturalisation requirements as an U.A.E. national.[3] The federal government responded with the creation of a committee on naturalisation in 2004 in the Ministry of Interior, which swiftly issued a decision reminding individual emirates and other government entities that the correct proof of U.A.E. nationality domestically/internally is possession of a family book, rather than a passport.

The first policy to name statelessness directly came in late 2005, when the federal government issued a decision to expedite the search for solutions for those without nationality (referred to as 'Bidoon' in the decision's title) (U.A.E. Federal Supreme Council, 2006). This decision came at the conclusion of a national census that revealed significant irregularities and a significant chunk of the population excluded from the count of citizens (U.S. Ambassador to U.A.E., 2006). The same year, Refugees International had produced the first known report on statelessness in the U.A.E. (Lynch, 2005). Eventually, federal authorities devised a solution to eliminate statelessness by turning a wide range of settled non-citizens into 'migrant workers', a legal category that the U.A.E. best knows how to administer, given that migrants form 89% of the U.A.E. population. The tools used here were familiar to democracies with significant stateless populations, but their deployment had a somewhat innovative twist (Lori, 2019).

The U.A.E. included in its systematic digitalisation of identity documents a registration campaign for people without nationality documents, most of which concluded in 2008. This came at a great cost to those regularised in terms of loss of status, employment, education, and (not insignificantly) time (Lynch, 2010; Zacharias, 2018). The novelty of the U.A.E.'s approach was its choice to 'regularise' the status of residents without nationality documents by acquiring an 'economic citizenship' passport from the Union of the Comoros (U.S. Department of State, 2013). This invention had traceable antecedents in the U.A.E.'s discourse around statelessness. The Emirates had previously conceptualised its stateless population as visa overstayers who had burned their passports, for example (Muawia, 2005). It also drew on the practices of neighbouring Kuwait (as developed in Benswait, this volume; Alshammiry, this volume), where authorities often called on stateless residents to come forward with their 'true nationality'.

Indeed, it is a long-standing Kuwait resident, the Syrian-French entrepreneur Bashar Kiwan, who thought up the scheme to extend Comoros citizenship to stateless people in the Gulf (U.S. Ambassador to Madagascar and Comoros, 2008; Abrahamian, 2015). Although Kiwan planned to market this idea to Kuwaiti authorities, his sales pitch only took off in the U.A.E. One reason for the U.A.E.'s quick acceptance of the idea of en-masse citizenship re-assignment had to do with the relative obscurity of statelessness as an issue of public concern to Emirati media and elites. Unlike Kuwait, where the stateless Bidoon are championed by a small group of academics and some tribal political formations, in the U.A.E. statelessness had simply not emerged as a unified popular concern (for discussion on Bidoon in Kuwait, see Benswait and Alshammiry in this volume). As shown above, individual emirates created a 'buffer' between federal policies and local incorporation (Lynch, 2010). An additional reason why the U.A.E. opted for this solution may lie with the fact that, unlike Kuwait, it does not possess a democratically elected legislature akin to Kuwait's parliament and most government decisions are not subject to public debate.

The Comoros economic citizenship programme and its effects

The Union of Comoros is composed of a collection of islands in the Mozambique Channel, which runs between Mozambique and Madagascar. The Comoros economic citizenship law (ECL) was passed by the Comoros National Assembly in November 2008, the same month that the U.A.E. concluded its registration campaign for stateless residents. The ECL itself is a short and internally inconsistent statute whose passage caused significant tumult in the parliament and was subject to a 2018 parliamentary commission investigation. The investigation concluded that the Comoros president at the time had already sold an unknown number of Comoros 'economic citizenship' passports to the U.A.E. months before the passage of the ECL, and that the law itself was but an exercise in rubber-stamping the programme (Union of Comoros National Assembly, 2017).[4]

The U.A.E.–Comoros deal was a bilateral agreement between a wealthy nearly-absolute monarchy and a client state, whereby the client state received direct remuneration and indirect benefits in exchange for providing documentation for a group of U.A.E. residents without nationality who have been 'pre-approved' by the U.A.E. The Comoros investigation into the ECL's origin determined, by comparing records from the company that printed Comoros passports with collective 'naturalisation' decrees, that more than 47,000 individuals in the U.A.E. were issued a passport under the ECL (Union of Comoros National Assembly, 2017). In interviews, current Comoros passport holders in the U.A.E. reported that they received calls from their emirate's passports office prompting them to apply for the passports. Meanwhile, Comoros citizenship was described as the path to naturalisation in a series of official government press releases from the summer of 2008. My interviewees also reported learning about the passports from friends or relatives. Once transformed into a citizen of a country unknown to them, the Comorians also officially became foreigners in the U.A.E. and were ushered into the process of receiving residence visas. At first, this residence visa process was facilitated for the Comorians. Unlike most migrants in the U.A.E., new Comorians did not need an employer or an Emirati relative to serve as a visa sponsor. In recent years, this initial flexibility has been withdrawn, and the vestigial documentary proof that 'Comorians' were once stateless locals is being lost to the digitalisation of identity documents.

For the U.A.E., this transformation eliminated the indeterminacy and deliberation that would accompany the existence of a 'non-non-citizen' class. A newly formed class of Comorian migrants usefully negates the existence of second-class citizens. The legal fiction of the 'Comoros economic citizen residing as an expatriate in the U.A.E.' emerged to accommodate the limitations of the U.A.E. legal system (and to some extent the international legal order, where government-sanctioned identity is paramount). U.A.E. immigration and citizenship laws, like those of many other countries around the world, do not permit devices of partial or 'potential' inclusion.

On the receiving end of the economic citizenship, there is no incentive for the U.A.E. 'Comorians' to 'self-deport', but they are very much motivated to remain law-abiding citizens who stand in line and wait their turn for citizenship (Zacharias, 2018). Further, as evidenced by the limbo of an unfortunate 'deportee' in 2018, Emirati Comoros passports do not even entitle their holders to enter the Union of Comoros, let alone reside there (Mukinda, 2018). The Comoros passports are thus an effective vehicle for social control, which locks in place an underclass of non-citizens through a documentation process that limits both socio-economic and international mobility, but does not eliminate the hope of eventual incorporation. This underclass of citizens-in-waiting and their pain-staking culling-out for naturalisation further serve to demonstrate to the Emirati citizens that their elite ranks will only be joined by the 'best and brightest' applicants who stand to enrich Emirati society in tangible and immediate ways. For example, the U.A.E. (like most other Gulf Cooperation Council countries) has naturalised professional athletes and opened up conscription in the national army of the U.A.E. to Comoros passport holders.

Beyond the contracting parties and the subjects of their agreement, negative externalities and confusion abound, exacerbating the human cost to belonging to the Comorian minority. In the case of international mobility, Comoros has struggled to explain to the world the precise status of its 'economic citizens'. Records obtained from the U.S. Department of State through Freedom of Information Act requests reveal that U.S. consulates in the U.A.E. understood the process through which the Comorian minority was formed. In recognition that these Comoros passport holders were indeed Emirati locals, the consulates devised a two-stage visa application process for the new Comorians. First, applicants were informed that their Comoros passport did not fulfil the legal definition of a valid travel document because it did not entitle its bearer to reside in Comoros.[5] Then, visa applicants were informed of a 'waiver' process whereby they were required to prove their 'non-immigrant intent' and strong ties to the U.A.E., often measured by a well-compensated white-collar job and bank account balances. A very small portion of applicants were issued visas (U.S. Department of State, 2018).

In late 2017, the U.S. embassy in Abu Dhabi attempted to gain buy-in from EU member states in order to approach the Emirati Ministry of Foreign Affairs for a memorandum of understanding to share the list of Emirati Comoros passport recipients (U.S. Department of State, 2018). For those Comoros passport holders who manage to leave the U.A.E. for a country with a statelessness determination procedure (such as the United Kingdom), proving statelessness was challenging if they held a passport perceived as real enough for authorities to presume nationality. Even judicial review decisions (including in cases for which I contributed expert testimony) fail to analyse the incompatibility between the Comoros ECL and the rest of the Comoros nationality and constitutional framework. That is, they fail to recognise that the Comoros 'economic citizen' is a legal fiction invented for another jurisdiction's purposes only.

The lens of the 'legal fiction'

The U.A.E.'s programme inflicted and exacerbated human rights violations on the recipients of Comoros economic citizenship. While I use this chapter to focus on the need to shift the analytical angle used to understand what took (and is taking) place, these rights violations must also be acknowledged. The analytical angle of the 'legal fiction' makes it possible to articulate the work that Comorian economic citizenship does for the Emirati state and its state-building project.

The new Comoros minority is made up of members of a range of minority groups who are invisible in the official census categories. This grouping of minorities is diverse and, like the very concept of 'statelessness' in Arabic, hard to capture succinctly. A non-exhaustive list of sub-groups includes: 1) descendants of once-nomadic tribes that have been on the territory of today's U.A.E. for generations; 2) people with ties to communities on both sides of the Persian Gulf, who were forced to permanently settle in the U.A.E.; 3) those whose ancestors came with the British Empire and found it impossible to leave when the Empire withdrew in 1968; and 4) descendants of groups that suffered mass expulsions throughout the twentieth century – such as the Manga Arabs of Zanzibar, Asians exiled from East Africa, and (most notably) Palestinians.

I suggest that the construction of Comoros economic citizenship in the U.A.E. should be understood as a form of 'legal fiction'. The notion of 'legal fiction' is widespread in the common law, extending from the British archipelago through the former British dominions, and persisting in post-colonial jurisdictions including the U.A.E. (and the United States, among others). Lon Fuller (1930–1931) famously referred to 'legal fictions' as 'false statements not intended to deceive' (367). Most legal fictions are inoffensive to a lay observer. Pragmatic views of legal fiction persuasively elicit their utility for our societies (Lind, 2015). This can be seen in the legal personhood of U.S. corporations, for example or the personality of a ship (Lind, 2015: 95). Even scholars embracing the utility of legal fictions acknowledge the harm of fictions of 'falsification', however, which create confusion and incoherence and whose effects are felt outside of the legal system (Lind, 2015: 83). One example of this latter variety is the doctrine of *terra nullius*, used notably to justify the colonial regime of dispossession in Australia, in that it 'juxtaposed retroactively the legal proposition that the Colony of New South Wales was practically unoccupied in 1788 against the extralegal fact that the Colony had hundreds of thousands of inhabitants' (Lind, 2015:106).

The trouble with the legal fiction of 'Comoros economic citizenship' presented here is that it seeks to fundamentally transform human lives on a large scale for the purposes of maintaining superficial coherence in formal law and policy. The result legitimates a legal order in which the only form of citizenship transmission is patrilineal *jus sanguinis*, where naturalisation does not and cannot exist by right. I propose that this state of affairs is symptomatic of the crisis of citizenism worldwide (see Bloom, 2018). The constructs associated with statelessness in the U.A.E. discussed here expose the fundamental contradiction in the governance of national belonging. In some areas of state practice, citizenship is treated as a legal fiction of convenience; in others, as a quasi-biological, primordial quality whose determination is a process of 'discovery' rather than attribution.

Conclusion

The U.A.E.'s mass purchase of Comoros passports and their subsequent distribution to the country's residents registered as 'without nationality documents' sought to reconcile policy incoherence over time, as well as between the federal and local (individual emirate) level. While the U.A.E. created a mechanism for 'eliminating' statelessness, the lived experience of statelessness (or, the limbo of non-incorporation) in the U.A.E. remained intact. This experience reveals the pitfalls of any project to end statelessness merely nominally.

Notes

1 This chapter draws on interviews and investigation concerning distinct groups of stateless persons in the U.A.E. Interviews were conducted in the context of a project on statelessness in the Middle East carried out by the author at the International Human Rights Clinic (IHRC) at Boston University School of Law from 2015 until 2019. The IHRC project emerged from the research of Boston University Professor Noora Lori, whose book *Offshore Citizens: Permanent Temporary Status in the Gulf* (2019) examines the UAE's population management stratagems.
2 The distinction between 'nationality' and 'citizenship' in English is subject to extensive discussion elsewhere. A convoluted legalistic distinction between the two is exploited by states who seek to 'assign' their stateless persons to other plausibly responsible states.
3 A translation of this order is held by the author.
4 The scathing investigation report did not end the ECL, nor did it result in the invalidation of passports already issued. Instead, the programme was frozen, such that passports were no longer issued to new-born children of passport holders. Also, the printing of new passport booklets was discontinued and passports were renewed by stamping a sticker on the expired passport, extending its validity for five years. For most of 2020, due to the Covid-19 pandemic, the Comoros Embassy in Abu Dhabi was closed. In August 2020, Comoros passport holders awaiting renewal were notified via WhatsApp that their passports would not be renewed, without further explanation.
5 U.S. diplomatic missions were repeatedly assured by Comoros authorities that residence or free entry to Comoros were not rights associated with the U.A.E. bidoon passports.

References

Abrahamian, A. (2015) *The Cosmopolites: The Coming of the Global Citizen* (New York: Columbia Global Reports).

Bloom, T. (2018) *Noncitizenism* (Abingdon, Routledge).

Fuller, L. L. (1930–1931). 'Legal fictions', *Illinois Law Review*, 25:4, 363–399.

Gulf News (2008) 'Saif recommends 25 ministry employees for UAE citizenship', *Gulf News*, 22 July [Online]. Available at http://gulfnews.com/business/visas/saif-recommends-25-ministry-employees-for-uae-citizenship-1.119527 (Accessed 24 June 2020).

Hall, D. J. (1969) 'UAE Committee on Immigration, Nationality and Passports,' letter to G. P. Wall (political agent in Bahrain), 9 September, Foreign and Commonwealth Office (FCO) 8/993 [Online]. Available at www.agda.ae/en/catalogue/tna/fco/8/993/n/2 (Accessed 24 June 2020).

Hawley, D. (1970) *The Trucial States* (London: George Allen & Unwin Ltd.)

Jamal, M. A. (2015) 'The "tiering" of citizenship and residency and the "hierarchization" of migrant communities: The United Arab Emirates in historical context', *International Migration Review*, 49:3, 601–632.

Lind, D. (2015) 'The pragmatic value of legal fictions', in M. Del Mar and W. Twining (eds) *Legal Fictions in Theory and Practice. Law and Philosophy Library, Volume 110* (Heidelberg: Springer): pp. 83–109.

Lori, N. (2019) *Offshore Citizens: Permanent Temporary Status in the Gulf* (Cambridge: Cambridge University Press).

Lynch, M. (2005) 'Lives on hold: The human cost of statelessness', *Refugees International* [Online]. Available at https://reliefweb.int/sites/reliefweb.int/files/resources/0BF295ED3E8AB5B3C1256FA9003537EB-Stateless_RI_Feb_2005.pdf (Accessed 24 June 2020).

Lynch, M. (2010) 'United Arab Emirates: Nationality matters', *Refugees International* [Online]. Available at www.refugeesinternational.org/blog/united-arab-emirates-nationality-matters (Accessed 24 June 2020).

McCarthy, D. J. (1969a) 'U.A.E. Committee on Immigration Nationality and Passports', letter from the Arabian Department, FCO 8/993, 29 September [Online]. Available at www.agda.ae/en/catalogue/tna/fco/8/993 (Accessed 25 June 2020).

McCarthy, D. J. (1969b) 'Union of Arab Emirates: Nationality Proposals', letter to the Nationality & Treaty Department, FCO 8/993, 7 October [Online]. Available at www.agda.ae/en/catalogue/tna/fco/8/993 (Accessed 25 June 2020).

Muawia, I. (2005) 'No stateless people in UAE', *Khaleej Times*, 24 March [Online]. Available at www.khaleejtimes.com/article/20050324/ARTICLE/303249949/1002 (Accessed 24 June 2020).

Mukinda, F. (2018) 'Meet "stateless" man who has been stranded at JKIA for four months', *Nairobi News*, 6 April [Online]. Available at: https://nairobinews.nation.co.ke/life/stateless-man-stranded-jkia (accessed 14 November 2020).

Nyrop, R., Benderly, B. L., Newhouse Carter, L., Cover, W. W., Eglin, D. R., Kirchner, R. A., Moeller, P. W., Mussen, W. A., Pike, C. E., and Shinn, R. (1977) *Area Handbook for the Persian Gulf States* (Washington, D.C.: American University Foreign Area Studies).

Political Agency Trucial States, Dubai (1961) Letter to British Residency in Bahrain attaching 'Draft nationality regulations for the Trucial States', 13 March (FO) 371/157060 [Online]. Available at www.agda.ae/en/catalogue/tna/fo/371/157060 (Accessed 24 June 2020).

Political Agency Trucial States (1967) 'Trucial Council agenda', telegram 15, 25 March, FCO 8/825 /196 [Online]. Available at www.agda.ae/en/catalogue/tna/fco/8/825 (Accessed 25 June 2020).

Potter, L. G. (2017) 'Society in the Persian Gulf: Before and after oil', Georgetown University Qatar, Center for International and Regional Studies, Occasional Paper No. 18 [Online]. Available at https://repository.library.georgetown.edu/bitstream/handle/10822/1045467/CIRSOccasionalPaper18LawrencePotter2017.pdf?sequence=1&isAllowed=y (Accessed 25 June 2020).

Seccombe, I. J. (1983) 'Labour migration to the Arabian Gulf: Evolution and characteristics 1920–1950', *Bulletin (British Society for Middle Eastern Studies)*, 10:1, 3–20.

Union of Comoros National Assembly (1979) 'Loi No. 79-12 du decembre 1979 portant code de la nationalite Comorienne' ['Nationality Code of the Comoros'], Law No. 79-12 [Online]. Available at http://comoresdroit.comores-droit.com/wp-content/dossier/code/nationalite.pdf (Accessed 7 July 2020).

Union of Comoros National Assembly (2008) 'Loi relative a la citoyenneté économique en Union des Comores' ['Economic Citizenship Law'] [Online]. Available at http://citizenshiprightsafrica.org/wp-content/uploads/2016/07/Comoros-Economic-Citizenship-Law-2008.pdf (Accessed 7 July 2020).

Union of Comoros National Assembly (2017) 'Rapport de synthése, rapport de la Commission d'Enquete Parlementaire sur la loi relative à la citoyenneté économique' ['Synthesis report, report of the Parliamentary Enquiry Commission into the law relating to economic citizenship'] [Online]. Available at https://tinyurl.com/y7mtq282 (Accessed 24 June 2020).

United Arab Emirates (U.A.E.)(1971, amended in 2004) *Constitution of the United Arab Emirates* [Online]. Available at www.constituteproject.org/constitution/United_Arab_Emirates_2004.pdf (Accessed 7 July 2020).

United Arab Emirates (U.A.E.) (1975) *Federal Law No. 10 for 1975 Concerning Amendment of Certain Articles of the Nationality and Passports Law No. 17 for 1972* [Online]. Available at www.refworld.org/docid/3fba19484.html (Accessed 7 July 2020).

U.A.E. Federal Supreme Council (2006) *Resolution (2) of 2005 Concerning the Problem of Stateless Persons (the Bidoon)*, 28 September [Online]. Available at https://lexmena.com/law/ar_fed~2005-12-03_00002_2020-01-27/ (Accessed 7 July 2020)

U.A.E. Minister of Interior (1974a) *Ministerial Resolution No. 1 of 1974 (Concerning the Validity of Emirates Passports)*, 17 January.

U.A.E. Minister of Interior (1974b) 'Announcement to citizens to cancel local passports to prevent the use of these passports for travel overseas', 12 March.

U.A.E. Minister of State for Cabinet Affairs (1989) 'Proof of citizenship', *Circular*, 19 June [Online]. Available at https://elaws.moj.gov.ae (Accessed 7 July 2020).

United Nations Human Rights Council (2010) 'Report of the Special Rapporteur on contemporary forms of racism, racial discrimination, xenophobia and related intolerance, Githu Muigai, Addendum Mission to the United Arab Emirates', 31 March [Online]. Available at https://documents-dds-ny.un.org/doc/UNDOC/GEN/G10/125/76/PDF/G1012576.pdf (Accessed 7 July 2020).

U.S. Ambassador to Madagascar and Comoros, R. Niels Marquardt (2008) 'Comoros National Assembly passes (sort of) economic citizenship law', Cable telegram to Washington, D.C., 5 December, released by WikiLeaks [Online]. Available at https://wikileaks.org/plusd/cables/08ANTANANARIVO809_a.html (Accessed 7 July 2020).

U.S. Ambassador to U.A.E. (2006) 'UAE census results finally released', Confidential telegram sent from Abu Dhabi to Washington, D.C., released by WikiLeaks [Online]. Available at http://wikileaks.wikimee.org/cable/2006/08/06ABUDHABI3204.html (Accessed 24 June 2020).

U.S. Department of State (2013) 'Country reports on human rights practices for 2012: United Arab Emirates' [Online]. Available at www.state.gov/j/drl/rls/hrrpt/2012humanrightsreport/index.htm (Accessed 24 June 2020).

U.S. Department of State (2018) Records released in response to freedom of Information Act Request F-2017–01556 (on file with author).

World Bank (n.d.) 'International migrant stock (% of population): United Arab Emirates' [Online]. Available at https://data.worldbank.org/indicator/SM.POP.TOTL.ZS?locations=AE (Accessed 8 May 2020).

Zacharias, A. (2018) 'Special report: Ten years on, the UAE's stateless people reflect on how life has improved and on the challenges ahead', *The National*, 5 September [Online]. Available at www.thenational.ae/uae/special-report-ten-years-on-the-uae-s-stateless-people-reflect-on-how-life-has-improved-and-on-the-challenges-ahead-1.767367 (Accessed 24 June 2020).

Figure 6

All faces

Arison Kul

I am here showing Papua New Guinea tribal faces. We are always connected to something physically or spiritually around us or distant from us. That is stronger than countries and passports.

21

Supra-national jurisprudence: Necessary but insufficient to contest statelessness in the Dominican Republic

Bridget Wooding

I had my first taste of nationality stripping at a 2007 international symposium on migration and nationality in Santo Domingo in the Dominican Republic. Francophone Haiti takes up the east of the island of Hispaniola, with hispanophone Dominican Republic to the West. Halfway through the symposium, participants received news that the Central Electoral Board (CEB) responsible for the Civil Registry was questioning the validity of the birth certificate of Sonia Pierre, the Amnesty International and Kennedy Foundation laureate who founded the Movement of Dominican-Haitian Women (MUDHA) (see Ramirez, 2007). The legal counsel David Baluarte, who participated in the Inter-American Court of Human Rights' (IACtHR) emblematic *Case of the Yean and Bosico Children v The Dominican Republic* (IACtHR, 2005) on the right to Dominican nationality and was in attendance at the symposium, observed: 'That would be nationality stripping.' He worried it would leave people without citizenship anywhere. While this threat to Pierre turned out be sabre rattling, that was not the case for many other Dominicans of Haitian ancestry.

This incident typifies the uneasy yet apparently necessary relationship between the Dominican state and the inter-American human rights system. The latter remains the last line of defence regionally for human rights defenders when national legislation is deficient, or when discriminatory practices persist without local remedies. Following a decade of restrictive measures on migration and nationality matters, in late 2013 the Constitutional Tribunal in Santo Domingo issued a ruling which effectively denationalised more than 130,000 Dominicans of mainly Haitian ancestry. Despite some limited pushback achieved by civil society actors and their allies at home and abroad, and notwithstanding official rhetoric to the contrary, this extreme violation of human rights is far from being redressed. International statelessness advocates identify the situation in the Dominican Republic as being in particular need of attention (Institute on Statelessness and Inclusion, 2020a). This chapter charts underwhelming progress and underscores the need for civil society on the ground to push for better governance to guarantee minority groups and their family members proper integration and belonging in Dominican society.

Context

For more than a decade at the turn of the twenty-first century, progressive sectors and conservatives in the Dominican Republic debated the need for and content of a new migration law to replace the obsolete 1939 regulatory framework, which was almost exclusively dedicated to outmoded Haitian groups. It was difficult to reconcile polarised proposals. The migration management arm of the Ministry of the Interior (DGM) wrote in 2016 with diplomatic understatement that the dynamic had been 'protracted and sinuous'. The law was eventually adopted in 2004, but there was no regularisation plan. The Dominican Republic is the only country in the Americas to never have a regularisation plan while hosting such a large number of irregular migrants, notably Haitians.

This 2004 migration law attempted to interpret expansively one of the conditionality clauses on *jus soli* (the principle that citizenship should be allocated to those born on a particular territory) such that the 'in transit' exception for parenting Dominican children (previously legally defined as ten days) would now come to encompass all immigrants with irregular migration status. This enlarged definition of 'in transit' was intended to codify an impediment to foreigners with irregular migration status registering their children born in the Dominican Republic as Dominicans (Hintzen, 2016). Subsequently, the new Constitution of 2010 introduced a new conditionality clause, stating that children whose foreign parents were not residing legally in the country would no longer receive Dominican birth certificates (Constitución de la República Dominicana, 2010).

Meanwhile, the battle lines were drawn between civil society actors, defending the rights of Dominicans of Haitian ancestry, and the Dominican authorities. The Dominican-Haitian Women's Movement (MUDHA), with legal support from organisations in the United States, brought a test case through the Inter-American human rights system. In 2005, this test became the first case found against the Dominican Republic, using this supranational mechanism for legal redress. Dilcia Yean and Violeta Bosico, two girls born in their homes in *bateyes* (settlements located around sugarcane plantations), were taken by their mothers to register their births as small children. The girls' mothers were Dominican nationals with Dominican ID cards (*cédulas*) and their fathers were Haitian migrant workers. Civil registry officials found that the girls' mothers did not provide sufficient documentation for late registration and denied the requests. In consequence, the civil registry denied the girls evidence of the Dominican nationality that they needed to study, impeding social mobility for them in Dominican society.

The mixed nationality of the girls' parents gave the Inter-American Court of Human Rights (IACtHR) the option to decide the case without addressing the question of who was a qualifying foreigner. However, the court did address the responsibility of the Dominican State to guarantee its nationality to children born in its territory to Haitian parents. It ruled that the suggestion that the 'in transit' exception would be linked to migratory status was inappropriate, and emphasised that birth in the territory should be the only relevant criteria in cases in which a child did not have a right to any other nationality. Nevertheless, because the girls' mothers were Dominican, these questions were not overriding in the girls' claims to Dominican nationality.

The backlash was not slow in coming. While ostensibly 'cleaning up' the Civil Registry (as the IACtHR had ordered) through two administrative dispositions of the Central Electoral Board (CEB) issued in 2007, incipient denationalisation occurred (Junta Central Electoral, 2007a and 2007b). The arbitrary denial of Dominican birth certificates for children born to Haitian parents formalised what had been denounced over decades as anti-Haitian discrimination. This was compounded by nationality deprivation of those who already had their papers. These Dominican documents were now being called into question and arbitrarily suspended where foreign parents were involved. They experienced 'both the denial and deprivation of citizenship and a deliberate lack of access' (Blitz, 2009). Although theoretically nationality-neutral dispositions, Haitian migrants comprise 87% of migrants and mostly have irregular status (ONE, 2013 and 2018). This deprivation of access to birth certificates, ID cards, and/or Dominican passports to people who had already been recognised as Dominicans by the state (and who had obtained copies of their documents in the past) amounted to nationality stripping and a serious limitation of their fundamental rights.

Some scholars suggest that international human rights advocacy in primarily international fora before 2005 may have had the net effect of hardening Dominican nationality law and policy (Martinez, 2014). This scholarship argues that the international spotlight enabled the elite conservative sectors in the Dominican Republic to be let off the hook, since they could successfully allege foreign interference on national sovereignty matters. Notwithstanding, most local and international advocates hold that the supra-national legal challenge was possibly the best option available at the time, recognising the Dominican Republic had signed up to the Court's jurisdiction in the late 1990s. These human rights defenders believed that domestic laws were likely to continue to evolve restrictively in line with discriminatory practices underway against Haitian migrants and their family members.

As attempts at policy dialogue proved unfruitful around the CEB's stealthy manoeuvres, in 2012 there was a turn towards strategic litigation. Thus, special appeals processes (*recurso de amparo*) were brought on behalf of persons being nationality stripped. Dominican civil society organisations presented more than sixty such actions representing some 250 affected persons. Despite favourable judgments in many cases, the CEB refused to comply with the order to hand over suspended documents immediately.

Sentence 168-13 of the Constitutional Court and its aftermath

In 2013, the Dominican Constitutional Court (CC) heard the case of Juliana Deguis Pierre, a young woman whose *cédula* had been seized by the Civil Registry in line with the CEB 2007 administrative dispositions. Sentence 168-13 of the CC decision ('*La Sentencia*') concluded that the 'in transit' exception had always been intended by legislators to cover four groups of non-immigrants, including temporary workers and their families. The Court ordered the CEB to review all births registered from 1929, which was the first year that the 'in transit' exception appeared in the Dominican Constitution, until 2007 to ensure that no children of foreigners 'in transit' had mistakenly been registered as Dominican nationals (Tribunal Constitucional, República Dominicana, 2013).

Political scientists define a 'focusing event' as a sudden and dramatic occurrence, like a natural disaster or some other kind of external shock to the status quo. The Haiti earthquake in 2010 was just such a sudden event, for instance. Because of its scale, it generated unprecedented solidarity with Haiti from many sectors in the neighbouring Dominican Republic (Fine, 2013). It could be argued that the Sentence, or *La Sentencia* as it became known, was also a focusing event of a very different nature. *La Sentencia* generated widespread outrage against what was perceived as an anti-Haitian reinterpretation of the Constitution to retroactively strip the citizenship of Dominicans of Haitian ancestry in contravention of human rights protections against discrimination and deprivation of nationality. The United Nations High Commissioner for Refugees (UNHCR) estimated that 133,770 people were left stateless as a result of the decision (Acento, 2016).

As fallout from *La Sentencia*, the overdue National Regularization Plan for Foreigners with Irregular Migration Status (PNRE) was decreed in late 2013, according to the mandate of the CC. There is consensus among progressive and conservative sectors alike regarding the need for the plan. Dominican civil society took a pro-active stance and approached the authorities from early 2014 with a view to cooperating and, indeed, sharing suggestions as to how to incorporate a gender perspective and best practices from other regularisation experiences in the Americas. The competent authorities within the Ministry of Interior and Police were initially enthusiastic, especially when – in their schema of things – *all* of those tens of thousands of persons denationalised under Sentence 168-13 would be obliged to register as foreigners.

Remedial legislation from the Dominican State became imperative when few gave credence to the official line that nationality-stripped persons would not be stateless because they might acquire Haitian nationality. The likelihood of this happening was slim. In May 2014, the Dominican legislature unanimously passed Law 169-14 (Congreso Dominicano, 2014) as its proposed solution to the crisis.[1] Consultation with civil society was minimal, but most concerned organisations believed that it was necessary to keep the door open for solutions rather than slamming it shut because of perceived inadequacies of the new law.

Law 169-14 ordered the restoration of Dominican nationality to approximately 61,000 individuals who had acquired Dominican nationality by birth in the national territory, but who were technically denationalised as ordered by the Constitutional Court ('Group A'). The law also created a path to naturalisation for those individuals who had been born in the Dominican Republic prior to 2007, but had never acquired nationality documents ('Group B'). The IACHR, invited by the Dominican Government to visit in late 2013 as a means to assuage international uproar, had already advised about the likely 'ripple effect' of *La Sentencia* on unregistered people born in the Dominican Republic of foreign ancestry.

'Group B' comprises individuals who considered themselves Dominican nationals by birth ('unrecognised citizens'), according to the prevailing interpretation of the Constitution at the time of their birth (Gibney, 2014). The solution that they naturalise through a procedure that required them to declare themselves Haitian nationals, before potentially naturalising after two years have elapsed, was unacceptable to many. These social and political implications of the proposed solution were entwined with bureaucratic complications and tight timeframes. As a result, there were only 8,755 applications from individuals in 'Group B'. This number fell far below initial estimates of the number of people who would qualify to naturalise under this provision of the law, which the Dominican government believed would be at least equivalent to numbers in 'Group A' – and for whom there is now no window of opportunity under Law 169-14.

Lastly, new regional jurisprudence was added to the mix in mid-2014, with the case of *Expelled Dominicans and Haitians v The Dominican Republic* (IACtHR, 2014), co-litigated by a Dominican, Haitian, and United States civil society coalition.[2] The Court analysed the right to nationality with regard to two groups of petitioners: Dominican nationals whose nationality documents were disregarded by authorities at the time of their expulsion, and persons who had been born in the Dominican Republic, but were unable to acquire nationality documents and were subsequently expelled. This second group was germane to the girls Yean and Bosico, who were born in the Dominican Republic and denied birth registration. The main differences were that the parents of the petitioners in *Expelled Dominicans and Haitians* did not have Dominican nationality documents, and the Dominican state was actively arguing that they were not entitled to Dominican nationality as the children of foreigners 'in transit'.

Several months later, there was a knee-jerk negative reaction from the Dominican state to the regional court decision on this case, alleging that their adhesion to the jurisdiction of the regional Court had never been finalised properly in the late 1990s and suggesting immediate withdrawal from the regional human rights system. To date, this threat has proven hollow. The Inter-American Human Rights Commission (IACHR) retorted that this eventuality would not affect those cases already decided by the Court against the Dominican state, whose jurisdiction would remain until full domestic compliance happened (OBMICA, 2015: 157). The nonchalance with which the Dominican state articulated this threat evidences an ambivalent relation with the Inter-American human rights system, not too dissimilar from several other states in the Americas. '*Obedezco pero no cumplo*' (I obey but I do not comply) is a phrase that was used in Spanish America throughout much of the colonial period to describe the attitude of local colonial officials towards the rule of the Spanish Crown. It aptly sums up latter-day relations of some member states of the Organization of American States (OAS) with regard to court decisions of the Inter-American human rights system.

Nevertheless, the Dominican Republic is sensitive to international opinion. In late 2015, the migration policy arm of the Ministry of the Interior and Police in Santo Domingo organised an international seminar where, *inter alia*, Dominican officials sought to show they were open to discussing migration and nationality matters with peers from the region and Spain. In the circumstances, the Dominican Foreign Affairs Ministry was surprisingly frank as to the furore caused by the denationalisation debacle. The official minutes of the discourse of a Foreign Affairs Ministry functionary Ambassador Josué Fiallo, two years on from *la Sentencia*, at this international seminar in Santo Domingo reads:

> The situation of irregularity and uncertainty in which the descendants of Haitian migrants found themselves provoked a grave political and institutional crisis. The Government, noted the Ambassador, did not have the tools with which to confront the situation, such that it was obliged to create an ad hoc technical team and draw up a new legal framework to placate the social and legal situation around the descendants of immigrants. Additionally,

the government found itself with a multitude of situations which affected decision-making.

(MIP/Instituto Nacional de Migración RD, 2015: 29,
author's translation from Spanish)

Compared to international norms for addressing statelessness, the legal framework developed and operated in the country since 2014 is inadequate, but nevertheless gives human rights defenders some space to restore the rights of nationality-stripped persons. The High-Level Segment on statelessness of the UNHCR Executive Committee of the High Commissioner's Programme (Excom) in Geneva in October 2019 was an important milestone where states had the opportunity to report on progress in reducing statelessness midway in the UNHCR-promoted ten-year campaign to eradicate statelessness by 2024. The civil society background report on the Dominican Republic to this gathering reported underwhelming progress thus:

> NGOs also remain deeply concerned with the continued failure to rectify the arbitrary deprivation of nationality of Dominicans of Haitian origin in the Dominican Republic. Five years after Law 169-14, which supposedly provided a path to restored nationality, only 27,000 of the 61,000 people identified in the Civil Registry audit by the government as eligible for documents have received them. Furthermore, of the 8,755 Dominicans who registered to receive documents for the first time, only 5,671 have received a form of permanent residence, and none have had their citizenship recognized.
>
> (unpublished document, summarised in UNHCR, 2019: 2)

The Dominican state's written statement at this Swiss summit offered no new commitments on reducing statelessness, reiterating that under the current operation of Law 169-14 and other legislation on nationality there was no possibility of statelessness in the Dominican Republic.

Perspectives on reducing statelessness

International dialogue on human rights and the Dominican Republic focuses on effective access to birth registration and a nationality without discrimination. The clearest example is the latest Universal Periodic Review (UPR), which culminated in January 2019. Multiple organisations and coalitions, as well as states, issued observations and recommendations on the topic. At the national level, positive developments occurred in 2018 and 2019 with spaces opening for policy dialogue between the state and Dominican NGOs. Notably, roundtables on the implementation of public policies and human rights, brokered by the IACHR, were likely agreed to by the Dominican authorities in a bid to be removed from the Human Rights Commission's so-called 'black list'. (In 2017, the Dominican Republic was among the least well-performing territories in the Americas. In subsequent years, it was removed from the list.)

Hopes were high when the first requests were lodged in 2018 for the naturalisation of beneficiaries of Law 169-14. Mobile brigades operated in select communities to facilitate the identification and documentation of people in Group A who no longer had access to their papers. The principal challenge remains, however, that the state fails to recognise that there are persons who are overlooked under the operation of Law 169-14 and hence remain stateless or at risk of statelessness. This is so despite the fact that civil society drew attention, in dialogue, to 10,263 persons who have been biometrically identified as deserving of solution despite never having had access to Dominican papers (OBMICA, 2019: 277). A blind eye is being turned towards this critical mass of non-citizens.

Ultimately, the actions of the Dominican state centre on four key failures: First, it refers to the successful application of Law 169-14 and denies statelessness in country. Second, it is ambivalent regarding recommendations and jurisprudence derived from the Inter-American human rights system. Third, it questions estimates of persons affected by *La Sentencia*, despite the fact that these estimates are obtained from official surveys carried out in 2013 and 2017, respectively (ONE, 2013 and 2018). Fourth, it fails to confront pressure groups hostile to Haitian immigrants and their descendants. In the light of recent developments and since the state complies weakly with the IACtHR decisions (Corte IDH, 2019a and 2019b),[3] Law 169-14 is the only instrument which civil society, supra-national supervisory organs of human rights, and the state itself has to advance towards more sustainable solutions on statelessness.

Without minimising the results of policy dialogue in recent years, progress will be limited until there is a mechanism for dealing with the citizenship status of unregistered people born in the country to foreign parents before 2010, as well as a more robust application of Law 169-14. Should policy dialogue continue without such developments, the credibility of the state at home and abroad will be weakened by egregious human rights violations stemming from statelessness. Despite obvious disagreements between concerned civil society actors and the Dominican state on the criteria contained in *La Sentencia*, all would benefit if Law 169-14 were to achieve its objective.

Legislation is necessary but insufficient without a mobilisation of the affected persons to plead their own cause and without a groundswell of public opinion sensitive to the issues. On the latter, the most recent survey *Public Opinion in Latin America* presents troubling and contradictory trends. First, fewer people in the Dominican Republic are supportive of the right to nationality of descendants of Haitians born in the Dominican

Republic. Approval dropped from 42.1% in 2006 to 34% in 2019. Second, support for regularising undocumented Haitians is also falling – from 38.7% in 2006 to 27.3% in 2019. By contrast, a slightly higher percentage believe there is discrimination in the Dominican Republic, rising from 44.5% in 2014 to 46.9% in 2019 (LAPOP, 2019). The net results suggest that human rights defenders have their work cut out for them in influencing public opinion and countering conservative pressure groups.

The Haitian state bears some responsibility for the weak implementation of the Dominican Republic's National Regularization Plan (PNRE) because it fails to provide the documents required by its nationals in a timely manner, despite good intentions (République d'Haïti, 2014). Persistent political instability and attendant protests have virtually paralysed Haiti since mid-2019 – a period known in Haitian Creole has *peyi lok*. Consequently, international engagement on behalf of their nationals abroad has been scant; many long-term irregular migrants could not gain Dominican Republic residency because they lacked essential documents. Residency status is essential long term because the Dominican Constitution of 2010 allows foreigners with such status to document their children born in the Dominican Republic as Dominicans, hence preventing potential statelessness for these offspring. Those who cannot regularise their status, or who were regularised but accorded a non-resident status, will not be able to access Dominican nationality for their children.

Conclusion

Successful supra-regional litigation since 2005 has undoubtedly served the purpose of drawing attention to flagrant human rights abuses, but challenges remain in the Dominican Republic for leveraging this advantage and pushing for better governance of traditionally excluded groups. Paradoxically, more attention on the international stage given to the denationalisation crisis, unleashed in 2013 in the Dominican Republic, has led to intransigence in the country by successive governments, alleging that the Dominican Republic is sovereign on nationality matters, hence foreign interference is not welcome.

In terms of global advocacy coalition building, however, it is important for human rights defenders on the ground that the international Institute on Statelessness and Inclusion (ISI) dedicated a year of action to the deprivation of nationality globally, launched in March 2020. Accordingly, the Dominican Republic was one of five regional situations with noteworthy statelessness (along with Kenya, Malaysia, Jordan, and North Macedonia) featured in an international video seminar in May 2020, spearheaded by

ISI and including the impact of the Covid-19 pandemic on stateless persons (Institute on Statelessness and Inclusion, 2020b).

This chapter has traced the mixed results of civil society contestation and demonstrated the need for an even greater push for better governance to guarantee minority groups and their family members' proper integration and belonging in Dominican society. The state's overriding argument at home and abroad – that the remedial legislative framework to counter the adverse effects of denationalisation has solved the problem – is viewed very differently by those tens of thousands of denationalised persons who have not yet obtained the Dominican papers to which they are entitled, seven years after the implementation of Law 169-14. While acknowledging deficiencies in both the content and operation of the legislation, civil society activists are reticent to criticise the law because that might adversely affect those persons who, against all odds, have regained their Dominican papers through this remedial mechanism. The issue, civil society organisations hold, is how to move beyond a more robust operation of this naturalisation law, which is necessary but not sufficient in order to achieve durable solutions.

To its credit, the state has carried out various surveys on migrants and their descendants born in the Dominican Republic, but this data is not routinely used for policy making. The so-called 'Haitian question' is so sensitive in the Dominican Republic that most major political leaders prefer to pander to minority nationalist and nativist points of view, which posit that Haitian migrants and their descendants born in the country represent a so-called 'Pacific invasion' by the neighbouring country.

For definitive progress to be made, the stalemate between the state and international norms espoused by the inter-American human rights system and other international human rights bodies needs to be addressed. In this regard, an evolution in the national context should be highlighted. In common with other countries in Latin America, the Dominican Republic has experienced (in 2019 and 2020) social unrest and unprecedented mobilisations advocating for more responsible political leadership. Discontent over postponed municipal elections, for instance, led to the establishment of a broad non-partisan coalition of mainly young people seeking to challenge the hegemony of the incumbent Partido de la Liberacion Dominicana (PLD) party, which has ruled for the better part of two decades. Representative youth groups, which mobilised around this objective, included an organisation of denationalised persons called *Reconoci.do*, comprised of young Dominicans of Haitian ancestry affected by *La Sentencia* (Lister Brugal, 2019). This positioning is promising, signifying denationalised people entering the ranks of new vibrant civil society coalitions and potentially advancing common causes using strategic intersectionality.

Mobility dynamics are in flux across the island of Hispaniola in the era of Covid-19, hinting at new spaces opening up for civil society contestation of human rights abuses, including the deprivation of nationality (Wooding, 2020). In this context, and at the time of writing, it remains to be seen whether better governance emerges to address statelessness following presidential elections slated for 2020 in the Dominican Republic. Universalising from the Dominican Republic case may be useful in other contexts where supra-regional jurisprudence is sought to address statelessness. As demonstrated in this Caribbean setting, high-level, landmark judgments are necessary but do not suffice to achieve full compliance without ratcheting up grassroots activism and a groundswell of favourable public opinion.

Notes

1 Appeals against the constitutionality of the law have been made by Conservative sectors, senators of the Fuerza Nacional Progresista party, and nationalist members of the so-called Comité Dominicano por la Solidaridad con Haití, but the Constitutional Court has yet to decide on these.
2 The October 2013 court hearing in Mexico, where the author delivered an expert witness testimony, importantly took into account the notorious sentence which had been handed down by the Dominican Constitutional Court just one month earlier.
3 Two resolutions from the IACtHR in late 2019 underline that the state has failed to report on its lack of compliance since 2014 in respect of the four cases under the regional court's jurisdiction. It required that this be remedied by early 2020. Moreover, in the resolution on the case of Narciso Gonzalez (the only case unrelated to Haitian migrants or their descendants), the Court observes that this lack of compliance to inform on and carry out sentences seems to be a generalised position of the DR in all the cases under which it is being supervised (Corte IDH, 2019b: para 19).

References

Acento (2016) 'ACNUR reitera que existen 133,770 personas apátridas en la RD, y que podrían ser más' [Online]. Available at https://acento.com.do/2016/actualidad/8313829-acnur-reitera-que-existen-133770-personas-apatridas-en-la-rd-y-que-podrian-ser-mas/ (Accessed 30 May 2020).

Blitz, B. (2009) 'Statelessness, protection and equality', *Forced Migration Policy Brief* 3, Refugee Studies Centre, University of Oxford [Online]. Available at www.refworld.org/docid/4e5f3d572.html (Accessed 30 May 2020).

Centro para la Observación Migratoria y el Desarrollo Social en el Caribe (OBMICA) (2015) *Estado de las migraciones que atañen a la República*

Dominicana 2014 ['State of migrations affecting the Dominican Republic 2014'] (Santo Domingo: Editora Búho) [Online]. Available at http://obmica.org/index. php/publicaciones/informes/126-estado-del-arte-de-las-migraciones-que-atanen-a-la-republica-dominicana-2014 (Accessed 24 July 2020).

Centro para la Observación Migratoria y el Desarrollo Social en el Caribe (OBMICA) (2019) *Estado de las migraciones que atañen a la República Dominicana 2018* ['State of migrations affecting the Dominican Republic 2018'] (Santo Domingo: Editora Búho) [Online]. Available at http://obmica.org/index. php/publicaciones/informes/279-estado-de-las-migraciones-que-atanen-a-la-republica-dominicana-2018 (Accessed 24 July 2020).

Congreso Dominicana (2014) 'Ley No.169-14' [Online]. Available at https:// migracion.gob.do/transparencia/wp-content/uploads/2019/10/Ley-No-169-14-de-Naturalizaci%C3%B3n.pdf (Accessed 24 July 2020).

Constitución de la República Dominicana, 26 January 2010 (G.O. No 10561) [Online]. Available at http://dominicana.gob.do/index.php/pais/2014-12-16-20-52-13 (Accessed 24 July 2020).

Corte IDH (2019a) 'Resolución de la Corte inter-americana de Derechos Humanos del 22 de noviembre de 2019 caso Nadege Dorzema y otros vs. República Dominicana. Supervisión de Cumplimiento de Sentencia' ['Resolution of the Inter-American Court of Human Rights of 22 November 2019 case Nadege Dorzema and others v. Dominican Republic. Supervision of Compliance with the Sentence'] [Online]. Available at www.corteidh.or.cr/docs/supervisiones/nadege_dorzema_22_11_19.pdf (Accessed 24 July 2020).

Corte IDH (2019b) 'Resolución de la Corte inter-americana de Derechos Humanos del 22 de noviembre de 2019 caso González Medina y Familiares vs. República Dominicana. Supervisión de Cumplimiento de Sentencia' ['Resolution of the Inter-American Court of Human Rights of 22 November 2019 case González Medina and family members v. Dominican Republic. Supervision of Compliance with the Sentence'] [Online]. Available at www.corteidh.or.cr/docs/supervisiones/ gonzalezmedina_22_11_19.pdf (Accessed 24 July 2020).

Fine, J. (2013) 'Emergent solidarities: Labor movement responses to migrant workers in the Dominican Republic and Jordan', Report to Solidarity Center, Rutgers University [Online]. Available at www.solidaritycenter.org/wp-content/uploads/ 2014/11/Rutgers.Emergent-Solidarities.Migration.pdf (Accessed 30 May 2020).

Gibney, M. (2014) 'Statelessness and citizenship in ethical and political perspective', in A. Edwards and L. van Waas (eds) *Nationality and Statelessness under International Law* (Cambridge: Cambridge University Press): pp. 44–63.

Hintzen, A. (2016) 'Cultivating resistance: Haitian-Dominican communities and the Dominican sugar industry' (PhD thesis, University of Miami).

Institute on Statelessness and Inclusion (2020a) *The World's Stateless: Deprivation of Nationality* (Nijmegen: Wolf Legal Publishers).

Institute on Statelessness and Inclusion (2020b) Webinar: Statelessness in a global pandemic' [Online]. Available at www.youtube.com/watch?v= gPGDPmNDnMU&mc_cid=d4a9ae15f0&mc_eid=5fc38751a8 (Accessed 24 July 2020).

Inter-American Court of Human Rights (IACtHR) (2005) *Case of the Yean and Bosico Children v The Dominican Republic* [Online]. Available at www.corteidh.or.cr/docs/casos/articulos/seriec_130_%20ing.pdf (Accessed 24 July 2020).

Inter-American Court of Human Rights (IACtHR) (2014) *Case of Expelled Dominicans and Haitians v The Dominican Republic* [Online]. Available at http://corteidh.or.cr/docs/casos/articulos/seriec_282_ing.pdf (Accessed 24 July 2020).

Junta Central Electoral (2007a) 'Estricto cumplimiento a la Ley No. 659 sobre Actos del Estado Civil y sus modificaciones al firmar las Actas de Nacimiento o Cualquier documento' ['Strict compliance with Law No. 659 on the Certificates of the Civil Registry and its modifications on signing Birth Certificates or any document'] [Online]. Available at www.acnur.org/fileadmin/Documentos/BDL/2012/8902.pdf (Accessed 24 July 2020).

Junta Central Electoral (2007b) 'Resolución que establece el Procedimiento para Suspender Provisionalmente la Expedición de Actas del Estado Civil Viciadas o Instrumentadas de Manera Irregular' ['Resolution which establishes the procedure for temporary suspension of the issuance of flawed civil registry certificates or those initiated irregularly'] [Online]. Available at www.acnur.org/fileadmin/Documentos/BDL/2012/8899.pdf (Accessed 24 July 2020).

Latin America Public Opinion Project (LAPOP) (2019). 'Proyecto de Opinión Pública de América Latina' ['Project on public opinion in Latin America'], Informe, Vanderbilt University [Online]. Available at www.vanderbilt.edu/lapop-espanol/publicaciones.php (Accessed 30 May 2020).

Lister Brugal, E. (2019) 'Dominican Republic, Democracy without the rule of law?' *Revista sobre acesso a justicia e direitos nas Americas Brasilia*, 3:3, 186–202.

Martinez, S. (2014) 'The price of confrontation: International retributive justice and the struggle for Haitian-Dominican rights', in G. Andreopoulos and Z. Arat (eds) *The Uses and Misuses of Human Rights: A Critical Approach to Advocacy* (New York: Palgrave): pp. 89–115.

Ministerio de Interior y Policía/Instituto Nacional de Migración (2015) 'Memoria', Seminario-Taller Administración Pública y Gestión Migratoria [Online]. Available at https://issuu.com/inmrd/docs/inm_relatoria_seminario_migracion_w (Accessed 24 July 2020).

Oficina Nacional de Estadística (ONE) (2013) *Primera encuesta nacional de inmigrantes en la República Dominicana, ENI-2012* ['First national survey of immigrants in the Dominican Republic, ENI-2012'], Informe General (Santo Domingo: Oficina Nacional de Estadística).

ONE (2018) *Segunda encuesta nacional de inmigrantes en la República Dominicana, ENI-2017* ['Second national survey of immigrants in the Dominican Republic, ENI-2017'], Informe General (Santo Domingo: Oficina Nacional de Estadística).

Ramirez, J. M. (2007) 'Critican que quieran anular acta nacimiento Sonia Pierre' ['They criticise the wish to annul the birth certificate of Sonia Pierre'], *Hoy*, 31 March.

République d'Haïti (2014) 'Arrêté accordant à toute personne dépourvue d'acte de naissance, un délai de cinq (5) ans pour faire régulariser son état civil' ['Decree granting anyone without a birth certificate, a period of five (5) years to have their civil status regularised'], *Le Moniteur*, 10.

Tribunal Constitucional, República Dominicana (2013) 'Sentencia TC/0168/13' ['Sentence TC/0168/13'] [Online]. Available at www.refworld.org.es/pdfid/5d7fcd99a.pdf (Accessed 24 July 2020).

United Nations High Commissioner for Refugees (UNHCR) (2019) 'NGO statement on statelessness' [Online]. Available at www.statelessness.eu/sites/www.statelessness.eu/files/Civil-Society_Coalitions_Statement_Statelessness.pdf (Accessed 24 July 2020).

Wooding, B. (2020) 'Mobility challenges across Hispaniola in the era of Covid-19', COMPAS Coronavirus and Mobilities Forum, University of Oxford, 15 April [Online]. Available at www.compas.ox.ac.uk/2020/new-mobility-challenges-across-hispaniola-in-the-era-of-covid-19/ (Accessed 30 May 2020).

22

Civil society advocacy to address statelessness: Using norms to promote progress on the Global Action Plan to End Statelessness

Melissa Schnyder

This chapter explores how civil society organisations (CSOs) working to end statelessness use norm-based advocacy strategies to effect political and social change in relation to the United Nations High Commissioner for Refugees' (UNHCR) Global Action Plan to End Statelessness ('Action Plan'). The focus here is on CSOs, which include local-level community groups, national and regional non-governmental organisations (NGOs), and regional networks of individual experts. Highlighting specific examples from a content analysis of CSO documents, public statements, and discourse, the chapter analyses how CSOs attempt to 'foreground' and dismantle problematic social norms that relate to causes of statelessness. In addition, it examines how CSOs use two strategies – *normative reframing* and *normative innovation* – to advance alternative norms in their place. The analysis shows how CSOs have used normative reframing in terms of human rights norms to build momentum for change in relation to Action 2 of the Action Plan (ensure that no child is born stateless), with a regional focus on Europe. Additionally, it illustrates how CSOs are currently using normative innovation to advance a normative framework based on a combination of equality, inclusion, and anti-discrimination norms to generate more progress on Action 3 (remove gender discrimination from nationality laws), an area that has seen less success.

Because norms play a role in both formal and informal institutions, efforts to advance normative change are significant in that they can lead to institutional reform (Raymond and Weldon, 2013) and can address intractable problems (Raymond et al., 2014). Past research has documented this across a range of issues including biofuels (Delshad and Raymond, 2016), climate change (Raymond et al., 2014), women's rights (Raymond and Weldon, 2013; Raymond et al., 2014; Jewkes et al., 2015), and child marriage (Shawki, 2015). Thus, although statelessness is the focus here, the conclusions of this research potentially hold relevance to civil society advocacy in other issue areas.

This chapter proceeds in several sections. First, a brief contextual section provides background on the Action Plan. Next, the theoretical framework on norm-based strategies is described. The ensuing section analyses how normative reframing and normative innovation are evident in CSO advocacy related to Actions 2 and 3 of the Action Plan. The concluding section summarises key points and presents topics for future research.

The Global Action Plan to End Statelessness

UNHCR's Action Plan reflects the global-level institutional framework that contextualises CSO advocacy efforts. Launched in 2014, the ambitious goal of the Action Plan is 'to bring an end to statelessness within 10 years by resolving existing situations and preventing the emergence of new cases of statelessness' (UNHCR, 2014a: 4). To support this, it outlines ten actions to be developed over ten years. These include resolving current situations of statelessness, preventing statelessness in cases of state succession and due to discriminatory laws and practices, ensuring birth registration and better nationality documentation, promoting accession to the statelessness conventions, and improving data collection and analysis (UNHCR, 2014a: 1). The focus here is Action 2, ensure that no child is born stateless, and Action 3, remove gender discrimination from nationality laws.

Progress on these actions largely depends on the political will of the international community (UNHCR, 2014b: 8). Although there is more work to be done (particularly on Action 3), gains have been made in recent years as more states are strengthening safeguards to prevent statelessness and closing loopholes in policy and practice. Before turning to an analysis of CSO actions, the next section explains two norm-based strategies that CSOs use to influence national and regional politics, and therefore policy and action, while building momentum in support of eradicating statelessness.

Norm-based strategies for change

Normative reframing and normative innovation have been analysed in research that assesses advocacy efforts towards social and political change on troublesome policy issues (Raymond and Weldon, 2013; Raymond et al., 2014; Delshad and Raymond, 2016). What makes these strategies noteworthy is that advocates have employed them with some degree of success, particularly in issue areas characterised by strong opposition and powerful vested interests. The goal involves changing what is considered the 'standard of appropriate behavior' (Finnemore and Sikkink, 1998: 891), and thus setting the stage for social and political change.

Normative reframing, the first norm-based strategy, involves reconceptualising an issue in terms of an alternative existing norm that suggests different behaviours or policies compared to the status quo (Raymond et al., 2014; Raymond and Weldon, 2013). Advocates first highlight the weakness of 'fit' between the status quo norm and the issue at hand, then apply an alternative norm that they argue is a better fit (Raymond et al., 2014). In reframing the issue, they apply the strongest possible norm(s) in order to strengthen the legitimacy of the newly proposed norm and render it difficult to infringe upon (Raymond et al., 2014).

Normative innovation, the second strategy, involves the deliberate creation of new norms in an issue space (Raymond et al., 2014). Unlike normative reframing, which is used when advocates view the status-quo norm as a poor fit to the issue, normative innovation is used when the status-quo norm is viewed as fundamentally illegitimate. Thus, it involves the outright rejection of an undesirable norm, after which advocates offer an alternative norm that supports the desired change. In the process of promoting new norms, advocates also create new categories and concepts (Raymond and Weldon, 2013; Raymond et al., 2014).

Both strategies begin with 'foregrounding,' or calling attention to, weakening, and dismantling a status quo norm (Raymond et al., 2014). Advocates then have the opening to create change by employing normative reframing, normative innovation, or both. As other chapters in this volume have shown how statelessness is perpetuated, the strategies of focus here may hold potential for generating momentum towards change. The following sections illustrate how advocates working to end statelessness use these strategies to build momentum and bring about change in relation to Actions 2 and 3 of the Action Plan.

Foregrounding undesirable norms in the context of Actions 2 and 3

CSOs advocating for progress on Action 2 (ensure that no child is born stateless) engage in foregrounding by highlighting status quo norms that they deem problematic, and attempting to weaken their influence. In Europe, advocates working to end childhood statelessness have foregrounded problematic norms that tolerate the shirking of official responsibility on matters of stateless children. For example, the European Network on Statelessness (ENS) is a network of NGOs and individual experts committed to addressing statelessness in Europe. ENS calls attention to this in explaining that 'new cases of statelessness have emerged, mainly among children and most significantly because the measures in place to prevent statelessness from being passed on from stateless parents are inadequate' (European Network on Statelessness, 2014: 3). In short, ENS plainly states that 'the lack of a thorough commitment and diligent efforts to prevent childhood stateless-ness is currently the most significant ongoing cause of new cases of stateless-ness in the region' (European Network on Statelessness, 2014: 3).

Similarly, problematic norms that relate to the shirking of state responsi-bility are foregrounded in the pan-European #StatelessKids campaign. The campaign calls attention to these norms in its statement: 'Regrettably state-lessness continues to arise because European states are failing to ensure that all children born within Europe's borders or to European citizen parents acquire a nationality. It is a problem that is entirely solvable, yet over half of European countries don't have necessary safeguards in place to protect chil-dren from statelessness' (European Network on Statelessness, 2019). These brief examples illustrate how advocates emphasise problematic norms involving the lack of political will to address some of the root causes of childhood statelessness. Their statements use language that highlights the shirking of official responsibility and avoidance of state obligations as set forth under the Convention on the Rights of the Child.

A second type of norm that CSOs foreground in relation to both Actions 2 (ensure that no child is born stateless) and 3 (remove gender discrimin-ation from nationality laws) are cultural norms that undergird and reinforce discrimination against specific groups of people. Such 'subaltern status' norms refer to accepted standards that reinforce the marginalisation of spe-cific groups (Scott and Lawson, 2002). In foregrounding these norms, the interlinkages between childhood statelessness and gender discrimination become clear. As Maureen Lynch and Melanie Teff (2009: 31) explain:

> Inequitable laws also create childhood statelessness… the nationality of a child born to parents from different countries is still a concern when laws treat men and women differently. Where citizenship is determined exclusively by the father's nationality, stateless fathers, single women, or women living apart from their husbands face numerous barriers to registering their children.

In relation to Action 2, advocates have argued that the protection of chil-dren depends upon certain norms, explaining that '[o]ne of these principles is that of non-discrimination. This means that discrimination on the basis of the status of the child or the child's parents is not allowed' (European Network on Statelessness, 2014: 5).

Similarly, advocates who focus on removing gender discrimination from nationality laws (Action 3) foreground culturally rooted norms relating to gender roles and the low social status of women. Recently, civil society in

Lebanon and Malaysia have called on their governments to end gender discrimination in nationality laws. In Malaysia, for example, the Joint Action Group for Gender Equality attempts to weaken such norms in stating that '[t]hese discriminatory laws, which affect the lives of many Malaysians and their families, are inconsistent with the spirit of the Federal Constitution, which guarantees equality and prohibits gender discrimination' (Joint Action Group for Gender Equality, 2019). Similarly, in Lebanon, the Arab Women's Right to Nationality Campaign organised a recent demonstration, noting that 'we press for lifting all forms of injustice and discrimination against women, starting with the adoption of a law that gives the Lebanese woman the right to pass nationality to her family members' (CRTDA, 2019a). The critiques in these campaigns highlight norms of gender-based discrimination and the shirking of state responsibility, which contradict the Convention on the Elimination of all Forms of Discrimination Against Women (CEDAW), in attempts to call attention to and weaken them.

After a particular norm has been foregrounded, advocates must then offer an alternative norm to take its place. To better understand which norms are promoted in efforts to end childhood statelessness and remove gender discrimination from nationality laws, the following sections examine how advocates use normative reframing and normative innovation.

Normative reframing to address Action 2: Ensure that no child is born stateless

Normative reframing involves offering a strong alternative norm to replace the foregrounded norm. In seeking the strongest norms possible, it is not uncommon for CSOs to leverage human rights norms to reframe childhood statelessness. The human rights reframing strategy is underpinned by principles of international protection. These principles are laid out in existing international frameworks, such as the 1948 Universal Declaration of Human Rights and the 1990 United Nations Convention on the Rights of the Child (CRC). The CRC is 'the world's most widely ratified human rights treaty' (UNICEF, 2019) and, as such, represents a strong basis for human rights norms that CSOs draw upon.

An analysis of ENS campaign documents and media reports provides examples of how CSOs use rights-based norms to reframe childhood statelessness. ENS uses right-based framing to reposition the issue away from a private family problem to one of state obligation. ENS does this by arguing that '[n]o child chooses to be stateless; no child deserves to be... excluded from accessing their rights' (European Network on Statelessness, n.d.: 1). They explain that 'over half of European countries don't have necessary safeguards in place to protect children from statelessness' (European Network on Statelessness, 2019). Furthermore, they affirm that '[c]hildren affected by statelessness did not choose this status. Nor do they somehow exist as free agents without any attachments to a family, a community, a place or a home. They have the same connections as anyone else... Yet their country is letting them down...' (European Network on Statelessness, 2015: 1).

The best interest of the child is a strong human rights norm that ENS promotes throughout its campaigns and reports. One report, for example, states that:

> While almost all countries in the region have some law provisions designed to protect against childhood statelessness, remarkably few provide all children born in their territory who would otherwise be stateless the opportunity to acquire nationality immediately upon or as soon as possible after birth – a provision that is clearly in the best interests of the child.
>
> (European Network on Statelessness, 2015: 1)

Moreover, ENS draws upon several human rights norms in reporting:

> [I]t is vital to recall that the right to acquire a nationality is a right of every child. Even if the circumstances of the child's conception or birth are complex (even perceivably controversial), the best interest of the child to be protected from statelessness must prevail over any questions which may arise from his or her parents' status or choices. Similarly, a child's right to preserve his or her identity, including nationality, must be assured – including where the parents' action is what jeopardises this.
>
> (European Network on Statelessness, 2015: 1)

Specifically, the promoted human rights norms include those relating to non-discrimination (Article 2 of the CRC), the best interest of the child (Article 3 of the CRC), and the right of every child to preserve an identity, to include nationality (Article 8 of the CRC). Using these norms to reposition the issue of childhood statelessness reinforces states' obligations and the need for more targeted national-level action, particularly in complex cases including 'children born to irregular migrants or to refugees, children of same-sex couples, children commissioned by European parents through international commercial surrogacy and children who have been abandoned' (European Network on Statelessness, 2015: 1).

Together, these brief examples show how normative reframing involves arguing against the 'fit' of certain norms to the issue at hand, then promoting an existing norm in its place. By reframing childhood statelessness as a human rights matter, as opposed to a private matter or an intractable global problem, ENS can more easily place accountability upon specific states and target specific areas of weakness in law or policy that prevent governments from meeting their obligations as established by relevant international conventions. In addition, human rights reframing makes it harder for states not to take action to close legal and policy loopholes that lead to childhood statelessness, particularly if they are signatories to other relevant international human rights conventions such as the Convention on the Elimination of All Forms of Racial Discrimination or CEDAW.

Normative innovation to promote progress on Action 3: Remove gender discrimination from nationality laws

Action 3 of the Action Plan calls on the world's governments to remove gender discrimination from nationality laws. CSOs are currently using norm-based advocacy strategies to target national policies in efforts to generate more progress on this particular Action (Khanna, 2017). The presence of gender discrimination in nationality laws is a root cause of statelessness (Harrington, 2019), as women's inability to pass on their citizenship to their children and spouses can result in family separation. Examples of gender-discriminatory provisions in national law include denying women the right to pass citizenship to a non-national spouse, and formally linking women's citizenship to their marital status. Today, twenty-five countries deny women the right to pass their nationality to their children as men can, and approximately fifty countries have some gender-discriminatory provisions in place (Harrington, 2019). Moreover, in these environments children can be left stateless because women lack the same rights as men to confer nationality, illustrating the interrelation between Actions 2 and 3.

CSOs in these environments can take cues from CSOs in other policy sectors and employ normative innovation to promote transformative change and propose new identities and concepts (see Shawki, 2015). As a strategy, normative innovation begins by arguing against the fundamental character of a status quo norm (Raymond et al., 2014). Unlike the situations of normative reframing discussed earlier, the following examples highlight an explicit rejection of an existing norm as opposed to presenting arguments about its 'fit' to the issue. Innovation involves creating a new norm or combining several pre-existing norms in innovative and creative ways, and promotes new behaviours by establishing new rules, categories, concepts, and/or identities.

In this process, CSOs highlight status quo norms supporting gender discrimination and unequal treatment, rejecting their content, as the examples below illustrate. To fill the normative void, their campaigns promote a new normative framework based on the combined norms of citizenship equality, inclusion, and anti-discrimination, thereby legitimising the equal treatment of women. Although these norms in and of themselves cannot be considered very new per se, they are innovatively interlinked to legitimise new ways of thinking, promote new behavioural standards, and encourage fundamental change. The equality norm reflects a social value that emphasises the concept of social justice pertaining to opportunities of different societal groups, in this case based on gender (Lutz, 2001; Fukuda-Parr, 2016). It underlies the position that inequality is morally wrong and unfair (Sen, 2000). Linked to this is the inclusion norm, which refers to a democratic practice involving the incorporation of marginalised groups in political and social processes (Young, 2000). Equality norms are currently codified at the international level in CEDAW, which stipulates that 'States Parties shall grant women equal rights with men with respect to the nationality of their children' (United Nations General Assembly, 1979: 3).

In Lebanon, the current nationality law stipulates that foreign spouses of Lebanese men can obtain citizenship after one year, but the same does not apply to foreign spouses of Lebanese women. Furthermore, the current law grants citizenship 'only to children born to a Lebanese father, those born in Lebanon who would not otherwise acquire another nationality through birth or affiliation, or those born in Lebanon to unknown parents or parents of unknown nationalities' (Human Rights Watch, 2018). Consequently, children of a Lebanese mother and foreign father are not granted citizenship, a situation which showcases the interrelationship between Actions 2 and 3, and illustrates the obstacles Lebanese women face in passing citizenship to their children. For two decades, Lebanese activists such as Frontiers Ruwad Association and the Collective for Research and Training on Development – Action have campaigned for a more equitable nationality law, attempting to innovatively conjoin norms of citizenship equality and anti-discrimination.

To illustrate, the 'My Nationality is A Right for Me and My Family' campaign has organised sit-ins and demonstrations to promote the norm of citizenship equality. This norm forms the basis of a draft bill prepared by the campaign 'demanding equal treatment between men and women' in citizenship law (CRTDA, 2019a), in order to 'persuade [the Legislature] to play fair and enact a legislation that restores women's incomplete citizenship' (CRTDA, 2019a). As campaign coordinator Karima Chebbo states, 'Where is the right of the woman stipulated by the Constitution? Aren't we entitled as Lebanese women married to non-Lebanese to give nationality to our kids?... We want a detailed draft that talks equality among all citizens without exceptions. We demand equality, citizenship and rights' (CRTDA, 2019a). Furthermore, activists call on politicians 'to enact an all-inclusive and fair nationality law that plays fair to women' (CRTDA, 2019b).

The language of fairness, equality, and anti-discrimination is evident in CSOs' advocacy work. CSO activists interlink these norms in novel ways to foster new identities, rules, and concepts – a telltale sign of normative innovation (Raymond et al., 2014). In interviews with Lebanese women and their non-citizen children, for example, Human Rights Watch (2018) noted their 'second class' identity, as inequality in current law 'robs them of their Lebanese identity'. In addition, the Collective for Research and Training on Development – Action uses the concept of 'legal colonization' in its discourse. It has called for the overthrow of 'legal colonialism' through the hashtag campaign #DownWithLegalColonialism, as part of which it states: 'Real independence… is achieved with the enactment of an unprejudiced nationality law which ensures gender equality' (CRTDA, 2018). Here, activists are intentionally creating a new concept (a hallmark of normative innovation) to promote combined norms of equality and anti-discrimination.

In addition to Lebanon, Malaysia presents a second case of gender discrimination in nationality laws. There are three problematic provisions in existing Malaysian law (Joint Action Group for Gender Equality, 2019):

1. Citizenship is conferred to children born overseas to Malaysian fathers, but not Malaysian mothers;
2. Malaysian fathers are unable to confer nationality to their children if the children are not born within a legally recognised marriage;
3. Although the foreign spouses of Malaysian men only have a residency period of two years before being able to claim citizenship by registration, the residency period is ten years for foreign spouses of Malaysian women, and then their spouses must apply for citizenship through naturalisation.

CSOs in Malaysia are working to dismantle the institutionalised gender discrimination that can cause statelessness, and to leverage the power of equality norms to promote new ways of thinking on citizenship and belonging. The Joint Action Group for Gender Equality (2019) promotes democratic norms of citizenship equality in arguing that 'all citizens must be treated as equal before the law and, thus, be given equal right to confer nationality on their children and spouses, regardless of gender'. Reinforcing international norms on gender equality, they write that '[w]e must leave no one behind and ensure that our nationality laws uphold gender equality, in line with the UN Sustainable Development Goals' (Joint Action Group for Gender Equality, 2019). Sisters in Islam (2017), another Malaysian CSO, is a signatory to an open letter which states that '[c]itizens must have equal right to confer nationality on spouses, children'. The letter discusses the need 'to achieve substantive equality by addressing systemic barriers women face daily such as unjust laws, poor implementation of laws and limited access to the justice system due to strained economic conditions, to mention a few' (Sisters in Islam, 2017). The Foreign Spouses Support Group, another CSO, complements the efforts of other organisations in leading a citizenship task force 'to put forward 13 recommendations to the Government and put pressure on parliamentarians to ensure equal nationality rights for all Malaysians is achieved' (Indramalar, 2018). This group argues that quality of life should be 'assured with equality, non-discrimination...' (Foreign Spouses Support Group, n.d.), pointing out that Malaysian women who do not earn a minimum of RM2000 per month cannot sponsor their non-Malaysian husbands. Instead, they must find a sponsor who meets the income requirement. This requirement is problematic for returning graduates who marry a non-citizen, therefore '[t]his discriminatory policy on Malaysian women should be removed in line with the Convention on the Elimination of All Forms of Discrimination Against Women (CEDAW), which Malaysia has ratified' (Foreign Spouses Support Group, 2018). A similar discourse is practised by the Sarawak Women for Women Society, which calls on lawmakers to review laws 'so they comply with CEDAW principles and provisions and can effectively operate when couples are from different ethnic communities and/or live in different places' (Sarawak Women for Women Society, 2016: 1), and more generally advocates for promoting norms of women's equality (Sarawak Women for Women Society, 2019).

Together, these CSOs interlink norms of citizenship equality and gender equality to promote a new standard, advancing new ways of thinking within the national context on systemic barriers that impact women's ability to achieve citizenship based on full civil and political rights. Although these examples draw on established norms, advocates scaffold and combine them in novel ways to promote transformative change. Thus, individual norms can sum to something greater, an innovative normative framework in which the status quo is fundamentally reimagined.

Conclusion

This chapter shows how CSOs working to advance progress on Actions 2 and 3 of the Action Plan utilise two norm-based strategies across different national and regional contexts with the aim of pressuring governments to reform citizenship and nationality laws. In the context of Action 2, CSOs use strong international human rights norms to reframe the issue of childhood statelessness. To promote more progress on Action 3, CSOs working within different national contexts leverage the global momentum around the broader issue of ending discrimination against women, using this progress to promote innovative norms that combine citizenship equality, inclusion, and non-discrimination in their respective domestic contexts. Each strategy can reduce the prevalence of statelessness by shifting the norms that underpin formal and informal institutions that allow statelessness to occur.

Norm-based advocacy can be a particularly powerful tool where issues of statelessness overlap or intersect, as in the case of childhood statelessness and gender-based discrimination in nationality law, where progress in one area can result in 'spillover effects' into related areas. In addition, CSOs using norm-based advocacy to address Actions 2 and 3 not only create more momentum around these specific Actions, but also around broader issues of statelessness, such as preventing denial, loss, or deprivation of nationality on discriminatory grounds (Action 4) and preventing statelessness in cases of state succession (Action 5). The case studies in this chapter add examples showing how norm-based strategies can be used to address persistent global problems. More research is needed to investigate how norm-based strategies are being used by civil society actors across different country contexts to address different problems that contribute to statelessness in order to better assess the conditions under which they are most effective in producing reform. Changing the norms governing a particular issue of statelessness can be a promising point of intervention for political actors seeking institutional change.

References

Collective for Research and Training on Development (CRTDA) (2018) 'On Independence Day: My Nationality campaign calls for knocking down legal colonization' [Online]. Available at https://crtda.org.lb/node/16255 (Accessed 10 September 2019).

Collective for Research and Training on Development (CRTDA) (2019a) 'My Nationality sit-in demands fair law for women' [Online]. Available at https://crtda.org.lb/node/16253 (Accessed 9 August 2019).

Collective for Research and Training on Development (CRTDA) (2019b) 'Minister Safadi backs My Nationality campaign' [Online]. Available at https://crtda.org.lb/node/16258 (Accessed 9 September 2019).

Delshad, A. B., and Raymond, L. (2016) 'Normative framing and public attitudes toward biofuels policies', *Environmental Communication*, 10:4, 508–524.

European Network on Statelessness (n.d.) 'Fact sheet 2: Statelessness and rights' [Online]. Available at www.statelessness.eu/sites/www.statelessness.eu/files/Factsheet%202%20-%20statelessness%20and%20rights.pdf (Accessed 9 September 2019).

European Network on Statelessness (2014) 'Preventing childhood statelessness in Europe: Issues, gaps and good practices' [Online]. Available at www.statelessness.eu/resources/preventing-childhood-statelessness-europe-issues-gaps-and-good-practices (Accessed 19 June 2020).

European Network on Statelessness (2015) 'No child should be stateless' [Online]. Available at www.statelessness.eu/sites/www.statelessness.eu/files/ENS_NoChild Stateless_final.pdf (Accessed 10 September 2019).

European Network on Statelessness (2019) '#StatelessKids – None of Europe's children should be stateless' [Online]. Available at www.statelessness.eu/statelesskids-no-child-should-be-stateless (Accessed 2 September 2019).

Finnemore, M., and Sikkink, K. (1998) 'International norm dynamics and political change', *International Organization*, 52:4, 887–917.

Foreign Spouses Support Group (n.d.) 'Our vision' [Online]. Available at http://foreign-spouses.simplesite.com/429388501 (Accessed 12 September 2019).

Foreign Spouses Support Group (2018) 'Muslim marriage in Malaysia' [Online]. Available at http://foreign-spouses.simplesite.com/429400391 (Accessed 13 September 2019).

Fukuda-Parr, S. (2016) 'Equality as a valued social norm, inequality as an injustice', in International Social Science Council and University of Sussex (UK) Institute of Development Studies (eds) *World Social Science Report 2016: Challenging Inequalities; Pathways to a Just World* (Paris: UNESCO and the ISSC): pp. 263–264.

Harrington, C. (2019) 'Getting to 100%: New video on the importance of ending gender discrimination in nationality laws', European Network on Statelessness Blog [Online]. Available at www.statelessness.eu/blog/getting-100-new-video-importance-ending-gender-discrimination-nationality-laws (Accessed 16 August 2019).

Human Rights Watch (2018) 'Lebanon: Discriminatory nationality law' [Online]. Available at www.hrw.org/news/2018/10/03/lebanon-discriminatory-nationality-law (Accessed 12 September 2019).

Indramalar, S. (2018) 'Nationality laws are unfair', *The Star Online*, 26 July [Online]. Available at www.thestar.com.my/news/nation/2018/07/26/nationality-laws-are-unfair-allow-women-to-have-equal-citizenship-rights-as-men-govt-urged (Accessed 8 September 2019).

Jewkes, R., Flood, M., and Lang, J. (2015) 'From work with men and boys to changes of social norms and reduction of inequities in gender relations: A conceptual shift in prevention of violence against women and girls', *The Lancet*, 385:9977, 1580–1589.

Joint Action Group for Gender Equality (2019) 'Citizens must have equal right to confer nationality on spouses, children', *Malaysia Kini*, 24 March [Online]. Available at www.malaysiakini.com/letters/469433 (Accessed 17 August 2019).

Khanna, M. (2017) 'State of the world's stateless', *World's Stateless Report* [Online]. Available at www.worldsstateless.org/state-of-the-worlds-stateless (Accessed 17 August 2019).

Lutz, M. A. (2001) 'On the norm of equality', *International Journal of Social Economics*, 28:10/11/12, 782–799.

Lynch, M., and Teff, M. (2009) 'Childhood statelessness', *Forced Migration Review*, 32, 31–33.

Raymond, L. (2016) *Reclaiming the Atmospheric Commons: The Regional Greenhouse Gas Initiative and a New Model of Emissions Trading* (Cambridge, MA: MIT Press).

Raymond, L., and Weldon, S. L. (2013) 'Informal institutions and strategies for social change', Workshop on Informal Institutions and Intractable Global Problems

Issue Brief [Online]. Available at www.purdue.edu/discoverypark/environment/docs/Informal_Inst.pdf (Accessed 5 August 2019).

Raymond, L., Weldon, S. L., Kelly, D., Arriaga, X. B., and Clark, A. M. (2014) 'Making change: Norm-based strategies for institutional change to address intractable problems', *Political Research Quarterly*, 67:1, 197–211.

Sarawak Women for Women Society (2016) 'Women calling for change' [Online]. Available at http://sarswws.org/wp-content/uploads/2016/07/manifesto-all.jpg (Accessed 13 September 2019).

Sarawak Women for Women Society (2019) 'About us' [Online]. Available at http://sarswws.org/about-us/ (Accessed 13 September 2019).

Scott, D., and Lawson, H. (eds) (2002) *Citizenship Education and the Curriculum* (Westport, CT: Ablex Publishing).

Sen, A. (2000) 'Social justice and the distribution of income', in A. B. Atkinson and F. Bourguignon (eds) *Handbook of Income Distribution*, vol. 1 (Amsterdam: Elsevier Science BV): pp. 59–85.

Shawki, N. (2015) 'Norm-based advocacy and social change: An analysis of advocacy efforts to end child marriage', *Social Alternatives*, 34:4, 57–62.

Sisters in Islam (2017) 'Press statement: Why RUU355 is not a law with feminist ideals' [Online]. Available at https://aliran.com/civil-society-voices/2017-civil-society-voices/sis-ruu355-not-law-feminist-ideals/ (Accessed 7 September 2019).

United Nations Children's Fund (UNICEF) (2019) 'For Every Child, Every Right' [Online]. Available at www.unicef.org/reports/convention-rights-child-crossroads-2019 (Accessed 11 November 2019).

United Nations High Commissioner for Refugees (UNHCR) (2014a) 'Global action plan to end statelessness' [Online]. Available at www.refworld.org/docid/545b47d64.html (Accessed 3 September 2019).

United Nations High Commissioner for Refugees (UNHCR) (2014b) 'Ending statelessness within 10 years', UNHCR Special Report. Geneva: UNHRC [Online]. Available at www.unhcr.org/ibelong/special-report-ending-statelessness-within-10-years/ (Accessed 3 September 2019).

United Nations General Assembly (1979) *Convention on the Elimination of all Forms of Discrimination against Women* [Online]. Available at www.ohchr.org/documents/professionalinterest/cedaw.pdf (Accessed 19 June 2020).

Young, I. M. (2000) *Inclusion and Democracy* (Oxford: Oxford University Press).

23

The construction of a Brazilian 'hospitality policy' and the adoption of a new legal framework for stateless persons

Thiago Assunção

Brazil's 'hospitality policy' includes novel provisions to enable recognition of statelessness and to provide a route to citizenship for stateless persons. Brazil has built a policy for asylum seekers based on the value of hospitality throughout the last decade. The government implemented a humanitarian visa in order to receive migrants escaping from natural disasters, as well as other situations not covered by existing international refugee law. This policy was institutionalised with the adoption of a new migratory legislation in 2017, in which statelessness also received unprecedented treatment. This took place under the presidency of Michel Temer, which lasted from August 2016 until December 2018. In the Brazilian context, therefore, statelessness is framed in the language of migration and asylum.

A statelessness determination procedure was adopted for the first time in Brazil, and in 2018 two sisters of Syrian origin were recognised as stateless. In October 2018, they became Brazilians through the inauguration of a facilitated naturalisation process for stateless persons. The adoption of this innovative policy was influenced by the activism of Maha Mamo, one of the sisters who later benefited from it. Mamo is known worldwide as an enthusiastic advocate for the cause of stateless persons. She has travelled abroad with the support of the United Nations High Commissioner for Refugees (UNHCR) as part of their #IBelong Campaign. This chapter analyses the new Brazilian legislation related to statelessness, in light of the successful case of Maha Mamo. The chapter ultimately seeks to understand how a particular set of policies has affected the lives of stateless persons, how a stateless person was able to influence policy change, and how statelessness is now addressed nationally in Brazil.

Brazilian hospitality in the context of international human mobility

Notions of hospitality are important to Brazilian self-identity. This provides important context for Brazil's so-called 'hospitality policy'. The historian Sérgio Buarque de Hollanda (1995), in his masterpiece *Raízes do Brasil* (*Roots of Brazil*), famously portrayed the Brazilian character with the distinctive trace of generosity and 'hospitality'. According to him, the Brazilian contribution to the world would be the cordiality of its people, a virtue which he said was recognised by the foreigners who visit the country. By considering the typical Brazilian as a 'cordial man', Hollanda (1995) does not make a value judgement related to kindness or good manners. The reference is instead to the emotive way Brazilians treat each other, as well as their extreme informality. Austrian writer Stefan Zweig (2013) is known for his descriptions of his own expressions of statelessness. Zweig lived in Brazil in the 1940s and he observed that 'any newcomer is received warmly, and everything is facilitated in the most helpful manner'. In his book, which sets out his impressions of the Brazilian culture and society, he expressed admiration for the ethnic diversity of the national population, composed of immigrants from different continents (Zweig, 2013: 125–130).

While it is important not to paint too rosy a picture – particularly since Brazil's history is also marked by slavery and the subjugation of Indigenous peoples – the country's advanced refugee law and innovative practice of 'humanitarian visas' are worthy of consideration. Even though racism and the situation of many Indigenous peoples remain problematic, Brazil can be described as a multi-ethnic society, with a long history of receiving migrants from different parts of the world. The reception of Haitians and Syrians on humanitarian grounds, for instance, and the adoption of a new migratory law (including a fresh regulation of statelessness) help make Brazil a worthwhile country to be studied as a reference for humanitarian policies in the context of international human mobility (Doyle and Macedo, 2018).

Brazil as an emergent destination for asylum seekers

Statelessness is addressed in Brazil within the context of asylum, addressing the specific needs of stateless refugees (see Tucker, this volume). Brazil signed the 1951 Convention relating to the Status of Refugees in 1952 and ratified it in 1960. The re-democratisation was a turning point not only for the country's political and social landscape, but also for its humanitarian openness.[1] In fact, 'since the end of the military rule in 1985, the apparent political indifference to refugees gave way to a more liberal application of migration rules to the benefit of refugees' (Fischel de Andrade, 2015: 167).

The 1997 Brazilian Refugee Act (Law 9,474) is considered to be an advanced legislation on the subject (Jubilut, 2006). The Act adopts the same definition of a refugee as featured in the 1951 UN Convention. The innovation comes in Item III, which partially adopts the 'extended definition' of the 1984 Cartagena Declaration – much broader than the definition found within the UN Convention – to protect those who, 'owing to serious and widespread violations of human rights, is obligated to leave his country of nationality to seek refuge in another country'. This is, no doubt, a major merit of the national law (Jubilut, 2007: 191).

In addition, the 1997 Act extended refugee protection to stateless persons who meet the refugee definition. That is, they are outside their country of habitual residence and cannot (or do not want to) return to it due to one of the five kinds of persecution stated in the law. This means that a stateless person in Brazil could receive protection only if they are also subject to persecution or widespread human rights violations. That person would be then a 'stateless refugee'. While not all stateless persons are refugees, this was a key context of statelessness in Brazil, before the adoption of the new legislation in 2017.

Therefore, Brazil is considered a leader in the protection of refugees in Latin America. This is 'according to the amplitude of its legal protection framework and environment of cooperation between governmental organs responsible for dealing with the institute of refuge, the UNHCR and the civil society' (Lacerda and Gama, 2016: 61). This corresponds to the rise in the number of asylum seekers in the country. Applications grew from 966 in 2010 to 28,670 in 2015 (Secretaria Nacional de Justiça, 2017). Until December 2018, the backlog of applications for refugee status was more than 160,000 (Secretaria Nacional de Justiça, 2019), of which more than half were from Venezuelans.

The Brazilian policy of 'humanitarian visas'

In 2010, a devastating earthquake in Haiti killed more than 100,000 people in the area of the capital, Port-au-Prince. Haiti is the poorest country of the Americas. The catastrophe displaced more than two million people in a few days. Many Haitians were forced to flee the calamity to neighbouring countries in Central America and the Caribbean. Notably, the UN stabilisation mission in Haiti was established by the UN Security Council in 2004 and was led by Brazilian forces until its end in 2017. A large number of Brazilians were engaged with this mission at the time of the earthquake. The year 2010 was also a good economic moment in Brazil; the average GDP between 2001 and 2010 was 3.6%, with a growth of 7.5% in 2010 (IBGE, 2013). As a result, the country became an important destination for the Haitian diaspora.

Upon arrival, many Haitians applied for refugee status, which would allow them to reside and work legally in Brazil. However, the Brazilian National Committee for Refugees (CONARE) understood that they were not refugees. That is, they did not fulfil the definition of persecution present in the National Refuge Law. What happened next was a turning point. The CONARE decided to send the case to the National Council of Migrations (CNIg) for analysis. After discussing the extraordinary situation, the CNIg issued an administrative resolution (97/2012), establishing a special visa for the Haitians for humanitarian reasons.

The humanitarian visa solution was new for Brazil. It provided an unprecedented solution for people who need protection in case of a natural disaster (Gediel and Casagrande, 2015). It filled a gap, allowing the Haitian migrants to settle in the country and work legally. The lesson in this case stemmed from the cooperation among different governmental institutions in order to offer an innovative humanitarian response, complementing the existing refugee protective norms, despite the lack of a specific provision. The initiative was praised by the UNHCR, since it solved an emergent situation – a solution that would be repeated later in the case of Syrians escaping from civil war and seeking safety in Brazil. In 2013, CONARE issued resolution 17/2013, allowing Syrians affected by armed conflict to get humanitarian visas at Brazilian diplomatic missions in order to safely arrive in Brazil and then apply for asylum (Rodrigues et al., 2017).

Statelessness law, advocacy, and activism in Brazil

Brazil was silent on the question of statelessness, except for the reference to 'stateless refugees', in its national refugee law. The only reference in ordinary migratory law was related to the concession of passports for people of 'indefinite nationality'. In this way, statelessness was seen as a migratory status. Brazilian understandings of statelessness centred not so much on statelessness in its own territory, but rather risk of statelessness for Brazilians born overseas. This background helps us to understand how the hospitality policy was extended to address statelessness when there was no statelessness determination procedure.

Stateless Brazilians abroad

While there is currently no major problem with statelessness stemming from inside the country – mainly because anyone born in Brazil is considered Brazilian (*jus soli*), even those born to foreign parents, provided they are not at the service of their country (according to Article 12, I, *a*, of the 1988

Constitution) – it was not always like that. After a change in the Constitution in 1994, around 200,000 Brazilian children were at risk of becoming stateless (see Moulin, 2015). Revision amendment no. 3 stated that, to obtain Brazilian nationality, a child born abroad to a Brazilian parent should reside in Brazil and opt for the Brazilian nationality. If they remained abroad, they would be ineligible for citizenship.

The 1994 constitutional change sparked protests from part of the three million Brazilians living abroad. Two categories of the Brazilian diaspora were particularly concerned: those who had no intentions of going back to Brazil, and those who lived in countries with *jus sanguinis* traditions (such as Germany, Switzerland, Italy, and Japan). In these *jus sanguinis* countries, children born to two Brazilian parents would be left stateless. They would not have the chance to leave the country of residence legally, nor to visit relatives in Brazil, since they would not have access to a travel document. The only case by which a child born overseas could obtain Brazilian citizenship from a parent was if that parent was working abroad for the Brazilian government.

Brazilian families living abroad created an online campaign called *Brasileirinhos Apátridas* ['stateless Brazilian children'] with a website to promote awareness about their problem. Their case attracted the attention of the civil society and media. Parents living abroad started to organise meetings and media interviews, and to lobby Brazilian diplomats and lawmakers. Protests took place in several cities around the world, including in front of the UN headquarters in Geneva.

Finally, in 2007, the National Congress approved the Constitutional Amendment 54/2007, by which the child of a Brazilian mother or father born abroad would be a Brazilian national. It would be sufficient for the child to be registered in the Brazilian consulate. The amendment put an end to years of uncertainty for the parents who felt connected to their country of origin and wanted their children to have the chance to share their citizenship, and perhaps to move freely to their country of origin in the future.

There were political reasons that opened space for this change. Public opinion in Brazil had become concerned with the mistreatment of Brazilians abroad, including tourists. Moreover, the political power of emigrants had risen, since the number of Brazilian emigrants able to vote jumped from 104,660 in 2006 to 200,392 in 2010 (Moulin, 2015: 87). As a result of the 2007 amendment, the Brazilian state has adequate Constitutional provisions on nationality to avoid new cases of statelessness arising among children born abroad to Brazilian parents (Godoy, 2010). The initiative was praised by the UNHCR, which cited the case in its compilation of good practices concerning the Global Action Plan to End Statelessness (UNHCR, 2015).

Statelessness within Brazil

Though Brazil ratified both the 1954 and the 1961 UN Statelessness Conventions, it remained in breach of the applicable international law by not fully implementing them. According to the Ministry of Justice, there were around 1,650 stateless individuals in the country in 2017.[2] Without any procedure to ascertain if those persons really had nationality or not, most of them could actually be nationals of third countries but without the appropriate documentation to prove it.

That situation changed completely with the adoption of the new migratory act in 2017 (Law no. 13,445). The legislative reform was result of more than twenty years of activism of social movements, considering that the old migratory law was still from the time of dictatorship in the country (Law 6,815 of 1980). Organisations such as *Conectas Direitos Humanos* (Conectas Human Rights) and *Instituto Migrações e Direitos Humanos* (Migration and Human Rights Institute) played a vital role in lobbying the lawmakers in the Congress about the need to update the legislation (for more on the role of civil society in legislative change in this area, see Wooding, this volume; Schnyder, this volume). The result was the final approval of a bill which gained support from the government (at the time led by President Michel Temer), as well as the opposition in Congress.

Two main innovations were broadly welcomed. First, there was the incorporation of the visa for humanitarian purposes, created for the *ad hoc* situations of Haitians and Syrians. This visa serves as an innovative form of complementary protection, and its incorporation into law is a practical example of the Brazilian hospitality policy created in the last ten years. Second and the most important here, there was the adoption of an entire chapter on the protection of stateless people and the reduction of statelessness. This has been influenced by the 2014 UNHCR campaign to eradicate statelessness by 2024, as will be considered below (see also Schnyder, this volume). The new act finally created a statelessness determination procedure in the country, albeit subject to further regulation.[3] It granted stateless persons who had entered the country from elsewhere the same rights of any resident migrant, including the right to documentation, free public education, healthcare and social security, and the right to work legally in Brazil.

How does this new procedure work? Since the new legislation entered into force, stateless persons in Brazil may fill out an application to be recognised as stateless. Then, the state verifies if the individual is really not a national of any other country. If the person is recognised as stateless, the new law provides a mechanism for them to naturalise as Brazilian citizens.

This naturalisation should occur in a maximum of 30 days. If the individual has no interest in naturalising as Brazilian, they are automatically offered permanent residence in the country as a stateless person. As I have noted previously, 'the approval of a specific statelessness regulation in Brazil configures a very important development in the area, turning the country into a place where people in this situation can count with clear rules and appropriate solutions for addressing their case' (Assunção, 2019: 279). This results in a policy which fulfils the hospitality paradigm mentioned before, as well as the Latin American so-called 'spirit of Cartagena' (Barreto and Leão, 2010).

After the launch of the UNHCR (2014) #IBelong Campaign,[4] Maha Mamo, a stateless refugee living in Brazil, started to advocate for the rights of stateless people all over the world. Mamo was born in Lebanon from Syrian parents with different religions (Christian and Muslim), which is not recognised by Syrian law. As Lebanon does not apply *jus soli* as a rule, Mamo and her siblings did not receive Lebanese nationality. They faced many difficulties from growing up with a sense of displacement and lack of belonging, which led Mamo and her sister to search for information about statelessness via embassies in other countries (UNHCR, n.d.). The only one that responded positively was the Brazilian embassy, since by that time the Brazilian government had in place an 'open doors' policy towards Syrians escaping war. She then travelled to Brazil with her sister and became a stateless refugee in the country.

Mamo started to raise her voice for the cause and was interviewed by newspapers and television channels. She began to travel with the support of UNHCR to spread awareness about the statelessness problem around the world (UNHCR, n.d.). At the same time, the new migratory bill was in discussion in the Brazil parliament. Mamo's fame helped stakeholders give attention to statelessness in the new law. The advocacy performed by civil society actors was important to the development of the law, as was the technical assistance of the UNHCR office in Brasilia. Maha Mamo no doubt raised the profile of the statelessness issue in the country, appearing on TV programmes and at conferences always with the Brazilian flag on her back – thanking the country publicly for its warm welcome. Eventually, her saga arrived at a happy end, since Mamo and her sister were the first two individuals who benefited from the new legislation. They became Brazilians through facilitated naturalisation for stateless persons in October 2018. Maha, in fact, was surprised by the conferral of her naturalisation by representatives of the Brazilian government at a side event during the 69th Session of the UNHCR Executive Committee in Geneva (UNHCR, 2018).

Conclusion

Brazilian innovation on the issue of statelessness includes the adoption of progressive asylum and migratory practices as part of a broader 'hospitality policy'. There was especially a movement forward in the country after the launch of the UNHCR's (2014) #IBelong Campaign, in part stimulated by the case of Maha Mamo and her family. Also influenced by the social activism of non-governmental organisations (NGOs) and the attentive work of the UNHCR office, the result was the inclusion of statelessness in the new migratory act (Law no. 13,445 of 2017) and a facilitated naturalisation procedure for those officially recognised as stateless, or those who would become stateless otherwise. Mamo's case can be considered a success, not only for the solution of a statelessness situation, but also due to the impact that a stateless activist had in raising awareness of statelessness in Brazil and worldwide.

The adoption of a statelessness determination procedure in Brazil has been followed by other countries in South America. Paraguay adopted new legislation in 2018 with similar provisions (Law no. 6,149). Uruguay did the same (Law no. 19,682) the same year, and Argentina did so in 2019 (Law no. 27,512). In 2019, Colombia reformed their nationality law by conceding nationality for children born to Venezuelan parents in Colombian territory, whether they were in a regular or irregular migratory situations, in order to avoid statelessness (Law no. 1997), with the support of UNHCR, IOM, and UNICEF (UNHCR, 2019). These developments – and a generally more permissive treatment of nationality attribution than in other parts of the world – make Brazil and the region more broadly an important case study for global leaders. It is important to keep advancing solutions for statelessness, and hopefully other states in the Americas (and beyond) will be inspired by the recent events and legislative reforms, in order to take immediate action towards the eradication of statelessness.

Notes

1 In 1989, Brazil withdrew from the geographical reservation established by the 1951 Convention, and in 1990 overturned the reservations previously made to Articles 15 and 17 of the Convention.

2 Information provided by the Brazilian Federal Police, under request of the author, through the Law of Access to Information. The official response was dated 29 August 2017.

3 The adoption of Decree no. 9.199/2017, which regulated the Law, and the edition of the Interministerial Ordinance no. 5 (February 2018) established the specific procedure to be followed by stateless persons in the country.

4 The UNHCR's #IBelong Campaign website is available at www.unhcr.org/ibelong/

References

Assunção, T. (2019) 'Statelessness in Brazil: From invisibility to the invitation for becoming a citizen', *Revista de Estudos e Pesquisas sobre as Américas (UnB)*, 13:1, 279–307.

Barreto, L. P. T. F., and Leão, R. Z. R. (2010) 'O Brasil e o espírito da Declaração de Cartagena' ['Brazil and the spirit of the Cartagena Declaration'], *Forced Migration Review*, 35 [Online]. Available at www.fmreview.org/sites/fmr/files/FMR35brasil.pdf (Accessed 28 March 2020).

Brasileirinhos Apátridas (n.d.) Homepage ['Stateless Brazilian children'] [Online]. Available at http://brasileirinhosapatridas.org/ (Accessed 28 March 2020).

Doyle, M., and Macedo, G. C. (2018) 'Brazil and the future of the international mobility regime', *Monções: Revista de Relações Internacionais da UFGD*, 7:14, 250–271.

Fischel de Andrade, J. H. (2015) 'Refugee protection in Brazil (1921–2014): An analytical narrative of changing policies', in D. J. Cantor, L. F. Freier, and J. P. Gauci (eds) *A Liberal Tide? Immigration and Asylum Law and Policy in Latin America* (London: School of Advanced Study, University of London): pp. 153–184.

Gediel, J. A. P., and Casagrande, M. M. (2015) 'A migração haitiana para o Brasil: bases teóricas e instrumentos político-jurídicos' ['Haitian migration to Brazil: Theoretical bases and political-legal instruments'], *Monções: Revista de Relações Internacionais da UFGD*, 4:8, 97–110.

Godoy, G. G. (2010) 'Considerações sobre recentes avanços na proteção dos apátridas no Brasil' ['Considerations on recent advances in the protection of stateless persons in Brazil'], *Caderno de Debates Refúgio, Migrações e Cidadania*, 6:6, 61–72.

Hollanda, S. B. (1995) *Raízes do Brasil* [Roots of Brazil] (São Paulo: Companhia das Letras).

Instituto Brasileiro de Geografia e Estatística [Brazilian Institute of Geography and Statistics] (IBGE) (2013) 'O Brasil em números (2013)' ['Brazil in numbers (2013)']. Centro de Documentação e Disseminação de Informações [Online]. Available at https://biblioteca.ibge.gov.br/visualizacao/periodicos/2/bn_2013_v21.pdf (Accessed 28 March 2020).

Jubilut, L. L. (2006) 'Refugee law and protection in Brazil: A model in South America?', *Journal of Refugee Studies*, 19:1, 22–44.

Jubilut, L. L. (2007) *O Direito Internacional dos Refugiados e sua Aplicação no Ordenamento Jurídico Brasileiro* [International Refugee Law and its Application in the Brazilian Legal System] (São Paulo: Método).

Lacerda, A. L., and Gama, C. F. (2016) 'O solicitante de refúgio e a soberania moderna: A identidade na diferença' ['The asylum seeker and modern sovereignty: Identity in difference'], *Lua Nova*, 97, 53–80.

Moulin, C. (2015) 'Mobilizing against statelessness: The case of Brazilian emigrant communities', in R. E. Howard-Hassmann and M. Walton-Roberts (eds) *The Human Right to Citizenship: A Slippery Concept* (Philadelphia, PA: University of Pennsylvania Press): pp. 78–94.

Rodrigues, G., Blanes Sala, J., and Siqueira, D. C. (2017) 'Visas and qualifications: Syrian refugees in Brazil', *Forced Migration Review*, 56 [Online]. Available at www.fmreview.org/latinamerica-caribbean/rodrigues-sala-desiqueira (Accessed 12 July 2020).

Secretaria Nacional da Justiça (2017) 'Refúgio em números', 3rd edition. Available at www.justica.gov.br/news/brasil-tem-aumento-de-12-no-numero-de-refugiados-em-2016/20062017_refugio-em-numeros-2010-2016.pdf (Accessed 10 November 2017).

Secretaria Nacional da Justiça (2019) 'Refúgio em números', 4th edition [Online]. Available at www.acnur.org/portugues/wp-content/uploads/2019/07/Refugio-em-nu%CC%81meros_versa%CC%83o-23-de-julho-002.pdf (Accessed 10 November 2019).

United Nations High Commissioner for Refugees (UNHCR) (n.d.) 'Maha Mamo, refugiada apátrida no Brasil, fala sobre os desafios de uma vida sem nacionalidade' ['Maha Mamo, a stateless refugee in Brazil, talks about the challenges of a life without nationality'] [Online]. Available at www.acnur.org/portugues/noticias/noticia/maha-mamo-refugiada-apatrida-no-brasil-fala-sobre-os-desafios-de-uma-vida-sem-nacionalidade/ (Accessed 20 June 2017).

United Nations High Commissioner for Refugees (UNHCR) (2015) 'Good practices paper – Action 1: Resolving existing major situations of statelessness' [Online]. Available at www.refworld.org/docid/54e75a244.html (Accessed 28 June 2017).

United Nations High Commissioner for Refugees (UNHCR) (2018) 'Brazil makes dream of belonging come true for stateless activist' [Online]. Available at www.unhcr.org/news/latest/2018/10/5bb6394a4/brazil-makes-dream-belonging-true-stateless-activist.html (Accessed 12 July 2020).

United Nations High Commissioner for Refugees (UNHCR) (2019) 'Colombia acts to ensure children born to Venezuelan parents are not left stateless' [Online]. Available at www.unhcr.org/news/briefing/2019/8/5d4937754/colombia-acts-ensure-children-born-venezuelan-parents-stateless.html (Accessed 12 July 2020).

Zweig, S. (2013) *Brasil, um país do futuro* [Brazil, a country of the future]. Translated by K. Michahelles (Porto Alegre: L&PM).

24

Ideological governance of citizen and non-citizen others in Kuwait

Areej Alshammiry

The nation-state is an organiser of social relations and practices, as well as the representations of difference among people who exist on its territory (Sharma, 2015: 129). Through a study of the Bidoon in Kuwait, this chapter presents the role of education in the symbolic representation of the nation. The cultural politics of the authoritative 'narratives of nationhood' promoted by government institutions and their knowledge platforms highlight a narrow narrative of the nation with the effect of *exalting* a particular group whose members embody the official characteristics of the nation (terminology from Thobani, 2007). The case of the Bidoon in Kuwait helps to demonstrate how, while certain human beings come to be 'exalted' and constituted as nationals, others are cast as 'strangers'. The national project constructs these 'strangers' as 'undeserving' of membership in the polity (Thobani, 2007: 5).

The role of public education in constructing the situation for the Bidoon in Kuwait is particularly important to consider. First, the Bidoon represent a prime example of in situ statelessness (the language of in situ statelessness is challenged in Fazal, this volume). Second, it provides a clear example in which national identity formation functions as 'exaltation', in which statelessness (and other forms of non-citizenship) is co-produced with citizenship. Third, statelessness in Kuwait was produced during state succession. This indicates the inextricable relationship between nation-state formation and statelessness and the ongoing (re)production of both (see also Kuzmova, this volume; Vollmer, this volume).

Bidoon statelessness in Kuwait

To understand the historical and contemporary making of the Bidoon statelessness, I trace their production in relation to the ideologies that are embedded in the constructions of Kuwaiti citizenship and national identity. The state assimilates identities and nations from outside its sovereign jurisdiction and into its mandate to enable subjectivity though recognition on its own terms. This enables it to create the national subject, stateless subject, or any other subject. These subjects become recognised according to the state's own legal frameworks and needs as a project of formation, with a predetermined national identity for further reproduction.

Over 100,000 stateless people live in Kuwait. They are known as 'the Bidoon' and constitute about 10% of the Kuwaiti national population. Some estimates suggest that the actual number of Bidoon exceeds 200,000, though this number still excludes those who have been exiled or who migrated to other countries for citizenship (Human Rights Watch, 1995). The term 'Bidoon' is a colloquial term in Arabic meaning 'without'. It is also used informally to signify any person who is 'Bidoon Jinsiya' [without citizenship] or [without nationality] in Kuwait. Before the term existed, those who became 'Bidoons' were known by their tribal background and affiliation, mostly as Arab Bedouins.

Over the years, and specifically since the 1959 nationality law in Kuwait, the Bidoons' material and ideological conditions have developed in ways that have produced an ideological and ontological separation from the citizen body. They have come to be seen as a different class or ethnic group. This was made possible by shifting their legal classifications, marginalising them into isolated social and physical realms, erasing their historical conditions of existence and ties with land, and painting them as 'unlawful' people through state propaganda (see also Benswait, this volume).

The majority of Bidoon people derive from a Northern nomadic tribal background. These tribes travelled and resided in the deserts of the Arabian Peninsula for generations prior to the establishment of the modern state of Kuwait. The first nationality law in Kuwait was established in 1948. However, it was not applied effectively, and many nomadic Bedouins were exempt from it as borders remained flexible. Further, the law specified that only those who settled in Kuwait prior to 1920 were considered citizens, which made it naturally discriminatory towards many tribes who travelled regularly and settled for short periods of time due to seasonal changes as a way of life. Nonetheless, the 1948 nationality law remained open to *jus soli* citizenship for those who have settled in Kuwait for ten years. However, due to geopolitical tensions in the early 1950s and the wave of Arab nationalism across the region, there were local impacts on members of the population who formed a political opposition party. This led to the dropping of the *jus soli* citizenship and the restricting of citizenship and voting rights in order to minimise the effect and increase of potential opposition against the regime, which led to the forming of the amended 1959 nationality law (Beaugrand, 2018: 78). Between 1959 and 1965, committees for nationality registration took place in the old town of Kuwait (now Kuwait City). While some tribes who were settled in the suburbs were naturalised, the rest were excluded from this process.

Dominant literature on the Bidoon specifies that the reasons for exclusion were because they lived far away in the desert areas and were unaware of the registration process or 'failed' to register. Other reasons contributing to their exclusion are rarely mentioned. First, some people ignored the concept of having documentation and state borders because it went against their ways of living and being as nomadic peoples (Human Rights Watch, 1995). As such, many individuals were unable to provide formal proof of their residence within the borders during the period of citizenship registration. Second, witness testimonies or affidavits became necessary to the process of registration. For some, this was impossible to provide. Finally, some of those who would become 'Bidoon' tried to register after the deadline. They were offered second-class citizenship but refused it on the grounds that it was discriminatory and hierarchical.[1]

Many Bidoon had either documentation that proved their affiliation and residency through employment, or 1965 census papers, but without being naturalised. The Kuwaiti government promised to naturalise the Bidoon who held proof of the 1965 census data – which according to the Nationality Law of 1959 is a requirement to be eligible for citizenship – but this promised naturalisation did not materialise. Until 1986, the Bidoon had access to all the same rights as citizens, except political participation (Human Rights Watch, 1995). In 1986, the Kuwaiti government changed the status of the Bidoon, making them 'illegal', stripping them of all the rights they used to enjoy. The government has since continued to make promises to naturalise Bidoons with a 1965 census proof of registration, though this has still not materialised (Al-Othman, 2012; Kuwait Times, 2019; Saleh, 2019).

The shifts in the classifications of the Bidoon, from 'Badiyat Al-Kuwait' [Kuwaiti tribes], 'Bidoon Jinsya' [without nationality] (where the term 'Bidoon' originates), to having 'Ghair Muhadadin Al-jinsiya' [undetermined nationality], to 'Muqim bi Sura Ghair Qanooniya' [illegal resident] demonstrate the intentional erasure of the Bidoon's history and land affiliations by the state. It also homogenised people with diverse backgrounds into one legal category. This stripped them of their agency and autonomy as diverse tribes that have long resided in the area now known as Kuwait. This strategy of denationalisation (Human Rights Watch, 1995) developed social, economic, and psychological impacts on the Bidoon (see Benswait, this volume). Further, these legal categories created a new ontological status that fits within the legal frameworks of the sovereign state, along with categories for other forms of non-citizenship like 'foreign residents' (locally known as 'wafidun' [migrants]). Evidence of the ideological impacts of these government practices and other forms of knowledge production appear in the debates on the Bidoon's eligibility for citizenship.

In recent years, Bidoon activists have been more vocal about their right to Kuwaiti citizenship. This has included revealing their living conditions to the public to gain support (Amnesty International, 2019; Beaugrand, 2014 and 2018). This has led to growing debates on Kuwaiti media platforms about nationality and national identity. On these platforms, some Kuwaitis argue there are 'deserving' and 'non-deserving' Bidoon based on whether or not they have acquired documents through processes like the 1965 census. Some Kuwaitis reject Bidoon inclusion. This is framed as being in order to protect Kuwaiti national identity (see *The New Arab*, 2019). These narratives are not new to the public. They have been used by preceding governments and have shaped public opinions relating to citizenship, including the Bidoons' right to citizenship, for a long time.

Power structures and dominant discourses continue to promote false information about Bidoon in Kuwait. This includes framing the Bidoon as a 'problem' that needs to be solved and a 'ticking bomb' (Al-Monitor, 2012) that causes anxiety for the government. Meanwhile, there have been growing xenophobic discourses against the migrant populations in Kuwait. This has included calls to 'fix the demographics' or 'population imbalance' (Eldemerdash, 2015), deport 'unlawful migrants', and nationalise their occupations (see Al-Hashem, 2019). The use of this language demonstrates that non-Kuwaitis are untrustworthy. They are often blamed for corruption and the unemployment of citizens (Al-Hashem, 2019), while the historical and ongoing contributions of migrant labour for state-building during its development stages is left out of the conversation (Eldemerdash, 2015).

The educational apparatus

A state's public education system plays a key role in producing and reproducing its ideological formation. I trace the ideological formations of the Kuwaiti nation-state in its educational curriculum and textbooks. This enables an understanding of how public opinions are formed about citizenship and nationality laws. I analyse a grade four public-school textbook called *My Nation* (MOE, 2018) to draw connections between the ideological constructions of the Kuwaiti nation-state in education and their manifestations in other state structures and discourses.

The textbook begins with a definition of a state and describes the concept of a sovereign territory and its borders alongside other independent sovereign territories.[2] On the next page, there is a picture of a customs agent in an airport speaking to a child. The child is telling the agent about his nationality as 'Kuwaiti'. The child explains that he 'belongs to Kuwait' and 'lives on its land and holds its identity'. The child goes on to describe Kuwait as having 'a sovereign authority governing the relationship between its people'. Below that conversation is a drawing of the territorial map of Kuwait followed by an exercise that asks students to read sentences under pictures of other children holding flags of other countries. The student reading this text is asked to identify with the children pictured, and to write his or her name and nationality on a blank picture of an identification card in the exercise part of the introductory section (MOE, 2018: 13–17).

The introduction of the book carries a significant ideological meaning. It hails the readers as national subjects through their recognition in national categories. It also depends on an abstract recognition of formal citizenship while equating it to national identity to construct one's existence. Furthermore, it normalises the idea of borders and sovereign territory, disregarding non-citizenship (specifically statelessness) and assuming everyone belongs to a nation naturally. This notion of national belonging through citizenship and territory, although disputable in the historical national literature, suggests that the understanding of nationality is built upon the conflation of territory, citizenship, and identity as a homogenous entity (Beaugrand, 2018).

Crucially for the Kuwait context, national symbols have significant roles in the historical national narrative. The textbook draws on islands and desert prairies as Kuwaiti landscapes. However, it does not give the desert the same level of significance with historical meaning other than nature. There are pages describing the history of pearl diving and marine life and other pages highlighting the activities that took place in the town near the coast, but the desert received almost no attention in a similar manner. Even the sections that discussed the settlement of the 'founding Kuwaitis' highlighted their migration through the sea. This is especially ironic, considering Kuwait has a large tribal citizen population whose ancestors were settled in the deserts of the region. The lack of emphasis on the desert ignores the histories of tribes as part of the official national narrative. Thus, it perpetuated the prejudice against Bedouin tribes (Beaugrand, 2018), which contributes to the erasure of Bidoon histories as predominantly Bedouins (Kennedy, 2016).

Literature on Kuwaiti history has largely focused on the project of modern nation building while separating from its historical transnational affiliations (Alrabei, 2018). In doing this, the nation-state asserts itself not as a new entity, but as one with a much longer history. This includes the erasure of the conditions of its origins. In order to assert its credibility, the

Kuwaiti nation-state presents itself as if it has always been on the world map. This erasure of transnational and nomadic histories is a widespread phenomenon in the world, including the Gulf where tribes lived and travelled freely (see Kazmova, this volume; Spertfeldt, this volume). The concept of nomadism was considered a threat to the governments of the new Gulf states, and erasing their histories was crucial for the nation-building project (Beaugrand, 2018). This has in turn left many nomadic tribes vulnerable to state violence.

Another section of the Kuwaiti school textbook discusses the ways in which population increases happen. It includes two photos: one of newborn babies in a hospital room, the other of the baggage claim area at the airport. The people in the latter picture are predominantly members of Kuwait's visible migrant communities. Under the first picture is the phrase 'natural increases in population'. Under the second picture is the phrase 'unnatural increases in population'. On the same page, there is a diagram showing the ratio between so-called 'Kuwaitis' and 'non-Kuwaitis' in Kuwait (30% Kuwaitis, 70% non-Kuwaitis) (MOE, 2018: 75).

The textbook exhibits various messages that connect to the hegemonic ideology of nationalism and belonging that produces the current structure of exclusion of non-citizens in Kuwait. First, it projects an idea that being born in the nation-state is the only natural way to belong to it, and inflows of migrants give rise to unnatural increases in the population. This type of content implicitly demonstrates that anyone who is a migrant is unnatural to the nation. This feeds into xenophobic public discourses against non-citizen residents, including the Bidoon, as 'outsiders' to the nation (Eldemerdash, 2015). This is a tactic of fearmongering. Second, it shows how governance of Kuwaiti identity depends on both homogenising diverse groups to manage their differences and creating a dichotomy of Kuwaiti and non-Kuwaiti.

These processes are not only evident in the educational context. They can be found across forms of official Kuwaiti government communication. It is common that official government announcements and newspaper agencies frame their stories around the nationality of the subject of the story and classify numbers into national categories. This reinforces xenophobic attitudes towards particular groups (Al-Khonaini, 2020). In reality, both the Kuwaiti citizen population and the Bidoon and immigrant populations in Kuwait are diverse. Indeed, these various groups overlap with each other in many ways.[3] Nevertheless, these similarities are erased and assimilated into an abstract and manageable category of difference within the legal and national framework.[4] In contexts where citizenship performs as nationality, structures of governance orbit around discourses of national identity.

Representations of non-citizen other(s):
The narrative of the Iraqi invasion of Kuwait

Positive representations of non-citizens do exist in Kuwait. That is, while some successful stories about the Bidoon and immigrants are celebrated, they are seen only as individual achievements and not as reflective of the national communities they belong to.[5] This is in contrast to what happens with respect to the majority population. Stories of successful individuals in the national population in Kuwait are celebrated as a national achievement,[6] while negative ones are dissociated as anomalous.[7] On the other hand, negative representations of non-citizens are attributed to the entire collective. This can be seen through a consideration of the roles played by various individuals in one of the most significant events in Kuwait's national story.

The 1990 Iraqi invasion of Kuwait marks one of the most significant events in Kuwait's history as a nation-state. Stories of resistance, unity, and sacrifices in the face of the enemy during the war have shaped the Kuwaiti national identity since that time. However, narratives of the war have also been used to demonise the Bidoon, mostly painting them as traitors who have joined the Iraqi popular army (Human Rights Watch, 1995). These representations ignore how the Bidoon have been part of the resistance and were under gunpoint when asked to join. They also ignore that the majority were part of the Kuwaiti resistance during that time. The Bidoon constituted 90–95% of the armed forces (Human Rights Watch, 1995: 29). Many were even among those taken by the Iraqi army and held as hostages (Human Rights Watch, 1995). Instead of mentioning this contribution to the Kuwaiti war effort, official narratives often focus on how some Bidoon and immigrants supported or joined the Iraqi popular army with no emphasis on the context or the fact that the majority resisted and fought (Human Rights Watch, 1995: 23; Eldemedrash, 2015). This was an army recruited by the Iraqi forces during their occupation. It is suggested, then, that the Bidoon in fact betrayed the people of Kuwait after years of living among them and receiving benefits from the state and are originally Iraqis claiming to be Kuwaitis (Human Rights Watch, 1995; Eldemerdash, 2015). This in turn fuelled the anti-Bidoon policies that emerged in the aftermath of the war like leaving many Bidoon in exile or laid out from the army and other jobs (among other things).

These narratives take the examples of a few who have been coerced into joining the Iraqi army and associate their actions with the entire group. This in turn feeds into discourses on immigrants and Bidoon as being dangerous and untrustworthy, with divided loyalty. As forms of exaltation, these representations enable the nation to see itself as unified in the face of threats. These threats come not only from outside of their borders, but from those whose bodies exist inside Kuwait but are represented as embodying an out-side threat. Despite the fact that both Kuwaiti citizens and the Bidoon both served loyally and a few only were coerced into the Iraqi army, this exaltation emphasises the loyalty and sacrifice attributed to the national subject, as well as the disloyalty and treason attributed to the Bidoon.

The exalted subject of the nation-state

The conditions for granting citizenship, as well as the processes of migration and inclusion, have always been important tools for national formation (Thobani, 2007; Sharma, 2015; Alrabei, 2018). As such, calling for inclusion of stateless persons into state membership without challenging the nationally defined structures of citizenship which exclude them cannot end statelessness (Tonkiss, 2017: 246). Such structures are designed to recognise specific 'produced' national traits (Eldemerdash, 2015). However, many individuals may lack these traits. As a result, individuals will be excluded from the national collective on the basis of criteria made for a few. In this way, national identity is an exalted identity, made through self-representation in relation to the excluded Other.

Master narratives of Kuwaiti nationhood define the national character relationally. Stuart Hall (1992) calls these processes 'narratives of nation-hood' (293). For Hall, these narratives create representations of the nation and its national identity. In doing this, they justify the entitlements of the citizen to the benefits and welfare of the state, and by extension justify the exclusion of others from the same rights. In the Kuwaiti national imaginary, the Bidoon are framed as strangers to the nation, and presented as making ridiculous claims to citizenship rights.

Kuwaiti national narratives take as their point of departure the authentic and lawful character of its nationals. In labelling Bidoons as 'illegal residents', the state correlates negative features of unlawfulness and deceitfulness with them. It simultaneously correlates positive (and aspirational) characteristics of lawfulness and authenticity with nationals. This puts the national subject at the top of a state-constructed moral hierarchy. Examples of these negative features include government statements that demonstrate they have documents proving the affiliation of many Bidoon people to other neighbouring countries, making their claims to the right of citizenship seem invalid and dishonest (Alanba, 2011). Yet, they have never displayed these documents nor referred any Bidoon to court for fraud.

There is an invisible discourse happening in parallel with the rhetoric of the Kuwaitis being 'authentic' citizens. This invisible discourse naturalises citizens as 'natives' to the nation, and non-citizens as outsiders who do not belong. It is commonly reiterated by officials that Bidoons should prove their 'true origin' and that 'Kuwait is for Kuwaitis', indicating only 'true Kuwaitis' belong (see Izzak, 2018; Al-Duwaisan, 2019; Al-Hashem, 2019; Izzak, 2019). These claims are situated within paradigms of original membership that assume everyone naturally belongs to a state (Cole, 2019). Such assumptions imply by extension that the Bidoon would also naturally belong to a state, just not to Kuwait. This drives a myth of 'authenticity', which relies on reducing belonging and nationality to a formal document (Alrabei, 2018). Thus, such arguments implicitly form ideas that those who are citizens of Kuwait belong to it naturally. This obscures the ways in which the nation-state is a modern establishment built on multiple settlements and created with legal structures that recognise some humans and exclude others. This is where we can see the ideological connections with state education as a process of interpellation of national identity through legal recognition only.

Anti-migrant discourses act as gatekeeping mechanisms to nationality, too. Many non-citizen residents living in Kuwait were born in the country, or have lived in Kuwait for most of their lives. Many have no alternative nation-state with which to associate themselves. Despite this, they are consistently assumed to be more loyal to their 'national origin'. Their existence is reduced to their labour capacities and any belonging they may have is seen to derive from this alone. Theirs is a permanent–temporary status of membership that remains conditional and ideologically outside the national boundaries.

Viewing national identity through the lens of exaltation suggests that these processes of exclusion affect even citizens who face marginalisation. The framing of non-citizenship as a danger to the nation not only affects the Bidoon and immigrants. It also impacts Kuwaiti women who marry non-Kuwaitis. Discourses on women's right to pass their nationality to their children and spouses show similar tensions. Kuwaiti women are restricted from passing nationality to their children and spouses. This means that the children of Kuwaiti women with Bidoon men may be left without access to any citizenship (e.g. see Al Barazi and Tucker, 2017). This is rooted in the patriarchal underpinnings of familial and national structures in Gulf nation-states, which render access to citizenship through the male figure. However, while there is a gender discrimination component to this, it intersects with a structure of racism and nationalism that together shape nationality laws and the politics of inclusion and exclusion (see Buterman, this volume; Brennan et al., this volume). Not only is there a rejection of complete agency and citizenship for women, but there is also a rejection of the idea that certain undesired groups can be included as citizens. There is an ethnic and racial idea of what makes someone a 'proper' national subject (Eldemerdash,

2015), and it gets intertwined with women's freedom in extending that citizenship to those who may not fit this idea. As such, structures of racism and patriarchy operate in inter-constitutive ways in restricting nationality in Kuwait.

Reframing statelessness in Kuwait: The national–stateless–migrant trialectic

Stateless people, migrants, and all non-citizen Others play crucial roles in the project of nation building. They are ideologically and materially intertwined with the constructions of nationality and citizenship. These Others are passively engaged in the politics of identity and belonging that re-inscribe them into the nation-state as new types of subjects to encounter. In this way, they also shape national identity. There is, then, what can be called a 'trialectic' in the construction of Kuwaiti national identity (terminology from Veracini, cited in Lowman and Barker, 2015: 28). A 'trialectic' describes a complex set of practices, discourses, and identities generated and imposed from the top to the bottom. The trialectic producing Kuwaiti national identity is premised on the perception of three subjectivities created by the sovereign: Kuwaiti national, immigrant Other, and Bidoon Other.

As figures constituted to be incommensurable with the national subject, both the Bidoon Other and the immigrant Other play vital roles in how the national subject sees themselves and their national community. The encounters of the Bidoon and the immigrant with the national subject determine how the Kuwaiti national is formed. The national subject is shaped through a process of differentiation among various Others which it encounters. In their exclusion and representation as threats to the national identity, these strangers become ontologised as strangers and are ideologically necessary to form and sustain the characteristics that the national community embodies.

Conclusion

In this chapter, I stress the need to look beyond the legal causes associated with statelessness in order to explore the foundational problems that produce it. I urge us to expand the frameworks to explore the ontological and ideological questions of identity and belonging within the nation-state. In problematising and challenging the assumptions people have about who they are and what this means for their place in the world, we challenge the legal and political structures that form and are formed by these ideologies.

The nation-state depends on the creation of ontologies and ideologies to govern differences between diverse groups of people within its territory. It uses representations, classifications, and narratives in knowledge platforms like education and media in order to reproduce its nation and sustain its sovereignty. In problematising the making of Kuwaiti citizenship as a process of exaltation and exclusion of different subjects, we can see how Bidoon statelessness is inherent to the processes of producing the national subject. Thus, rather than calling for simple inclusion of stateless people, we must approach statelessness by diving deeper into the problematic formations of nationality laws and the ways in which they are fundamentally built on specific forms of exclusion. This is a necessary commitment in order to re-imagine the ways in which citizenship can be amended to end Bidoon statelessness, and further exclusions.

Notes

1 Interview conducted by author with Bidoon activist, June 2018.
2 Quotations from the textbook are translated from the original Arabic by the author.
3 The different national groups also share similar tribal backgrounds, similar religious sects, and are involved through kinships.
4 Susan Kennedy Nour al Deen (2018) discusses how the discourses on Bedouin citizens and conflicts between 'badu' and 'hadar' in Kuwait neglect how the Bidoon are part of that category as predominantly Bedouin tribes, and how they are affected by the state prejudices against Bedouins even more than citizens with tribal roots.
5 For instance, a former Bidoon football player has been celebrated for being a prominent player for the national football team. Although he has the right to citizenship, the media and government framed his naturalisation as a result of his contributions to the reputation of Kuwait though his athletic skills (Eremnews, 2016).
6 Media platforms combine and frame stories of individual achievements as national pride. See: https://twitter.com/anjazq8?lang=en.
7 Crime reporting on citizens often states their occupation or gender rather than nationality. This is in contrast to the reporting of crimes committed by non-citizens, where the headlines state their nationality in bold fonts.

References

Al Barazi, Z., and Tucker, J. (2017) 'Challenging the disunity of statelessness in the Middle East and North Africa', in T. Bloom, K. Tonkiss, and P. Cole (eds) *Understanding Statelessness* (Abingdon: Routledge).

Al-'الفضالة: تجنيس البدون حملة إحصاء 65 وما قبله شريطة الإقامة بصفة دائمة' (2011) Alanba-
  Fadhalah: Naturalizing the Bidoon holding the 1965 census proof with the
  condition of consistent residency'], *Alanba*, 13 June [Online]. Available at www.
  alanba.com.kw/ar/kuwait-news/203926/13-6-2011 (Accessed 15 June 2020).

Alrabei, T. (2018) 'Bidun poets and Kuwaiti literary history', *Journal of Arabian
  Studies: Arabia, the Gulf, and the Red Sea*, 8:2, 193–207.

Al-Duwaisan, F. (2019) 'Political dialogue [Al-Hiwar Al-Seyasi]', *ATV Kuwait*
  [Online]. Available at www.youtube.com/watch?v=_aeeEBEc8Z8 (Accessed 5
  June 2020).

Al-Hashem, S. (2019) 'Political dialogue [Al-Hiwar Al-Seyasi]', *ATV Kuwait*
  [Online]. Available at www.youtube.com/watch?v=8c5XCtFgiFU (Accessed 5
  June 2020).

Al-Khonaini, A. (2020) 'How Covid-19 stress-tested relations between residents and
  citizens in Kuwait', *Gulf International Forum*, 29 April [Online]. Available at
  https://gulfif.org/how-covid-19-stress-tested-relations-between-residents-citizens-
  in-kuwait/ (Accessed 5 June 2020).

Al-Monitor (2012) 'Kuwait's "stateless" class: A ticking time bomb', *Al-Monitor*,
  12 May [Online]. Available at www.al-monitor.com/pulse/culture/2012/05/the-
  stateless-issue-kuwait-bomb.html (Accessed 3 November 2019).

لمى العثمان: الجويهليون العنصريون دفنوا ضمائرهم في مقابر جماعية وأسسوا حزباً (2012) Al-Othman, L.
  يتعرض لكرامات الناس وأصولهم' ['The racists have buried their consciousness in a mass
  grave and created a party that disrespects the dignity and ancestry of people'],
  Sabr, 12 May [Online]. Available at www.sabr.cc/2012/05/12/57699/ (Accessed
  15 June 2020).

Amnesty International (2019) 'Kuwait: Authorities crackdown on protesters
  demanding citizenship rights' [Online]. Available at www.amnesty.org/en/
  latest/news/2019/07/kuwait-authorities-crackdown-on-protesters-demanding-
  citizenship-rights/ (Accessed 3 November 2019).

Beaugrand, C. (2014) 'Framing nationality in the migratory context: The elusive
  category of Biduns in Kuwait', *Middle East Law and Governance*, 6:3, 173–203.

Beaugrand, C. (2018) *Stateless in the Gulf: Migration, Nationality and Society in
  Kuwait* (London and New York: I.B. Taurus).

Cole, P. (2019) 'Taking statelessness seriously', *Statelessness and Citizenship Review*,
  1:1, 161–164.

Eldemerdash, N. (2015) 'Being and belonging in Kuwait: Expatriates, stateless
  peoples and the politics of citizenship', *Anthropology of the Middle East*, 10:2,
  83–100.

رسمياً.. فهد العنزي يحصل على الجنسية الكويتية' (2016) Eremnews ['Officially, Fahad Al-Enezi
  acquires Kuwaiti citizenship'], 15 August [Online]. Available at www.eremnews.
  com/sports/football/arab/545737 (Accessed 13 June 2020).

Hall, S. (1992) 'The question of cultural identity', in T. McGrew, S. Hall, and D.
  Held (eds) *Modernity and Its Futures: Understanding Modern Societies, Book IV*
  (Cambridge: Polity Press): pp. 273–326.

Human Rights Watch (1995) 'The Bedoons of Kuwait: "Citizens without
  citizenship"' [Online]. Available at www.hrw.org/reports/1995/Kuwait.htm
  (Accessed 5 June 2020).

Izzak, B. (2018) 'Expats blamed for rampant graft in Kuwait', *Zawya*, 15 March [Online]. Available at www.zawya.com/uae/en/legal/story/Expats_blamed_for_rampant_graft_in_Kuwait-SNG_112038233/ (Accessed 5 June 2020).

Izzak, B. (2019) 'MPs call on government to cut expat numbers by 50%', *Kuwait Times*, 11 March [Online]. Available at https://news.kuwaittimes.net/website/mps-call-on-government-to-cut-expat-numbers-by-50/ (Accessed 5 June 2020).

Kennedy, S. (2016) 'The stateless Bedouin in Kuwait society: A study of Bedouin identity, culture and the growth of an intellectual ideal' (PhD thesis, University of Adelaide) [Online]. Available at https://digital.library.adelaide.edu.au/dspace/bitstream/2440/119698/2/02whole.pdf (Accessed 10 October 2019).

Kuwait Times (2019) 'Govt. determined to resolve bedoons problem: Saleh', 25 August [Online]. Available at https://news.kuwaittimes.net/website/govt-determined-to-resolve-bedoons-problem-saleh/ (Accessed 5 June 2020).

Lowman, E. B., and Barker, A. J. (2015) *Settler: Identity and Colonialism in 21st Century Canada* (Halifax: Fernwood Publishing).

Ministry of Education (MOE) (2018) *My Nation Kuwait [Beladi Al-Kuwait]*, Ministry of Education for Kuwait [Online]. Available at https://school-kw.com/file/1663/ (Accessed 5 June 2020).

Saleh, A. (2019) 'National Assembly panel to discuss bedoons' proposed bill next week', *Kuwait Times*, 3 November [Online]. Available at https://news.kuwaittimes.net/website/national-assembly-panel-to-discuss-bedoons-proposed-bill-next-week/ (Accessed 5 June 2020).

Sharma, N. (2015) *Home Economics: Nationalism and the Making of 'Migrant Workers' in Canada* (Toronto: University of Toronto Press).

The New Arab (2019) 'Kuwait promises "fair solution" for stateless Bidoon population, but rejects citizenship', 23 July [Online]. Available at https://english.alaraby.co.uk/english/news/2019/7/23/kuwait-promises-solutions-for-bidoon-population-but-rejects-citizenship (Accessed 5 June 2020).

Thobani, S. (2007) *Exalted Subjects: Studies in the Making of Race and Nation in Canada* (Toronto: University of Toronto Press).

Tonkiss, K. (2017) 'Statelessness and the performance of citizenship-as-nationality', in T. Bloom, K. Tonkiss, and P. Cole (eds) *Understanding Statelessness* (Abingdon: Routledge): pp. 241–254.

25

'We are *not* stateless! You can call us what you like, but we are citizens of Myanmar!': Rohingya resistance and the stateless label

Natalie Brinham

We are not stateless! We are already part of a state! We have built our Myanmar nation. We also have all our documents. Why are they [international lawyers] calling us stateless?

These are the words of one of many Rohingyas seeking safe return to their homeland. Such individuals feel that their identities and their futures are being negatively impacted both by the production of statelessness in Myanmar and by the label 'stateless' that frames understandings of their persecution in international discourses. For Rohingya, this label can profoundly affect international approaches to securing their futures in Myanmar and beyond. Why Rohingya resist, reject, or adopt the 'stateless' label has not yet been explored in academic literature. This chapter begins to fill that gap, using an empirical approach.

Based on narrative research with Rohingya in Bangladesh, Malaysia, and India between 2017 and 2019 with 100 participants in focus groups and interviews,[1] this chapter considers how Rohingya negotiate, resist, and problematise the labelling process. It explores Rohingya narratives relating to their identity documents and citizenship with a focus on how and why they resist the categories and labels that frame them domestically and internationally as 'stateless'. Legal definitions and social labelling are intertwined and mutually enforcing. This chapter first focuses on the categorisation of Rohingya as 'stateless' as a legal definition. It then considers the term as a social label. It concludes by suggesting that until the categorisation of 'stateless' can deliver tangible human rights and protection benefits for Rohingya populations globally, the term will remain contested. All the Rohingya narratives within this research asserted that state-led attempts to strip them of their citizenship should be viewed within the broader context of state crime.[2] Their demands are for recognition and restoration of their citizenship in Myanmar as an integral part of the pursuit for safety, justice, and restitution.

'Stateless' as a legal definition

Rohingya have been described as *de jure* stateless by human rights organisations and bodies since the mid-1990s (Human Rights Watch, 1996). The United Nations High Commissioner for Refugees (UNHCR) established a presence in Rakhine State in Myanmar in 1994 to monitor the mass repatriations of Rohingya from Bangladesh to Myanmar. Securing identity documents for returnees and other Rohingya in Myanmar was at the forefront of UNHCR negotiation and advocacy strategies. The term 'stateless' to describe Rohingya fell into common usage at this time. Rohingya statelessness is generally described as resulting from the 1982 Citizenship Law (see Socialist Republic of the Union of Burma, 1982), passed by the military government of General Ne Win. The new law severely restricted the acquisition of citizenship through criteria other than membership of the ethnic groups listed by the Council of the State as pre-colonial. Rohingya were not included on the list of 135 ethnic nationalities and there was no alternative category available to them.

The 1982 law also introduced a tiered system of citizenship with members of the listed national ethnic groups at the top. A different set of rights and rules was applied to each category. The evidentiary requirements to qualify for lesser forms of citizenship including 'naturalised citizenship' are high,[3] and this law contains no safeguards against statelessness (ENS and ISI, 2019). From 1995 until 2015, Rohingya were provided with 'white cards' or 'temporary registration cards', which were ordinarily given to those who needed replacement citizenship cards. The vast majority of Rohingya have been unable to secure citizenship documents since the 1982 law came into effect. Since the 1990s, the Myanmar state has claimed that Rohingya are racially 'Bengali', so cannot be full citizens under section 3 of the citizenship law. The ethnic/racial groups that legally belong are decided at the full discretion of the Council of the State, according to section 4.[4] As a result, Rohingya are 'not considered as national(s) by any state under the operation of its law' and were accordingly defined as stateless (United Nations, 1954: Article 1.1).

During the period of military rule from the 1990s until 2012, international agencies mostly confined legal analysis of Myanmar citizenship frameworks to where they failed to comply with international law and resulted in statelessness (Brinham, 2019). Legal analyses were muted on two issues. First, they ignored whether most Rohingya had been recognised as Myanmar citizens under the 1948 provisions prior to the enactment of the 1982 Citizenship Law. Second, they generally did not consider the widespread practices by state authorities of confiscating and/or destroying Rohingya's identity documents, which could be used as evidence of citizenship. According to Rohingya accounts, such practices have been widespread and have occurred intermittently since 1974. Rohingya have been consistent in stating that they used to hold the same documents and enjoy the same rights as all other citizens of Myanmar. As more evidence of such state practices surfaced after 2012 – which marked the first major wave of state-sponsored violence against Rohingya since the period of military rule – legal researchers increasingly focused on these two issues.

The 1982 Citizenship Law stipulates in section 6 that those who were citizens before the law came into force shall remain citizens. Thus, by showing that Rohingya were formerly considered citizens but lacked evidence due to the arbitrary removal, destruction, or non-issuance of identity documents, researchers challenged the categorisation of Rohingya as *de jure* stateless, showing how they were entitled to status under the existing legal framework. They suggested instead that Rohingya were *de facto* stateless or 'presumed' stateless (Cheesman, 2017a; Nyi Nyi Kyaw, 2017). During the same period, UNHCR was also in the process of providing further guidance on the interpretation of the 1954 Statelessness Convention. In 2014, they clarified the meaning of 'under the operation of its laws'. Whether a person is considered to *not* to be a national is described as a 'mixed question of fact and law' (UNHCR, 2014: article 23). This guidance was provided in order to give legal clarity to the long-standing conceptual confusions between *de jure* and *de facto* statelessness. Accordingly, regardless of whether it was law or practice that rendered them so, Rohingya are still considered stateless since Myanmar (and all other states) officially deny their right to citizenship.

Following the mass expulsions of close to three-quarters of a million Rohingya from Myanmar to Bangladesh in 2016 and 2017, there was increased access for human rights researchers to affected Rohingya populations. Now able to congregate in groups with fewer safety concerns, Rohingya refugees began to gather and collect old documents relating to their citizenship, land rights, and to past state recognition of their Rohingya identity. As social movements gained momentum, Rohingya demanded Myanmar's recognition of their group claim to citizenship as a precondition of repatriation to Myanmar. As part of this demand, they resisted attempts by the Bangladesh government and UNHCR to collect their biometric data. This was a pre-emptive attempt to prevent their data being shared with Myanmar and risk being documented or categorised as 'stateless' or 'foreign' upon return (Brinham, 2018).

At this time, some Rohingya demanded that international researchers stop calling them 'stateless' and stop condoning the existing verification and documentation schemes in Myanmar. Within this context, the Independent International Fact Find Mission (IIFFM) report described Rohingya as *de facto* stateless against the grain of other reports. The report shifted the framing of the production of their statelessness away from the content of the 1982 Citizenship Law alone to focus on the unlawful and arbitrary practices of Myanmar's state authorities relating to registration and identity cards (UNHRC, 2018: 110–119). This approach inserted the voices of Rohingya that had strongly rejected the 'statelessness' label.[5] Underlining this, Rohingya genocide survivors were brought from the refugee camps in Bangladesh to speak at the Human Rights Council in Geneva for the first time in March 2019. In Mohib Ullah's impassioned speech, he stated: 'We are *not* stateless. Stop calling us that! So, we want to go home... with our rights and our citizenship. You can call us what you like – we are citizens of Myanmar'.

This clearly restated the Rohingya rejection of the 'stateless' label. Nevertheless, international lawyers working on the issue reasserted that Rohingya were *de jure* stateless according to international legal definitions. They raised concerns that the term '*de facto* stateless' muddied the legal waters. They noted that clarity was important in order to correctly identify the violation of rights and advocate internationally on the right to nationality. They argued that rather than discard or alter the term 'stateless' to refer to the Rohingya, it was important to reclaim and reassert it as an extreme and arbitrary violation of rights, and an imposed legal condition.[6]

However, as the legal category 'stateless' is discussed, disputed, and reasserted in international human rights circles, Rohingya resistance to the term has grown, along with their demands to have their identities recognised as 'Rohingya' and as citizens of Myanmar. This has left the human rights community that works on statelessness in an uncomfortable position. As Amal de Chickera stated at the World Conference on Statelessness and Inclusion in June 2019:

> As an advocate working in the international law space, how do I reconcile that the Rohingya are legally stateless – and that is an important advocacy message because we are fighting for the right to a nationality – with the notion and the belief among Rohingya that this term is imposed on them and that it is being used to undermine their connection and their claim on Burmese citizenship?

Beyond the legal binary: 'Stateless' as a social labelling process

Over decades, Rohingya have had externally ascribed terms and categories imposed on their group as part of a process of 'Othering', including terms like 'Kalar'[7] and 'Bengali'. Focus group participants and interviewees identified the term 'stateless' as an additional term used to Other them. They said that this term damaged their identity as a people that belonged to Myanmar's Rakhine region. Participants described feelings of hurt, anger, disempowerment, and anxiety that resulted not from the legal condition of statelessness, but from the labelling process itself.

Some rejected the term based on popular understandings that suggest stateless people are 'nowhere people' without a state or homeland. Others engaged with the term as relating to state recognition and the law. Discussions explored how the state in Myanmar has recognised Rohingya as citizens and when/if that recognition was withdrawn. They considered the content and legitimacy of the citizenship law and the gaps between the citizenship law and the practices of state authorities. They also discussed how law functions (and fails to function) in Rakhine society, and the similar lack of access to citizens' rights provided to those who hold citizenship cards (Rohingya, Myanmar Muslims, and ethnic nationalities).

The vast majority of Rohingya participants believed that the legal binaries of 'stateless person' and 'citizen' failed to capture how the Myanmar state had slowly eroded their citizenship status, rights, and identity over many decades. Some participants described how the issue of state recognition of their citizenship in Myanmar had been reduced in international legal circles to the question of whether or not they had been issued with particular ID cards. A common sentiment, for example, was: 'It is only that we do not have the right documents. We are already citizens'. They backed this up by describing how their citizenship had been recognised in various ways by the state before and after the ID card schemes were rolled out according to the 1982 Citizenship Law (from 1989 onwards).

Rohingya could participate in national and local elections, such as voting and standing for public office, until 2015. They paid formal and informal taxes and worked in public sector jobs ordinarily reserved for citizens, including in state education and health sectors, the judiciary, and public administration. They joined the state security forces, including the police force and army. Some continued to draw state pensions from these roles even after they were denied citizenship cards. Asked when Myanmar had cancelled their citizenship, participants came up with wide-ranging responses relating to their enactment of citizenship and to different state ID card schemes. Some Rohingya interviewees and focus group members argued they were still citizens and that the state's ongoing controversial attempts to roll out a new ID card scheme for Rohingya known as the National Verification Cards (NVCs) would potentially reify and give material form to the stateless category. Similar to the findings of other anthropological studies on ethnic classification, the ID cards were commonly understood not as objects that reflected objective facts about their legal status, but rather created the categories themselves (Lehman, 1967; Leach, 1973; Mamdani, 1996; see also Benswait, this volume, and Vollmer, this volume).

There were very few participants who noted that their citizenship was 'cancelled' prior to the time when the term 'stateless' came into common usage in the mid-1990s.[8] In fact, several participants felt that the labelling process itself helped 'make' them stateless. While the identification of stateless persons is a key strand of international advocacy approaches, for many Rohingya the negative implications of the label was not balanced by international advocacy gains. Stemming from this – and from concerns about the current lack of international protection and action – was a resentment and mistrust of some UN agencies and international non-governmental organisations (INGOs) that had been operating in Myanmar. This was expressed by one participant, who explicitly blamed international organisations for statelessness:

> Because [the] UN told us to take the white cards [from 1995], they made us stateless... I hate that the UN started calling us stateless in the 1990s. It started from UNHCR. It is wrong. We are citizens... It [the 1982 Citizenship Law] was the genocidal law, but it was the UNHCR who were describing us as stateless. We are not stateless, we are citizens.

Throughout this research, Rohingya participants referred back to the fact that the designation of them as 'stateless' since the 1990s has brought no meaningful improvements in terms of access to protection, rights, or services in Myanmar, Bangladesh, Saudi Arabia, and Malaysia. The term thus holds little strategic value. In the context of long-term intergenerational displacement, where hope of return to Myanmar was diminished, the term 'stateless' was more acceptable than for those who had experiences of home in Myanmar. One participant observed: 'If people say that we are stateless, of course there should be special things for the stateless... like a right to travel or to survive'. That is, if there were protections or benefits associated with the term, then it may be more acceptable to them.

Stateless as a term that produces discourses of unbelonging

Many Rohingya participants resisted the 'stateless' label on the basis that it had long played into Myanmar's discourses of exclusion and entrenched popular understandings that Rohingya did not fully belong to Myanmar. One participant observed that '[i]t is our right to be citizens of the country, no matter whether they recognise us; we are still and still will be the people of the land. That is the reason we are denying we are stateless'. Another noted: 'Stateless [suggests] we were originally stateless – that we are not like locals'. That is, they felt that using the label 'stateless' risked affirming the state discourses that had systematically erased their history in Rakhine and Myanmar.

Rohingya focus groups explained how the conditions of statelessness were not created by the law alone, but also by Myanmar's practices of erasing Rohingya identity and thereby altering social relations. Rohingya as a term connotes belonging to both Rakhine state and to Myanmar. It is thereby a claim to full citizenship. Imposing state categories denoting foreignness was described as a key state strategy of identity erasure. 'Bengali' was the incorrect label imposed by Myanmar that created exclusion, and 'stateless' was the unwanted label imposed by international agencies that underlined that exclusion. The two processes were viewed as working side-by-side, influencing both domestic and international understandings of Rohingya identity as something 'Other' than fully Burmese, which all research participants consistently underlined was wrong.

This Otherness was described as being exacerbated by the INGOs and international agencies operating in Myanmar, which used the term 'stateless' while simultaneously avoiding use of the term 'Rohingya'. Many participants understood this to have undermined Rohingyas' identity as a group belonging to the Rakhine region and reproduced notions of unbelonging. The UN and INGO approach in Myanmar has been characterised by 'quiet diplomacy' and engagement with the military and civilian governments. This is pragmatic, ensuring that they maintain access to the country. Agencies including UNHCR have used euphemisms and descriptors instead of the term 'Rohingya' in meetings with or documents accessed by the Myanmar government (UNHCR Style Companion, 2012). The term 'stateless Muslim' was sometimes itself used as a euphemism to describe Rohingya (for example: McKinsey, 2012). Attempts to engage with the military and civilian governments in Myanmar often led UN agencies to downplay the role of the state in anti-Rohingya persecution. This included reference to 'communal violence' to describe what Rohingya called 'state violence' and 'genocide' (Cheesman, 2017a).

This was mirrored in international analyses of Myanmar's practices relating to citizenship and to the enumeration and registration of Rohingya populations. Published documents often evaded the issue of the unlawful and persecutory practices of the Myanmar state in relation to Rohingya citizenship. Rather than tackling the inherent racism in Myanmar's laws and institutions head on, they instead emphasised adjustments that could be made to existing administrative and legal frameworks to improve access to citizenship (Center for Diversity and National Harmony, 2019). This was viewed by research participants as legitimising both the militarised state and the military's laws. The global push for legal identities such as SDG 16.9 and the World Bank's ID4D (World Bank Group, 2018; Bloom, this volume) arguably also began reducing the right to nationality to the right to registration and ID documents (Oppenheim and Powell,

2015; Van Waas, 2015; Gelb and Manby, 2016; Manby, 2018; Bloom, this volume).

'Stateless' as a label and its connection with repatriations

Even as thousands of Rohingya fled across the border into Bangladesh in 2017, international attention turned to securing their right of return to Myanmar through repatriations. Though the vast majority of Rohingya were consistent in wanting to return when circumstances allow, past forced repatriations were also in their collective memories (Brinham, 2017; Crisp, 2018). Rohingyas organised and presented demands on the preconditions of return, based on the failures of past repatriations to secure their futures in Myanmar. The thrust of all the demands contained three interlinked elements: safety and security, direct return to their lands, and citizenship.

Citizenship as a precondition to return has become a key sticking point (Potter and Kyaw Win, 2019). Rohingya research participants recounted how citizenship and equal rights were not secured prior to previous returns from Bangladesh. Instead, the ID schemes that were later brought in under the premise that they would provide legal identities and pathways to citizenship (such as 'white cards' and NVCs) resulted in a further deterioration of their legal status, access to rights, and identity in Myanmar (Brinham, 2019; Fortify Rights, 2019). They expressed concern that the notion of their statelessness in the context of repatriations set the bar lower than that of other returning refugees in human rights terms. In contrast, they demanded citizenship restoration and recognition of their Rohingya identity to enable them to return on an equal footing with other populations of Myanmar.

There is a growing awareness of the potential for registration and ID schemes elsewhere to 'lock in statelessness' by labelling undocumented persons as non-nationals, including in the Dominican Republic, India, and various African and Asian contexts (Estonia: Vollmer, this volume; Dominican Republic: Wooding, this volume; Kuwait: Benswait, this volume). In some situations, this has led many key international actors, including UNHCR, to take more nuanced position on registration and documentation (Chaudhuri and König, 2018; Hayes de Kalaf, 2019; Manby, 2018).

Legal identities and pathways to citizenship

Research participants' most frequent objection to the statelessness discourse, as it related to them, was that it failed to effectively locate citizenship withdrawal within the wider processes of state persecution and failed to hold the military and civilian government responsible for the denial.[9] One focus group participant said: '[Citizenship denial] is their way to drive out all the people from the Burma side. The... Burma government used new policies including the new [1982] citizenship law... This is the master plan of the Burmese government'. That is, citizenship denial was understood as a pre-planned state strategy that aimed to ensure the state-led violence and mass expulsions of Rohingya since the 1970s resulted in their *permanent* physical removal from the territories of Myanmar.

This softly-softly approach of international organisations and bodies included discussion of expanding the scope of 'naturalisation' provisions within the existing law; a focus on reducing administrative barriers within the existing law; providing legal identities through state registration, ID card schemes, and biometric data collection; 'trust-building' and 'conflict resolution' approaches to ID card schemes; and 'capacity building' for law makers in Myanmar. Such 'pathways to citizenship' are still recommended as initial steps for expediency, before addressing the inherent issues of discrimination within the law and the state institutions that continue to produce and reproduce Rohingya statelessness (Advisory Commission on Rakhine State, 2017). Many Rohingya participants believed that such approaches legitimised discriminatory laws by reinforcing notions of their 'Otherness' and 'foreignness', and side-stepping their needs for restitution and justice. Additionally, approaches promoting 'naturalisation', 'verification', and registration require Rohingya to forsake their group identity, meaning that an individual's acceptance of identity cards is often viewed as 'selling out' to the state practices of identity erasure (Brinham, 2018 and 2019).[10]

Within the context of Myanmar's citizenship law – which affords full citizenship almost exclusively on the basis of membership of a group – nationality as an individual right and a collective identity are virtually indivisible (Socialist Republic of the Union of Burma, 1982: section 3; see also Cheesman, 2017b). International technical and financial support for state ID schemes within these paradigms is thus viewed with intense mistrust and frustration, as validating Myanmar's false narratives that Rohingya have never belonged to the country. Focus group participants voiced concerns that international organisations can, perhaps inadvertently, legitimise Myanmar's persecutory state ID schemes. For example: 'For the white card, UNHCR provided help. It was a tool of genocide. So is the NVC'. Rohingya have demanded that the parameters of policy discussions on their citizenship are considered within the broader approaches of state crime and international justice that seek accountability, restitution, and reparations. Although statelessness is often linked conceptually to genocide and atrocity crimes (Arendt, 1958; Blitz, 2017), Rohingya voices remind us that in practice the reduction of statelessness has become divorced from notions of state crime and welded to the international desirability of identity documents for all.

Rohingya have made some progress in this respect. International lawyers are consciously drawing attention to the fact that Myanmar is solely responsible for rendering Rohingya stateless and has violated its obligations under international law. According to this position, the issue should be rectified through significant changes in the law and/or state institutions that lead to the reinstatement of Rohingya's former citizenship. The recommendations of the IIFFM, for example, included the speedy restoration of Rohingya citizenship and an overhaul of the institutions that underpin it such as the security sector and the judiciary (UNHCR, 2018: 420–430).

The human rights violations associated with enforcing Myanmar's latest ID card scheme – NVCs since 2015 – are now well documented (Fortify Rights, 2019; Potter and Kyaw Win, 2019). Most international agencies no longer consider this verification process a viable way to secure legal identities or pathways to citizenship. However, the problems of the NVC scheme need to be understood within the broader international approaches to statelessness that underpin it and have been in place since the 1990s.

Conclusion

Some Rohingya have argued that the term 'stateless' influenced popular discourses that negatively impacted their identity claims, had very little strategic value in terms of social action or claiming rights, and profoundly impacted international policy discussions about repatriations and their possible futures in Myanmar. In rejecting the label, participants demand that the international human rights community recognise the arbitrary deprivation of their citizenship as an extreme violation of their rights for which the state is culpable. Further, the label of 'stateless' in the countries with the largest Rohingya populations is yet to be endowed with access to protections, rights, and services. Until that time, the 'stateless' label for Rohingya will most likely remain undesirable to those it describes.

It is not simply a lack of legal grounding or conceptual confusion in international discourses and media of the term 'stateless' that undermines Rohingya identity and belonging. It is also the language, the silences, and the policy approaches of international organisations that have surrounded the term. Approaching the production of Rohingya statelessness in Myanmar within a state crime context and as an issue of international justice can potentially mitigate some of the side effects of the label. Further, understanding the production of statelessness as an extension or tool of state persecution, rather than a series of administrative barriers and errors, could potentially shift the paradigm and broaden the parameters of policy discussion to incorporate the legitimate concerns of Rohingya and other affected populations.[11] Rohingya are demanding that the international human rights community finds ways of approaching citizenship as an issue of international justice requiring restitution. Now is the time for active listening.

Notes

1 Focus groups and interviews took place in Malaysia, Bangladesh, India, and Europe. They were conducted in Rohingya language, Burmese language and, where applicable, English. A total of 12 interpreters took part in this process, including checking the interpretation. The names of all participants and interpreters are withheld for safety reasons in line with the QMUL ethics review.

2 State crime is defined as human rights abuses committed by states in pursuit of organisational goals (Green and Ward, 2004).

3 Unlike the 1948 citizenship rules, there are no provisions in the 1982 Citizenship Law to naturalise through marriage or long-term residence. The category of 'naturalised citizenship' in the 1982 Citizenship Law instead refers to those who can prove that their families lived permanently in Myanmar prior to independence in 1948.

4 Most Rohingya have also been unable to secure Bangladesh citizenship. Although the citizenship laws in Bangladesh have *jus soli* and naturalisation provisions, in practice Rohingya born in Bangladesh or married to Bangladeshis have been excluded from citizenship through civil documentation procedures (Hoque, 2016). However, it is important to note that the overwhelming thrust of the narratives in this research was of Rohingya claiming their right to citizenship in Myanmar, not the countries into which they had been displaced.

5 Some of this research took place before the report came out, so it was not possible to ask all participants if the term *de facto* stateless was more acceptable to them. Nonetheless, of those asked only one expressed that the term *de facto* stateless was preferable to *de jure* stateless.

6 As discussed during a World Conference on Statelessness panel entitled 'Strengthening a unified human rights voice on the Rohingya', The Hague, The Netherlands, 27 June 2019.

7 'Kalar' is a racist term denoting a lack of belonging and is used to describe Muslims or people of South Asian appearance.

8 Although many Rohingya actively rejected the term stateless, not all did. This chapter considers only those who rejected it.

9 In March 2020, I travelled with a group of Burmese and Rohingya for a study tour to the Jewish ghettos of Krakow and the Auschwitz labour and death camps. Comparisons were repeatedly made by the group between Myanmar and the Nazi use of ID cards, both to stigmatise and strip groups of their rights and agency.

10 'Selling out' and shame relating to the acceptance of NVCs were common themes in my research.
11 The Institute of Statelessness and Inclusion, for example, based on consultation with Rohingya communities, frames their statelessness within the concepts of genocide and citizenship stripping. See: Institute of Statelessness and Inclusion, 2020, 'Human rights and Covid-19: What now for the Rohingya?' https://files.institutesi.org/Covid19_The_Rohingya_Briefing_Paper.pdf (Accessed 16 November 2020).

References

Advisory Commission on Rakhine State (2017) 'Towards a peaceful, fair and prosperous future for the people of Rakhine: Final report' [Online]. Available at www.rakhinecommission.org/app/uploads/2017/08/FinalReport_Eng.pdf (Accessed 22 July 2020)

Arendt, H. (1958) *The Origins of Totalitarianism*, 2nd enlarged edition (London: Allen and Unwin).

Blitz, B. (2017) 'The state and the stateless: The legacy of Hannah Arendt reconsidered', in T. Bloom, K. Tonkiss, and P. Cole (eds) *Understanding Statelessness* (Abingdon: Routledge): pp. 70–84.

Brinham, N. (2017) 'Breaking the cycle of expulsion, Repatriation and exploitation for Rohingya', *Open Democracy*, 26 September [Online]. Available at www.opendemocracy.net/beyondslavery/natalie-brinham/breaking-cycle-of-expulsion-forced-repatriation-and-exploitation-for-r (Accessed 30 January 2018).

Brinham, N. (2018) '"Genocide cards": Rohingya refugees on why they risked their lives to refuse ID cards', *OpenDemocracy*, 21 October [Online]. Available at www.opendemocracy.net/natalie-brinham/genocide-cards-why-rohingya-refugees-are-resisting-id-cards (Accessed 10 July 2020).

Brinham, N. (2019) 'Looking beyond invisibility: Rohingyas' dangerous encounters with papers and cards', *Tilburg Law Review*, 24:2, 156–169.

Center for Diversity and National Harmony (CDNH) (2019) *Myanmar's Citizenship Law: An Analysis* [Online]. Available at www.cdnh.org/publication/myanmars-citizenship-law-an-analysis/ (Accessed 22 July 2020).

Chaudhuri, B., and König, L. (2018) 'The Aadhaar scheme: A cornerstone of a new citizenship regime in India?' *Contemporary South Asia*, 26:2, 127–142.

Cheesman, N. (2017a) 'Introduction: Interpreting communal violence in Myanmar', *Journal of Contemporary Asia*, 47:3, 335–352.

Cheesman, N. (2017b) 'How in Myanmar "National Races" came to surpass citizenship and exclude Rohingya', *Journal of Contemporary Asia*, 47:3, 461–483.

Crisp, J. (2018) '"Primitive people": The untold story of UNHCR's historical engagement with Rohingya refugees', *Humanitarian Exchange*, 73, 13–15.

European Network on Statelessness (ENS) and Institute on Statelessness and Inclusion (ISI) (2019) 'Statelessness in Myanmar: Country position paper' [Online]. Available at https://statelessjourneys.org/wp-content/uploads/StatelessJourneys-Myanmar-final.pdf (Accessed 22 August 2020).

Fortify Rights (2019) ' "Tools of genocide": National verification cards and the denial of citizenship of Rohingya Muslims in Myanmar' [Online]. Available at www.fortifyrights.org/downloads/Tools%20of%20Genocide%20-%20Fortify%20Rights%20-%20September-03-2019-EN.pdf (Accessed 10 July 2020).

Gelb, A., and Manby, B. (2016) 'Has development converged with human rights? Implications for the legal identity SDG', Centre for Global Development [Online]. Available at www.cgdev.org/blog/has-development-converged-human-rights-implications-legal-identity-sdg (Accessed 17 November 2018).

Green, P., and Ward, T. (2004) *State Crime: Governments, Violence and Corruption.* (London and Sterling, VA: Pluto Press).

Hayes de Kalaf, E. (2019) 'Making foreign: Legal identity, social policy and the contours of belonging in the contemporary Dominican Republic', in G. Cruz-Martínez (ed.) *Welfare and Social Protection in Contemporary Latin America* (Abingdon: Routledge): pp. 101–117.

Hoque, R. (2016) 'Report on citizenship law: Bangladesh', EUDO Citizenship Observatory [Online]. Available at https://cadmus.eui.eu/bitstream/handle/1814/44545/EudoCit_2016_14Bangladesh.pdf?sequence=1&isAllowed=y (Accessed 22 July 2020).

Human Rights Watch (1996) 'The Rohingya Muslims: Ending a cycle of exodus?' [Online]. Available at www.hrw.org/legacy/summaries/s.burma969.html (Accessed 10 July 2020).

Leach, E. (1973) *Political Systems of Highland Burma* (Abingdon: Routledge).

Lehman, F. K. (1967) 'Ethnic categories in Burma and the theory of social systems', in P. Kunstadter (ed.) *Southeast Asian Tribes, Minorities, and Nations* (Princeton, NJ: Princeton University Press): pp. 93–124.

Mamdani, M. (1996) *Citizen and Subject: Contemporary Africa and the Legacy of Late Colonialism* (Princeton, NJ: Princeton University Press).

Manby, B. (2018) ' "Legal identity" and biometric registration in Africa', *Newsletter of the American Political Science Association's Organized Section on Migration and Citizenship*, 6:2, 54–60.

McKinsey, K. (2012) 'High Commissioner for Refugees wraps up mission to Myanmar, Thailand', UNHCR, 13 July [Online]. Available at www.unhcr.org/50000ff96.html (Accessed 11 November 2019).

Nyi Nyi Kyaw (2017) 'Unpacking the presumed statelessness of Rohingyas', *Journal of Immigrant and Refugee Studies*, 15:3, 269–286.

Oppenheim, B., and Powell, B. M. (2015) 'Legal identity in the 2030 Agenda for Sustainable Development: Lessons from Kibera', Kenya Foundations, O. S. [Online]. Available at www.justiceinitiative.org/uploads/0a6472de-a975-4a3b-b3ad-2b979891d645/legal-identity-2030-agenda-lessons-kibera-kenya-2051216.pdf (Accessed 22 July 2020).

Potter, R., and Kyaw Win. (2019) 'National Verification Cards – A barrier to Rohingya repatriation', Burma Human Rights Network [Online]. Available at www.bhrn.org.uk/en/report/1090-national-verification-cards-a-barrier-to-rohingya-repatriation-full-report.html (Accessed 10 July 2020).

Socialist Republic of the Union of Burma (1982) *Burmese Citizenship Law* [Online]. Available at www.refworld.org/docid/3ae6b4f71b.html (Accessed 10 July 2020).

United Nations (1954) *Convention relating to the Status of Stateless Persons* [Online]. Available at https://treaties.un.org/Pages/ViewDetailsII.aspx?src=TREATY&mtdsg_no=V-3&chapter=5&Temp=mtdsg2&clang=_en (Accessed 11 July 2020).

United Nations High Commissioner for Refugees (UNHCR) (2012) *UNHCR Style Companion* [Online]. Available at www.refworld.org/docid/4fe30f9a2.html (accessed 21 May 2017).

United Nations High Commissioner for Refugees (UNHCR) (2014) 'Handbook on protection of stateless persons under the 1954 Convention relating to the Status of Stateless Persons' [Online]. Available at www.unhcr.org/dach/wp-content/uploads/sites/27/2017/04/CH-UNHCR_Handbook-on-Protection-of-Stateless-Persons.pdf (Accessed 10 July 2020).

United Nations Human Rights Council (UNHRC) (2018) 'Report of the independent international fact-finding mission on Myanmar' [Online]. Available at www.ohchr.org/EN/HRBodies/HRC/Pages/NewsDetail.aspx?NewsID=23575&LangID=E (Accessed 22 July 2020).

Van Waas, L. (2015) 'The right to legal identity or the right to legal ID?', European Network on Statelessness blog [Online]. Available at www.statelessness.eu/blog/right-legal-identity-or-right-legal-id (Accessed 17 December 2018).

World Bank Group (2018) 'Identification for development: ID4D annual report 2018' [Online]. Available at https://id4d.worldbank.org/sites/id4d.worldbank.org/files/2018_ID4D_Annual_Report.pdf (Accessed 22 July 2020).

26

United Stateless in the United States: Reflections from an activist

Ekaterina E

I remember the train trip back from Washington, D.C., to Seattle after I had been definitively told by my embassy that the return home was impossible, and that I no longer had any rights to consular assistance. I was told that I was not considered a national of my home country under the operation of its law. For decades, I thought I was simply undocumented. Apparently things were a lot more complicated. I had no nationality.

I was staring out into the darkness with the sound of Pink Floyd's 2014 song 'Louder Than Words' in my headphones. The official music video features the Central Asian landscape. I was born there. My father's ancestors roamed the region for thousands of years. My mother's colonial Russian roots in Central Asia are four generations deep. How can I not belong to a place where I was born, a place that surely must be a part of my very DNA?

How can I, a human being living in the modern world, someone who has been – at least by my own estimations – a decent person, a community volunteer, and a consistent tax-payer my entire adult life be denied a request to self-deport in order to be with my family, to be by my gravely ill father's side?

How can I not belong to my own country, not be allowed to return home?

My story begins in the Soviet Republic of Uzbekistan, where I was born and raised. Three months after my 16th birthday in 1994, I arrived in the United States on a scholarship to study for a year as a high school foreign exchange student.

To travel, I was issued a Soviet document. During this time, my country was in crisis because the Soviet Union had recently collapsed. Many Russians, an ethnic minority in Uzbekistan, were in a state of panic. Hundreds of thousands of people were fleeing the country in fear of persecution. Russian-speaking TV channels were shut down and there were outbursts of violence throughout our city.

Fearing for my safety, my family urged me to stay in the U.S. and try to continue my education there.

I applied for scholarships to colleges but was unsuccessful, and an unfortunate experience with an unscrupulous immigration attorney resulted in me ending up without a status. I was an undocumented teenager on the streets of America.

I did my best to survive. I painted, sold flowers, worked as a nanny, living my human life as best I could. Yet, despite many attempts, I was not able to adjust my legal status nor gain the privilege of a U.S. citizenship.

The next twenty years of my life saw me through a productive, creative long-term marriage, achievements in the field of art, and several awards, including – ironically – a nomination for Citizen of the Year for my volunteer community work.

In 2014, I learned that my father was dying of cancer and that my mom was very sick, as well. I decided to deport myself so I could finally return home to be with my family. This decision did not come lightly. I had to make a choice between a life I had built in the U.S. and what was likely my last chance to reconnect with my father.

To leave the U.S. as a deportee with a record of more than twenty years as an undocumented alien almost certainly meant that I would never be able to return. I made my choice, but my embassy told me that return home was impossible. My choice had been taken from me, my only way home – closed.

Not a national. A citizen of nowhere. A ghost.

As the train sped down the tracks, I stared at my reflection in the glass. I was still the same person I was yesterday, except that now I had a new word to describe myself: stateless.

I typed 'statelessness' into the search bar on my phone only to be engulfed by stories of war and genocide, abandonment, suffering, and violation. I learned that there are millions of people around the globe living without nationality.

In that moment, however, I was the only stateless person I knew. I had lost my citizenship before obtaining a new one. I was nothing. An empty bubble of darkness, written out of existence, cut off not only from my family, but from the rest of the human race without an apparent way back.

During the following months, I searched for any information I could find about statelessness. I desperately wanted to connect with someone, anyone, who could understand or relate to my story. Buried in academic research papers and United Nations High Commissioner for Refugees (UNHCR) manuals, statelessness seemed inaccessible and confusing. I followed stories of the Rohingya, attempted to read political theory, and struggled to explain my strange status to my closest friends and family. Nobody I spoke with had ever heard of statelessness before.

My father died in December 2015, on the other side of the world. At 37, I found myself with my heart in pieces, my sense of self – shattered. My life was crumbling around me as my marriage collapsed. I fell into a deep depression, contemplating suicide.

An unexpected break came when I read an article in *Newsweek* about Tatianna Lesnikova, a stateless woman from the Ukraine living in the U.S. whose story had gained publicity around 2014 (Dulai and Mendoza, 2015). Tatianna lost her nationality when she fled her country to seek asylum in the U.S. with her youngest son after the government targeted her eldest for being politically outspoken. Denied asylum, she had lived in limbo in the U.S. for decades. Her story resonated with my own. Long-term family separation is a wound that never quite closes.

I reached out to her via Facebook and she answered. A piano teacher living in Massachusetts, she radiated strength, resilience, and a bit of resignation as she spoke of her solitary efforts to resolve her situation.

Tatianna had testified before the U.S. Congress, had given interviews, and served as the 'face of statelessness in the US' in UNHCR advocacy campaigns.

'One drop of water makes a hole in the stone, if dripping long enough', she said, and then insisted that I connect with Nikolai Levasov, who was 'looking for other stateless persons' as well as the UNHCR Protection Unit in Washington, D.C.

I was no longer alone. There were others.

I will never forget my first phone call with Nikolai. It must have lasted two hours. Our stories were very similar, as he too grew up in the former Soviet Union and like myself was living in the United States without a nationality. Levasov writes of his own journey:

> *My first exposure to stateless human rights violations started, as with many stateless individuals, with my own personal case. I knew I was stateless in the United States and was desperately trying to renew my travel document to assist in my immigration case.*

> *When contacting the consulate and the Ministry of Internal Affairs offices of my country, I learned that I was not qualified to renew because I lacked citizenship. My arguments that this was my only source of identification had no bearing within the existing legal framework.*

> *This was the first time I realized that there might be absolutely no protection for people like myself. I took matters into my own hands and reviewed the*

referenced law. It had been changed while I was abroad and now denied me rights to renew my documents. Being an ethnic minority in my own country I felt even more segregated and discriminated against.

This is when I first reached out to UNHCR hoping that I was protected by international law. However, I underestimated the power of domestic law. At that point I was still very naïve, thinking that there was an existing solution to protect me against detention and family separation.[1]

The need to organise became clear. Isolated, solitary drops of water needed to become a torrent if we were to make a dent in the monolithic face of the legal system of a nation without statelessness in its vocabulary, or even a basic awareness of the fact that stateless persons exist in its territory. And we did exist.

In Philadelphia, a young woman of Armenian-Ukranian descent living in the U.S. since age eight was bravely telling her story at local events. In Milwaukee, a doctor and a community leader for the Rohingya was raising a family and looking for solutions. A young Bidoon woman detained and traumatised as a teen in New York was supporting her siblings and elderly mother. In Maryland, a man who survived torture during the Eritrean/Ethiopian conflict was working twelve-hour shifts on minimum wage. All stateless, just like me.

What began as a search for answers grew into a conversation. For months we exchanged emails, pouring over the Universal Declaration of Human Rights, exchanging ideas around the possibility that the answers we were seeking simply did not exist. That it was maybe up to us to come up with them.

We met as a group for the first time at the UNHCR regional office in Washington, D.C., in December of 2017. I still remember that morning as we stood waiting to be let into the building with our steaming cups of coffee in hand, absorbing each other's stories in wonder.

Some of us were born into statelessness, some became stateless because of conflicts in nationality laws, some fell through the cracks during tectonic political shifts such as state succession.

A woman from Kuwait, a man from Myanmar, several of us from the former Soviet Union, a man from Ethiopia – what did we have in common? Strangers, flung together by fate and bound by a strange circumstance, we were humans who every country on earth considered a foreigner. And in that moment, as we laughed and cried, and hugged – our shared humanity shone like a silver thread in the tapestry of our diverse backgrounds, places of origin, ethnicities, gender identities, ages, and religious beliefs. We found each other and never looked back.

UNHCR provided a safe space for us to gather, as well as support to take some initial steps as a fledgling organisation. Several non-stateless individuals – a visionary and kind-hearted organisational consultant, a brilliant young human rights defender, and an eagle-eyed academic expert – all deeply passionate about the issue, immediately flanked our small group, further strengthening our sense of solidarity and purpose.

Before long, we decided to launch ourselves as an independent organisation. We soon held a paper in our hands, a document legitimising *United Stateless* as an official non-governmental organisation (NGO). As a non-profit, we have become real in the eyes of the law. As stateless individuals, however, we were yet to be seen or recognised.

While the United States is a party to the 1967 UN Protocol Relating to the Status of Refugees, it has never signed the 1954 Convention Relating to the Status of Stateless Persons, nor the 1961 Convention on the Reduction of Statelessness. At the time of writing, there are no definitions of statelessness in the legal framework of the U.S., nor is there a procedure for the determination of a person's stateless status. There is no way for a stateless person to leave the U.S. to try to address their statelessness elsewhere.

We understood early on that to succeed in our chosen mission – 'to build and inspire community among those affected by statelessness, and to advocate for our human rights' in any effective way, we would have to face and overcome a host of challenges.

We were a grassroots fledgling organisation driven by volunteers – mostly stateless, with very limited resources, and a lofty goal of changing national policy in an environment rife with anti-immigrant sentiment.

Our issue was unheard of domestically and there were no statistics to rely on. Our constituents were uncounted, unprotected – living in limbo in the shadows of a system that both rejected and entrapped them.

Levasov writes about one of our early projects:

> When I initially started learning about statelessness, I spent hours every day reading through all the related information available. I didn't have a systematic approach – in fact, most of my research was conducted via smartphone on the NYC subway. I did, however, discover a common theme, in that there were no reliable statelessness statistics out there and most published papers and articles referenced different estimated numbers.
>
> One particular source – the Global Detention Project (GDP) – cited the U.S. stateless population as zero. This was particularly disturbing to me as an actual stateless person and a grassroots activist for human rights.
>
> When I reached out to GDP with a request to correct their data error, their reply was that they are by no means statelessness experts and obtained their

data from the UNHCR database. They were right – the UNHCR database did state that stateless people did not exist in the United States.[2]

I remember staring at the 'zero' next to the United States in the online database of the world's leading authority on statelessness. That strange sense of dissociation washing over me. I felt small – reduced to nothing, and yet oddly powerful. Our very existence was enough, all we had to do was voice it.

We launched our #WeAreNotZero campaign, which mostly consisted of writing letters and asking questions. The effort eventually culminated in a submission of a report to the United Nations Human Rights Council at the 36th Session of the Universal Periodic Review in collaboration with the Institute on Statelessness and Inclusion (ISI) and The America's Network on Nationality and Statelessness (Red ANA).

In October 2017, the Center for Migration Studies in New York (CMS) initiated a project to try to map the stateless population in the U.S. United Stateless assisted by participating in interviews and helping get the word out to the members of the stateless community. In January 2020, CMS released the results of the study, finding that 'the population in the United States that is potentially stateless or potentially at risk of statelessness is larger and more diverse than previously assumed, albeit with the caveat that severe data limitations make it impossible to provide precise estimates of this population' (Kerwin et al., 2020). CMS's analysis revealed that an estimated 218,000 U.S. residents are 'potentially stateless' or 'potentially at risk of statelessness'.

Clearly, we have our work cut out for us.

What lies ahead? A vast uncharted territory – millions of minds to educate, an arduous legal struggle for justice, thousands of voices to bring out of the shadows.

A stateless story almost invariably stems from traumatic events caused by this or another nation's laws or practices rooted in racial, gender, ethnicity, or religion-based discrimination. In light of this, we expect to cross paths with activists in many spheres and make new allies, and hopefully not only finally resolve the question of where and how we belong, but help bring about a more humane world and a more just society.

The United Nations exists to 'achieve international co-operation in solving international problems of an economic, social, cultural, or humanitarian character, and in promoting and encouraging respect for human rights and fundamental freedoms for all without distinction as to race, sex, language, or religion' (United Nations, 1945: 1.1.3). United Stateless exists to advocate for the rights of human beings who have been expelled from the world of nations, the system of states. United Stateless has to exist because we, the stateless, exist.

Notes

1 Email communication with the author, reproduced with permission.
2 Email communication with the author, reproduced with permission.

References

Dulai, S., and Mendoza, M. (2015) 'Stateless: The ultimate legal limbo', *Newsweek*, 10 April [Online]. Available at www.newsweek.com/stateless-ultimate-legal-limbo-319461 (Accessed 6 June 2020).

Kerwin, D., Alulema, D., Nicholson, M., and Warren, R. (2020) 'Statelessness in the United States: A study to estimate and profile the U.S. stateless population', New York: Center for Migration Studies [Online]. Available at https://cmsny.org/wp-content/uploads/2020/01/StatelessnessReportFinal.pdf (Accessed 12 June 2020).

United Nations (1945) *Charter of the United Nations*, entry into force 24 October 1945.

Figure 7

We are not immigrants

Fred Kuwornu

'We are not immigrants', one of them says, 'we do not come from another country, we did not cross any border. We are here since the beginning of our life'.

At present, there are thousands of young people who were born in Italy, speak Italian fluently, have studied in Italian schools and have lived only in Italy and yet are not entitled to Italian citizenship. Many of them do not have access to any citizenship at all.

The film *18 IUS SOLI* puts together the stories of eighteen guys and girls of Asian, South American, or African descent who were born and raised in different regions of Italy. If you watch the film with your eyes closed there is no way to tell they come from immigrant families, their accents are so thick, so Italian that, some of them say, people on the bus or in restaurants are so surprised to hear them speak that way and they do ask. Yet people ask why they speak Italian so well. Let's make it clear to them all… they are Italian, that's why.

Index

Page numbers with an *f* refer to a figure or a caption; *n* indicates a footnote. Pseud. indicates a pseudonym.

EU authorised representative for GPSR:
Easy Access System Europe, Mustamäe tee 50,
10621 Tallinn, Estonia
gpsr.requests@easproject.com